The Human Side of Organizations

Second Edition

Stan Kossen

Merritt College

Harper & Row, Publishers
New York Hagerstown Philadelphia San Francisco London

Chapter Opening Photographs by Karil Daniels
Cover Design by Michael Rogondino
Cartoons by Steve Byram
Project Coordinator: Thomas E. Dorsaneo
Printer and Binder: R.R. Donnelley and Sons Company

The Human Side of Organizations, Second Edition
Copyright © 1975, 1978 by Stanley Kossen

For information address:
Harper & Row, Publishers, Inc.
10 East 53rd Street
New York, N.Y. 10022

Library of Congress Cataloging in Publication Data

Kossen, Stan
   The human side of organizations.

   Bibliography
   Includes index.
   1. Personnel management.   2. Organizational behavior.   3. Interpersonal relations.   I. Title.
HF5549.K664   1978   658.3   78-754
ISBN 0-06-384719-1

Contents

4 The Sum of the Parts Is . . .   75
The Dynamics of Small Groups

part two   Leaders Need People   103

5 Everybody *Needs* Something—What *Motivates* You?   105
Human Needs and Motivation

17 It All Relates to the Bottom Line   407
Organizational Responsibilities Toward Society

18 Which Direction Is the Future?   427
A Prognosis

DEAR READER:

You are about to explore the human side of organizations. In one sense, an organization exists wherever there are two or more persons. For our purposes, the term *organization* can relate to business organizations, governmental bodies, social organizations, cause-oriented groups, and even family units.

Although not inevitable in every instance, wherever there are two or more persons, *potential* conflict exists. However, do people who have to make decisions (and who doesn't?) in this problem-beset world have to wait until after a crisis before they act? Wouldn't it be far more desirable if potential discord and organizational problems were anticipated and prevented? Perhaps problems could be prevented in far more instances than they are at present if individuals in organizations could develop greater sensitivity toward *human* problems.

A book about human relationships should not be a "how to" presentation. There are no ten simple rules that will enable you to resolve all problems. What should the book be then? It should assist you in developing a keener awareness of and sensitivity toward the needs, sentiments, and attitudes of individuals—including yourself—in organizations, in sharpening your perceptions, and in improving your ability to make effective decisions both on and off your job.

Voluminous materials have already been published in the field of human relations, yet there seems to have been no significant decline in the quantity and intensity of discord and misunderstandings that presently prevail in organizations. There has continued to remain a paramount need for a text on human relations that stresses the practical, the so-called "real world," and omits the highly sophisticated, often incomprehensible, and excessively theoretical approach. This book, I hope, fills that void.

Many of you who read this text may tend to identify with management. However, you ordinarily will not begin your careers in managerial positions. As a result, you will have the subordinate's responsibilities of getting along with other workers, as well as working with and through individuals, both within and without the organization. Even if your intentions are not to become a manager, you can benefit from this book. Although the expression may sound a bit trite, human relations truly *is* the responsibility of everyone in an organization. It is to be hoped that the study of human relations will assist you in becoming more sensitive to human behavior and in anticipating problems before they occur, or in resolving them after they have already occurred.

The text that you are holding at the moment doesn't contain the traditional approach to the study of human relations. Although many standard—and necessary—concepts are included, they are presented in a style that shouldn't threaten you, as do some texts on human relations.

The style of writing is intended to be at a level that you can understand with a minimum of effort, rather than one that tends to talk down to you. A book needn't be excessively scholarly to be useful. Texts written in an overcomplex fashion generally turn off students before they've had the opportunity to develop an interest in the subject.

Professor Leo Rosten, quite unknowingly, has summarized my intentions in this text:

> Education, the pearl beyond price, does not much help the *writing* part of a writer. Nor does scholarship. Intellectuals seem to me to place too high a premium on the sheer ingestion of data. Since they confuse obscurity with profundity, is it surprising that they mistake bibliography for brains? The tragedy of the uncreative scholar is that he has spent so many years in autopsy that his mind has become a morgue.[1]

As you read this text, you will discover another departure from the traditional approach. Topics that previously have been largely ignored or inadequately covered are given prominence: *listening, the nature of prejudice and discrimination in organizations, the employment of women, problems of the aging and the handicapped, and the problems of alcohol and drug abuse in organizations.*

The final section of this text examines both *personal* and *external* human relations. Untraditional emphasis is given to concepts related to the maintenance of your own personal mental and physical health. You can't fully separate your personal existence from your work existence, even though some managers seem to prefer—and even expect—that you will. Personal problems, in actuality, are often organizational problems. This section also discusses some of the responsibilities and problems that managers at present have toward their employees, society, and the environment in which they function.

You'll notice that *learning objectives* have been included at the beginning of each chapter. Take a good look at them; they are there to assist you. You probably like to know where you're about to go in a particular chapter; the learning objectives can help you find out. They also can serve as a checklist to enable you to see if you have studied the chapter well.

Terms and questions have been placed in the margins of many pages. They are intended principally to point up the importance of the paragraphs they represent, as well as to serve as quick references. The margin

[1]Leo Rosten, *The Return of H*Y*M*A*N K*A*P*L*A*N* (Harmondsworth, England: Penguin Books, 1968), pp. 16, 17.

questions are not always answered in the text but, instead, are there to provoke you into thinking deeper about the topics.

I sincerely hope that you will find studying this text not only a beneficial experience, but an enjoyable one as well. You have now read this note. Much more significant is what you will feel after reading this text. If at any time you would like to express your views (either positive or negative) or recommendations about any of the sections, please feel encouraged to write to me. Only through feedback *from you* will I ever know if my efforts were useful *to you*. Until then, good luck—and now let's start focusing on *the human side of organizations*.

Stan Kossen

Stan Kossen
Merritt College
Oakland, California

TO THE INSTRUCTOR

The response to the first edition of *The Human Side of Organizations* has been extremely gratifying. Over 100 colleges and universities have adopted the book since its publication. Based on the feedback I've received from users of the text, my principal goal seems to have been achieved: to develop materials designed to appeal to and interest students in basic and practical organizational behavior and human relations concepts. I wanted to avoid overloading them with the multitude of erudite theories that tend to turn off—rather than to excite—students facing their first course in human relations, industrial psychology, or organizational behavior. Typical of the "fan mail" received from satisfied students is the following sent by a Mesa College student: "I didn't know they made textbooks so readable, enjoyable, and full of knowledge."

Can't learning be enjoyable?

Merely the Beginning. . . .

But the end—contrary to the omnipresent prophets of doom—is not near, nor is it even close! No writer can afford to rest on his or her laurels and feel that the "ultimate in new and different textbooks" has finally been achieved. Fresh ideas and concepts are continually being developed, as are new applications of long-established concepts. Mindful that most everything can be improved, my editors and I set out to discover what specific modifications might make the revised edition of *The Human Side of Organizations* even more usable to instructors and students—without sacrificing any of its previous attributes. To do this, questionnaires were mailed to users of the text; the response was excellent.

A reflection of your needs

The second edition of *The Human Side of Organizations,* as well as the revised student learning guide and instructor's manual, reflects the input that you—the users of the first edition—provided. If you are a first-time user, or are considering adopting this edition, you should quickly discover why the text has appealed to instructors and students who have used it in the past. Summarized below is an overview of the organization plus the principal features and improvements embodied into this edition.

Organization of the Text

The Human Side of Organizations is divided into four parts:

Understanding people

1. *Humans Are People*—four chapters designed to help the reader develop insight, sensitivity, and an improved understanding of people—both leaders and followers—in organizations. Includes chapters that discuss an overview of human relations, and concepts of perception, communication, and group behavior.

Understanding leadership

2. *Leaders Need People*—six chapters designed to assist organizational leaders in developing, maintaining, and improving the organizational climate. Includes chapters that discuss concepts of needs and motivation, organization, leadership techniques and problems, morale, and the dynamics of change.

Understanding present-day problems

3. *Constraints on Organizational Behavior*—five chapters designed to assist present and future managers in understanding and dealing with forces that tend to constrict leadership activities. Includes chapters on unions, the nature of prejudice and discrimination, employment problems of women, the aging and the handicapped, and the organizational problems associated with alcohol and drug abuse.

Understanding and improving self, understanding managerial responsibilities, and preparing for the future

4. *From Here to Eternity*—three chapters designed to help readers maintain their own mental and physical health; understand the responsibilities and problems that managers currently have toward their employees, society, and the environment of which they are a part; and understand some of the future directions that human relations concepts are likely to take.

Improved Organization

More logical relationships

As a reflection of first edition user preferences, chapter order and the organization of specific chapters have been slightly rearranged. For example, the topic of listening, a basic and integral part of the communication process, has been incorporated into the chapter on communication. The discussion of adjustive reactions (human response to frustration) has been merged with the chapter on human needs and motivation, where the topic relates more logically.

New and Updated Materials

Factory fresh!

Various up-to-date and practical materials have been added to the second edition. These include:

1. A completely new chapter on *small group behavior*, including basic concepts related to transactional analysis and interviewing.
2. A practical overview of a well-known management tool, MBO (*management by objectives*).
3. A discussion of how *creativity* can improve the problem-solving process.
4. A new theory, *Derived X*, a practical extension of Douglas McGregor's X-Y theories.
5. A new law, *Kossen's Law (K's Law)*, an offshoot of Parkinson's Law.
6. A discussion of *current industry experiments and practices*, including flexible working hours and job sharing (twinning).
7. A discussion of the major problems associated with managing the "new breeds," such as the *knowledge worker*.

8. Current materials on *special employment groups,* such as minorities and women, including women in management positions.
9. A completely *revised and updated bibliography* following each chapter.

Additional Case Materials

Expanded choice of case materials

Also included is a wider variety and choice of case materials following each chapter. Although almost all of the previous short cases have been retained, eleven new cases have been added; these are slightly more complex and are intended for those instructors who prefer cases with greater depth and involvement.

New Illustrations

New artwork

Although the basic format with notes, questions, and terms printed in the wide margins has been retained, *all new artwork* appears in this edition in order to maintain a lively and up-to-date appearance.

Improved and Expanded Student Learning Guide

A better student resource

The learning guide has been improved and expanded to include projects and applications related to the text materials. Also included in each learning guide chapter is a short reading designed to enrich the student's understanding of selected human relations topics. Learning guide questions have been improved throughout.

Improved Instructor's Guide

In addition to its original basic features, the instructor's guide has been broadened to include a separate quiz for each chapter. Each quiz consists of twenty-five objective questions related to the text. These can be removed from the manual and reproduced by photomechanical means. Also included for instructor use are two mid-term examinations and a final examination, also suitable for reproduction.

Continued User Satisfaction Intended

Wanted— continued feedback

I hope that you, the users of the second edition of *The Human Side of Organizations,* will continue to find it a useful, as well as enjoyable, teaching tool, one that is not only interesting and easily read, but that also contains the basics you want your students to learn. I also hope that you will continue to provide me with constructive feedback and input. Your interest will help me continue to develop the materials that can make your teaching activities more satisfying and enjoyable. Best of success with your students!

S. K.

ACKNOWLEDGMENTS

Bestowing adequate recognition on all who have provided assistance and encouragement during the writing of both the first and second editions of this book is, indeed, a difficult task. The list of individuals who have influenced my thinking in the area of human behavior is practically without end. Nonetheless, at the risk of inadvertently omitting some, I should like to offer my sincere gratitude to the following:

George Provol, Carol Pritchard, Tom Dorsaneo, Karryll McBane, Jack Jennings, and the entire San Francisco staff of Canfield Press, who provided me with technical assistance and psychological sustenance during all phases of the revised manuscript's preparation.

A special round of kudos is in order for my students who, in my opinion, are among the best judges of the quality of a text.

Mary Boice, U. S. Office of Rehabilitation Services; Rod Carter, California State Department of Employment; Howard Gilbert, Gilbert Industries; Charles P. Haywood, Bay Area Urban League; Evan Hodgens, U. S. Department of Labor; Harold E. Mackin, Occidental Life Insurance Company; Marshall D. McClure, American Management Associations; George Renquist, Moore Business Forms; John E. Ringer, The Clorox Company; Robert Sager, U.S. Bureau of Narcotics and Dangerous Drugs; and Gary Simpson, Kaiser Aluminum and Chemical Corporation, all of whom provided valuable information and assistance.

Special appreciation is also extended to the following professors who provided me with helpful suggestions during the revised manuscript development phase of *The Human Side of Organizations:*

Joseph Abbruscato
Maricopa Technical
Community College
Arizona

Alfred A. Adelekan
St. Paul's College
Virginia

James W. Anderson
Fullerton College
California

Diane Blasius
Normandale Community College
Minnesota

Valerie M. Bockman
Pima Community College
Arizona

Stephen C. Branz
Triton College
Illinois

Morris Bryson
Bryson and Associates
California

Fred Capellas
Sacramento City College
California

ACKNOWLEDGMENTS

B. Crabtree
Palo Verde College
California

Ray Curtis
Lorain County
Community College
Ohio

J. R. Dempsy
University of Detroit
Michigan

Carol Giers
Orange Coast College
California

Evelyn Grace
Tarrant County Junior College
Texas

Richard Gradwohl
Highline Community College
Washington

Richard Green
Orange Coast College
California

Ethyl Hanson
Portland Community College
Oregon

Donald Hucker
Cypress College
California

Larry A. Hudson
Polk Community College
Florida

Michael D. Hughmanick
West Valley College
California

John F. Hulpke
College of Marin
California

E. Bruce Isaacson
Mesa College
Colorado

Brian James
Merritt College
California

Don Johnson
Portland Community College
Oregon

Jim Kerr
Phoenix College
Arizona

Stan Laney
Central Texas College
Texas

Robert Markwith
American River College
California

Edward W. Morius
Linn-Benton
Community College
Oregon

E. J. Napier
Northern Kentucky University
Kentucky

Paul Newmark
Laney College
California

Leo R. Osterhaus
St. Edwards University
Texas

ACKNOWLEDGMENTS

Leonard L. Palumbo
North Virginia
Community College
Virginia

Geoffrey A. Turnbull
Pasadena City College
California

W. H. Robinson, Jr.
Hillsborough Community
College
Florida

Betty Van Meter
Laney College
California

Nora Jo Sherman
Tarrant County Junior College
Texas

Fred Weber
Saddleback College
California

William E. Stratton
Idaho State University
Idaho

Mike Wirth
College of Alameda
California

I also want to convey my deepest love and appreciation to my wife, Sonna, especially for her ability to survive, for the third time, the preparation of another textbook. As with the first edition, Sonna extended me patience, understanding, and direct assistance during the entire preparation of the text. Publication deadlines, even with experience, seem to get no easier to endure. The various stresses and strains would indeed be difficult to endure without a strong, loving, and supportive person like Sonna.

And to Jeremy Stuart, my five-year old son, I want to extend my thanks and express my amazement for his never—not even once!—confusing my manuscript materials for his drawing paper. I wouldn't be the least bit surprised to see him writing his own book in the very near future!

one

Humans Are People

When you finish this chapter, you should be able to:

1. **Summarize** the nature and limitations of the study of human relations.
2. **Contrast** formal with informal organizations.
3. **List** four major types of organizational human relationships.
4. **Trace** the human relations movement.
5. **List** the major causes of the expanding popularity of human relations.
6. **Explain** the necessity for organizational order and predictability.
7. **Relate** the importance of situational thinking in problem solving.
8. **Summarize** the advantages of the case study and role-assuming approaches.

You see things;
and you say "Why?"
But I dream things that never were;
and I say "Why not?"
—from George Bernard Shaw's *Back to Methuselah*

"Human relations just doesn't work! You try to be nice to people and they'll walk all over you! We tried job enrichment, job enlargement, and all that other fancy ivory tower stuff down at our plant. It was a waste of time. Everybody knew before we tried all those things that they wouldn't work. After all, *our* business is different. And besides, I don't care what you say, people are people."

Have you ever overheard comments like these around organizations? They're really quite common. Unfortunately, some organizational members will say that something doesn't *work* when in reality it hasn't *been worked;* that is, from the beginning, people haven't really been sold on trying the idea. Far too frequently, built-in cynical attitudes have caused sound programs to be squelched before they've been given any sort of a fair trial.

To illustrate, let's assume that a week ago you purchased a shiny new car but haven't driven it yet. This morning while waiting for a bus you meet Baldwin, one of your business associates:

Baldwin: I hear you bought a new car. How does it run?
You: It doesn't.
Baldwin: It doesn't run? How come?
You: I really don't know.
Baldwin: When did you try it?
You: Try it? I haven't really tried it yet.
Baldwin: Then how do you know it doesn't run?
You: Because I haven't tried it yet!

How does *not working* differ from *not worked?*

This bit of circular reasoning helps to point out the necessity for avoiding the confusion between something *not working* and something *not worked.* Few organizational activities work well unless people want them to.

A vital assumption of this book is that *human relations can and does work,* especially in organizations where positive attitudes and ample understanding of the human side of organizations exist. The development of

4

an understanding of human behavior is not easy but it's essential if organizational conflict and strife are to be resolved.

Organizations and Human Behavior

Is conflict inevitable?

Did you notice the title of this chapter—"1 + 1 = Organization"? Wherever there are two or more persons, there is, in effect, an organization; and wherever there are two or more persons, there is the potential for conflict resulting from a myriad of causes. Conflict is not necessarily inevitable, but with the numerous differences among individuals both in the ways in which they perceive and in the strengths of their needs, conflict among human beings is likely to be common in organizations.

Considerable discord also stems from difficulties in communication. Misunderstandings frequently result from differences in which organizational members interpret words and actions.

Is all conflict bad?

We can readily observe disharmony all around us, ranging from the relatively mild differences of opinion between two good friends to the brutal and destructive dissension among nations. The communications media bombard us daily with examples of human conflict. Not all types of disagreements are harmful. Some types of conflict, or differences of opinion, can be quite beneficial to organizations by bringing fresh ideas to the surface.

What Is Human Relations?

organizational behavior

human relations

The terms *organizational behavior* and *human relations* will be used interchangeably in this text. Some scholars prefer to make a distinction between the two terms. *Organizational behavior* is considered by some to be a body of theoretical knowledge, while *human relations* is considered a skill. Whether the distinction between the two terms is a practical one can be debated. Theoretical knowledge, of course, can usually help a person develop better human relations skills, something that operating managers need in order to be effective with subordinates.

Human relations as a field or skill involves the application of the various behavioral sciences, such as psychology, sociology, and anthropology. There is, however, a significant difference between human relations and the other fields. For example, psychology is concerned primarily with the scientific study of the human behavior of individuals—*why* people behave as they do. Sociology is concerned chiefly with the scientific study of groups—*why* groups behave as they do.

How does human relations differ from other behavioral sciences?

Human relations is likewise concerned with the *why* of people and their groups, but goes considerably farther. In the study of human relations, in addition to the *why* we want to learn *what* can be done to anticipate, prevent, or resolve conflict among organizational members. The goals of organizations and the needs of members are difficult to satisfy in an atmosphere of perpetual conflict and strife.

action-oriented

In other words, the field of human relations is *action-oriented*, emphasizing the analysis, prevention, and resolution of behavioral problems within organizations.

What Human Relations Is Not

The field of human relations is extremely significant because of the many problems and conflicts that regularly occur among people in organizations. However, the intent of human relations awareness can easily be misunderstood. The purpose of learning human relations concepts, is *not*, for example, to enable you to discover clever techniques for winning friends and influencing people through personality development; *nor* to enable you to manipulate people as though they were puppets, but to assist you in working more effectively with other people in organizations.

What is the purpose of human relations?

Why study a field without *the* answers?

You will soon discover, however, that the study of human relations seldom provides the "correct" solutions to human problems, although an understanding of behavioral concepts should assist you in developing *better* solutions. Individuals who view events on a two-valued basis (right or wrong, good or bad, one-answer philosophy) are often frustrated when they first confront a human behavior course in which this approach does not work.

There is a popular cliché that "human relations is just plain common sense." The application of sound humanistic concepts to organizational behavior would seem to be plain common sense, but if this is true, why does there seem to be so much conflict and strife in organizations? For example, the U.S. Department of Labor reported that in 1976 alone more than 2½ million workers were involved in work stoppages amounting to more than 38 million workdays idle during the year. This number was nearly 7 million workdays above the 1975 total. Maybe common sense is not as common as many people would like to believe!

How common is common sense?

What Is An Organization?

In later chapters we will discuss organizations in considerable detail. For our purposes now, however, we should discover what is meant by the term *organization*. We have already learned that an organization can include two or more persons. Any two individuals can experience some of the behavioral problems that can be found in larger organizations.

Organizations, however, can be far more complex. If you have ever worked for a company, you may have observed something called an organization chart, which is really sort of a guide to people's positions and their relationships in the *formal* organization. However, if you ever spend a fair amount of time in any organization, you are likely to discover considerable *informal* interaction taking place among individuals. These informal activities and relationships will not be found in any company manual or organization chart.

Two Patterns of Structure

A major distinction to be remembered is that in any organization you will usually find two principal patterns of structure, the formal and the informal:

formal organization

1. The *formal organization* is the planned structure and relates to the official lines of authority and responsibility ranging from the board of directors and president to the operative workers.

informal organization

2. The *informal organization* relates to any natural self-grouping of individuals according to their personalities and needs rather than to any formal plan.

As mentioned in the To the Reader section, the term *organization,* for our purposes, can include not only business organizations, but also governmental units, social organizations, cause-oriented groups, and even families.

four types of human relationships

There are *four types* of human relationships, whether formal or informal, with which we shall be concerned in this text:

1. Those between management and the workers
2. Those among the workers themselves
3. Those among managerial personnel
4. Those between members of the organization and the community

A Separate Field of Study

What *kind* of
experience is
the best teacher?

Some people seem surprised to learn that the human side of organizations has been established as a separate area of study. For many years have the words been uttered: "Experience is the best teacher." Although experience *can* be a good teacher, people do not always learn from experience alone. Experience, itself, may be *bad* experience; sometimes it becomes final. A careless driver who is fatally injured in a head-on collision has no other chance to learn from his or her experience.

The Human Relations Movement

We need not delve too deeply into the historical background of human relations. However, some relatively recent and significant events are generally recognized as having influenced the greater human awareness that, we hope, exists today.

Farmers Leave the Soil

**How ya gonna keep'em
down on the farm. . .?**

The stage was set for the human relations movement during the beginnings of industrialization in the mid-1800s, when farmers moved off the land and into towns in hope of improving their situations. Conditions in the early factories left much to be desired. Employees had to work extremely long hours with low pay and were treated not unlike pieces of processed pigskin leather. Horrible working conditions persisted (some persons would argue that they still persist!) until the early years of the present century. There was little humane concern for the worker before the 1920s and 1930s. Managers tended to regard workers merely as factors of production fortunate to be employed.

Along Came Taylor

*father of
scientific management*

Not necessarily noted for his humanitarian views, F. W. Taylor entered the organizational scene in the early 1900s. His principal concern in organizations was for efficiency and as a result he became known as "the father of scientific management." Even though he focused somewhat coldly on efficiency as an organizational goal, maintaining that just as

8

well-designed machinery can be made to operate more efficiently so can people, Taylor did bring needed attention to the human being in organizations.[1]

The Effect of Hawthorne

*father of
human relations*

A series of research studies in 1927 is said to have first established human relations as a separate field. They were undertaken at the Hawthorne works of the Western Electric Company in Chicago by the late Elton Mayo (known as the ''father of human relations''), F. J. Roethlisberger, and their colleagues at Harvard.

The main study involved altering the work environment of a group of production workers in the Relay Assembly Test Room. During the experiment, twenty-four different working conditions were changed, sometimes being improved, and sometimes worsened. Regardless of the changes made, however, production rates kept climbing.

Many present-day students of human behavior are somewhat amazed at how basic the results of the study were. In short, the researchers discovered that when workers are treated as human beings rather than as robots, and when they have the feelings of pride and personal worth on their jobs, as well as the opportunity to get things off their chests, morale and productivity tend to rise.

*Hawthorne
effect*

A new expression was born out of the Hawthorne studies, the *Hawthorne effect:* this refers to *any improvement in worker performance that is the by-product of attention and feeling of self-worth*. The workers studied at the Hawthorne works had received more attention than a typical grandmother gives her grandchild at Thanksgiving time.

The Depressing Effect of the 1930s

**What caused the
workers' unrest?**

The shock effect of the Great Depression of the 1930s, with almost 25 percent of the American labor force unemployed in 1933, stimulated the cohesiveness and militancy of labor union groups, and management discovered the need to develop an entirely new style of industrial relations. The anti-union efforts of the leaders of industry seemed to only increase militant activities. The judicial and legislative branches began to reverse their previously unsympathetic stands toward collective bargaining. Workers' ''sitdowns'' became common practice. In 1937, for example, the General Motors Corporation agreed to recognize the United Automobile Workers after employees had taken over the plant for almost three months.

[1]Frederick W. Taylor, *The Principles of Scientific Management* (New York: Harper and Brothers, 1911).

A significant, albeit tragic, event occurred in 1937 when ten persons were killed and eighty wounded during a Memorial Day clash between police and members of the Steel Workers Organizing Committee at the plant of the Republic Steel Company in South Chicago. These and other events set the tone for a new consciousness toward the role of human beings in organizations.

The Present Role of Human Relations

Since World War II, the growing awareness of the human side of organizations has at times approached the proportions of a fad. Not everyone is convinced of the usefulness of a positive approach to human relations —after all, fear *does* motivate. However, too much irreversible change has taken place within our social structure for sensitive organizational members to ignore human factors. The principal causes of the expanding popularity of human relations at present include:

Why is human relations probably here to stay?

1. A significant increase in the *general educational level* of today's workers who, as a result, demand more from their employers.
2. Workers' groups *protected by the courts*, as they were not before the 1930s.
3. More *managers* who are *university trained* and have a greater understanding of human behavior.
4. Publicity about problems of employment among *minority groups, women,* and other *special employment groups,* problems that require a greater awareness and sensitivity on the part of management.
5. The possible *weakening of the "work ethic,"* requiring managers to develop newer attitudes toward work as a major pursuit.
6. The changing *work environment*—more specialization of work activities and larger scope of operations—which requires a greater degree of managerial effectiveness in working with and through organizational members.

Why aren't there "rules" of human relations?

As we enter the 1980s, we see that human relations is not yet, nor will it ever be, an absolute science. There are neither magic formulas nor lists of "ten simple rules" that can be applied to specific problems. Human beings cannot be poured into test tubes like so many grams of a chemical for the purpose of controlled experiments. Consequently, there is not likely to be complete agreement about which behavioral concepts are the most acceptable. James G. Miller once said, "Organizational theory is a field without a large body of empirically established fact."[2] However, there are concepts, *if learned and applied*, that can aid us in preventing and resolving conflicts.

[2]James G. Miller, "Living Systems: The Organization," *Behavioral Science* 17, no. 1 (January 1972):174.

The Individual in Organizations

What is it that motivates you to work? Do you feel that unless you work, your wants for food, shelter, or a car will go unsatisfied? The income you receive for working helps to satisfy such material wants.

Personal Needs Affect the Organization

How do *your* needs affect *your* work?

Individuals like yourself bring their personal needs to the organizations in which they work. These needs are partially material and economic, partially psychological and social. The personal needs of the employees can have significant effects on the organizations themselves. For example, one's personal needs strongly influence his or her interest and motivation on the job. Managers, especially, should attempt to understand human needs because of the ways in which they influence the attitudes and behavior of employees.

Organizations Need Order and Predictability

Can an organization survive without order?

Try to imagine any organization attempting to accomplish specific goals without some sort of order or guidelines. "Everybody doin' his own thing" may seem desirable in some situations, but most organizations, regardless of how progressive, would find survival under such conditions extremely difficult. An organization without some structure could be compared to an airport that has no ground or air control over the airplanes using the facility. Imagine the chaos that probably would develop.

Almost any well-run organization for which you work is likely to have a set of rules—sometimes called *policies, procedures,* or *guidelines*—designed not to restrict creativity but to assist its members in the accomplishment of organizational goals. You are also likely to find in most organizations some rules that seem reasonable and others that appear ridiculous. Utopia is a difficult place to find. Since you will probably never find an organization that in your mind seems perfect, your next best approach when seeking a position might be to attempt to find one that provides you with a reasonable amount of satisfaction according to your own values. Organizations, like people, have personalities. You probably feel more comfortable around some types of personalities than around others.

Why don't all rules seem reasonable?

required versus

emergent systems

Most well-mannered organizations, therefore, will have some order and predictability, referred to as their *required system* (the formal organization). But, regardless of how energetically the management enforces and coordinates formal policies, *emergent* or informal types of behavior related to personal needs will tend to evolve. The needs of workers cause many behavioral situations that are not to be found in any company manual and should be handled on an individual basis.

The Organizational Climate

Organizations, just like the state of California, have climates, and, like California's, the climate is not always sunny and favorable. One of the major purposes of this book is to expose you to some modern human relations concepts that, when effectively applied, can assist you in understanding and influencing the atmosphere of organizations.

Who is responsible for human relations?

As mentioned in the To the Reader section, human relations is the responsibility of *everyone* in an organization. *Managers* have the primary responsibility for the establishment of a favorable human relations climate, but the *subordinate* and *operative* members of organizations also have strong influence over the climate and should share the responsibility for it.

Requirements for Improving Human Relations

Since workers tend to follow as they are led, how they follow will be significantly influenced by the human relations climate established by the management of the organization. Managers cannot order human relations to be improved. Nor can they assume that all changes affecting human beings will always bring the desired results. However, human relations in organizations can be improved. Adams has provided us with a concise laundry list of six requirements of any human relations program.[3]

What makes an effective human relations climate?

1. Know what employees consider important in their work—their needs and wants.
2. Be a good listener.
3. Develop effective vertical communication lines from employees to management, from management to employees, and horizontally among workers.
4. Develop wage incentive plans.
5. Set up procedures to handle on-the-job grievances.
6. Provide leadership.

Decision Making in Organizations

Regardless of your position in an organization, you have to make decisions in your daily activities. Your personal life is also beset with decision-making responsibilities. Any decisions that you make about

[3]Thomas J. Adams, *The Business of Business* (San Francisco: Canfield Press, 1976), p. 430.

human relations problems are strongly influenced by your past experiences, your perceptual skill, and the assumptions that you have about a particular situation.

There are numerous ways to make decisions. Some are made on the basis of fallacious generalizations, snap judgments, intuition, and hearsay. There are, however, more scientific and logical approaches that can and should be followed. The next chapter discusses how your perception skills influence your decisions and offers some suggestions as to more scientific approaches to problem solving.

Rational Decisions Within the Limits of Time

In the everyday world we don't have endless amounts of time to spend in analyzing problems. To save time in the longer run, we should attempt to gather as much useful information as possible (within the time available) about a specific problem before making up our minds. Before attempting to define a particular problem, we should try to see the situation as it *really* is and not as we *think* it is.

Situational Thinking

When confronting a particular problem, you should remember that each situation is different from others in certain respects. You may have previously confronted a similar problem, but chances are that it was not identical. For example, assume that you are a supervisor who must resolve a serious conflict between two subordinates. You recall how you resolved a similar situation in the past and decide to employ the same techniques. Will they work? Perhaps. Perhaps not. Sometimes attempts with the same solution will backfire because of the individual differences among the persons involved in the problem.

situational thinking   Therefore, when confronting problems one might do well to apply *situational thinking*, a method of confronting human relations problems by *drawing on past experiences and knowledge, but recognizing that each situation is unique and may require a distinct solution*. There is nothing particularly wrong with looking to the past for assistance, but one should recognize that the present and future are not always identical to the past.

The Case Method Approach

Modern courses in human relations are seldom limited to lectures. A far more practical and demanding approach—the case method—has been developed. Your personal abilities in human relations are more likely to be increased through the study, contemplation, and discussion of "real life" situations than through the more traditional methods of study. Lectures may be useful in certain circumstances, but are far less effective than case methods in assisting students of human behavior to work with and through others.

How do you benefit from cases?

In studying cases, you will discover no magic formulas or sets of major principles that can be plugged into specific problems. Newcomers to the case method approach soon find that they are confronted with a variety of vicarious experiences that help to sharpen their sensitivity toward others. Cases also provide the opportunity for a person to apply various concepts to different situations. Every situation is unique and, therefore, cannot be approached with a standard set of rules or "correct" answers.

Role Assuming

> All the world's a stage,
> And all the men and women merely players;
> They have their exits and their entrances;
> And one man in his time plays many parts.
> Shakespeare[4]

You're always you—but the *same* you?

Every day we find ourselves assuming different roles in various circumstances. You may not like the phrase "assuming a role." After all, you are a real person who doesn't need to assume or play roles. But are you *precisely* the same person with your father as you are with a friend of the opposite sex, or with your spouse? Do you interact in exactly the same fashion with the president of a large corporation as you do with your dog or a baby? Think about it—we all tend to assume different roles in different circumstances.

Various experiences can change our roles for any given situation. Have you, for example, ever been displeased with the role you assumed or the behavior you displayed during a conflict with someone for whom you cared deeply?

The Value of Role Assuming

How can you practice human relations?

An invaluable part of a course in human relations can include the use of role assuming. Situations in a classroom are not exactly identical to situations you may confront at work, nor can you acquire skills solely

---

[4]*As You Like It*, act 2, scene 7.

from lectures or books. You may have discovered that you cannot become skillful in a sport, such as tennis, skiing, or golf, only by reading a "How to" book on the subject. You must practice.

role assuming

The same condition holds true for a human relations course. You must practice the application of effective human relations concepts in order to learn the skillful use of them. *Role assuming* is the concept of creating a more realistic situation, usually one of human problems and conflicts, and then acting out the various parts.

Saying is not doing.

There is the tendency when asked what *you* would do about a given problem to respond with, "Well, if I were the supervisor, I would. . . ." In the real world of organizations you don't resolve problems in such a fashion; you must engage in certain types of action usually involving face-to-face conversation and interaction. Role assuming should, therefore, closely approximate a real situation and afford the participants the vicarious experiences that enhance their sensitivity, growth, and development.

The Good Old Days

Our society has changed since farmers decided to move to the towns during the Industrial Revolution. Sometimes we don't recognize some of the progress that we've made in our human relationships. For an example of the "Good old days," take a look at a set of rules posted by a Boston office manager in 1872.

Rules For Office Employees

1. Office employees each day will fill lamps, clean chimneys and trim wicks. Wash windows once a week.
2. Each clerk will bring in a bucket of water and a scuttle of coal for the day's business.
3. Make your pens carefully. You may whittle nibs to your individual taste.
4. Men employees will be given an evening off each week for courting purposes, or two evenings a week if they go regularly to church.
5. After thirteen hours of labor in the office, the employee should spend the remaining time reading the Bible and other good books.
6. Every employee should lay aside from each pay day a goodly sum of his earnings for his benefit during his declining years so that he will not become a burden on society.
7. Any employee who smokes Spanish cigars, uses liquor in any form, or frequents pool and public halls or gets shaved in a barber shop, will give good reason to suspect his worth, intentions, integrity and honesty.

8. The employee who has performed his labor faithfully and without fault for five years, will be given ~~an increase~~ of five cents per day in his pay, providing profits from business permit it.

[According to the Boston *Sunday Herald* of October 5, 1958, a Boston office manager, cleaning out a file in preparation for his firm's move to a new location, came across these office rules for 1872. He wanted to read them to his office force, but the members all were out on one of the day's several coffee breaks.]

Summary

Human relations, like other behavioral sciences, attempts to explain human behavior. Human relations, however, goes beyond explaining *why* individuals or groups behave as they do. It strives to determine *what can be done* in a positive way about human behavior that may disrupt organizational objectives.

Organizations, and the potential for conflict, exist wherever there are two or more persons. Larger organizations consist of both *planned* or *formal* and *natural* or *informal* structures. The latter is a result of the personal needs that organization members bring to their groups.

The field of human relations is relatively young and is said to have first become recognized as a result of the research studies at Hawthorne made by Elton Mayo and his associates.

Organizations, to survive effectively, require a reasonable amount of *predictability* and *order*. The human relations climate in organizations should be determined by their managements; however, human relations is the responsiblity of *everyone* in organizations.

Individuals attempting to resolve problems rationally should apply *situational thinking* and recognize the need for obtaining relevant information within the time available.

Case studies and role assuming can aid students in developing human relations skills by providing them with vicarious and closer-to-real-life experiences.

Terms and Concepts to Remember

Organizational behavior	Hawthorne effect
Human relations	Required systems
Action-oriented	Emergent systems
Formal organization	Case method approach
Informal organization	Situational thinking
Types of human relationships	Role assuming

Questions

1. Explain the distinction between something that doesn't *work* and something that hasn't been *worked*.
2. Are all types of organizational conflict harmful? Explain.
3. What benefits can be derived from studying a field, such as human relations, that doesn't provide the "correct" answers to all behavioral problems?
4. Explain the major difference between the study of human relations and the study of other behavioral sciences, such as psychology.
5. Do you feel that managers, in order to accomplish their goals more effectively, should attempt to prohibit the emergent or informal organization? Explain.
6. What have been some of the principal causes of the recently expanding popularity of human relations?
7. How do the personal needs of employees relate to organizations?
8. What potential dangers can you foresee for an excessively ordered and predictable organization?
9. What is a major advantage of the case method approach over a human relations training program that is limited to lectures alone?

Other Readings

Bass, Bernard M., and Barrett, Gerald V. *Man, Work, and Organizations—An Introduction to Industrial and Organization Psychology*. Boston: Allyn and Bacon, 1972.

Chesler, Mark, and Fox, Robert. *Role-Playing Methods in the Classroom*. Chicago: Science Research Associates, 1966.

Davis, Keith. *Human Behavior at Work*. 5th ed. New York: McGraw-Hill, 1977.

Landsberger, Henry A. *Hawthorne Revisited*. Ithaca, N.Y.: Cornell University Press, 1958.

Magnuson, Karl O. *Organizational Design, Development, and Behavior*. Glenview, Ill.: Scott, Foresman, 1977.

Miles, Raymond E. *Theories of Management: Implications for Organizational Behavior and Development*. New York: McGraw-Hill, 1975.

Sanford, Aubrey C. *Human Relations: The Theory and Practice of Organizational Behavior*. Columbus, Ohio: Merrill, 1977.

"Solved: The Mystery of the Hawthorne Effect." *Psychology Today*, December 1976, p. 40.

Applications

The Precision Parameter Co.

The Precision Parameter Co. is an electronics firm whose general offices are located in Sunnyvale, California. The firm has separate divisions located in Annandale, Virginia, and Tucson, Arizona, each involved with similar activities and employing approximately 175 to 200 employees. The company is principally a manufacturer of components for electronics equipment, such as hand-held calculators, digital watches, and video games that can be attached to television sets.

Pam Hill, Personnel Vice-President, recently analyzed statistical data from each manufacturing unit and discovered a wide discrepancy between the activities of the Tucson plant and its Annandale counterpart. Ms. Hill discovered that the Tucson plant, compared to Annandale, had:

1. nearly double the rate of employee turnover
2. a 35 percent higher incidence of accidents on the job
3. three times more absenteeism
4. 65 percent more tardiness

Ms. Hill asked the plant managers at both locations to supply her with production figures and discovered that the Tucson plant also had:

1. lower levels of production
2. higher levels of wasted materials and customer-rejected products

Ms. Hill decided to call the two plant managers, Steve Branz of Annandale, and Jim Albritton of Tucson, to Sunnyvale for a conference. The following conversation took place during the meeting:

> *Ms. Hill:* Gentlemen, each of us here is interested in furthering the goals and objectives of the Precision Parameter Company. I want you to know that I haven't called this meeting to criticize anyone, merely to uncover some information so that we can improve our operations at all of our locations in the future.
>
> I personally feel that people are one of our most important resources. I also feel that we might be able to do a more effective job of managing if we knew more about the attitudes of our employees at the production level, and so. . . .
>
> *Mr. Albritton:* Ms. Hill, with all due respect to you, ma'am, I know exactly what you're gonna say. I've been through sessions like this before with personnel people and . . . well . . . they're all just about alike. They sit up there smugly in their

office towers dreaming up new ideas. You're gonna tell me that my division isn't operating as efficiently as Steve's, aren't you? Well, I wanna tell you this. His situation is completely different from mine. You can't get the same types of employees in Tucson that you get in Virginia. They're all either young people who have lost the good old-fashioned work ethic that we all used to have, or they're old and ready to retire, rock back and forth in their chairs, and bask in the warm Arizona sun. I know those production employees. Heck, I used to be one of 'em myself. All they're interested in is their paycheck.

Ms. Hill: Jim, there certainly is the possibility that employment conditions *are* different in your area, but I want to assure you that I'm not here to criticize. Nothing is perfect, but perhaps we three can put our heads together and come up with some ideas on how we might improve things.

What I would like is for us to attempt to develop material that we might incorporate into an employee attitude survey. If we can find out what our employees like and don't like about working for Precision, then perhaps we'll be in a better position to manage more effectively and to retain valuable employees. Let's give it a good positive effort. What do you say?

Questions

1. What do Jim's statements reveal about his attitude toward workers in his plant? In what ways might he be contributing toward the poor results at the Tucson plant?
2. Assume that you are Steve Branz. What broad areas of employee concern would you include in an attitude survey? Develop a list of survey questions that could apply to each of these broad categories.
3. How can the information uncovered in the survey help the managers improve working conditions?

The Clara Dong Case

Clara Dong has been a staff member of a Dallas, Texas, residential care home for the aged for the past eleven years and is admired and respected for her ability to deal with the residents of the home. You, her supervisor, have often claimed that Clara can deal effectively with virtually any of the problems that arise during a normal working day and is more efficient than anyone else on your staff.

Among her co-workers Clara is an informal leader. She is well liked and has a dry wit that contributes to her reputation as a "great person."

Last January, you noticed a change in Clara's behavior. She seemed to be surly and short-tempered. Her fellow workers managed to kid her out of this mood. Several weeks later, Clara's efficiency began to drop. She complained of severe headaches and began to withdraw from contacts with the rest of her work group. The quality of her work has continued to be poor and she seems to be a different woman. Last Monday she came to work drunk. Several of the group covered for her. They took her into the women's room and attempted to sober her up.

You happened to go into the women's room to brush your teeth after lunch and noticed Clara and the women.

Question

What should you do about this situation?

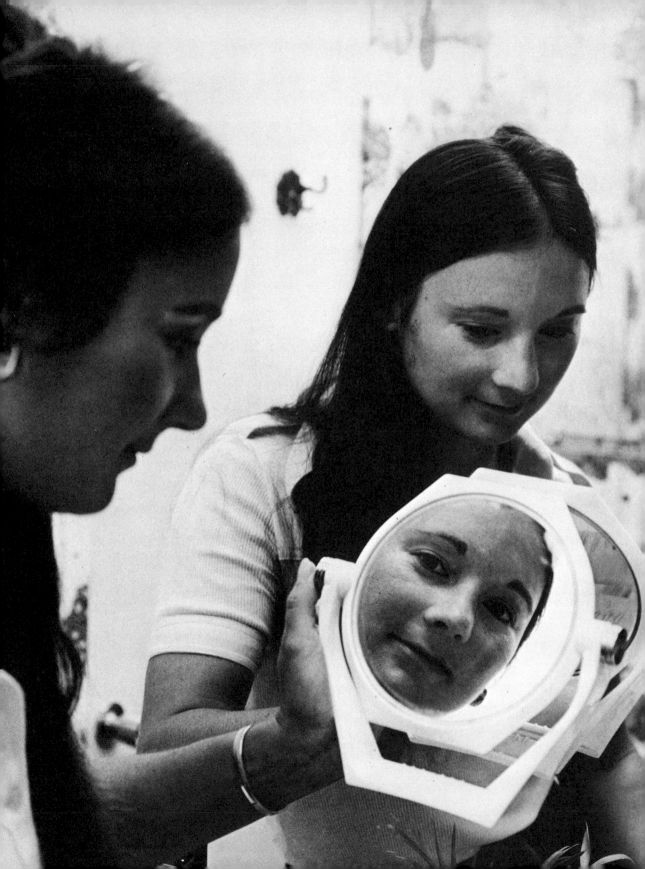

When you finish this chapter, you should be able to:

1. **Recognize** the difference between a fact and an inference.
2. **List** the factors that influence what a person sees in a given situation.
3. **List and describe** at least five pitfalls in logical reasoning.
4. **Summarize** the scientific method approach to problem solving.
5. **Describe** how creativity can aid the problem-solving process.

Aide: I see they have painted
the streetcars.
President Coolidge (while
riding through Detroit): Yes.
At least on one side.
—Attributed to Calvin Coolidge

Creativity is seeing what
everyone else sees,
but thinking what no one
else thinks.
—Albert Szent-Györgyi

Why do you go to college? To get answers, right? If you agree, perhaps you had better dwell a bit longer on this subject. Have you ever noticed that answers that seemed at one time to be "correct" are frequently discovered to be incorrect later? We need to feel secure, and we often feel considerably more secure when we believe that there are absolute answers to perplexing questions. Perhaps Bertrand Russell hit the nail squarely on the head when he said, "Those who believe themselves to be absolutely right are often absolutely wrong!"

The Importance of Seeing What's Really There

In this chapter we are going to explore some of the major concepts of perception in the hope that a better understanding of them will assist you in perceiving organizational situations more accurately.

We all have observed how different individuals seem to perceive the same situation dissimilarly. You merely have to take a ride in your automobile to observe some of the extreme differences in the perceptions of other drivers (and who knows what they are thinking about you!). Have you ever attended judicial courtroom proceedings and observed the pronounced differences in the perceptions of the same situation by defendants and plaintiffs?

A Perceptual Tendency

mental set

There is a human tendency to believe that what *we* see is the truth. If there is a difference of opinion, it must be the other guy who is off base. Many people, however, tend to perceive what they want, *or are set*, to see, *regardless of reality*. We call this type of perception *mental set*.

Why should you want your head drycleaned?

If we are going to confront human relations problems objectively, we must attempt to develop the ability to see things as they really are, not as we are set to see them. A prime (and dreadful-sounding) objective of this chapter is the *cleansing and confusing of your mind*. You'll see what is meant by this statement as we progress.

A Perceptual Enigma

Take a look at figure 2-1. What do you see? Most observers will see a woman. Approximately how old is the woman? Does she appear young, possibly in her twenties? Or does she look rather old, probably in her sixties? Or does she seem to be middle-aged? Make a decision before you read further.

So, about how old is she?

Figure 2-1.

25

About half of those who observe the picture will typically feel that the person is a young woman. Others will contend that she looks quite old. A few will say that she appears middle-aged. Still others will argue that there are *both* an old and a young woman in the sketch. Which did you see? Look at the picture again for a few moments and see if your original perception changes. If you saw the young woman, look for the older one. Did you see the older one first? If so, try to see the young one. *Both are actually there*. If you see only one woman and are disturbed by this, you

frustration could be experiencing a phenomenon called *frustration*, a feeling described as "dissatisfaction arising from unresolved problems."

If at first you observed only one woman, what might have been the reason? Could you have been mentally set to see only one? Why did you see only the young (or the older) woman at first? The point is this: Sometimes we don't immediately see the entire meaning in a situation; accurate perception may take some intense effort. Numerous organizational problems are a result of poor or incomplete perception.

Preset Judgments Can Sink Ships

Have you ever known anyone whose mind seems to be already made up on a subject before he or she has gathered enough facts to make an accurate judgment? We all are probably guilty of such inflexibility at times.

Here's a short sea story about a sailor who didn't have the opportunity to make the same mistake in perception twice. In 1912 there was a ship, proclaimed to be virtually unsinkable: the *Titanic*—named after a giant in Greek mythology. Her builders were so absolutely certain (remember Bertrand Russell?) of her indestructability that too few lifeboats were provided for the passengers. The world was dismayed when the highly acclaimed vessel failed to complete her maiden voyage from Southhampton to New York. Captain Smith, the *Titanic's* skipper, apparently set in his perceptions, perceived a small hunk of floating ice that, unfortu-

Why did Captain Smith goof? nately, turned out to be a massive submerged iceberg. A fatal gash ended the voyage prematurely. The ship sank and took 1,513 lives with her! How might this incident relate to problems of perception in organizations?

Judgments Should Leave Room for Error

We all must make judgments and decisions in our daily lives without first

Can you *really* "size up" a person right away? acquiring all of the facts, but we should realize that sometimes our picture of reality will be accurate while at other times it will not. Have you ever found yourself making judgments about other people based solely on their clothes? Retail sales personnel have sometimes lost sales after assuming that a tattered looking person could not afford the goods.

Do you tend to judge a person by his handshake? A popular cliché states that "a *real man* shakes hands with firmness and strength—not like a fish." However, within many cultures, both in America and abroad, a firm handshake is an indication of lack of warmth.

When dealing with problems of human relationships, attempt to acquire relevant facts before making up your mind. False assumptions will usually result in false conclusions. Most of your judgments should be flexible and allow room for possible error.

Another Perception Puzzle

Are details important? Read the short sentence in figure 2-2 below. Have you read it? Okay. Will you now reread it and count—that's right, *count* the number of times that the letter *F* appears. How many do you see?

Figure 2-2.

> FINISHED FILES ARE THE RE-
> SULT OF YEARS OF SCIENTIFIC
> STUDY COMBINED WITH THE EX-
> PERIENCE OF MANY YEARS.

Did you count three *F*s? Most readers will; others will count four or five; still others will find six. There are six. Did you see them all immediately? If not, why not? Did you overlook half of the letters—the *F* in the word *of*? Unimportant detail, you may say, but you were specifically requested to count *F*s, weren't you? In a human relations problem could you afford to overlook 50 percent of the relevant details?

A Typical Family Scene

Would you like to meet yourself? Now let's look at a different type of quiz. Improving your human relations skills is far easier when you have acquired greater self-understanding, and there are tests designed to tell you something about yourself. Figure 2-3 is a picture of the Shuck family. Take a careful look at the picture. Then, based on what you see, answer whether the statements below the picture are *true*, *false*, or *cannot be answered at all*.

Figure 2-3.

	True	False	?
1. There are three people and a dog in the room.	___	___	___
2. The Shuck family owns a television set.	___	___	___
3. The Shuck family consists of Mr. Shuck, Mrs. Shuck, and Jeremy.	___	___	___
4. Mrs. Shuck is having a before-dinner cocktail.	___	___	___
5. Mr. Shuck smokes cigars.	___	___	___
6. Jeremy is doing his homework while watching TV.	___	___	___
7. They have a dachshund for a pet.	___	___	___
8. They are watching a nighttime TV program.	___	___	___
9. Mr. Shuck is a stockholder.	___	___	___
10. The Shucks subscribe to *Time*, *Business Week*, and *Ebony*.	___	___	___
11. Mrs. Shuck is upset at Mr. Shuck.	___	___	___

Answers to Perception Quiz

From what you were able to observe in the picture on the preceding page, *none* of the statements could be said to be true or false. All should have been answered with a question mark.

1. This question points out a problem in semantics. There are three people and a dog in the room, *but there may be more*. You cannot see the entire room. In fact, both the photographer, Howard Rodkin, and your author were in the room when the photograph was taken. If you had seen the *entire* room and were asked for the number of persons in the room, wouldn't you be likely to have said five?

2. The Shuck family *may* own a television set, but do we know this to be a fact? The set could be rented, or they might not even be in their own house.

3. From the picture do we really know what the Shuck family consists of? There may be more members of the family than are in the picture.

4. Is it a cocktail, a glass of water, or what? Do we really know from the picture?

5. Mr. Shuck may smoke cigars; he may not. Is it possible that someone else left the cigar there? Who knows, perhaps Mrs. Shuck smokes them.

6. Do we know from the picture what Jeremy is really doing? Have you ever attempted to *appear* to be doing one thing while *doing* something else?

7. Is the dachshund necessarily theirs? Couldn't they be dogsitting? Are there any other possibilities?

8. People often have lights on during the daytime. Can we really tell from the picture whether it is day or night?

9. Anyone can buy *The Wall Street Journal*, which is a news as well as a financial paper. Possession of the *Journal* does not automatically give one capitalist status!

10. Do the Shucks necessarily subscribe to the publications? Couldn't they possibly buy them at a store, be given them by a neighbor, or check them out of a library? Do we know for a fact where the magazines came from? All we really can do is to draw inferences.

11. Can we really tell from a photo how Mrs. Shuck feels?

The purpose of this quiz is to stress the differences between *facts* and *inferences*. Read on and you will discover what those differences are.

Facts versus Inferences

Most of us are fairly impressed by facts. Many persons look with envy upon the person who seems to have all the answers. Quiz shows have continually been one of the favorite types of daytime and family hour television programs. Detective stories continue to be popular with many individuals who enjoy reading about others clever in hunting down facts. There is nothing wrong with facts. Perhaps they deserve your respect. But are you clear about what a fact actually is? Do you know the important distinctions between *facts* and *inferences?*

A Consensus Definition

A fact may be defined as "anything that we agree to be true." If the general consensus of society is, for example, that the earth is flat, we could say that we have established a fact—according to our definition—and that the earth *is* flat. Quite often a consensus is correct; occasionally it is not. For years no one saw anyone fall off the edge of the earth, yet people went right along believing that the earth was flat. The Catholic Church once excommunicated a nice Italian boy by the name of Galileo for refuting the established "facts" on the subject of the gravitational attraction of the earth's mass; that is, the law of gravity. So you see that the consensus definition of a fact can often fall flat on its face, gravitationally speaking.

HEY, GUISEPPE, WILL YOU LOOK AT THAT? IT'S GALILEO TOSSING SOME BALLS OFF THE EDGE OF THE EARTH AGAIN!

An "Actual" Fact

One of Mr. Webster's definitions of a fact is the "quality of being actual." Without becoming excessively philosophical, when can we say that an event is "actual"? For example, is it a fact that John, an employee of your organization, has recently become lazy on the job? Or is his idleness something that you have observed and internally *feel* to be a fact? Is he actually lazy or have you inferred it? Perhaps John has some personal problems that have changed his normal behavior on the job.

Is Oakland a fact or an inference?

The point of this discussion is that it is important for you to differentiate between facts and inferences. Many things are well-documented facts, such as the population of Oakland, California, but facts such as this are really history and change rapidly.

Where is the line between fact and inference?

The fine line between fact and inference is difficult to see, but the distinction is important. For example, assume that you are a professor who has just finished giving an examination, and an apparently troubled student anxiously asks to speak with you. She states that she saw two students cheating, saying that she knows they were cheating because she saw one pass a piece of paper to the other during the exam. Is it a fact or an inference that the two students cheated? Your assumptions as the professor might significantly influence your action in such a case. True, passing notes during an exam is questionable behavior, but were the students actually cheating? We can infer that they were, but could we logically state our opinion as a fact?

The following is a summary of some of the major differences between statements of fact and inferences.[1]

Inferences	*Facts*
1. Are made any time—before, during, and after observation.	1. Are established after observation or experience.
2. Go beyond what one observes.	2. Are confined to what one observes.
3. Represent only some degree of probability.	3. Represent as close to certainty as anyone ever gets.
4. Usually generate disagreement.	4. Tend to get agreement.
5. Are unlimited in number.	5. Are limited in number.

Possibilities, Probabilities, and Certainties

In a sense that may sound strange we could state that all facts are really inferences with differing degrees of probability. The nearer an inference

[1]*Fundamentals of Management* (USPS Training and Development, Postal Service Management Institute, n.d.), p. 164.

If something is *possible*, is it necessarily *probable*?

is to certainty, the closer it is to being a fact. All this may sound a bit philosophical, but perhaps it could be made clearer with the use of a probability scale (see figure 2-4). For example, one could state that the book that you are reading at this moment has been made from poisonous paper. Is such a statement one of fact or inference? Is it possible that if you ripped off a corner and munched on it you would expire? Certainly it is *possible*, but is it *probable?* Remember that almost anything can be said to be possible (could occur), but far fewer things are probable (are *likely* to occur).

PROBABILITY SCALE

No Chance					Probable				Certain
1	2	3	4	5	6	7	8	9	10

Figure 2-4.

Let's look at a final example of this topic. Assume that you are a law enforcement officer watchfully walking your beat along Telegraph Avenue in Berkeley, California, and you observe a long-haired youth loitering on the sidewalk. Then you discern next to the young fellow's faded-green right tennis shoe what appears to be the remains of a previously smoked marihuana cigarette—an inference that would be ranked fairly low on the probability scale. Next you dutifully pick up the object, smell it, and decide that the probability of the cigarette's being marihuana has moved up to about nine on the scale. Should you cite the young man for possession? You know for a "fact" that the cigarette is marihuana, but does your police training tell you whether it is a fact or an inference that the cigarette belonged to the long-haired youth? Where would you place his *possession* on the scale? Is it likely that you could convince an objective jury that the cigarette absolutely belonged to the young man?

Decisions in the real world of organizations must be made. Within our limited time we must somehow attempt to make *certainties out of probabilities*. Yet we must remember to be flexible in our thinking and realize that what we believe to be a fact at this moment could turn out later to be not even a good inference. Leave some room for possible error, and be willing to alter your approach when new "facts" are discovered.

The Determinates of Perception

Numerous factors influence your perception, that is, the way in which you see a particular situation. Among the more significant are:

What influences the mental photo you take?

1. Hereditary factors
2. Environmental background and experiences
3. Peer pressures
4. Projection
5. Snap judgments
6. Halo and tarnished halo effects

Hereditary Factors

Who made the choice—you or your parents?

You didn't have much influence in the choice of your parents or grand-parents. You may have been merely the result of a gleam in your father's eye. However, they had a considerable effect on who and what you are. In science courses you can learn in some detail how hereditary factors influence offspring. For our purposes, however, it is sufficient to understand that in addition to things such as the shape of your nose and the size of your feet, your parentage also determines your vision and color acuity. For example, if you are myopic (nearsighted), what you see without your glasses will differ from what a person with 20/20 vision sees. Or, like one out of about ten American males, you might have a color-weak tendency (popularly called color blindness), and will see many objects differently from a person with normal color perception. Your vision and ability to perceive colors will often affect your eligibility for particular careers, such as those of airline pilot, commercial artist, or interior decorator.

Environmental Background and Experiences

Is a house always a home?

Environment probably has a greater influence on what you see in a given situation than anything else. For example, think about a babe-in-arms deriving her necessary nourishment from her mother's breasts. If during her early years she continually hears from her parents such utterances as, "Those people are lazy . . . they don't really want to work . . . those people stink . . . those people are cheap," the infant has a good chance of emerging into adolescence with a firm belief in such statements. After all, parents do provide the infant with her needs, determine what is right and wrong for her, and are practically her complete frame of reference when she is in her early formative stages.

Usually young persons will gravitate toward companions who share common beliefs and interests, and many of their early prejudices will tend to become reinforced or intensified. Educational experiences may change some beliefs but can have the reverse effect of making individuals defensive of their existing beliefs. Did you perchance find yourself becoming defensive when you took any of the perception tests?

The way you perceive any situation is significantly influenced by your past experiences. The next time, for example, you see the "How Many *F*s?" perception test, the chances are good that you will see the "truth" quite quickly.

Peer Pressures

How do your peers press you?

peer effect

Related to environmental experiences is the effect that our *peers* or friends have on what we see. Perception within groups is often different from individual perception.

An example of the *peer effect* took place in a classroom during a discussion of a human relations problem. After most of the students had developed firm opinions on the case, a latecomer entered the classroom. The professor decided to see if she would be influenced by what she believed to be the attitudes of the other students, so she was told that the class had considered the behavior of a specific person in the case to be ridiculous, and then asked if she agreed. She responded with an emphatic, "Yes!" The professor then confessed that the class had *not* felt that the situation was ridiculous. She then admitted that she hadn't even read the case, but felt as if she should go along with the group. Perhaps our desire for peer acceptance influences our perception more than we sometimes realize. Chapter 4 will explore in greater depth the influence of small groups on the behavior of individuals.

Projection

projection

Say, Pete, that's not Paul you're talking about— that's you!

"Everybody else cheats on their expense accounts, why shouldn't I?" If you haven't already heard that question, chances are that one day you will. There is a human tendency to attribute to others some of our own faults and motives, a characteristic called *projection*. But think quite seriously about a statement once made by the Dutch philosopher Spinoza: "When Peter talks about Paul, we often learn more about Peter than we do about Paul."

So if you assume, for example, that almost everyone cheats on expense accounts or examinations (or in politics!), might not your assumptions be related to your own behavior and values? When approaching human relations problems, be careful that your perceptions are not clouded by the projection of your own values into another person's situation.

34

Snap Judgments

How might *you* avoid *snapping* your *judgments?*

Have you ever known anyone who exclaims proudly: "I can size up a person right away!" Most of us from time to time are guilty of making *snap judgments* before we have gathered enough facts to come to valid conclusions. Frequently we attempt to solve a problem before we know what the problem actually is. Married couples who have lived together more than five years are still learning about each other. So hold back a bit. How can you possibly make a valid judgment about a person or a human problem after only a minute or two of exposure to the situation?

Halo and Tarnished Halo Effects

halo effect

Another human tendency that affects perception has been labeled the *halo effect*: a person is good at one thing and so is assumed to be good at something else—the assumption creating the halo.

For example, assume that you are a foreman or supervisor in a machine shop. Freddy Fnurd, a subordinate of yours, has been one of the best drill press operators in your section for over five years. A lathe operator is unexpectedly needed in another section. You recommend Freddy, assuming that he will also do well at the lathe. Freddy bombs! He may have excelled at one job, but he lacked the necessary skill or aptitude for the accomplishment of the other. Figuratively you had placed a halo over Freddy's head. Another example of the halo effect could be found in the situation in which two of your men have a violent fistfight on the job. One of the men is a personal friend with whom you regularly socialize off the job. Watch out for the tendency to place a halo over your friend's head by assuming that the other fellow must have been the cause of the conflict.

tarnished halo

Some supervisors are guilty of what could be termed a *tarnished halo* effect. For example, assume that there is a particularly incompetent man in your department who continually goofs in his job. You might place a tarnished halo over his head by assuming that he would not do well in any job on which you might place him. When perceiving people try to perceive them as they really are. Watch out for the tendency to place halos, shiny or dull, over their heads.

Was King Kong, scaler of tall buildings, a good dancer?

A Few Fallacies

In working with case materials or human relations problems, there are a number of pitfalls in logical thinking that you should make an effort to avoid:

1. The fallacy of composition
2. The fallacy of division
3. *Post hoc, ergo propter hoc*
4. Wishing it were so
5. Two-valued reasoning

The Fallacy of Composition

If it's true for you, is it true for everyone?

''Anybody can go to college if he really wants to. I didn't have any bread, but I worked nights, lifted myself up by the bootstraps, and got a college degree. If I could do it, anyone can!'' Is that statement necessarily true? What if a person has a disability or a large family to support and is living up to or beyond the limits of his or her income? What if a person has not had the good fortune to be born with the capacity for knowledge or the mental abilities of another? What if one came from an environment that discouraged intellectual growth? The exceptions could go on and on; in fact, the exceptions could become the rule!

There is, however, the tendency to assume that what is true for one person or situation is, therefore, true for all persons or situations. If you were to make such an assumption, you might be guilty of employing the *fallacy of composition*

fallacy of composition, more formally defined as the fallacy of *assuming that what is true of a part is, on that account alone, alleged to be true also of the whole.*

There are, of course, generalizations that are true. For example, if one person were to puncture an artery and then bleed profusely, we could be secure in generalizing that all individuals would experience similar bleeding upon puncturing an artery.

However, assume that you are observing a parade, and there are three rows of tall persons standing in front of you. If you stand on your tiptoes, you will undoubtedly be able to see more of the parade. But, if everybody stands on tiptoes, will anyone see any better? What was true for you alone was not necessarily true for all (except maybe the case of tired arches!). So be on guard against the use of the fallacy of composition.

Fallacy of Divison

fallacy of division

''Sunshine is good for everybody, so it certainly would be good for that pale white fellow under the beach umbrella. Why doesn't he get out into the sun?'' Such reasoning is an example of the *fallacy of division*, that is, *the assumption that what is true for the whole is necessarily true for each of its parts.* In other words, a person has learned somewhere that sunshine is good for people and decides that, therefore, it must be good for everyone. However, there are individuals who lack ample pigmentation of the skin and cannot tolerate the intensity of the sun's rays.

Here is an organizational example of the fallacy of division: Let's assume that a supervisor, Esther, recently completed a company-sponsored human relations training program. Esther learned that certain human relations techniques tend to increase the productivity of workers. If she assumes that results that are generally true will necessarily be true for every one of her subordinates, she may be applying the fallacy of division.

Be careful not to confuse the fallacy of composition with the fallacy of division; they are opposites.

Post Hoc, Ergo Propter Hoc (The Fallacy of False Cause)

after this, therefore because of this

Of course, if you are a college student you fluently speak and read Latin and therefore know the meaning of the phrase, *post hoc, ergo propter hoc*. Literally (just in case you don't speak Latin!) the words may be translated as, "after this, therefore because of this." The fallacy is formally defined as *the assumption that when one event precedes another, the first event necessarily causes the second*. A simpler way of illustrating the term is this: event A occurs and is followed by event B. If you assume that in every instance event A is the cause of event B, you may be guilty of *post hoc* reasoning.

Do showers cause colds?

For example, assume that yesterday, after a late dinner, you took a hot shower and immediately afterwards streaked completely nude through your front entrance into the cool night air to sit on the edge of the cold, damp concrete curb. This morning you came down with a miserable head cold. Did event A—the act of running outside dripping wet after the warm shower—cause event B—the cold? Not necessarily. What usually causes colds? Air? Or is it not rather a virus or germs? Besides, the incubation period of most colds is usually longer than one day. Perhaps you shouldn't have been so affectionate toward your sneezing friend two days ago!

Embarassed?

However, if a policeman had arrested you while you were sitting bare buttocked on the chilly concrete, perhaps we could find a relationship between the two events—your lounging naked in public and your arrest.

Another example: Assume that one of your subordinates is transferred to a different position within your department. Shortly thereafter the quality and quantity of her work begins to decline. What is the cause? Perhaps it is the transfer, but perhaps it isn't. Additional facts might indicate that she now has problems that bear no relationship to her new position. Once again, caution should be employed when making judgments about others. Perhaps there is no correlation between two consecutive events.

post hoc and *ad hoc*

One more thing: Don't confuse *post hoc* with *ad hoc*. *Ad hoc* (literally, *for this*) is a term often used to describe, for instance, a committee that has been temporarily established to work on a specific task.

Wishing-It-Were-So Philosophy

Have you ever wished upon a star?

We all tend to believe what we want to believe. If you have a vested interest in and are loyal to the company for which you work, you might believe that its practices are right regardless of how society perceives certain of its activities. Have you noticed how often environmentalists and oil company executives see things differently?

wishing it were so

Let's look at an organizational example of *wishing it were so*. Assume that you are a manager who has developed a program designed to give your workers a better understanding of the importance of high profits to your firm. You feel that, given the information, they too will see the importance. You may be in for a surprise the next time that the wage contract comes up for renegotiation. *Wishing something to be true does not make it so.* When confronted with human problems with conflicting and opposite views, you should be careful not to make what *appears* to be the favorable decision by substituting hope for logic.

Two-Valued Reasoning

Can something be *both* good *and* bad?

As the Asian American said to the native American, "Things aren't always either black or white!" That excessively corny pun may help to illustrate a human tendency to believe that in any situation there is only *one correct side*. To the person who engages in *two-valued reasoning*, situations are either right or wrong, good or bad—with no possibilities in between. You may have observed such a philosophy, expressed as, "we are right and they are wrong." Once you have dug more deeply into the problem, you will frequently discover that there usually is *more* than one right side to any problem. Organizational problems are seldom clearly divided into entirely right or entirely wrong positions. Be sure to look for those shades of gray in issues which seem to be clearly black or white.

two-valued reasoning

Can a situation have more than two sides?

Our language, unlike Asian languages, seems well-designed for the limited two-valued approach to reasoning. For example, we have no word in the English language for describing a person's being "a little bit pregnant." A woman, in the English language, is either pregnant or she isn't. We can, however, overcome the shortcomings of our language by applying *multi-valued reasoning* to organizational problems; that is by recognizing that in most situations there may be even *more* than two sides.

multi-valued reasoning

A Logical Approach to Problem Solving

There are numerous ways in which individuals approach problems. Some techniques are more effective than others. One widely-followed approach, a condensed modification of which follows, is called the *scientific method*.

scientific method

Step 1. What is the problem? Some persons dive energetically into their problems as would a wild cougar in quest of food. A far more effective approach to problem solving is first to *define the problem*. Sufficient facts about a problem have to be gathered to enable you to develop a reasonable definition. Over-eagerness in problem solving has often resulted in "good solutions" for the wrong situation. Furthermore, many capable employees have been fired from their jobs because the employer hastily and wrongly defined a problem.

define

Step 2. What are your recommendations for the solution to the problem? Note that "recommendations" is in the plural form. There seldom is only one solution to a problem. Often you will discover after making alternative recommendations that your second or third solution appears more realistic and reasonable than your first.

recommend

Step 3. What are the implications of your recommendations? This step is more important than it may first appear. Before actually carrying out any recommendations, you would be wise to *anticipate* the probable effects of each recommendation on the situation itself. By doing so, you may discover that some recommendations would create more problems than they resolve.

anticipate

Step 4. Carry out your "best" recommendation. After evaluating all of your alternatives, choose the recommendation that, in your judgment, will accomplish your desired objectives, and *apply* it to the problem. However, don't forget the concept of situational thinking. You may have to alter your plans during your efforts. Will you be ready for such contingencies?

apply

Step 5. Follow-up. The problem-solving process is not yet complete. To ensure that your actions accomplish your objectives, you should examine carefully the situation at a later (but not too late!) date.

re-examine

Step 6. Modify if necessary. If, in your re-examination, you discover that your goals have not been accomplished, you may have to study the problem again and apply other alternatives to it.

modify

Creativity and Problem Solving

A characteristic known as a creative mind can be tremendously effective in helping you develop sound alternatives to difficult problems. Let's take a brief excursion into the often-misunderstood area known as *creativity*.

What Is Creativity?

Creative minds of the past have developed a variety of definitions for the term *creativity*. What do you think of when you envision a creative person? Is she or he one of those oddball types who don funny clothes, wear their hair either too short or too long, and work, live, and play in environments that look as though a hurricane recently struck? To many people, this is the creative person. But isn't it what individuals *do* and what they *accomplish,* rather than how they look that makes them creative?

creativity

What, then, is *creativity?* Let's say that it's any thinking process that solves a problem or achieves a goal in an *original and useful way.* But few ideas, if we really think about it, are 100 percent fresh and new. Creative ideas can also result from examining established ideas and methods and building onto them. Creativity is also the ability to see *useful relationships among dissimilar things*. Try, if you will, to think of two objects or ideas that are not directly related but that could be synthesized into a third useful object or idea.

What Can Help You Become More Creative?

Can you imagine what you might accomplish by using your imagination?

You don't need to be a genius to be creative. What you do need is to use your imagination. Problem-solving activities are often more effective when you allow your mind to run free, sometimes even allowing it to go off into what at first appears to be insane directions. But look for useful relationships among seemingly unrelated objects and you are likely to develop ideas and solutions to problems that you previously felt incapable of handling.

A few of the acquired characteristics of the creative person include being *inquisitive and innovative,* being able to make *new applications of older concepts,* and being *receptive and open-minded to new ideas*. The negative person—the individual who feels new ideas won't work, even before they have been tried—finds it difficult to be creative. Managers should encourage their subordinates to be creative and innovative in their activities.

Most people, with sufficient desire and practice, can improve their creative ability. Why not give it a try? The feeling of having created useful ideas can even help improve your feelings toward your job and your personal life.

Summary

Perception, by which individuals acquire the mental images of their environment, is an important element of organizational behavior. You have to be able to perceive human relations situations accurately to be effective in preventing or resolving difficulties in organizations. A major purpose of this chapter, therefore, has been to assist you in developing greater sensitivity of perception. Perception tests reveal that we do not necessarily see an accurate or complete picture of a situation immediately. An awareness and application of certain perceptual concepts, however, can sharpen one's ability to see reality.

The differences between a fact and an inference are not always clear. Facts can be said to be inferences which appear at higher points on a probability scale. Facts may be disproved by new evidence. Flexibility in making judgments is, therefore, essential.

Both heredity and environment influence a person's perception of a given situation. Perception is also affected by the pressure of peers, the tendency to project one's own values onto others, snap judgments, and the halo effect.

An awareness of some of the major fallacies in logic can help eliminate or reduce the usual pitfalls of reasoning and perception.

The application of the scientific method and creativity to the solution of human relations problems can help reduce the number of failures or ineffective efforts.

Terms and Concepts to Remember

Mental set

Peer effect

Projection

Snap judgments

Halo effect

Fallacy of composition

Fallacy of division

Fallacy of false cause

Wishing-it-were-so philosophy

Two-valued reasoning

Multi-valued reasoning

Scientific method

Creativity

Questions

1. Give two examples of human relations problems that can develop as a result of your perceiving inferences as though they were facts.
2. Explain how heredity and past experience influence perception. How might education alter perception?
3. Would your perception of a political speech that you and three close friends had watched on television together be any different if you had watched it alone? Why or why not?
4. Give three examples of the halo effect that you personally have observed.
5. Determine the fallacies in the following statements:
   a. ''Every product that our firm has ever produced always outsold our competitors'. Our latest product, an electric banana peeler, will also outpace its competition.''

    b. "We recently hired a graduate of Sage State University and he is the sloppiest employee I've ever seen. That's the last time I hire anyone from *that* university!"

    c. "We've never had these types of problems in Department C before we sent Jones, the supervisor, to that human relations training program. I think we've had enough 'human relations' nonsense around here!"

    d. "Labor unions are harmful to a free-enterprise system and should be outlawed before it's too late!"

    e. "Of course I'm aware that Clarence has had no training or experience in management, but I'm sure that he will be able to handle that supervisory job. After all, he *is* my son."

    f. "Low tuition is why many students don't do well in college. If we were to raise tuition, students would be willing to study harder and, therefore, get better grades."

6. When attempting to solve human relations problems, why is step 3 of the scientific method, analyzing the implications of your recommendations, so important?

Other Readings

Fabun, Don. *Three Roads to Awareness—Motivation, Creativity, Communications.* Beverly Hills: Glencoe Press, 1970.

Gregory, Richard L. *Eye and Brain,* 2d ed. New York: McGraw-Hill (World University Library), 1973.

Osborn, Alex F. *Applied Imagination.* New York: Charles Scribner's Sons, 1960.

Samples, Bob. *The Metaphoric Mind: A Celebration of Creative Consciousness.* Reading, Mass.: Addison-Wesley, 1976.

Vernon, M. D. *The Psychology of Perception.* Baltimore: Penguin Books, 1962.

Application

The Slinky Sam Case

Assume that you are a law enforcement officer investigating the burglary at a house that had been empty for a previous weekend. The rooms had been freshly painted on Friday, so the occupants decided to rent a motel room rather than to endure the smell.

Upon their return, the owners discovered that a window had been forced open and expensive pieces of silver and china were missing from a cabinet across the room from the window. You discover a handprint on the fresh paint next to the cabinet, check the print, and determine that it belongs to Slinky Sam, a person with a history of convictions for burglary.

Questions

1. Is it fact or inference that a burglary occurred in the house?
2. Is it fact or inference that Slinky Sam had been in the room from which the valuable items were taken?

The Case of the Snapping Judgments

News Item, Houston. A short circuit fought off more than sixty police officers along the Houston ship channel before it was finally subdued. Plain clothes and uniformed officers spent the predawn hours chasing what they thought was someone peppering them with gunfire from atop one of the tanks. One officer said he had been shot in the heel of the shoe. Another graphically described slugs slamming into a road paved with oyster shells. Police threw themselves to the ground with each loud crack.

Fire trucks stood ready and police lobbed tear gas bombs into spots where they thought a sniper was hiding. In the first light of dawn two sheriff's deputies and four journalists came upon the culprit—in a one-inch piece of pipe. The "shots" were nothing more than the popping noise produced by water dripping through an opening into a conduit pipe, seeping through insulation tape, and shorting out a piece of No. 8 electrical wire. "I just goofed," said electrician R. A. Graves, who was called in to silence the wire. He said he forgot to put a plate on the outside of the pipe which keeps the wire inside waterproof. The richocheting noises which sent police scurrying for cover during the dark of night were produced by the outside pipe vibrating against the adjacent conveyor belt with each big pop. The plate that was missing from the pipe cost $2.50. The personnel used to hunt down the "sniper" cost Harris county and the city of Houston an estimated $3,000. *

Questions

1. What appears to be the main problem in the above incident? How might the problem have been avoided?
2. List at least five types of activities inherent in certain jobs that would tend to cause some people to perceive negative situations where none actually existed.
3. How might the above incident relate to you in your particular job?

*Adapted from "The Sneakiest Gun in Texas," *San Francisco Chronicle* (24 May 1968).

The Smelly Case

Abel Mann, division manager at Ajax Perfumes, was reviewing the production records for their best selling product, Smelnise. The information covered the last quarter and revealed a decreasing amount of production during the last two months. When Abel compared the Smelnise results with those of other Ajax perfumes, he noted that Smelnise had the lowest production record. Abel knew Smelnise was no more difficult to produce than any other Ajax product, yet Smelnise production was considerably below planned goals. Abel sat back in his padded executive chair, propped his feet on his spacious mahogany desk, loosened his tie, and began to reflect on this production problem.

Three months ago the production responsibilities for Smelnise had been assigned to Wanda Werk. Wanda had been with Ajax since graduating from Quality University with a major in chemistry. Wanda had taken top honors in a class of sixty-four students, and her last two years at the university had been paid for through a grant she won for her persistence, accuracy, and attention to detail on a chemical research project for the university. During the past three years at Ajax, Wanda had headed a small laboratory group validating ingredients for the various Ajax products.

The laboratory group, headed by Wanda Werk, was considered a hard-working and systemized team. It was the group's task to receive samples from each batch of ingredients used in all Ajax perfumes. Before each batch could be released, the laboratory technicians performed standardization tests on the samples and completed a validation form that was then presented to Wanda for her review and signature. Wanda personally participated with the technicians in some validations and periodically repeated the validation tests in order to confirm the technicians' results. Group morale was good, work performance was timely and accurate, and coordination with other departments at Ajax was favorable. The validation laboratory generally performed well above expectations, with Wanda receiving credit for the satisfactory performance. Her results had made her a prime candidate when Abel Mann was searching for a Smelnise production supervisor.

As Abel continued to reflect on the production problem, he wondered if he should again confer with Wanda. During their last conference, she had mentioned a need for retraining some of her quality controllers and subordinate supervisors. The interphone buzzer interrupted his thoughts.

''Mr. Mann, this is Charlie over in the warehouse,'' the interphone announced. ''Our inventory on Smelnise is getting low,'' the voice continued. ''Can you push up the production before marketing gets on our tail?''

Abel Mann dispatched Charlie with assurances that he would check into it and get back to him. As he clicked off the interphone, he knew he would have to stop reflecting and start acting. He had a problem that needed solving now.

Questions

1. What was the likely reason that Abel Mann selected Wanda Werk as production supervisor of Smelnise?
2. What pitfall of logical thinking may be involved if Abel Mann blames the lagging production on Wanda Werk? Explain.
3. What would be the quickest way for Abel Mann to replenish the warehouse temporarily?
4. Using the scientific method, define the steps necessary for Abel Mann to find a long range solution to Smelnise's production problem.

There's More to Communicating Than Meets the Ear

When you finish this chapter, you should be able to:

1. **Identify** the essential ingredients of effective communication.
2. **Summarize** the main characteristics of words.
3. **Explain** the problems associated with the use of feedback mechanisms.
4. **List** five methods for minimizing communication breakdowns.
5. **Describe** the nature of the silent languages.
6. **Cite** the benefits of effective listening habits to the organization and its members.
7. **Recognize** the difficulties that may arise when supervisors don listening "earmuffs."
8. **List** five types of listening responses.
9. **Contrast** "open" with "closed" questions.

> God gave us two ears and only one mouth.
> In view of the way we use these,
> it is probably a very good thing
> that this is not reversed.
>
> —Cicero

> Words are poor conveyors of meaning
> —in fact, it is a wonder
> that two people ever do
> understand one another.
>
> —Carl Rogers

Have you ever played the silly little group game of whispering a phrase or sentence into the ear of the person seated beside you who then passes the message on to the person beside him or her, and so on, until the message has been transmitted to everyone in the room? The results are sometimes startling. Frequently, the message becomes completely unrecognizable by the time it returns to the original sender.

Such an exercise helps to illustrate an important concept: *communication* can take place in a variety of situations, but for communication to be *effective* there must be *understanding*. One of the major causes of human relations problems in organizations today is the lack of effective communication. Often supervisors *assume* that they have communicated if they have made oral statements to their subordinates. And frequently leaders are virtually positive that they have communicated when they have transmitted a message in writing. Naturally, one does have to make certain assumptions in this world in order to function, but as one manager wryly put it, "When you *a s s u m e*, you often make an *ass* out of *u* and an *ass* out of *me*!"

Organizations cannot function effectively when communication skills are lacking among their members. The current chapter, therefore, will consider some of the major facets of communication and include an examination of the characteristics of words, the need for established feedback mechanisms, and the means for overcoming barriers to communication. We shall also explore some of the significant aspects of non-verbal communication and the importance of listening.

The Nature of Communication

We are continually surrounded by forms of communication during our day-to-day activities. For example, in the San Francisco-Oakland area of California there are at least eight television channels. Listed in the San Francisco newspapers are almost forty FM radio stations and twenty-five AM stations, all of which are technically classified as forms of communication. A station, however, is not necessarily communicating even when all of its power is on and an announcer is glibly chatting. What more than the power and station personnel is necessary? You may say, "This is obvious—the radio receivers must be tuned in to the broadcast." However, a radio may be tuned in to a station that is broadcasting, but there is one more essential ingredient of communication if it is to be effective: *understanding*.

What are the essential ingredients of effective communication?

Consequently, whether we are talking about a radio station or about you within your organization, there are *three essential ingredients* necessary for effective communication to take place:

1. A sender.
2. A receiver (or listener).
3. An understood message.

communication

Communication, therefore, can be defined as *a process of imparting information and understanding to one or more persons*. If there is no understanding, or if there is a misunderstanding, the ideas have not been effectively communicated.

Responsibility for Effective Communication

Who's responsible?

Who has the responsibility for ensuring that effective communication takes place? Both the *sender* of the message and his or her *listener* share the responsibility. As in the case of the radio station previously mentioned, the listener has to be tuned in to the message before effective communication results. You, however, have a considerable advantage over the broadcasting medium in your efforts to communicate. You can discover immediately if the receiver is tuned in. How? By attempting to acquire *feedback* from the listener. By *asking certain questions* you can discover if the receiver actually understood your message. Or, if you are on the receiving end of the communication, by *restating what the speaker said*, you can often determine whether you understood the message.

feedback

two-way process

Unfortunately, in organizations there is an excessive amount of one-way communication. By necessity, communication must be a *two-way process* in order to prevent the development of psychologically negative attitudes among the personnel of an organization. A feedback mechanism of some sort must be built into the communication process.

Characteristics of Words

Is a dictionary a source of the "correct" meaning of words?

A large part of our daily communication is transmitted by symbols that we usually call "words." When we attempt to engage in effective communication with others, we are really trying to impart *meaning* through the use of words. If our communication is to be understood, therefore, it would appear logical that we are going to have to understand the meaning of words. We all know where we can look for the "correct" meaning of words: the dictionary, right? Wrong!! Most lexicographers (dictionary makers) contend that the book that they prepare is merely a history book, one that shows how some words have been used at particular times and in certain contexts. You probably can think of numerous words that you use regularly in your daily conversation and that are understood but are not even in the dictionary.

Words as Inexact Symbols

Can you write down the meaning of the word *fast*? Think for a moment. Does the word imply motion, as in the case of a fast runner? Or does it imply lack of motion, as in a fast color or in she stands fast? Or does our little four-letter word also relate to eating habits, as in the case of a person who fasts or abstains from food during a holiday, such as Lent? What about the expression, "He was too fast on the first date." A large dictionary will offer at least fifty different "meanings" of the word *fast*. The same can be said for such words as *wind, wing, run, lie, air,* and many others. How, then, can we determine the true meaning of words?

Where is the meaning of a word?

First you have to get out of your head that *words* have meaning. The word is not the thing: the word is merely a symbol that represents different things to different people. The true meaning of a word is not in the word itself nor in the way the listener interprets the word. The meaning of a word is in the *sender* of the word or words. There are believed to be about six hundred thousand words in the English language. An educated adult in daily conversation uses about two thousand, of which the five hundred most commonly used have fourteen thousand dictionary definitions. Do you really think that you can guess the right meaning every time?

Therefore, if we want to discover the meaning of a speaker's words, the only way to be certain is to *ask* him or her what they mean when we are in doubt. Instead of wondering what the *words* in a message mean, a better approach is to wonder what the *speaker* means. A corny story might help to illustrate this point:

"Now," said the village blacksmith to the apprentice, "I'll take this iron out of the fire, lay it on the anvil, and when I

50

nod my head, you hit it.'' The apprentice did so, and now he's the village blacksmith!

Two ways, therefore, in which you can lessen the chance of communications failure between you and others are:

1. Don't assume that everyone knows what you are talking about.
2. Don't assume that you know what others are talking about without asking them questions to make certain.[1]

The blacksmith erroneously made the first assumption, and the imperceptive apprentice made the second!

Words with Regional Meanings

Just what is a "snail"?

Sometimes the *meanings of words are regional*. For example, usually when individuals refer to a snail, they are referring to one of those slimy, slow-moving gastropod mollusks with spiral shell that slithers along a freshly-cut lawn. In some parts of the United States a snail also means a sweet, round breakfast roll designed to be washed down with a fresh cup of morning coffee.

[1]Don Fabun, *Three Roads to Awareness–Motivation, Creativity, Communications* (Beverly Hills: Glencoe Press, 1970), p. 109.

The Development of New Meanings

What does the word *turkey* mean to you?

Words *develop new meanings* with the passage of time. Almost every decade brings forth a myriad of new meanings for old words. Often the parents of college or high school students cannot understand the conversations of their offspring. Many popular songs contain words that have specific meanings only to some listeners. The black community also has been a fertile and creative source of new meanings applied to old words.

The Development of New Words

Are you running out of *synergy*?

New words are continually derived as a result of the development of new industries or fields, as in the case of the word *astronaut*, which emerged from space exploration, or *software, firmware,* and *hardware,* from the electronic data processing field.

Tone Affects Meaning

The tone arranger rides again!

Finally, a *difference in tone can change the meanings of words*. "John, you've been doing a hell of a job around here," is a phrase that could convey praise or blame, depending on the tone of the speaker's voice.

In summary, therefore, we could state that we should remember five important factors about the meanings of words:

1. Words have many meanings.
2. Words sometimes have regional meanings.
3. Words develop new meanings.
4. New words are continually derived.
5. A difference in tone can change the meanings of words.

Up the Organization

An important facet of communication in organizations is its flow upward through the organizational hierarchy. Lack of upward communication cuts off an important lifeline vital to the overall health of any organization. Much in the way of *upward communication* takes place on a face-to-face basis, through various feedback mechanisms, or through the grapevine (to be discussed in chapter 4).

upward communication

Feedback—A Way to Facilitate Understanding

feedback

Feedback is *the process through which the originator of a message learns of the response to his or her communication.* Let's assume, for example, that you have asked your assistant Fran to close the door. Have you communicated? Perhaps you have, and perhaps you haven't. Or how about if you—a department manager—send a memo to the three supervisors who report directly to you. The memo asks them to attend a meeting on Friday morning at 9:00 A.M. Have you communicated? Once again, maybe you have, and maybe you haven't.

If your assistant Fran closes the door, and if your three supervisors attend the Friday morning meeting, then you might safely assume that you have communicated; they have all given you feedback. If your assistant doesn't respond—that is, doesn't close the door—or if she starts to clean the floor instead, you have still received feedback. Feedback, then, is what tells the source of any communication if a message has been interpreted as intended, or if it needs modification. Feedback can provide a clue as to what further communication might be necessary. Managers should try to establish channels for feedback in order to develop a better understanding of the attitudes, sentiments, and feelings of subordinates within their organizations.

"George, throw me down the stairs my hat. George? What are you doing? Say, George, why are you picking me up? Help!"

The Use of Suggestion Boxes

suggestion box

To develop feedback, some organizations have *suggestion boxes*, a tool that can be either used or misused. Too frequently, suggestion boxes are misused. An example of such misuse was once found in one of the largest

printing plants in the Pacific Northwest, an establishment consisting of more than 200 skilled employees. Employees passing through a particular corridor of the building could see, very firmly attached to the wall, a wooden box with the words "EMPLOYEE SUGGESTIONS" affixed to its side. Once out of curiosity, an employee opened the unlocked lid. The suggestion box looked more like a garbage receptacle than a mechanism for generating feedback. Inside the dusty container were unsightly hunks of well-masticated stale chewing gum, along with crumpled old cigarette and gum wrappers! What might the employees be attempting to suggest to the management?

Do litterbugs use suggestion boxes?

The employees seemed to feel that there was little use or purpose in placing anything other than garbage into the box since, in the words of one of the employees, "Management would only deep-six [place in the waste basket] our suggestions anyway!"

The usefulness of suggestion boxes is doubted by some students of communication. They argue that management's requirement that suggestions be written may discourage the presentation of useful ideas by employees who lack either the inclination or the ability to put their suggestions into writing.

Why should recognition be given to the submitter of suggestions?

However, if management does decide to employ the suggestion system, it should give recognition to the submitter, whether or not the idea is valid, in order to encourage the flow of ideas upward in the organizational chain of command. An employee usually feels that he or she is entitled to know why suggestions are rejected. Numerous firms provide not only an *explanation in writing* to the employees, but also a *discussion* of the reasons for the rejection or acceptance of an idea. A suggestion system can soon become viewed by employees as a farce if the suggestions are not acknowledged.

The Filtering of Communication

filtering

One of the major problems in organizations today is the *filtering* out of communications as they rise up to management levels. Quite frequently, managers assume that if they have not personally heard derogatory remarks from employees, there must be little, if any, dissatisfaction among the employees with the company's policies and procedures. If so much communication weren't filtered out so often, many managers would quickly discover that numerous employees detest their very managerial intestines! Frequently, managers or supervisors, even those with the best of intentions, will inform their employees that they believe in an *open-door policy* and that any time any individual wants to see them, all the person need do is drop in.

open-door policy

In too many cases an open-door policy really means that the door is open for managers to walk out.[2] Usually there are few, if any, workers who feel inclined to walk through their bosses' so-called open doors because of various psychological or status barriers between the managers and themselves. Even where open-door policies have been announced, many employees have found that upon attempting to walk through the "open door," they were stopped and asked, "Do you have an appointment with Mr. Lockout?"

If managers really want to discover how their subordinates feel about the operations of an organization, they must walk through the portals themselves and engage in some observant exploration. This is not to say that an open-door policy should never be attempted. Some managers are very effective in developing the credible attitude that an open door actually exists. When employees believe such an attitude exists, an open-door policy can, in many instances, be used as an effective tool of management.

And Down the Organization

Have you ever noticed that during your day-to-day activities, you are bombarded with communications of all types. As your clock-radio gently awakens you early in the morning, intermittent messages about the weather and traffic conditions, advertisements about a "pre-fire sale" at the Felonious Furniture Factory, and a host of other proclamations tickle your tympanic membranes. As you sleepily sip your morning coffee, you are mercilessly assaulted by seemingly endless advertisements on various topics, ranging from cures for itchy piles to opportunities for taking advantage of increasing land values by buying, "before it's too late," a piece of virgin land in "blissful Viscid Valley."

On the way to work, you pass countless outdoor advertising posters, store-front neon signs, and theater marquees, all vying mightily for your attention. On arriving at your place of employment, you meet a union organizer who hands you a leaflet. You enter the building and pass a company information rack stuffed with pamphlets about safety and health education. A few steps beyond is the bulletin board. In your mail slot are five memos, the latest issue of the company's magazine, and a copy of the organization's annual report.

At 2:00 P.M. your payroll envelope is handed to you. Between a notice from your credit union and an announcement of a forthcoming company picnic you discover your paycheck.

We have indicated only part of the barrage of communication by

[2]Keith Davis, *Human Behavior At Work* (New York: McGraw-Hill, 1977), p. 402.

which you are assaulted in a single day. It could be safely concluded that the competition from all sources for your mental attention is indeed prodigious.

The Downward Flow of Communication

downward communication

We've already discussed the importance of understanding feedback and its relationship to the flow of communication *upward* through the hierarchy of an organization. Equally important are the numerous channels or approaches available for effective communication *downward*.

selective reception

Don't hear everything you believe.

Unfortunately, employees are bombarded with such tremendous volumes of downward communication that they often resort to *selective reception;* that is, they hear or see the information they are set to hear or see and tune out much of the rest. Any person who has regularly attempted to convey information to others recognizes how difficult the process is. In any group there seems to be a certain percentage of individuals who fail to get "the word."

If your job requires the use of downward communication in an organization, it is essential that you strive to be understood. Certain precautions can be taken and approaches used in order to minimize communication breakdowns. Among them are:

1. Use face-to-face communication.
2. Develop empathetic speaking and listening habits.
3. Don't create credibility gaps.
4. Choose more effective times for communication.
5. Avoid wordiness.

Let's now examine each of these factors separately.

Face-To-Face Communication

Why are face-to-face communications more effective?

Face-to-face communication is felt to be more effective than written orders because the sender can receive feedback immediately and discover if he or she has been understood. The impersonal characteristics of a memo or letter can be easily misunderstood, especially when information· of a negative nature is being conveyed.

While employed as a sales representative for an office equipment company, a person we'll call Victor Vendor discovered that personal meetings with his customers, rather than impersonal written communication, more effectively resolved problems or conflicts that had developed between them and his company. By asking certain questions and by listening empathetically to the answers, Vic regularly discovered that the problems seemed to diminish.

Developing Empathetic Speaking and Listening Habits

empathetic speaking and listening

Hey, man, don't call me boy!

Empathetic speaking and listening are also essential for effective communication. Some persons create communication barriers because they seem to lack the understanding that some words or phrases are felt to be derogatory and offensive to others. An example may be taken from a course in human relations in which a student, a retired Chief Petty Officer, appeared to be attempting to convince the other members of the class, of whom about half were black, that he was not prejudiced. During a class discussion, the former naval man stated, "When I was in the Navy, I had a couple of colored boys working for me, and we had a good working relationship." The face of every black person in the room immediately registered disgust. The student later admitted to the class that he was not aware of the connotation of the phrase "colored boy." Can you place yourself into the shoes of a black person who historically has been called "boy," regardless of his age, by his boss?

The important point is to try to *know your audience* and *be sensitive to their needs and feelings* when you speak and listen; otherwise, you may short-circuit important communication networks.

The Avoidance of Credibility Gaps

What may happen when action does not follow words?

Credibility gaps are quite common between management and workers in organizations. To prevent the cynical distrust of the communication that flows downward in an organization, you should remember that *words are not substitutes for action*.

Assume, for example, that one of your subordinates, Ms. Anne Earnest, complains to you about the excessive glare of the sun shining through her office window, informing you that the blinding sun reflecting off her desk makes work extremely difficult, if not practically impossible. If you promise to remedy the problem, but fail to do anything, you are likely to discover that Anne will tend to disbelieve many of your statements in the future.

Some managers feel that a simple statement such as, "I'll see what I can do about that problem," will placate the worker. However, when dealing with others you should be aware that they will frequently remember the promises you have made. The chasm of disbelief will widen with each failure on your part to deliver what you promised.

Effective Timing of Communications

There's no time like good timing.

Assume that one evening you finally made the decision to ask your boss on the following day for the raise in pay that you feel is long overdue. All night you tossed and turned in bed trying to frame the most tactful and

57

persuasive plea for the pay increase. The next morning, however, you observed that your boss scarcely noticed the employees and appeared to be extremely harried upon her arrival to work. Nonetheless, your mind is set; your courage is at its peak. You bravely walk through the "open door" of your boss's office, and politely, but firmly, ask her for a raise, and suddenly—BANG!! You feel as though you are reliving the 1906 San Francisco earthquake. Your boss shouts, "Can't you see I have some important things on my mind?" And you realize that you must have picked the wrong time for the right question.

What is the best time for important communications?

Optimum timing is as important as the choice of words in many situations, whether you are talking to your parents, children, friends, superiors, subordinates, or customers. The best time to attempt to convey important communications face-to-face is *when your message is competing the least with other situations affecting the listener*. However, your message is most likely to be considered and listened to when it provides a *solution to a problem* affecting the receiver.

Avoiding Wordiness

A young college student, Miss Ima Anxious, while enrolled in her first course in college English, was required to study and learn the definitions, spelling, and usage of ten pages of vocabulary words each week. As a serious student of the English language, Ima was quite proud of her scores on the weekly tests. In fact, she felt that she should display her newfound knowledge by using the words in a term paper assignment modestly entitled, "The History of Insurance." So she began: "As the adoption of the Constitution gave birth to a fairly sound financial system in the United States, conditions for corporate enterprise were copiously ameliorated."

"Copiously ameliorated"? What was Ima actually trying to say? Didn't she mean "greatly improved"? Apparently clarity wasn't the major concern of a conscientious freshman who wanted to parade her scholarly knowledge.

Far too frequently written communications within organizations appear to have been prepared by ambitious freshmen like Ima. Many members of the United States Navy discover that a memo is often referred to as a "promulgation." Another example of wordiness once existed in a naval barracks where posted neatly over a drinking fountain was the notice: "Expectoration into drinking apparatus is expressly prohibited." About nine out of ten persons who were asked the meaning of the word "expectoration" didn't have the foggiest notion of its meaning. One person thought that the word might mean "to urinate"! A curious sailor decided to investigate its meaning, opened Mr. Webster's famous (but wordy) book, and discovered that one definition of the verb "to expectorate'' is ''to spit.'' Perhaps the simple admonition, ''Don't spit in the fountain!'' would have sufficed.

A manager with a large insurance company once said that he believed all communications should be delivered with a *K.I.S.S.*, which meant *"Keep It Short and Simple."* Perhaps you should regularly ask yourself, ''What is the major objective of any communication that I desire to make to others?'' Communication is not effective unless there is *understanding,* which should be a major goal of any communication. Do not overcomplicate your messages. If there were a fire in your office or plant, you probably wouldn't exclaim, ''It is mandatory that we attempt to extinguish the portentious pyrogenation.'' You would be understood much more readily if you merely shouted, ''Let's put out the fire!''

However, written communication, before it can be understood, must *attract the attention* of those to whom you are aiming it. Imagine this notice tacked to a bulletin board:

MEMORANDUM TO ALL EMPLOYEES CONCERNING
REGULATIONS AND RESTRICTIONS APPLICABLE TO
EQUITABLE ALLOCATION OF VACATION PERIODS
FOR THE YEAR 1980

Would you really expect many employees to spend much of their valuable coffee break perusing such a memo? A simple and readable title would be more apt to attract the attention of the employees.

MEMORANDUM
TO: ALL EMPLOYEES
FROM: PERSONNEL DEPARTMENT
SUBJECT: VACATION SCHEDULES, 1980

Silence Is Not Always Golden—Other Facets of Communication

Most of the time when you think about communication you probably think of either *spoken or written words*, but these are only two types of communication. There are also the *silent languages*, those that do not use words but such things as overt actions (such as body language), failures to act (such as not saying ''hello'' to someone), and even factors such as space, height, and status symbols.

The Body Speaks!

Whether you realize it consciously or not, you're communicating each time you make a gesture or a glance at a person. The motions people make with their bodies (or sometimes don't make!) often communicate messages of various sorts. Such communication isn't always accurate or effective, but it is communication nonetheless. For example, assume that after you arrive at your job one morning you pass in the hallway a co-worker who gives you an unusual glance, or at least a glance that appears to you to be strange. You might wonder for the rest of the day what that glance meant. Some employees seldom greet others whom they pass in hallways or work areas. Instead, their faces seem frozen. Sometimes a person might feel that a frozen stare is an indication of displeasure.

Inactivity Communicates

How does lack of activity communicate?

Assume that you, a supervisor in an organization, are habitually cordial toward your employees each morning as you arrive on the job. You seldom forget to say hello to anyone. However, one morning you wake with pressing problems on your mind, problems that demand your immediate thought and attention. As you pass the receptionist on that particular morning, your mind might be one million light years away, and you hardly notice him. Have you attempted to communicate anything to the receptionist? No, not consciously; yet, you might have communicated something. He may start wondering, "What did I do? Why didn't the boss say 'Good Morning' to me today?"

Nonverbal communication might include the failure to compliment individuals on the quality of their work. Many employees feel that the only time anyone comments on their activities is when they have done something wrong. You should find that one way favorably to influence fellow employees or subordinates in your organization is *to recognize and acknowledge good work when you see it*. If you only communicate or discuss what the workers are doing when they have done something wrong, they will soon feel that they aren't appreciated in your organization. As V. Wilcox wryly stated, "A pat on the back is only a few vertebrae removed from a kick in the pants, but is miles ahead in results."

Communicating with Handshakes

Put 'er there fellah.

Handshakes are another way of communicating. Americans are sometimes accused of being a nation of snap-judgment makers. Frequently, one will hear the statement, "He shakes hands like a fish, not a man." However, if you travel to different parts of the world, you will quickly discover that not all of the world's citizens shake hands like your fellow Americans. Nor do all Americans shake hands in an identical fashion. For example, a tremendous amount of communication passes between black hands when they are shaken by Afro-American "brothers" and "sisters."

60

Care to arm wrestle?

In many of the Latin countries, handshakes are very soft and gentle, without the vigorous up and down movements common in the United States and Germany. In northern European countries, such as Germany, you frequently might feel that you are in a contest of strength with a native handshaker who seems to be testing his grip on your hand. In France, however, if your right hand or arm is occupied holding packages, you may shake hands with your left hand without being regarded as impolite. Some persons while reclining at a Riviera beach even use their feet!

Shake a leg?

Other Silent Languages

space

The use of *space* is another factor that can affect communication. You would probably speak differently in a large lecture hall or conference room from the way you would when whispering near to a person's ear. In office situations space may tell us something about the patterns of authority among the various employees. If you observe two department managers, one with office space twice as large as the other, you might safely assume something about their relative authority in the organization.

height

Height also tends to "speak" to us. An executive suite would seldom be found in the basement of an office building. In our culture, *higher* is assumed to be better than *lower*. Have you ever heard of anyone aspiring to "descend" the ladder of success?

status symbols

Status symbols tend to be visible indicators that relate to individuals and often tell us something about their ranks within organizations. Items that might appear trivial to an outsider can become important influences on the morale of employees, such things as a telephone on, or a wastebasket near, an employee's desk. Some executives would prefer a rug on their office floors over pay raises. Any items that people perceive as significant can serve as symbols of status among organizational members.

Often, however, there is *miscommunication* in the silent languages. Have you ever had an experience whereby you felt that you were actually smiling at someone who then asked, "What's wrong? What did *I* do?" At times people will perceive what they are set to see regardless of what you might have intended them to see.

Hearing Isn't Listening

Were you a born talker? Soon after your birth you undoubtedly learned the effectiveness of communication in the form of crying. You may have let loose with a wail at 3:00 A.M., and mama or papa came running. Later in your life, while in high school or college, you may have had the opportunity to take courses in speech, public speaking, or composition. By the time you leave college, you probably will have had a considerable amount of experience and possibly further training in talking and writing. Most of your day is spent in verbal communication, but have you ever had formalized training in listening? Probably not, if your educational experiences have been typical of those of most students.

Considerable resources have been expended on educational facilities designed to improve one's ability to speak and to write, even though a person usually spends close to half of his or her day listening and very little time writing. A baby certainly does not appear to be a born listener. And, unfortunately, an excessive number of adults have had no formalized training in the development of more effective listening skills and techniques. A growing number of private organizations and schools, however, have become aware of the need for training in listening. A number of training films and materials have been developed by institutions, private firms, and associations. The purpose of this section is to present some significant—but often ignored—concepts designed to develop better listening habits.

The Importance of Listening

Management will find difficulty in receiving feedback from subordinate personnel without developing techniques of listening. Often, however,

Figure 3–1. An example of two listening "experts." Reprinted with permission of Publisher—Hall Syndicate.

the rushed and harried supervisor feels that he or she just cannot find enough time to listen to the workers. Some supervisors, however, discover that time spent on effective listening can be as valuable as a capital investment and can save them a valuable resource—time.

What are the benefits of effective listening?

Effective listening habits are important for *all* organizational members, not only managers. Employees should learn the techniques of better listening in order *to maintain good relationships* with those who deal with their organizations. Furthermore, costly *accidents* and *expensive errors* can often be avoided when employees listen to their superiors and co-workers. Effective listening habits can also *prevent misunderstanding and rumors* from developing in an organization.

There are other important reasons for developing effective listening habits. For example, the Bureau of National Affairs has developed a ''laundry list'' of ten important concepts related to effective listening. Think about how *you* might employ each one of them.

1. Everyone likes to feel important.
2. People perform better when they know their opinions and suggestions are listened to.
3. Supervisors must use the expertise and experience of employees —and be able to elicit this expertise from subordinates.
4. Attention paid to small gripes often prevents their blossoming into big grievances.
5. Supervisors who don't get all the facts often make poor decisions.
6. Supervisors who jump to conclusions lose the respect of their subordinates.
7. To do a good job of listening, supervisors must plan time for it in their busy schedules.
8. Listening requires full attention to the speaker; it is impossible to listen intelligently while the mind is preoccupied with something else.
9. Listening habits are deeply embedded in the personality and are related to other personality traits, such as obstinancy, empathy, and so on.
10. Correction of bad habits is a slow process, and must be self-motivated.[3]

The ''Earmuff'' Problem

Judging from the frequency that important feedback communication is filtered or miscommunicated, you might think that some supervisors in

[3]An excerpt from the ''Leaders' Guide,'' a pamphlet that accompanies the film *Listen Please* (Modern Management Films, Bureau of National Affairs, Washington, D.C., 1959).

organizations wear earmuffs in face-to-face communication. Effective listening is not a simple or passive activity; it requires concentrated effort and a certain amount of tension. The *earmuff problem* occasionally exists when managers perceive their role as authoritative, one that involves the initiation of action and decision making. To have to engage in a less conspicuous activity, such as listening, sometimes affects or hurts supervisors' egos, especially if they feel as though they only have control of a situation if they are doing the talking. However, if you were to ask some satisfied employees what they like most about their supervisors, frequently they would say, "I like my boss. She *listens* to me."

earmuff problem

Whether you are a manager or a worker, on or off the job, employees may approach you with their personal problems. Is this the time to tell them that you, too, have similar problems? Put yourself into the shoes of the other person. When you have a personal problem that you want to discuss with someone else, do you really want to hear about *his* or *her* problems? Does hearing about the other person's problems necessarily make you feel any better? Usually not. Often you are more concerned, consciously or subconsciously, about having the opportunity to get things off your chest.

Do troubled people want to hear *your* problems?

Effective listening by organizational members can be a form of *preventive maintenance*. Just as lubrication can prevent friction and the wear and tear of machinery, so can effective listening prevent friction and problems of human relations from developing in your organizational or personal life. Frequently for persons who have complaints or difficulties, the mere act of finding sympathetic listeners helps to "get things off their chests" and possibly to see the problems more objectively.

How is listening a form of preventive maintenance?

Developing Listening Skills

Listening is a skill to be developed, and the knowledge of how to make certain *listening responses* and how to *phrase questions* can greatly assist you in conveying to speakers that you are interested, attentive, and wish them to continue. Let's first examine some effective ways to elicit responses from your speakers.

Listening Responses

listening responses

Listening responses should be made *quietly* and *briefly* so as not to interfere with a speaker's train of thought. As with any tool, responses can be misused, ineffective, and counterproductive. Responses are likely to appear to be manipulative and unreal if they are not genuinely sincere. Responses are usually made when the speaker pauses. Five types of listening responses are:

The nod—nodding the head slightly and waiting.

The pause—looking at the speaker expectantly, but without doing or saying anything.

The casual remark—"I see"; "Uh-huh"; "Is that so?" "That's interesting."

The echo—repeating the last few words the speaker said.

The mirror—reflecting back to the speaker your understanding of what has just been said: "You feel that. . . . "

Phrasing Questions

Occasionally, a supervisor may notice that an employee's behavior or work habits have changed significantly. If a dependable employee with a record of good work suddenly starts coming to work drunk or having accidents on the job, the change may be a signal that a personal problem exists. Personal problems that affect an individual's performance on the job should become the concern of the employee's supervisor, who may be able to offer assistance when he or she can discover the nature of the problem. However, merely asking the worker, "Is there anything wrong, Joe?" will frequently elicit a negative response. There are far more *phrasing questions* effective ways of *phrasing questions* to enhance the possibility of receiving a more complete response. Questions may be phrased as *open* ques-*open and* tions, or as *closed* questions. Open questions usually generate better *closed questions* responses than do closed questions.

A question is *open* when phrased in such a way that it cannot be answered with a simple yes or no. For example, "Joe, I've noticed some changes in your work lately. What seems to be the problem?" The questioner who asks an open question, exercises patience, and says nothing until Joe finally responds, discovers more often than not that Joe will be more likely to express his inner feelings about a personal problem.

Why do *open* questions elicit greater response than *closed*?

A question is *closed* when phrased in such a way that it can be answered yes or no. For example, "Joe, do you have a problem?" Too frequently the answer will be: "No."

Psychiatrists and counselors regularly employ the open-question technique. Can you really imagine a psychiatrist saying to his or her patient, "Mrs. Jones, do you have a problem"?

Another illustration could be found in the case where you wish to discover an employee's attitude about a change in the organization. If you ask, "Betty, do you feel the recent change in your duties is fair?" she is likely to say yes because of fear or the status barriers between employee and supervisor. However, if you were to ask, "Betty, how do you feel about the recent changes in your duties?" you will be more than likely to find out some of her real attitudes and feelings.

Practice formulating questions by using the open-question technique. You may be surprised and pleased with your results. The following is a list of *key words* which determine whether a question is open or closed.

Open	*Closed*
Who	Is
What	Do
When	Has
Where	Can
How	Will
Why	Shall

Summary

Communication, the process of imparting information and understanding to one or more persons, requires, in order to be effective, a *sender*, a *receiver,* and an *understood message*. Words facilitate communication, but do not have meaning until themselves. They are like containers; their meaning is in the *user*. When in doubt about the meaning of a word, ask the user what he or she meant.

The frequency of communication failures can be lessened by neither assuming that everyone knows what *you* are talking about nor that you know what *others* are talking about without asking them questions to make certain. The meanings of words are not always clear since words often have many meanings, may be regional, develop new meanings, are newly derived, and are affected by tone.

Communication upwards through an organization is sometimes accomplished through the use of suggestion boxes, open-door policies, morale surveys, labor news publications, and effective listening techniques.

Communication downward in an organization is accomplished by memos, publications for employees, bulletin boards, information racks, financial reports, and payroll inserts. *Face-to-face communication* and *empathetic speaking and listening habits* enhance downward communication. Precautions against short-circuiting communication networks would include timing, brevity, and the prevention of credibility gaps.

The silent languages of body language, failure to act, space, height, and status symbols communicate without the use of words.

The other side of the communications coin is listening. Skill in listening is not easy to acquire, even though most of us were born with two ears and only one mouth. The art of good listening can be developed with practice. Much of our educational system has ignored the topic of listening until recently.

Terms and Concepts to Remember

Communication
Feedback
Two-way communication
Upward communication
Suggestion box
Filtering
Open-door policy
Downward communication

Selective reception
Empathetic speaking and listening
Silent languages
Earmuff problem
Listening responses
Open questions
Closed questions

Questions

1. What is communication?
2. What is necessary for effective communication to take place?
3. Explain the statement, "Words are like containers."
4. Explain the various processes through which feedback can take place in organizations. How might they be misused?
5. How does the concept of timing relate to communications?
6. Explain the statement, "Words are not substitutes for action."
7. What are some of the benefits, both to the organization and to its members, of the application of effective listening habits by managers and subordinates?

8. Why do some managers figuratively don "earmuffs" when their subordinates talk to them?
9. Why will relating your own problems probably not comfort a person who has approached you with a personal problem?
10. Give two examples each of open and closed questions. Why do open questions generally elicit greater response from the speaker?

Other Readings

Fabun, Don. *Three Roads to Awareness–Motivation, Creativity, Communications.* Beverly Hills: Glencoe Press, 1970.

Fast, Julius. *Body Language.* New York: Simon and Schuster, 1970.

Flesch, Rudolf. *How to Make Sense.* New York: Harper & Row, 1954.

Hayakawa, S. I., *Language in Thought and Action.* 3d ed. New York: Harcourt Brace Jovanovich, 1972.

"How to Listen and Why!" Washington, D.C.: BNA, Inc., 1965.

Jandt, Fred E. *The Process of Interpersonal Communication.* San Francisco: Canfield Press, 1976.

Nichols, Ralph G. "Listening is Good Business." *Management of Personnel Quarterly* 1, no. 2 (Winter 1962): 2–9.

Nichols, Ralph G., and Stevens, Leonard A. *Are You Listening?* New York: McGraw-Hill, 1957.

Wilhelm, Donald, Jr., revised by C. W. Ufford. *An Employee Suggestion System for Small Companies.* Washington, D.C.: Small Business Administration, 1964.

Applications

The Paragon Printing and Lithography Company

The Paragon Printing and Lithography Company is one of the largest printing and lithography firms in the southwestern United States, employing more than 180 persons and divided into two major divisions —Letterpress and Lithography. The company was formed in 1929 as an office supply firm, and gradually diversified its operations to include printing and lithography on a relatively small scale.

At the onset of World War II, the Paragon Company was called upon by the United States Government to print and publish military manuals. This increased activity resulted in the need for a tremendous expansion program. The office supply division was dissolved, and all subsequent activity was carried on in the printing and lithography trade.

In 1978, the major customer of the Paragon Printing and Lithography Company was still the United States Government, a situation that necessitated equipment capable of turning out tremendous quantities of printed matter, with the emphasis on *quantity* rather than quality.

The Camera and Platemaking Departments were, in effect, two separate departments under the supervision of Peter Vacher. In these departments were two people operating the two process cameras, six preparing the negatives, and four making plates for the lithographic presses. All of the personnel, including the supervisor, were members of the union.

Joe Matino, a journeyman lithographer in the Platemaking Department, had been with the company for seventeen years. Matino was classed as an "old-timer" by almost everyone in the plant, and he had seniority over all the personnel in his department. However, he was not classified as foreman of the Platemaking Department, which was regarded as a part of the Camera Department. The supervisor of both departments was Peter Vacher.

Peter Vacher was regarded by most of the men in his department as being "quite a capable man." However, the general belief among the people in the two departments was that Vacher never seemed very happy. On numerous occasions Vacher had complained vehemently about how poorly organized the management was. On one occasion he had said to Nat Stossen, an apprentice who worked the swing shift in the Platemaking Department and attended day classes at a nearby university, "As supervisor, I get it from both sides. I'm not supposed to get too friendly with the workers, but yet the management doesn't really accept me as part of management either. Those . . . won't even supply me with any cost information. The only way I can get it is to scrounge it out of Bill Johnson, the Purchasing Agent. How in hell do they expect me to be cost-conscious if I don't even know anything about costs! Actually, Nat, management won't confide in any supervisor who is in the union!"

A month later, Betty Hanson, who was one of the two production managers, telephoned Vacher and asked him to come up to her office right away.

> *Hanson:* Hi, Pete! Have a chair, will you?
> *Vacher:* Thanks, Mrs. Hanson. What can I do for you?
> *Hanson:* Well, at a recent meeting the Estimator revealed that he was having one hell of a time trying to determine accurately just how much he should charge for labor to each job, since he doesn't have any labor time standards to go by. What I want you to do, Pete, is to go back to your departments and establish some time standards for the various operations in the Platemaking and Camera Departments. For example, I want you to determine how long it takes for a platemaker to make each of the various sizes of plates that are made in the department. Then submit a report back to me by tomorrow morning at 9:00 A.M.
> *Vacher:* All right, Mrs. Hanson, I'll see what I can do.

Vacher went back to his departments to speak to Matino (the older platemaker).

> *Vacher:* Joe, they're on our backs again. Now they want to know how long it takes for you guys to make plates. Will you please determine some sort of standard time for making each of the four different sizes and types of plates? I've got to have this info before 9:00 A.M. tomorrow so I can give it to the "efficiency expert."
>
> *Matino:* What in hell's the matter with those crazy people upstairs? What do they think we are trying to do—put something over on 'em? Okay, I'll get it for you right away.

About half an hour later, Matino placed the report on Vacher's desk. When the swing shift reported to work the same afternoon, Matino complained to Hank Willows, the night shift journeyman platemaker, about his having established the new time standards.

> *Matino:* For some reason, Pete asked me to establish time standards for the platemaking in this department. I wrote down the new standard on this piece of paper for you, and be sure you don't go *under* it. Those characters upstairs are trying to check up on us, and if we put out too much work, we'll work ourselves plumb out of work. So what I did was set a standard that we can do real easy. So don't work too damn fast or you'll foul things up. Tell the 'professor,' your apprentice, about this.
>
> *Willows:* Sure will, Joe. I've seen this happen before in other shops. If you set the standard too high, they'll always expect you to make it, and then they'll give you hell if you don't. Don't worry about a thing!

Later that evening, Willows told Nat Stossen, his apprentice, to slow down, that a standard had been set, and that he was not to attempt to "work us out of work." Stossen accepted the order reluctantly.

The regular hours of the swing shift were from 4:00 P.M. until 12:00 midnight. At about 10:00 P.M., the night after the standards had been established, production in the platemaking department halted.

> *Willows:* Well, professor, let's go home. We've done all we have to do, and if we do any more we'll go over the standard.
>
> *Stossen:* Go home! It's only ten o'clock. We shouldn't go home yet.
>
> *Willows:* Don't worry, Nat, there aren't no supervisors on the swing shift so whose gonna know?
>
> *Stossen:* If you don't mind, I think I'll stick around a while

longer. I don't want to jeopardize my job. I've got two more years of college to do, and I don't know of any other job where I could make this kind of money and work hours that will enable me to finish school.

Willows: Heck, there are plenty of jobs where this one came from. Okay, suit yourself. But *don't* make any plates!

Every night thereafter Stossen took a textbook to work with him and studied from approximately 10:00 P.M. until 12:00 midnight.

Questions

1. What do you feel are the major problems in this case? What are some possible solutions?
2. Why do supervisors sometimes feel that they are on "the two horns of a dilemma," being neither managers nor workers?
3. Evaluate the leadership techniques of Vacher. Should he have established the time standards himself?
4. What was your evaluation of the approach which Stossen took? Was it ethically wrong for him to study on the job and to be paid for those hours?
5. If you had been Stossen and a manager made a surprise visit one evening at 10:30 P.M. after Willows had departed, what would you say to him?
6. What action would you take if you were a manager who dropped in one evening and observed that Willows was absent and Stossen was studying?
7. Explain the following statement: "Followers tend to follow as they are led."

"I Like Them, but I Didn't Order Them!"

Customers of the Ace Ferndock Spreader Company frequently place their orders by telephone. You, the office manager, have received increasingly more numerous complaints about the shipment of *unordered* goods to your customers.

After a detailed study you discover that the major problem relates to incorrect information, such as item numbers, quantities, and colors, having been taken down by your employees on the telephone order purchase forms.

Questions

1. What seems to be the major problem?
2. What would you do to correct the problem?

The Reticent Subordinates

Phyllis Freephall, an office manager with the Let Toil Paper Company situated in Norfolk, Virginia, sent a memo to her subordinates two weeks before the usual end-of-the-month staff meeting requesting topics for discussion at the forthcoming session.

As of two days before the scheduled meeting, none of the employees had submitted any topics, so Ms. Freephall assumed that the meeting might as well be canceled.

Questions

1. Does the lack of suggested topics necessarily mean that the employees would have nothing to say if the meeting were held as scheduled?
2. If the meeting were conducted, how might Ms. Freephall elicit comments from her subordinates?

A Communications Detour

Enjoy the following humorous use (or, rather, misuse) of the English language.

These statements allegedly were taken from actual letters received by a welfare department. They are presented in order to show what may happen when language arts communication goes astray both in reading and writing. Source unknown.

I am forwarding my marriage certificate and my six children. I had seven but one died which was baptized on a half sheet of paper.

I am writing to say that my baby was born two years old. When do I get my money?

Mrs. Jones has not had any clothing for a year and has been visited regularly by the clergy.

I cannot get sick pay, I have six children. Can you tell me why?

I am glad to report that my husband who was reported missing is now dead.

This is my eighth child, what are you going to do about it?

Please find for certain if my husband is dead. A man I live with now can't eat or do anything till he knows.

I am very much annoyed to find that you have branded my boy as illiterate as this is a dirty lie. I was married to his father a week before he was born.

I am forwarding my marriage certificate and my three children, one of which was a mistake as you will see.

In answer to your letter, I have given birth to a boy weighting 1011 lbs.

My husband got his job cut off two weeks ago and I haven't had any relief since. Unless I get my husbands money pretty soon I will have to lead an immortal life.

You have changed my little boy to a girl. Will this make any difference?

Please send money at once as I have fallen in error with my landlord.

In accordance with instructions I have given birth to twins in the enclosed envelope.

I want money as quick as I can get it. I have been in bed with the Doctor for two weeks and he doesn't do me no good. If things don't improve I will have to send for another Doctor.

When you finish this chapter, you should be able to:
1. **Describe** the purpose and nature of formal and informal groups.
2. **Summarize** the advantages and deficiencies of group decision making.
3. **Identify** the essential ingredients of transactional analysis (TA).
4. **List and describe** the principal types of interviewing styles.
5. **Summarize** the suggestions for conducting and participating in interviews.

Groups, like individuals, have
shortcomings. Groups can bring out
the worst as well as the best in
people.

—Irving L. Janis

Greta Garbo, glamorous Swedish-born film actress of the 1930s, and
Howard Hughes, famous industrialist of the 1960s and 1970s, had something in common. Both became world famous as a result of their group
activities, and both became obsessed in their later years with the desire to
avoid groups.

Although named best actress of the first half of the century by a *Variety* poll in 1950, Greta Garbo withdrew from most public contact and
became renown for her statement, "I want to be let alone." And Howard
Hughes, noted for his flight of a twin-engined Lockheed around the world
in three days and nineteen hours in 1938, as well as for his gigantic
industrial empire, seemed almost to become a figment of the journalistic
media's imagination, so rare were his public appearances in the latter part
of his life. It's lucky for both Garbo and Hughes that they never fell in
love and married, since their talents in the area of group dynamics and
interpersonal relations seemed to leave much to be desired.

**We'll
walk alone
together!**

A large body of theory related to the dynamics of group behavior has
developed. Our approach here will not be to explore in depth each of the
various theories, but, instead, to try to glean from past research those
ideas that can be applied in a practical manner to the everyday organizational behavior of small work groups.

Here a Group, There a Group,
Everywhere a Group-Group

Few of us ever find ourselves in the Garbo-Hughes position of being able
to avoid other people as they did. How much time, for example, are you
able to spend alone each day? Probably very little.

The chances are quite good that you are a member of a wide variety of
groups, such as household, school, social, religious, and work groups.
For most of us, being a member of groups is as normal as the daily
flowing in and out of the oceans' tides. In short, being a member of a
group or groups is usually a basic part of much of our lives.

Just What Is a Group?

group

Do you remember our mentioning in chapter 1 that whenever there are two or more persons there is, in effect, an organization? The same premise holds true for our meaning of the term *group*. Although not all scholars agree on the precise definition of a group, for our purposes we'll define the term as *two or more people who interact personally, or through communication networks, with each other.*

Were Adam and Eve a group?

Based on our definition, then, a husband and wife, an assembly team in a factory, and even the members of a large multinational corporation could be considered groups. Groups, as is fairly apparent, vary in size. Our principal focus in this chapter, however, will be on the behavior and problems associated with smaller groups, those that interact on a face-to-face basis rather than through interoffice or interdivision communiqués.

The Nature of Formal and Informal Groups

Regardless of the type of group we might discuss, most work groups have split personalities, so to speak. They have their *formal*—or *required* side—and they have their *informal*—or *emergent* side. Let's examine the principal differences between the two.

The What and Why of Formal Groups

required (formal) system

Most formal work groups are *required systems*. The required system consists of individuals who are positioned and coordinated for the purpose of attaining predetermined organizational goals and objectives. (Additional discussion of formal work organizations will be covered in chapter 6). Assume that you own a bicycle sales and rental shop and employ five people to help you achieve your planned objectives. Your organization has to have some sort of formal structure in order to achieve your goals of selling bicycles, providing service to bicycle enthusiasts, and making a profit.

Why must we be so formal?

The formal system, therefore, provides some degree of *order and predictability* in an organization. You assume, for example, based on your planning, that Suzy, Joe, and Karen—your staff of salespersons—will be on the job promptly at 9:00 A.M. each morning, as will Frank and Ernestine, both service repair workers. Your work group couldn't function effectively without some sort of a formal—that is, required, planned, or orderly—system.

Formal organizations, then, exist for a variety of reasons. Basically, formal groups:

1. Enable the *accomplishment of goals* much less haphazardly than do informal ones.
2. Facilitate the *coordination of activities or functions* of the organization.
3. Aid in *establishing logical relationships* among people and positions.
4. Enable the application of the concepts of *specialization and division of labor*.
5. Create more *group cohesiveness* as a result of a common set of goals.

The Informal Group Emerges

In the following chapter, we'll examine concepts related to human needs and motivation, concepts that are significant to the topic of small group behavior—especially to its informal aspects. Returning for the moment to your bicycle sales and service shop, it matters little whether you are what your workers consider a good or a bad boss from the standpoint of the existence of an informal organization. You, as owner-manager of the bike shop, can create a formal work group, but you *cannot* eliminate an informal one as long as you have an organization. The *emergent, or informal, system,* evolves in one form or another regardless of your personal wishes, although you can *influence* its activities and behavior.

emergent (informal) system

Why People Group into Groups

We've already discussed the purpose of formal groups. They are formed basically for the purpose of achieving goals and objectives. But couldn't the same be said about informal groups? Think about it for a moment. Don't informal groups also have goals and objectives? Don't most individuals have various sorts of psychological and social needs that require satisfying? Unfortunately, the required sytem seldom satisfies all individual needs. So informal groups—the emergent system—comes galloping to the rescue of small group members. But are informal groups a good or a bad thing?

Are they good—or are they bad—or both?

There is little doubt that informal groups sometimes create problems for organizations. They transmit false information (rumors) through the grapevine, resist change, and sometimes even develop goals that conflict with those of the formal organization. However, the informal organization also performs a variety of positive or useful functions. As already mentioned, groups help the individual members satisfy psychological and social needs. For example, in large plants and offices, a person could feel merely like an employee number instead of a human being if it were not for the opportunity to socialize and interact with other members of the group.

78

Conversely, the employee's personal needs may be *unsatisfied* if the members of the group ostracize or exclude him or her from social interaction. For example, a person whose work pace is faster than the norm for a particular group might be looked upon as a "ratebuster" or person trying to "show up" the other group members.

The Behavior of Groups

Groups, it has been observed, are dynamic. Managers often express amazement at the "strange" behavior of some employees when they are grouped together. It is important to realize, however, that all sorts of factors can influence behavior in groups, such as the membership of the group itself, the cohesiveness of the group, the work environment, and the grapevine as a means of informal communication among group members. Let's now take a brief look at each of these.

The Influence of Group Members

The sum of the parts is . . . than the whole!

social norms

Groups, as we know, are a lot like individuals. Both groups and individuals have distinct needs, personalities, and beliefs as to what constitutes acceptable or so-called normal behavior. But individuals often undergo a kind of metamorphosis when they become part of a group. And their concepts of "what ought to be" may become altered along with their personalities. Group standards, known as *social norms,* have a powerful influence over the group member who wants to be accepted by peers. The shy, retiring high school youth, for example, who seldom asserts him or herself when alone in an unfamiliar crowd may suddenly become boisterous and obnoxious when with friends. Most of us have observed the loud and aggressive behavior of packs of youths who, as individuals alone, would seldom behave in such a manner.

So one significant way in which the group influences the individual is by providing him or her with *power and security,* feelings of *strength.* Labor unions, as well as employer and medical associations, are vivid examples of groups that offer some degree of power and security to their members.

formal leader

informal leader

Certain individuals within a specific group may also have a significant influence over the group's members. An obvious example is a supervisor, a *formal leader,* who has been officially delegated particular rights, or authority, over his or her subordinates. In many groups there may also emerge an *informal leader,* a person who is able to influence other group members because of his or her age, knowledge, technical or social skills, or physical strength. In a sense, the informal group itself can assign a leadership role to a person.

The Cohesiveness of Groups—Sticking Together

group cohesion

Another common characteristic of behavior in groups is an emotional closeness or *group cohesion* that tends to exist among members. Groups provide the mechanism for giving people a sense of both identity and unity—something referred to as a feeling of *belongingness*.

belonging-ness

Some groups are highly cohesive. Their members stick closely together in spite of pressures to reduce their emotional ties. Other groups consist of members who couldn't care less about unity, solidarity, or group cohesiveness. They don't really feel part of a team. These people are merely a collection of individuals who may be technically members of the group, but whose needs are not satisfied by personal interaction with the group's other members.

Are we together or not?

For example, you may have observed some professors who are members of a group, such as a psychology department, but who seldom interact with other department members. They feel little in the way of unity or personal identification with their cohorts. Yet there are other individuals, such as members of a sales force who are widely dispersed geographically, who share a feeling of camaraderie and mutual identity. Professor John B. Minor suggests that there are three major factors that influence the degree of *unity* of a group. These are:

What tends to influence group unity?

1. The predominance of certain kinds of social motives or needs.
2. The capacity of the group to provide emotionally for its members.
3. The existence of a shared goal.[1]

Watch out, though! Group cohesion can be tricky. Individuals, for example, may develop cohesiveness either in harmony with *or* in conflict with the goals of the formal organization. Subgroups or cliques may form within a group. Certain members of a group may develop cohesion against other group members and ostracize them because of such factors as sex, race, age, or physical characteristics.

Work Arrangement Influence on Informal Groups

How might the arrangement of work influence informal groups?

Studies made by Michael Argyle indicate that the formal arrangement of the physical work flow influences the nature of the informal group. According to Argyle, employees who work side by side on assembly lines, for example, seem not to develop a group feeling; they tend to feel isolated from their fellow workers. Such a lack of group cohesiveness, Argyle contends, can provoke absenteeism and unfavorably affect job satisfaction, turnover, and productivity.[2] In order to overcome such problems,

[1]John B. Minor, *The Challenge of Managing* (Philadelphia: W. B. Saunders, 1975), p. 124.
[2]"Newsletter/Social Science," *Intellectual Digest,* March 1973, p. 72.

80

some firms have restructured their assembly lines to include teams of workers. In chapter 9 we shall discuss problems of morale in greater detail.

Communicating Along the Grapevine

Astute managers learn quickly that the informal group is something that cannot be squelched regardless of any misguided efforts to eliminate it. Informal communication will likely travel from group member to group member and throughout an entire organization even if rules are established to prevent such communication. For example, after the end of the Vietnam war, released American prisoners of war revealed that they had developed secret techniques and channels of communication, such as codes or signals, so that they could communicate, even between one prison camp and another. Some prisoners ingeniously drilled holes through their cell walls with barbed wire strands in order to develop communication networks.

If the premise is true that informal communication cannot be prevented, perhaps it can and should be used constructively to assist an organization in achieving its goals, and at the same time, help group members in achieving their goals.

grapevine

Considerable communication flows through a channel termed the *grapevine,* which is a means of *informal communication,* either oral or written, often considerably faster than the official channels. Wherever there are people, the grapevine seems to exist and frequently it transmits rumors. A *rumor* can be defined as a *statement or report without known authority for its truth,* or, put another way, as a *generally incorrect statement.*

Not only false information, however, travels along the grapevine; much information is accurate or at least partly accurate. Employees probably learn more about what goes on in an organization through the informal grapevine than they do from the official channels of communication. If you have ever worked in an organization, you may have noticed that it seems as though the first person from whom you usually find out new information is the custodian. In some instances, informal communication may even travel from another employee's spouse to your spouse and then to you. Informal communication travels from many sources and through many channels.

Can grapevines be squelched without making your feet purple and your face red?

Some managers seem to feel that the grapevine is a harmful and malicious means of communication and should be stamped out, a task that would be virtually impossible since informal communication is quite a normal activity among normal people. Since the grapevine is probably the fastest means of communication in an organization, it can be *useful* when employed as a *supplement to formal communication*, which tends at times to be extremely slow.

Rumors are usually not a serious problem in organizations where *trust exists* between the managers and the workers and where formal communication networks are used efficiently to keep employees well informed. If an organization has developed an effective feedback system, its managers should be able to become aware of rumors flying about. Managers, by providing accurate facts to informal leaders through the use of face-to-face communication, can frequently squelch false rumors before any damage is done.

Some managers have *weekly or semi-monthly meetings* with their employees in order to provide an outlet for questioning and correcting misinformation. Harmful rumors are not likely to be common in an organization where the normal channels of communication are kept open with factual information.

Group Problem Solving and Decision Making

group decision making

Two heads are even better than none!

meetings

Quite customary in many organizations is *group decision making*, an activity based on the old adage that "two heads are better than one." Although many decisions are made as a result of one-to-one interaction between two individuals, a considerable amount of decision making in today's organizations takes place in *meetings*. Most meetings are intended to accomplish either of two objectives: (1) to provide information, or (2) to solve problems. Let's take a brief look at some of the group dynamics and characteristics of such activities.

Planned and Unplanned Agendas

planned agenda

When managers call meetings for the purpose of providing information or for finding solutions to specific problems, they generally have a good idea of what should be covered during the meeting. In other words, they typically have a *planned agenda,* The planned agenda is useful in that it serves to guide the group's activities toward a pre-established goal. A planned agenda can help prevent a lot of scarce and valuable time from being eaten up needlessly.

hidden agenda

Although an agenda may be planned, one of the potential pitfalls of any meeting is the possibility that a *hidden agenda* will surface. A group member's hidden agenda is basically the attitudes and feelings that he or she brings to the meeting. The person's hidden agenda may be planned in advance of the meeting, or it may emerge spontaneously as the result of a disagreement with ideas expressed or a distrust of people conducting the session. In some instances, the person with the hidden agenda, either consciously or subconsciously, tries to place obstacles in the path of the formal agenda. A chairperson should weigh the validity of any hidden agendas that crop up and try to prevent them from sidetracking a meeting too far from its original purpose.

Brainstorming

brainstorming

A group activity that many have found useful for developing creative solutions to problems is termed *brainstorming*. A brainstorming session is one in which the group members can express themselves freely, regardless of how crazy or wild their ideas may appear to the other group members. The usual guidelines for brainstorming sessions are: (1) that the atmosphere be free of criticism, and (2) that no idea or thought be squelched by either the idea's originator or the group.

Brainstorming sessions have proven helpful in generating a large number of potentially useful ideas. In a freewheeling session there is a tendency for useful ideas to build on less useful ones. For example, the name of a new automobile could be developed by a group of individuals who say aloud every name that comes to mind during the session. After a long list of names is developed and recorded, an analysis could be made and the "best" one chosen.

Let's Form a Committee

committee

In some organizations, difficult decisions are often "referred to committee," either an *ongoing,* standing committee, or one established to handle a specific situation, an *ad hoc* committee. A *committee* can be defined as a group of two or more persons who officially meet together for the purpose of considering issues or problems related to the organization.

Are committees really useful for arriving at decisions? Using committees to accomplish goals is a practice not without critics. For example, the late Hendrik van Loon, Dutch-American historian, had this to say about committees: "Nothing is ever accomplished by a committee unless it consists of three members, one of whom happens to be sick and another absent." And an anonymous skeptic once said, "A camel is a horse designed by a committee."

Many people, however, hold the view that committees, when properly administered, are useful. They feel that committees can result in better decision making since—as with brainstorming—two heads can be more effective than one. They also argue that a greater input of ideas can occur in committee meetings, with one idea perhaps rising out of others. Further, several people with different types of knowledge, abilities, and experience might be able to see more facets of a particular problem than could one person.

Deficiencies in Group Decision Making

potential time waster

Although creative ideas do frequently result from group decision making, there are inherent dangers that one should continually guard against. For example, if meetings are not well planned, they are *potential time wasters*. A manager and his or her subordinates can find much of their time wasted through discussions of trivia—topics that do little to further the organization's goals and objectives.

dilute responsibility

Another danger inherent in the use of group decision making, such as in committees, is that they tend to *dilute responsibility*. Since decisions are arrived at by group consensus, no one person can be blamed for a bad decision.

groupthink

A further potential problem of group decision making lies in what has been called *groupthink*, which can be defined as the process of deriving negative results from group decision-making efforts as a result of in-group pressures. People do tend to be influenced by their peers. The influence of some group members' thinking can sway an entire group into pursuing an undesirable course of action. We've already discussed the nature of group cohesion, which can actually contribute to poor group decision making. Closely knit groups sometimes suffer from the "illusion of unanimity," that is, no one wants to break up the cohesiveness of the group. The group members become the victims of groupthink.

The misjudged sounds of silence!

Group leaders sometimes encourage a groupthink type of atmosphere at meetings—particularly when they've arrived at specific decisions before the meeting even begins! The other members are there merely to rubber-stamp predetermined decisions. Group leaders may also assume that silence on the part of the participants means consent or agreement to decisions actually made unilaterally by the leader.

costly delays

Group decision making can also result in *costly delays*. Other tasks must be neglected while committee members are in session, and sometimes important members arrive late or are absent altogether. There also tends to be more indecisiveness rather than candid and creative thought among committee members as they try to arrive at reasonable decisions and conclusions. Nietzsche, the German philosopher, long ago warned us about group behavior. He said that "madness is the exception in individuals but the rule in groups." In far too many cases, he seems to have been right!

tendency toward indecisiveness

In spite of the many potential pitfalls inherent in group decision making, it is likely to continue playing an important role in many organiza-

tions. However, when its limitations are recognized and sessions are properly planned, group decision making can lead to good ideas.

Analyzing Transactions—an Introduction to TA

trans-actional analysis (TA)

Another facet of group dynamics and interpersonal relations has received considerable attention in recent years. It is called *transactional analysis* (or *TA*). Originally developed by Eric Berne and further popularized by Thomas A. Harris, Dorothy Jongeward, and Muriel James, TA concepts have been studied and applied in recent years by an increasing number of individuals ranging from amateur psychologists trying to get their ''heads on straight'' to organizational managers trying to improve interpersonal relations within their work groups.

To *transact* is to ''carry on'' something. If you have a transaction with a real estate broker, for example, you are carrying on business of some sort—perhaps buying or selling a house. Transactional analysis is concerned with social transactions between people, that is, the way they respond to each other. The term *transactional analysis,* therefore, is considered to represent a body of knowledge related to social transactions between individuals.

What good is TA?

What good is TA? Well, according to its proponents, TA offers some highly significant benefits to those who learn how to apply its concepts. There are four ways in which TA is believed to be beneficial. It can help improve a person's ability to:

1. understand what's going on in face-to-face relationships.
2. maintain a supportive, "positive stroking" attitude toward others.
3. keep the lines of communication open.
4. accept him- or herself and others.

As you learn a few of the basics related to TA in this section, ask yourself how TA might help you achieve the four benefits listed above.

There are those who suspect that TA is a passing fad, which indeed it may prove to be. But there are others who contend that TA concepts are not really all that new but are merely catchy, novel ways of presenting some of Freud's long-established concepts related to the id, the ego, and the superego. Rather than be drawn into the great debate as to where TA came from and where it might go, a more practical approach is to examine how we might utilize TA concepts to improve our own understanding of the ways in which we interact with others and others interact with us.

There's a Bit of Ego in All of Us

trans-
actions

ego
estates

As members of small groups, we each find ourselves communicating in a variety of ways with other people. The various ways in which we interact with others, in the vernacular of TA, are called *transactions*, from which was derived the term *transactional analysis*. According to Berne, each of us interacts with others from one of three positions, or *ego states*. These

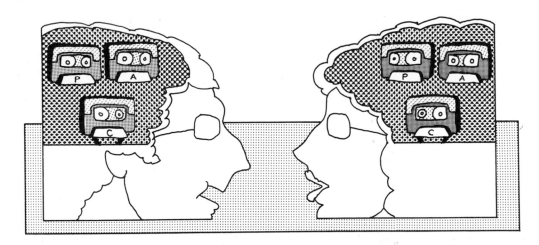

Figure 4–1. The three ego states, or positions, from which we interact with others.

positions, as indicated in figure 4–1, are the *parent ego,* the *adult ego,* and the *child ego.*

According to TA theory, each of us has all three ego states indelibly etched on our minds. Each ego state behaves as though it were a preprogrammed computor disc, or script, causing us to "transact" with others in specific ways. The *parent ego state* in you, for example, feels and behaves somewhat the way your mother and father (or the person who raised you) did. The parent in you may be either helpful or critical, or may be a combination of both, as your parents probably were. Your *adult ego state* is less emotional and demanding than your parent. It gathers facts and attempts to make sound decisions in guiding your transactions with others. Your *child ego state,* like the parent position, is more emotional. It causes you to behave with others in ways that you did when you were a child. It is the position that causes you to act in a natural and uninhibited way at a party or a ball game, or to almost throw a tantrum when you don't get your own way. The child ego state also provides you with feelings of joy and wonder, as well as those of rebelliousness and aggressiveness.

Transacting TA Business

Like hummingbirds flitting from flower to flower, people, during a typical day, flit from one ego state to another. Being able to sense where another person is coming from—that is, which ego state the person is currently in—can help you significantly in interacting with him or her.

According to TA theory, all conversations are a series of transactions, or interactions, between ego states. For example, when you and another person are conversing with each other, *your parent, adult,* or *child* is interacting with his or her *parent, adult,* or *child.* Your own effectiveness with others could improve with an understanding of the two major types of transactions we'll discuss now.

Uncrossed (Complementary) Transactions

The best kinds of transactions between people are the *uncrossed,* or *complementary, transactions.* In short, an uncrossed transaction is the type of transaction that gets the expected response, one that is usually appropriate for the situation. However, to be complementary a transaction doesn't have to be taking place between one adult ego state and another adult ego state.

Figure 4–2 shows an example of an uncrossed transaction. The boss asked a simple question and received a reasonable and appropriate answer. This sort of adult-to-adult transaction tends to keep communication lines open.

You know, for a moment there I thought I heard my daddy!

If I don't get my way, I'll hold my breath till you die!

The transactions people say.

uncrossed (complementary) transactions

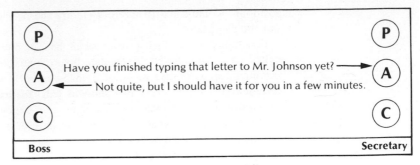

Figure 4–2. An example of an uncrossed adult-to-adult transaction.

A few subtle changes in the wording and tone of a message can bring out a completely different type of response. For example, figure 4–3 shows an example of the boss coming from a *child ego state,* and causing a *parent* response from the secretary.

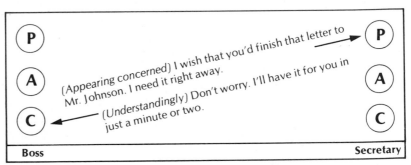

Figure 4–3. An uncrossed transaction originating in the boss's child ego state but eliciting a parent response from the secretary.

Or, as can be seen in figure 4–4, a *child-like* comment might activate the *child* in another person.

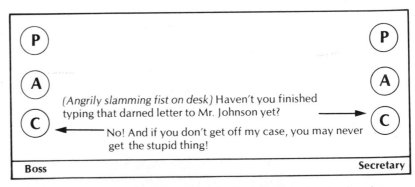

Figure 4–4. An uncrossed transaction originating in the boss's child ego state and activating a child response in the secretary.

Crossed (Uncomplementary) Transactions

Crossed, or *uncomplementary, transactions,* are those that evoke an unexpected or inappropriate response and are often the result of misunderstanding or resentment between two persons. When crossed transactions take place, the lines of communication become broken, and conflict usually develops. Crossed transactions can start and end from any ego state. Figure 4–5 illustrates a type of cross-communication that begins with the *adult* state and evokes a *child* response.

Complementary and uncomplementary transactions are not the only possible types of transactions, but they do provide us with the basis for a better understanding of the purpose of transactional analysis.

Figure 4–5. An example of a crossed transaction originating with the boss's adult and activating a child-to-parent response.

All Us Folks Need Some Strokes

All of us receive and give out *strokes* during our daily transactions with others. *Stroking* is the TA term for giving attention or recognition to another person. Strokes may be *positive,* as when you praise someone for the quality of his or her work; or they may be *negative,* as when you criticize a person for errors he or she may have made. Stroking—either positive or negative—may be given through words, touch, and a variety of actions, such as glances, smiles, or frowns. The way you listen to another person is also a form of stroking.

Giving an employee added responsibility might be interpreted as either a positive or a negative stroke. Can you figure out why? The answer relates to the next part of TA—the *life positions* that people tend to assume.

I'm Really OK . . . Aren't I?

In our personal interaction with others, we generally assume a certain mental state, or as TA terms it, a *life position.* Our life is related to the

Mirror,
mirror, on
the wall . . .

Today's
strokes
determine
tomorrow's
folks!

way we perceive ourselves and others during our transactions. How do you personally feel about yourself? In general when you look in the mirror, do you like what you see? Are you relatively confident about your abilities? Do you feel OK, or not so OK, about yourself? Does your self-image change when you are in certain groups or with certain people?

TA theory suggests that how we feel about ourselves and toward others is formed during our early years and relates to the strokes—both physical and verbal—we received as children. Young children, for example, who have repeatedly been told by their parents that they are stupid are likely to grow up feeling not too good about themselves. Or an infant who has been physically abused may grow up feeling the same way.

So how you feel about yourself relates significantly to the types of stroking you received in the past. This stroking has influenced your life position. But past and present stroking influence the way you feel about yourself in relation to others like your boss, your peers, your subordinates, your friends, acquaintances, and family. There are *four basic positions,* or ways of perceiving yourself relative to other people, according to TA theory. These are:

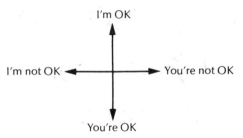

FOUR LIFE POSITIONS

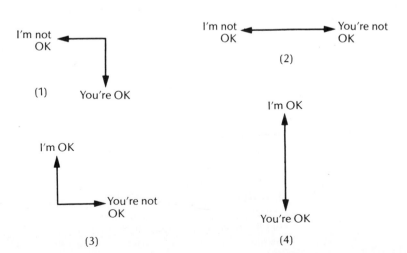

Although called "life positions," they need not be fixed for life. The healthy position to take, of course, is the I'm OK—you're OK one. By understanding yourself and others, and consciously attempting to accept your own limitations as well as those of others, you can find the OK-OK position an attainable goal. Giving positive strokes to others often results in your receiving positive strokes in return.

Can you expect to feel OK all the time?

Interaction with others, at work, at home, or in social situations, is far easier when you are able to accept yourself and to accept the people you are with. This doesn't mean that you have to like everything about everybody. But by recognizing that some good exists in most people, you should find feeling OK about them an easier task.

TA can also help you avoid certain conflicts with others by making it easier for you to recognize when crossed transactions have occurred. Positive strokes, sincerely applied, are powerful wonder drugs for curing communication illnesses and for making others feel OK about themselves and about you.

Really Small Groups—the Interview

interviewing

Another aspect of small group behavior that receives considerable attention in management literature is the process of *interviewing*. For our purposes, interviewing can be defined as *the act of consultation between a manager and a worker*. Most employees—whether they are managers or subordinates—are often involved with this form of interpersonal behavior, since interviews are used for a variety of purposes in organizations. The principal types of interviews are:

What are the main types of interviews?

1. Employment (to observe applicants for job openings)
2. Appraisal (to review an employee's performance)
3. Counseling (to aid employees with personal problems)
4. Disciplinary (to discuss an employee's behavior)
5. Grievance (to discuss an employee's complaints)
6. Morale surveys (to discover employee attitudes)
7. Exit (to assess reasons for employee terminations)

Styles of Interviewing

What determines the style of interview that should be used?

The particular style of interview employed generally depends on the *nature* of the interview and the *experience* of the manager. As with most activities, interviewers (as well as interviewees) should alter their styles to suit the particular situation. The most commonly used include the *structured, unstructured, group, and stress* styles of interviewing.

structured (patterned) interview

A *structured (patterned) interview* is one that usually follows a predetermined pattern. Frequently a specific set of questions, taken from a detailed form, are asked of the interviewee. The form is a guide to what questions are going to be asked, and it helps keep the interview on the track. Some interview forms include two sets of questions: (1) the specific questions to be asked during the interview and (2) questions not asked by the interviewer, but intended to help him or her interpret the significance of the interviewee's answers. (These latter usually appear directly below the primary questions and are often highlighted in a different color to make them distinguishable.) Some types of interviews, by their very nature (employment or disciplinary, for example), lend themselves to greater structure than do others (such as counseling or grievance) since managers, when involved with the former, usually know the specific ground they want to cover.

unstructured (nondirective) interview

An *unstructured (nondirective) interview* is one that attempts to avoid influencing the interviewee's remarks. Often a broad, general question is asked, and the interviewee is encouraged to answer in some depth. Open types of questions, such as ''How do you feel about your last job?'' or ''How did the problem between you and Hazel start?'' are usually asked. The interviewee, during an unstructured interview, tends to feel freer to express attitudes, desires, emotions, and problems. With certain types of interviews, such as grievance or counseling, the unstructured approach often serves as a beneficial safety valve by which employees can vent pressures or complaints. In such interviews, however, there is the inherent danger of getting sidetracked and wasting time on nonrelated topics, especially if the interviewee has a tendency to ramble.

''How do you feel about . . . ?''

group interview

A *group interview* is adaptable to a variety of situations. In one variation, several managers, or members of a board or panel, observe, challenge, and pool their impressions of the interviewee. Applicants for positions with a high degree of responsibility, such as sales or executive trainees, may be subjected to group interviews. Promotions in some governmental jobs also require the aspirants to go before a board or panel of interviewers.

Another variation of the group interview involves several candidates for a particular position being questioned and observed—as a group—by several managers. The group being interviewed may be questioned by the executive panel, its members observed as they interact with each other, or a combination of both may occur.

stress interview

The *stress interview* is one whose merit has been widely debated. With this approach, the interviewee is intentionally placed in a tense—possibly even abusive—situation in order to see how she or he responds to stress. The theory underlying this approach is that during stress, the ''true'' personality of the interviewee tends to emerge. It is debatable, however, whether a person has one ''true'' personality. Most individuals tend to react differently at different times to similar situations, depending on their moods at the particular moment.

Hey! Why'd you punch me in the nose?

Managers who use the stress technique feel that by introducing tension into the interview through insults or extremely challenging questions, the applicant can be observed in other than artificial "courtship-styled" behavior situations. A typical approach for inducing stress into an interview is for the interviewer to indicate that the applicant is obviously unfit and shouldn't be wasting the interviewer's time. The interviewer then observes the response of the applicant. An inherent danger in this approach is that the applicant might develop negative attitudes toward the organization and interviewer.

Wow! That turkey is weird!

Guidelines for Conducting Interviews

Regardless of the type of interview, the manager should have patience, knowledge of questioning and listening techniques, an awareness of and sensitivity toward nonverbal communication, and a basic liking and respect for people. Some types of interviews, such as disciplinary interviews, should be conducted privately in order to prevent embarrassing the employee. In general, however, the *technique* employed by the interviewer is far more critical to the interview's success than its setting.

Below are some guidelines for conducting more effective interviews.

What factors can improve your interviewing techniques?

Plan ahead. Know why you are there and what you want to accomplish. What do you want to find out?

Know something in advance about the person whom you are interviewing. Look at the person's application, personnel file, or any other relevant information before the interview.

Watch out for your own biases. Your task is to obtain information or provide assistance, not to feed your own ego.

Try to help the person you are interviewing relax and feel confident enough to communicate with you.

Don't make the mistake of doing all the talking; encourage the interviewee to talk.

Practice the concepts of good listening and phrasing questions.

Don't fight the clock. Try to arrange for enough time to conduct the interview so that the session does not become tense.

Control the interview. Some small talk may help to relax the person you are interviewing, but, in general, attempt to guide the interview in the direction of your objectives.

Never argue. Arguments usually prevent the attainment of your objectives.

Look beyond the employee's words. Is there a meaning that has not surfaced?

Maintain your alertness at the end of the interview. Much can be learned after the first "good-bye."

Guidelines for Being Interviewed

So far we have been examining the interviewing process mainly as a tool of management. But almost everyone, workers and managers, is interviewed periodically. So let's step now into the shoes of the person on the receiving end of an interview. How might you improve your image when being interviewed? The following is a list of guidelines that could help you.

How to succeed at being interviewed by trying.

Try to determine in advance why you are being interviewed and be prepared for the types of questions that will be directed at you.

Be certain to be prompt. Arriving late can cause you to get off to a bad start in the interview.

Make certain that your appearance is appropriate to the particular situation.

Bring **something** to do in case you have to wait to be interviewed. Writing a letter or reading a book can help you relax.

Don't be over-anxious to answer questions. Give complete, but brief, responses to questions—don't ramble.

Listen carefully to the interviewer. If you don't understand a question, don't fake your answer. Ask for clarification.

Be certain to take with you any background, reference, or statistical material you might need. If you are being interviewed for a job, do you have a resumé, or summary, of any data you might need?

Be polite and courteous throughout the interview. Don't forget to thank the interviewer for his or her time, shake hands, and say good-bye.

Summary

Everyone is a member of a variety of small groups. Organizational members should try to gain an understanding of the workings of group behavior—both formal and informal—because of its significant influence over them. Managers, too, have an influence over the small group. Work groups strongly influence the behavior and performance of their members—in either positive or negative ways.

Transactional analysis (TA) is a tool that helps us understand what happens when two ego states get together. Stroking is a way in which we express our feelings about others, and it strongly influences how others react to us.

Another aspect of small group behavior is the interview. We examined the structured, unstructured, group, and stress types of interview. An understanding of effective interview behavior can be helpful to both managers and workers.

Terms and Concepts to Remember

Group
Required (formal) system
Emergent (informal) system
Social norms
Formal leader
Informal leader
Group cohesion
Belongingness
Grapevine
Rumor
Group decision making
Meetings
Planned agenda
Hidden agenda
Brainstorming

Committee
Groupthink
Transactional analysis (TA)
Transactions
Ego states
Uncrossed (complementary) transactions
Crossed (uncomplementary) transactions
Strokes—positive and negative
Life position
Interviewing
Structured (patterned) interview
Unstructured (nondirective) interview
Group interview
Stress interview

Questions

1. Evaluate the following statement: "Formal groups, by their very nature, restrict our freedom. This would be a far better world in which to live and work if formal groups did not exist."
2. It has been said that informal groups help individuals satisfy their psychological and social needs. How might the informal group have the reverse effect—that is, create dissatisfaction in an individual group member?
3. What are social norms? In what ways might they make a supervisor's job easier? More difficult?
4. Why do members of groups tend to develop group cohesion?
5. What might cause a person *not* to want to be accepted by a group?
6. Evaluate the following statement: "Informal communication, because of the workings of the grapevine, cannot be controlled or influenced by a manager."

7. Is group decision making better than individual decision making? Explain some of the potential pitfalls to effective group decision making.
8. How might an understanding of TA assist organizational members?
9. What might be some of the ways, not discussed in the chapter, in which *stress* could be brought into an interview?

Other Readings

Berne, Eric. *Games People Play*. New York: Grove Press, 1964.

Harris, Thomas A. *I'm OK—You're OK*. New York: Harper & Row, 1969.

James, Muriel, and Jongeward, Dorothy. *Born to Win*. Reading, Mass.: Addison-Wesley, 1971.

————*Winning With People*. Reading, Mass.: Addison-Wesley, 1973.

Jandt, Fred E. *The Process of Interpersonal Communication*. San Francisco: Canfield Press, 1976.

Janis, Irving L. *Victims of Groupthink*. Boston: Houghton Mifflin, 1972.

Mills, Theodore M. *The Sociology of Small Groups*. Englewood Cliffs, N.J.: Prentice-Hall, 1967.

Applications

Meeting Madness

The Super Stress Surgical Instrument Company is a medium-sized firm located in an industrial park on the outskirts of Madison, Wisconsin. The company is principally involved with manufacturing surgical instruments and supplies for medical doctors and hospitals.

About a year ago, Margaret Gingrich, age 23, niece of the firm's founder, Marshall Gingrich, was hired to replace Randy Hunt, quality control supervisor, who had reached the age of retirement. Margaret had recently graduated from the University of Wisconsin where she had majored in industrial engineering.

Ken Giles, age 54, is the production manager of the Prosthesis Department, where artificial devices designed to replace missing parts of the human body are produced. Ken has worked for Super Stress for 15 years, having previously been a production line supervisor and, prior to that, a worker on the production line. Ken has almost two years of college, acquired mostly by attending occupational night courses at a local community college.

From their first meeting, it seemed as though Ken and Margaret could not get along together. There appeared to be an underlying animosity between them, but it was never too clear what the problem was.

Grover Garvin, age 45, is the plant manager of Super Stress. He has occasionally observed disagreements between Margaret and Ken on the production line. Absenteeism has also risen in Ken's department since Margaret was hired as quality control supervisor. Grover recently decided to write a memo calling for a meeting of all nine supervisory personnel in the production and quality control departments. The memo was worded as follows:

To: All supervisory personnel,
      production and quality
      control departments

From: Grover Garvin,   ____Please respond
        Plant Manager

Subject: Clarification of work roles.   **X**__No response necessary

---

I would like all of you to meet with me on Friday, July 8, at 9:00 A.M. in Room 23, at which time we will attempt to straighten out any misunderstandings and differences that seem to exist among production and quality control personnel.
Respectfully submitted,

Grover

Grover opened the meeting by explaining why he had called it, and then asked Ken for his opinion of the problem. The following conversation took place:

> *Ken:* That wonder girl you hired is too eager to find fault in our department. Until she was hired, we hardly ever stopped production. And when we did, it was only because of a mechanical malfunction. But "meticulous Margaret" has been stopping everything if one defective part comes down the line.
> *Margaret:* That's a lie, Ken. You know darned well. . . .
> *Ken:* Grover, our quality hasn't changed one bit. It's still the same consistently good quality it was before she came, but all she wants to do is hassle us.

Margaret: May I say something? Ken, you never have accepted me right from the beginning. I can remember some of the snide remarks and wisecracks you used to make behind my back. I heard them quite clearly!

George Daskarolis (Margaret's assistant): I have to back up Margaret, Grover. I think that everyone here knows that the rules permit quality control to shut down production if rejects exceed five an hour. This is all Margaret has been doing.

Ken: Now listen to me! Margaret starts counting the hour from the moment she gets the first reject. Randy never really worried about that obsolete reject rule when he was supervisor. She wants my department to look bad! Isn't that true, Lloyd?

Lloyd Cunningham (Ken's assistant): It sure is, Ken. Every time that lady halts production, she costs the company money, and the workers aren't able to earn their bonuses.

Twenty minutes later Margaret and Ken were still lashing out at each other. Grover decided that ending the meeting might be the best move for now. He promised to send out a memo clarifying the matter some time next week.

Questions

1. Should Grover have called a meeting to solve this problem? Why or why not? How might the meeting have been handled more effectively?
2. How do you feel about the rule calling for production to halt if there are more than five rejects in an hour? Should it have been enforced? Explain.
3. Identify where, if at all, group cohesion exists among the members of the meeting group.
4. What do you feel is the major problem in this case? The solution?

Doing Our Own Thing

Medical Claims Processing, Inc., is a company that was established by three computer specialists to service federal and state government medical care programs. MCP was an immediate success. After less than five years in business, the company was employing 1,000 people. Most observers felt that opportunities for continued growth would easily parallel the expanding government role in health care. MCP was viewed as being at the "state of the art" in the computerized processing of medical claims.

Chuck Armstrong, president of MCP, decided to explore systematically commercial opportunities to apply the company's technology to medical claims processing for unions and large corporate employee groups. Chuck felt there would also be opportunities for selling know-how to medical providers such as insurance carriers, hospitals, and clinics. For example, the MCP computers accumulated facts on health care usage that could be useful to the health care industry in planning and pricing health services.

To capitalize on this unique business opportunity, Chuck selected Jeff Sharp for this new assignment. Jeff had served for one year as a long-range planning analyst, and was now promoted to director of marketing research and authorized to hire a staff. Jeff prepared personnel requisitions for a start-up staff, including two project managers and one statistical analyst. The Human Resources (Personnel) Department initiated recruiting through its usual sources. Jeff found this process too slow, however, so he contacted two colleagues from days at Wharton School of Business, Steve Fenn and Dave Marcus, and sold them both on the benefits of joining MCP. Steve and Dave had recently completed MBA degrees and felt that the rapidly expanding health field might be a good place to start their careers. Jeff then arranged a transfer for Sandra Johnson, whom he knew for her excellent statistical experience in the long-range planning department.

One week after Steve and Dave accepted the positions as project managers, a woman telephoned to request an interview with Jeff Sharp. Judy Angelli had learned of the job opening from the placement office at San Jose State University. She told Jeff that she had an M.S. in statistics and was finishing an M.A. in health care services. The graduate studies in health care services was a new program. Jeff liked her background and decided to interview Judy, even though he had filled all budgeted jobs.

While studying at Wharton for his Ph.D. in business administration, Jeff became enthusiastic about participative management concepts. Now, as director of marketing research and running his own department for the first time, Jeff was going to practice participative management. He decided to implement participative management by scheduling a group interview—Jeff, Steve and Dave would group-interview Judy Angelli.

The interview began at 10:00 A.M. and continued through lunch. The following are a few exchanges from the interview:

> *Jeff:* Judy, the three of us represent the marketing research
> department of MCP. We have a mandate to identify marketa-
> ble expertise now in MCP or available to MCP. We will iden-
> tify demand, research the opportunity thoroughly, and prepare
> proposals for sale of consulting or data to health providers.
> As you can see, our objectives are broad, and we are explor-
> ing new territories where no one has walked before. Steve
> and Dave were research assistants to me while we were all

attending Wharton Graduate School of Business just over one year ago. When I got this promotion a few weeks ago, I called them immediately because of my confidence in them.
Steve: We all think alike. Some of our brainstorming sessions are truly exciting.
Judy: I've been a research assistant at the State University for Professor Hill. I enjoy the research environment—you know, all the freedom and challenge. I'm an independent person. Professor Hill and I couldn't agree on methodology for research, so he suggested I should seek other employment. I guess someday I'll be able to finish my second masters degree.
Jeff: Perhaps I told you on the telephone that we don't have budget approval for more than two project managers.
Judy: Yes, you told me. However, I felt that if I could meet you for an interview you would be impressed.
Dave: We have more statistical work already than Sandra can handle. Maybe we could get approval to hire Judy as a statistical analyst.
Judy: I don't want a clerical job. I want a management job. You know what I mean—with all my education I'm ready for real responsibilities.
Jeff: The pay would be less, but in this fast-growing company there's a shortage of good management candidates. There will be lots of opportunities.

Approval was granted to add one statistical analyst. Judy accepted the offer because she wanted the work and the starting pay was considerably more than she had earned as a student research assistant.

The group—Jeff, Steve, Dave, and Judy—began to function as one happy family. Sandra was a 9-to-5 person. She was well regarded by the group for her ability, but they all agreed her future was limited to analyst. The group dressed more casually than all other departments in corporate headquarters. Since they were in research, each member decided to arrive at the office about mid-morning, then work until well past dinner. After those long hours, stopping for pizza and beer was a favorite group "unwinding."

Four months after Judy joined the department she confronted Jeff with a demand for a pay increase. Jeff decided to meet with Harriet Morrison, vice president of the human resources department, to resolve the pay demand. The following is part of the conversation that took place between Jeff, Judy, and Harriet.

Harriet: Would you like to fill me in on this situation?
Jeff: Judy demands that her pay be increased to the same as

Steve's and Dave's—something to do, she said, with equal pay. She also demands overtime pay for the past four months. Judy knows that we are not "clock punchers." We have always included Judy in our evening brainstorming sessions because she has some good ideas. Now she wants to be paid like a clerk for overtime hours.

Judy: That's unfair. You promised me that I could get ahead. Steve and Dave have less education and less background in health care than I do. I've been managing projects the same as Steve and Dave; yet, their pay is $700 per month more than mine. I make the same salary as Sandra and she only has a BA and doesn't have the potential I have.

Jeff: Lately Judy has been out of control. Last week she wanted to send an invitation to a meeting to the heads of sales and the computer group. She even wanted to have an agenda—something we just don't do. I told her I'd send the memo. Next thing I knew she'd called a meeting with these two other department heads. Frankly, it made me look bad.

Judy: The idea to develop a client newsletter as a marketing piece was mine, and you agreed it was a good one. Why should you take credit for my idea? If I don't get the same pay as Steve and Dave, I'll file a charge of discrimination.

Harriet interrupted the meeting to excuse Judy so that she could discuss the resolution with Jeff. The two-party discussion continued as follows:

Jeff: I guess Judy doesn't fit my group. I don't like threats. I've been fair and open with her. I'll send out a memo requiring neckties and fixed hours, and I guess I'll fire her for insubordination.

Harriet: Maybe we're moving too fast. Before any action is taken, I want to review Judy's job description. She said she's managing projects. Is she?

Jeff: Only with my close supervision. Not like Steve and Dave. They show more initiative.

Harriet: Could I read the job descriptions you agreed to write for each of your new people?

Jeff: You can't describe research in a job description. My people are creative, not like the rest of the company. We don't want job descriptions.

Questions

1. Do you feel the group interview was a good selection tool? Why or why not?
2. Is this small group an "island" where casual attire, hours of work, and unstructured jobs are justified because they are in "research"?
3. Is it important that a member of the group be a statistical analyst or a project manager but not both? Explain.
4. Should participative management include group interviews, no-agenda meetings, and "one happy family" relationships? Explain.
5. Which elements of the MCP environment are significant to this group? Why?
6. What is the major problem in this case? The solution?

two

Leaders Need People

5

Human Needs and Motivation

Everybody Needs Something— What Motivates You?

When you finish this chapter, you should be able to:

1. **Describe** how **wants** differ from **needs.**
2. **Restate** in your own words the phrase "felt needs motivate."
3. **Understand** the effect of culture on needs.
4. **Explain** why a satisfied need ceases to motivate.
5. **Summarize** the motivational theories of Maslow and Herzberg.
6. **Recognize** the problems that unsatisfied needs can cause.
7. **Summarize** the major adjustive reactions to unsatisfied needs.

> If companies are to survive, they
> will have to change from
> management by movement to
> management by motivation
>
> —Frederick Herzberg

A college student, whom we'll call Irwin O'Luzer, once had a term paper due on a particular morning. The previous evening, while typing the final copy on his trusty electric portable typewriter, Irwin accidentally joggled the plug out of the electric outlet and discovered that, no matter how he touched the typewriter keys, he was frustrated in his attempts to type. Although not mechanically inclined, Irwin realized something was wrong. He had an unsatisfied need: electricity. Irwin's life would have continued without the manufactured machine, but he had a scholastic *goal* important to him, and the typewriter assisted him considerably in the quest for that goal. Many things that we think of as needs, such as Irwin's "need" for an electric typewriter, are actually wants, but we have been conditioned to feel them as needs. For example, you *need* food to sustain yourself, but do you need (or merely *want*) chicken cacciatori?

How do your *wants* differ from your *needs*?

The Importance of Human Needs

All of us have needs. Although we might be able to survive quite nicely in many situations without electricity, we cannot survive for long without food, drink, sleep, air to breathe, and a satisfactory temperature. These are all *basic*, *primary*, or *physiological needs*.

basic needs

We humans also have a variety of *secondary*, or *psychological needs*, which also tend to motivate us. Among these needs are included needs to feel secure, to be with other people, to be respected as human beings, and sometimes even to climb mountains. Such needs (also called *motives* because they move or motivate us to act) are not identical in all persons. Not everyone *needs* the same number of hours of sleep a night. Needs exist in each individual in varying degrees.

secondary needs

Needs and Motivation

Why learn about needs?

An awareness of the concept of needs, important for various reasons, is especially important for a greater understanding of your own behavior and of others with whom and through whom you work. If you ever become a manager or supervisor, you will discover that an understanding of the needs of your subordinates will greatly facilitate your attempts to motivate them. Employees and family members likewise can benefit from a knowledge of needs concepts.

If You Are a Manager

Managers get things done with and through people, and an understanding of concepts of needs is essential if management is to be effective. Managers should recognize, for example, that not all persons are motivated by the same incentives. One person might feel motivated to work harder by an increase in pay; another might barely respond to any change in income. Some individuals might be highly motivated by the opportunity to have more responsibility on the job; others may be frightened of additional responsibility.

Is work a nasty four-letter word?

Traditional types of managers believe that most people dislike work and will be best motivated by fear and financial reward. Such managers believe that since most individuals must work, they will respond more productively when the fear of suspension, demotion, or dismissal hangs over their heads. Fear can motivate in the *short run*, but often in the *longer run* it merely motivates individuals into seeking employment elsewhere.

How does the modern manager differ from the traditional?

The modern approach to motivational management makes greater use of positive factors, such as recognition, status, and responsibility, than of the negative factors preferred by the traditional manager. The modern manager recognizes that all persons have needs, and that not everyone places the same value or priority on the objects or situations that satisfy needs.

If You Are an Employee

How can you as an employee benefit from an understanding of needs and motivational concepts? The knowledge of what motivates a particular type of behavior can enhance your understanding of yourself and others. You should find that you become less irritated with the behavior of others when you are able to understand it. You may find it easier to solve problems between you and your boss or your co-workers if you have a better understanding of what motivates people.

If You Are with Family or Friends

The same premises can hold true for you if you are married, a parent, or even among friends. All behavior tends to be caused, and an understanding of some of the causes can significantly assist you in preventing and resolving human problems in a variety of situations.

Knowledge Can be Misused

Should organizational members be concerned with theory?

Watch out for the possibility of misinterpreting the intent of understanding human behavioral concepts. Individuals in organizations, for example, do not have the time to sit around in official "ivory towers" passing the hours merely contemplating their organizational navels, so to speak, and discussing theory among themselves. Most organizations do not, and indeed could not, cater to such academic pastimes.

Who wants to be a puppet?

Nor should we use an understanding of human behavior to manipulate others, a practice that has extremely dire connotations. Any tool can be used or misused. The major purpose of an improved understanding of motivation is to assist us in working *positively* with and through individuals in organizations. Other purposes are likely to develop counterproductive results.

Felt Needs Motivate

Look at the cartoon, an illustration of a basic motivational concept. Little Jeremy, growing rapidly, has a ravenous appetite. At the moment, he appears to be displaying his usual hunger pangs. He *feels* that he needs some of Mom's cookies, and until he gets some, he experiences a certain amount of *tension* and excitement. These feelings tend to motivate him to take some cookies, an activity that offers him *relief* (at least for the moment!).

need
↓
tension
↓
activity
↓
relief

In summary, needs create tensions. Tensions motivate action. Action can result in the accomplishment of a goal and/or the relief of tension. The achieved goal then can result in satisfaction, at least until the next tension arises.

For example, someone may say that you *need* an education, and he or she might be right, but if *you* don't feel the need, you are not likely to be motivated toward the activity that an education requires.

An example of the lack of motivational tension apparently existed in a student who seemed uninterested in preparing his assignments for a particular course. The professor asked the student to drop by the office for a counseling session one day, during which the student showed the professor his grade sheet from the previous term: two Fs, two withdrawals, and an incomplete. Asked why he was attending college, the student replied: "I'm not quite sure, but my mother wants me to go." A mother may want her son to attend college, but her wants are not likely to provide enough tension or feelings of need in her son. Somehow, the son has to discover, or be assisted in discovering, for himself why he may want or need a college education. To reiterate: a *felt* need motivates.

The Nature of Needs

What becomes important after bread?

As a person's basic needs become satisfied, other needs (called higher-order needs) become increasingly more significant. You must eat to live. If you are ravenously hungry, your first morsel of food might give you tremendous satisfaction. As you continue to eat, you may begin to experience what economists often refer to as "diminishing marginal satisfaction" from each additional portion of food. After a certain point (which varies with the individual), you discover that the basic need of satisfying your hunger drive has been met.

If you had been extremely hungry *and* extremely tired, one of your drives, or motives, might have been stronger than the other. For example, assume that you have not eaten or slept for two and a half days and someone leads you into a comfortable room. As you enter, you observe on one side of the room a perfectly broiled juicy T-bone steak and a tender baked potato smothered in sour cream and sprinkled with chives. On the other side of the room you see a comfortable-appearing queen-sized bed. Which of the two intense drives will you satisfy first? You would probably favor your hunger drive. After satiating yourself with a meal, your sleepy eyes would probably find that the bed has begun to look increasingly inviting.

Cultural Effect on Needs

Do *you* determine all of your needs?

The culture of our society has had a significant influence on our needs. Americans, for example, tend to drink large quantities of water; Germans, however, tend to drink little water, but lead the world in the per capita consumption of beer. If you travel at all through Europe with any of the natives, you will probably notice how your thirst for water seems much greater than that of your European friends. What might be the reason?

One reason is that the cultural background, or childhood training, of Americans is considerably different from that of, say, German or French children. Do you remember how twice a day in grade school your teacher would march you and your classmates to two places: the toilet and the drinking fountain? Americans expect to find drinking fountains in public buildings, but such amenities are still rare in much of the rest of the world. Technology also plays a part in the American "need" for water. Drinking fountains wouldn't make much sense in countries that still do not have water suitable for drinking.

Why is body odor offensive?

Advertising also is a cultural factor that strongly influences what we think we need. Most textbooks on the subject will admit that the creation of a demand is one of the major purposes of advertising. If you are convinced by advertising that natural body odors are offensive to others, you are more likely to spend money in order to reduce the "tension" that b.o. creates in you.

Cultural effects have likewise convinced workers in Spain to believe that they "need" a three- or four-hour lunch break, but, unlike Americans, they do not "need" to finish work before 5:00 P.M.; 7:00 P.M. suits them just fine. Nor do most Spaniards need to eat dinner before 10:30 P.M.

A Satisfied Need Ceases to Motivate

Is anyone ever *completely* satisfied?

If you have usually been able to acquire most of the food and adequate shelter you have needed, other motives may have become more important. Perhaps *security* (such as a good retirement plan) or *social approval* (such as becoming president of an organization) or other factors have become more important to you. The point to be made is this: As our basic, lower-order needs become satisfied, there is the tendency for other needs—termed *psychological* or *higher-order needs*—to increase in importance. The concept of a priority or hierarchy of needs was thoroughly developed by A. H. Maslow in his book *Motivation and Personality*.[1]

higher-order needs

A Stroll Down Needs Lane

Maslow's concepts[2] should appear clearer if you assume that you are going to take a leisurely stroll down a hypothetical street called Needs Lane, as illustrated in the cartoon. The temperature on this hot July day is

[1]Abraham H. Maslow, *Motivation and Personality* (New York: Harper & Row, 1954).

[2]There is much debate among behavioral science scholars about whose motivational theory is most reasonable. Besides Maslow, others, such as Douglas McGregor, Frederick Herzberg, Victor Vroom, and B. F. Skinner, have developed theories of motivation. For a comparison of theories see Gene W. Dalton and Paul R. Lawrence, eds., *Motivation and Control in Organizations* (Homewood, Ill.: Richard D. Irwin, 1971), pp. 337–375.

a broiling 102°F, and you have developed a prodigious thirst. To top it off, you thoughtlessly skipped breakfast this morning, are unusually famished, and your stomach is growling ferociously. Suddenly you notice the store with the address No. 1 Needs Lane.

Basic Needs Cafe

What happens when you've had enough french fries?

Ah, the Basic Needs Cafe is before you. Fortunately, you have some of last week's paycheck on you, so you enter the cafe and order a giant cheeseburger and a large root beer packed with ice. The air-conditioning feels magnificent. After you have eaten the cheeseburger, you are still hungry, so you order another, with a double side-order of crispy french fries smothered with thick sweet catsup. Your stomach now begins to feel somewhat stuffed. Your basic needs of hunger and thirst are satisfied. The "tension" of hunger no longer persists; a goal has been achieved.

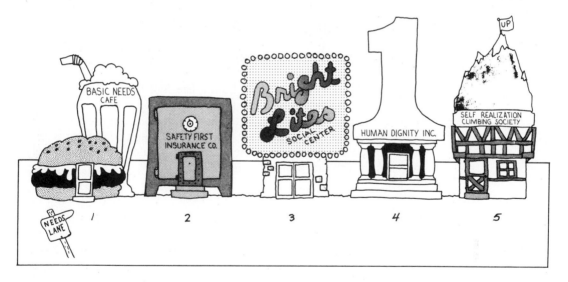

Safety-First Insurance Company

Have you ever thought about your old age?

You walk outside and come across the Safety-First Insurance Company at 2 Needs Lane. You are reminded of something about which you have been thinking for some time. You earn a fairly good salary, but are not able to save much of it. Recently you have begun to wonder what your old age will be like. How much security will you have? An affable life insurance agent catches you before you can get away and discusses a nifty old-age retirement plan with you. He points out that although some people die too soon, many others live much too long after they stop working and find themselves with inadequate funds to support themselves and their families. So you buy an annuity.

Bright Lites Social Center

Next you come to 3 Needs Lane, the Bright Lites Social Center. You broke up with your close companion three weeks ago last Friday, and you have been having some difficulty in meeting someone new. So you enter the Bright Lites and leave two hours later with a good score. You have acquired the names and phone numbers of three potentially interesting and unusually attractive persons.

Human Dignity, Inc.

Do you feel the need for self-esteem?

Continuing your merry journey down Needs Lane you pass Human Dignity, Inc. Curious about their activities, you enter the office. You discover that Human Dignity offers home study courses in accounting that lead to a CPA certificate. You have been doing quite well, thank you, as a bookkeeper for some years, but you certainly would like to be able to tell your mother that you are a Certified Public Accountant, rather than merely a bookkeeper. You sign up for the course.

Self-Realization Climbing Society

What in the world is at 5 Needs Lane? The Self-Realization Climbing Society. What a fascinating name for an organization. You feel satisfied with your day so far. However, wouldn't it be fun, at least occasionally, to feel that you are on "top of the world"? Not many people are able to climb the highest mountains in the world, but wouldn't it be exciting to try during your vacation next month? You sign up!

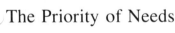

The Priority of Needs

levels of needs

Did you get the significance of our discussion of your trip down Needs Lane? The point, in case you missed it, is this: Human needs can be categorized into *various levels* (or a hierarchy), and each level of need has to be satisfied to some extent before the next level assumes importance. Maslow developed a concept that distinguished five levels of human needs, ranging from basic, lower-order needs to psychological, higher-order needs:

1. Basic physiological needs.
2. Safety and security needs.
3. Social and love needs.
4. Self-esteem, self-respect, and prestige needs.
5. Self-realization needs—the feeling of accomplishment.

Remember the french fries?

A cardinal point of the hierarchy-of-needs theory, as you should recall, is that a *satisfied need ceases to motivate*. Lower-order needs do not become unimportant to the person, but higher-order needs achieve greater significance for the individual as his or her basic needs become satisfied.

Is money the sole motivator?

For exampie, take the case of an employer who pays his or her employees more than the prevailing industry rate. The employer may feel that the employees are satisfied and would not think of withholding their services by going on strike. However, can you think of what might become more important to employees as their basic needs become relatively satisfied through the receipt of ample income? Perhaps various fringe benefits, such as a group health plan, or a center for social activities on the company's premises, or even such reflections of status as a title, one's own thermostat control in his or her office, or a private secretary rather than the use of a steno pool.

Perhaps the hierarchy-of-needs concept helps to explain the behavior of many young Americans today who appear to their parents not to appreciate the many material things with which their elders have provided them. Numerous young people have not felt the necessity to be particularly concerned about the satisfaction of their basic needs; food has always been on the table. Other psychological needs, such as those for love, self-respect, along with a desire for a decent social and economic environment for their fellow humans, may have become more important.

Needs Are Not Mutually Exclusive

Can more than one need be important simultaneously?

Many writers have presented the hierarchy-of-needs concept as a stepladder or pyramid, implying that as you lifted your body past one rung on the ladder of needs, you were finished with it. Needs, however, are not mutually exclusive. For example, refer to our trip down Needs Lane once again and assume that you emerged from the Bright Lites Social Center, not with phone numbers, but with a lively young companion. You had both been dancing strenuously and developed enormous appetites. So you return to the Basic Needs Cafe for two tuna fish sandwiches and thick milkshakes. More than one drive, in this case drives of hunger *and* social companionship, can be satisfied simultaneously when you and a date go out for dinner—if a tuna fish sandwich and a milkshake can be called dinner.

The Maintenance of Motivation

Herzberg's Motivation-Maintenance Model

Frederick Herzberg, a well-known management theorist, is probably best known for another theory of motivation—the ''motivation-maintenance model.''[3] Herzberg's research indicates that *two sets of factors* or conditions influence the behavior of individuals in organizations. The first set provides an almost *neutral* feeling among the workers of an organization, but *if withdrawn* creates *dissatisfaction*. These are called *maintenance* or *hygiene factors*. (The word *hygiene* was borrowed from the medical field where it refers to factors that help maintain, but do not necessarily improve, health.)

maintenance (hygiene) factors

motivational factors (satisfiers)

The second set is termed *motivational*. When present, it is said to *cause* job satisfaction, the factors serving as *motivators* or *satisfiers*. Absence of the satisfiers, however, will not cause dissatisfaction. The terminology may seem confusing at first so let's go into a slightly more detailed explanation of each set of factors.

Maintenance (Hygiene) Factors

First let's look at the following short list of what Herzberg calls "hygiene," or "maintenance," factors:

1. Company policy and administration
2. Supervision
3. Interpersonal relations with superiors, subordinates, and peers
4. Salary and certain types of fringe benefits
5. Working conditions

What are your hygiene factors?

According to Herzberg's research, maintenance factors such as these do not necessarily motivate workers in organizations. Can you figure out why? Mainly, such factors do not create satisfaction but, when absent, can lead to dissatisfaction among employees. An illustration to which you might relate may make the concept clearer. Assume that while attending college, you live with your parents who provide you with a regular, generous allowance. Your father, an engineer with an aircraft company, has been laid off as a result of a cutback in government national defense expenditures. Regretfully, he has to suspend your allowance. Having taken the allowance for granted, you might find that the absence of the allowance (a hygiene factor) creates a feeling of *dissatisfaction* in your mind (and wallet!), although while you had it, the allowance had had a neutral effect on your behavior and attitude.

Another example: Americans tend to take the availability of ice cubes for granted. Many refrigerators in the United States today even contain built-in automatic icemakers. The omnipresence of the frigid little cubes

[3]Frederick Herzberg, *Work and the Nature of Man* (Cleveland: World Publishing, 1966), and *The Managerial Choice* (Homewood, Ill.: Dow Jones-Irwin, 1976).

114

probably doesn't particularly turn you on. Travel to some other countries, however, and you will receive odd looks if you ask for ice in your drink. The absence of ice, therefore, for many Americans becomes what Herzberg would term a *dissatisfier*.

dissatisfier

Maintenance or hygiene factors in formal organizations would include sick leave, vacation, health and welfare plans, and most other personnel programs. Some managers have convinced themselves that a good fringe benefit program will motivate employees. Instead, such programs are usually taken for granted and (like your allowance) merely maintain, but do not create, satisfaction.

Motivational Factors (Satisfiers)

Now let's take a look at a completely different set of factors. The following list includes what Herzberg calls *motivational factors,* or *satisfiers*.

1. Achievement
2. Recognition
3. The job itself
4. Responsibility
5. Growth and advancement possibilities

What motivates you?

Factors like these are said to motivate indviduals. However, the absence of such satisfiers will not necessarily cause employee dissatisfaction.

For example, let's examine the position of a man at a large resort who waters plants, grass, and trees. If he feels that there is a chance to advance to, say, the position of gardener or landscape designer, he may be more satisfied with his job and be motivated to perform it more efficiently and productively. However, the lack of opportunities for advancement, other things being equal, will not necessarily reduce his satisfaction with his job.

A final word of caution: Perhaps with an understanding of the theory of motivational and hygienic factors you can see that employers who attempt to increase the motivation of employees by raising their pay may be in for a disappointment if the workers perceive the additional remuneration as a maintenance factor. Once a pay raise becomes a regular part of a salary or wage, it usually does little to provide additional motivation. An important consideration is this: The employees' actual perception of a motivational factor is of far greater importance than the manager's perception of it. A factor that merely maintains one person may motivate another.

See figure 5–1 for a graphic comparison of the Maslow and Herzberg theories of motivation.

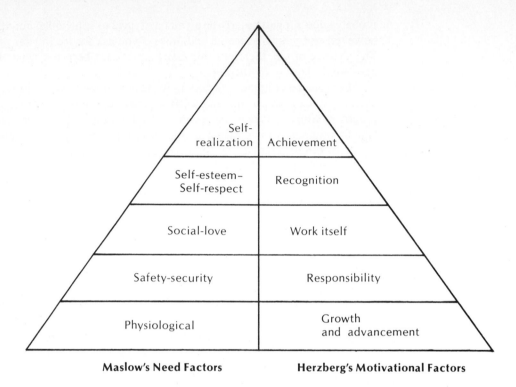

Figure 5–1. A brief comparison of the motivational theories of Maslow and Herzberg.

Frustration and Unsatisfied Needs

Have you ever observed a young child—assume he's a little boy—who was unable to have what he wanted? Do you remember his reactions? He may have tugged and pulled interminably on Mommy's blue jeans or Daddy's hand, whining, shrieking, and crying until either his wants were satisfied or he was distracted by another object. The young child was

frustration

What was your last frustrating experience?

experiencing what could be termed *frustration*, which is *the feeling of insecurity and dissatisfaction arising from unresolved problems or unsatisfied wants.*

You, too, undoubtedly have experienced certain frustrations from time to time. For example, perhaps you have been rejected by someone of whom you were quite fond, or maybe you were turned down for a job you eagerly wanted, or you may have been bypassed for a particular job promotion to which you had anxiously aspired.

Problems often arise when the needs of organizational members, either on or off the job, go unsatisfied for a long time.

adjustive reaction

The *mind*, either consciously or unconsciously, generally attempts to *cause* behavior designed to aid the frustrated person to adjust to an unresolved situation, a type of behavior termed *adjustive reaction*. Some adjustive reactions are *positively directed*; other reactions may be excessively *negative*. Some frustrations may result in *mild* adjustive reactions; others may be *extreme* and *emotional*. The intensity of a particular adjustment generally depends on two factors: the *type* of frustration *activity*, and the *previous experience* of the frustrated *person*. Psychologists have developed a variety of terms to describe the numerous types of adjustive reactions to frustration. In the next section you will learn of some typical reactions that individuals occasionally experience while attempting to cope with life's many frustrations.

Reactions to Frustrations

An understanding of psychological concepts, such as adjustive reactions, will certainly not enable you to lie wistfully on your cozy make-believe psychiatrist's couch, skillfully playing the roles of psychotherapists Carl Rogers or Erich Fromm, while sensitively treating your own complex mental problems or those of others. Any person with chronic and severe problems should seek professional assistance. However, an awareness of the major *adjustive reactions* may enable you to deal more effectively with the relatively normal stresses and strains of everyday living that can affect you and others in your organization.

When you recognize some of the adjustive responses in others, you should be able to be more empathetic and understanding of behavior that previously may merely have made you angry, frustrated, or disappointed.

The adjustive reactions with which we shall primarily be concerned are:

1. Compensation
2. Negativism
3. Resignation
4. Repression
5. Rationalization

6. Fixation
7. Obsessive thinking
8. Displacement
9. Flight
10. Conversion

Compensation

You have probably heard of persons born with physical handicaps who went on to achievements far beyond the usual capabilities of many individuals without similar misfortunes. Well-known are Franklin D. Roosevelt, former President; John Milton, poet; Ray Charles and Stevie Wonder, musical performers. Numerous people in work organizations have, for various reasons, striven with unusual zeal to attain certain self-imposed goals, which in some instances could be forms of adjustive reaction.

compensation

We are referring to the term *compensation* when we discuss a situation in which *an individual with feelings of inadequacy—either real or imagined—exerts him- or herself with extra effort in an attempt to overcome the insecure feelings.*

Some forms of compensation may be quite beneficial, or *positive*, while others are harmful, or *negative*. Positive compensation might be found in a person whose child died from a birth defect and who expends an inordinate amount of energy on helping handicapped or retarded children. Employees who feel that their abilities are inferior to that of co-workers may work particularly hard on certain projects in order to prove that they can do as well. Often the best college term papers received by professors are prepared by students lacking a certain degree of confidence, but who labor with extra vigor and energy on their projects. The best students seldom seem to feel that they have expended sufficient time on assignments.

What might determine whether a compensation is positive or negative?

Some persons may react in a *negative* fashion because of their feelings of inadequacy. They may become aggressive, pushy, overcritical, and sometimes even power-hungry. Some historians believe that Napoleon's ambitious military conquests may have been related to the shortness of his stature.

Negativism

An anonymous philosopher is alleged to have claimed, "If we all would only admit that we are insecure, then we would probably be less insecure." Individuals with typical insecurities tend to believe that other mortals don't feel the same as they; but, in actuality, there are few persons who are totally secure, regardless of their outward appearances.

The promotion on television of many products is directed toward the normal insecurities most people tend to have, such as the fear of rejection by others ("Spray one armpit and half the world will love you!"). Many "high achievers," for example, are driven by a fear of possible failure that makes them insecure.

negativism

How might others be affected by a person's negativism?

One of the unfortunate by-products of some people's insecurities is what can be termed *negativism*, a reaction defined as *the unconscious resistance to other persons or objects.* Take, for example, the hypothetical case of a supervisor named Hattie Ferndowner whose ideas at a particular supervisors' meeting have been totally rejected. Hattie originally thought that her proposals were good, but as a result of their rejection, she felt disappointed and frustrated. A reasonably secure and well-adjusted person might either have attempted to analyze the rejection of the ideas, or merely have dismissed the situation from her mind and gone on to other important matters.

Hattie, however, returned to her department, and for the rest of the day caustically picked apart nearly everything that her subordinates did. At the end of the day, Hattie regretted her actions even though she didn't fully understand the reasons for her negative behavior. In one sense, Hattie was not only "belittling," but she also was "being little." Some years ago Charles Reigner wrote an essay that may relate to Hattie's behavior:

> Life is too short to be little. Every one of us has his share of rebuffs and disappointments. When somebody says or does something that hurts us, our first impulse is to try to return the hurt. We want to fight back; but when we do so, we are just lowering ourselves to the plane of the attacker. When we exhibit littleness, we show that we have not attained maturity in our thinking and acting.
>
> It is the person who is in love with his work who gets the greatest measure of happiness and satisfaction in life. He is ready at all times to join hands with others in a good cause. Such a person has passed the adolescent state of dependence or near-dependence on others.
>
> Anybody who gets worthwhile things done will have some people say cutting and unkind things about him. They will

belittle his motives and question his actions. The worst thing one can do under such circumstances is to brood on the unkind things said about him.

Because we play small parts in the scheme of things is no warrant for our ever being little in our attitudes. A friend of mine who was once unjustly attacked said, ''I have enough pride not to give my attacker the satisfaction of knowing that what he said hurt me.''

Until people and nations actually mature in their thinking and acting, we are going to have tension and war. What can one person do? Well, he can resolve not to be little himself. He can act like a mature person, for life is too short to be little.[4]

Resignation

''You can't fire me, J.B. You know why? Because I *quit*, that's why!'' This statement to J.B. is the ultimate in resignation by an organizational member, but is only one of various types. The psychological term, *resignation* *resignation*, generally relates to a deep-seated, extremely intense type of frustration sometimes experienced by individuals. The condition may be long-lasting or temporary. Resignation can be defined as *the state of giving up, or withdrawing from one's involvement with a particular environmental situation.*

An example with which some students might identify relates to a term paper assignment. Assume that you have a ten-page term project due only two days from now. Also let's assume that you've already done all of the necessary background reading and research, but you are having extreme difficulty in ''putting it all together.'' And the excessive noise coming from a nearby room doesn't help a bit; it only tears apart any ideas flowing through your head.

You've sat in front of your typewriter for two hours, but you've produced only two paragraphs, both of which provide you with no personal satisfaction—and they'll probably please your professor even less! Finally, in disgust, you shout, ''To hell with it! I'll bat this darn thing out tomorrow night.'' You then lie down on your waterbed—and it's not even bedtime. Your decision to stop working and to do a less than adequate job tomorrow evening is a form of resignation.

There are other ways in which you might have adjusted more positively. You might have asked the people in the next room if they would lessen their noise, or you might have attempted to change your environ-

---

[4]Charles G. Reigner, ''Mature Thinking.'' Reproduced from the March 1966 issue of *The Rowe Budget*, p. 17, by special arrangement with, and permission of, the author, Charles G. Reigner, and the publisher, The H. M. Rowe Company, Baltimore and Chicago.

ment by going to a library, or to another room, if possible. Sometimes, however, the act of resignation appears, at least temporarily, to be the easy way out, but it neither gets your tasks completed nor provides you with feelings of accomplishment.

**Why might
resignation
seem to be
the easy way out?**

Another example: An employee—let's call him Joe—has received little praise for the progress he has made on a company project assigned to him. This lack of reinforcement—either positive or negative—frustrates Joe and might result in his no longer caring whether he does a good job. Joe could have asked his boss for comments, but instead chose resignation as a more natural way out.

Repression

"Oops! I'm sorry, boss—but I completely forgot to tell you about the Purdy Upsette Company. That big order they placed a while back, you remember? Well, they cancelled it last week."

This example of a lost account illustrates that a person may "forget" something, especially something psychologically disturbing, because of the sense of anxiety or guilt that it might arouse. When individuals *exclude certain experiences or feelings from their consciousness*, they are making an adjustive reaction called *repression*.

repression

**Why is it not
necessarily un-
desirable to
forget some things?**

Not all repression is necessarily negative. The human mind is a miraculous instrument, for it also tends to repress the unpleasant parts of many experiences. For example, years after a vacation, family members may remember the events that gave them pleasure, but they tend to repress, or forget, the less pleasant parts, such as the flat tire and lack of a spare one, the high prices at the gas stations, the biting mosquitoes, and the upset stomachs.

Persons who have experienced inordinate numbers of tragedies during their lives, such as accidents or the unexpected deaths of their loved ones, often appear later not to be excessively disturbed by the events. Nevertheless, initially they may have been profoundly affected by the experiences. The mind tends quite normally to repress unpleasant events, but the individual who continually focuses on distressing past experiences tends to find little enjoyment in the present.

Rationalization

"Shooot . . . I didn't really want that crummy promotion anyhow. Besides, that job will be nothing but problems for the turkey who got it. Actually, I'm darn lucky I didn't get it."

Have you ever overheard "sour grapes" remarks similar to the one quoted above? Individuals may actually mean what they say but often

rationalization

any reason but right one.

Why might some persons *rationalize* their behavior?

their remarks may be excuses for deeper, unconscious feelings. The psychological adjustive reaction involved here is termed *rationalization*, which exists when an individual *attempts to give plausible (rational)–but not necessarily true–explanations for specific, often undesirable, behavior.*

Another example of rationalization may be found in the person who says, "Everybody else cheats on exams, expense accounts, income taxes, and in politics; so why shouldn't I?" But does everybody else necessarily cheat? Not likely, but such a belief tends to make the person feel that his or her behavior is more acceptable. Even if increasing numbers of other persons' ethical values may have deteriorated, does this mean that you have to follow suit? If someone else were to punch him- or herself continually on the nose, and if you realized that such activity was foolish and undesirable, would you feel that you had to do the same thing? Imitating behavior that you feel is undesirable merely because "everyone else does it" is logically equivalent to saying, "If I don't smoke, somebody else will."

In effect, the person who attempts to justify behavior that he or she feels is undesirable—either consciously or unconsciously—is engaging in *rationalization*.

Fixation

"I'm going to look just one more time in that drawer for my keys." Have you ever had the experience of misplacing something, such as your car keys, and looking in the same place two, three, or more times? You may even have searched all of your pockets at least twice, but—alas—you repeat the pointless motions over and over and over again.

fixation

The reaction involved in such situations is termed *fixation*, which is *the process of maintaining an obsessive preoccupation with a particular type of behavior*, even though all reasonable evidence indicates a different approach to be more desirable.

How might *fixation* lead an organization down an undesirable path?

Assume, for instance, that you are an office manager and that one of your subordinates—let's call her Ms. Anna Mae Handy—informs you that a specific office form no longer serves any particularly useful function. If you give Anna Mae's remarks careful consideration, you may agree with her suggestion. But, instead, you might say to yourself, "I didn't ask for Anna Mae's advice. I make the decisions around here. We've always used that form in the past, and we're damned well going to continue to use that form in the future!"

In other words, your persistent following of an activity regardless of its utility—in this case, the use of an obsolete form—could be an example of *fixation*.

Obsessive Thinking

obsessive thinking

Another adjustive reaction is called *obsessive thinking*. The term—somewhat related to fixation—refers to *a condition whereby a person enlarges all out of realistic proportion specific problems or situations that he or she has experienced.*

For example, an individual employed in a dull, monotonous type of job requiring little in the way of active thinking or concentration may continually mull over personal or company problems in his or her mind. Perhaps the particular problems were not especially grave, but the obsession with them could create an exaggerated effect. And then the problem may appear gigantic to the individual.

How might obsessive thinking be avoided in work situations?

A mind that is kept occupied, however, has little opportunity for obsessive thinking. If the job could be redesigned, or if the person could be allowed to talk to other employees, the chances for obsessive thinking might be lessened.

Let's look at another example: Assume that you have a subordinate whose spouse is critically ill and currently bedridden in a hospital. The doctors doubt whether the patient will survive. Would telling the employee to take the week off necessarily serve as a release of tensions? Probably not; it is unlikely that the employee would be permitted to spend entire days at the hospital, and more than likely that he or she would be home thinking obsessively about little other than the problem. The opportunity to interact with others during periods of severe stress often helps individuals to focus their minds on topics other than their own personal problems.

Displacement

What personal motives might have caused the following immoderate (to say the least!) types of behavior?

Vandals, according to the Coast Guard, continually shoot out buoy lights and batter their way into untended lighthouses to shatter equipment.

A spokesperson for the Transportation Department says that vandals regularly tamper with rail switching equipment to cause trains to derail or collide with cars on sidings.

Zoo directors lament that individuals periodically break into zoos, spray animals with paint and chemicals, and free rare birds and deer.

A twenty-four-year-old man was arrested in Menlo Park, California, for having stomped a puppy to death.

123

displacement

Many of us occasionally experience similar—but far less extreme —reactions to frustration. The incidents mentioned above could have been examples of *displacement*, which may be defined as *the psychological process of redirecting pent-up feelings, or emotions, toward objects other than the main source of the frustration.*

When a particular situation affects a person's feelings of security, he or she may react by lashing out verbally (or, as we have seen, physically) at others. Prejudice toward other groups is often the result of an individual's own insecurities—and can be a form of displacement.

scapegoating

Scapegoating, or *blaming a particular person for one's own problems or insecurities*, is also a type of displacement. Henry L. Sisk, a professor of management, said of security:

> Those who are well adjusted and secure perceive positive traits in others, while those who are insecure and unable to recognize and accept their shortcomings tend to perceive others as having the same characteristics.[5]

Therefore, many of our negative reactions to others may really be our own psyches telling us (and others) something about ourselves. Remember, when Clarence talks about Suzie, we may learn a lot about Clarence and perhaps very little about Suzie.

Here's another brief example of *displacement:* Assume that you reject, abruptly and without any explanation, a subordinate's request for a particular afternoon off. What might have caused your reaction? Perhaps you were reprimanded earlier in the day by your own boss about something you had, or had not, done. You may be attempting to release your own frustrations and tensions by hassling your subordinate. Such behavior on your part is likely to create even more tension for you later.

[5]Henry L. Sisk, *Management and Organization*, 3d ed. (Cincinnati: South-Western Publishing, 1977), p. 307.

124

Flight

flight

The adjustive reaction to frustration or conflict termed *flight* could be confused with that of *resignation. Flight*, however, goes somewhat farther, and involves the actual *leaving, or running away from, a particular situation that causes frustration or anxiety.* Resignation may involve an apathetic, "don't-give-a damn" attitude about the problem but, unlike flight, does not necessarily involve leaving the source of conflict or frustration.

For example, during the war in southeast Asia, especially during the late 1960s and early 1970s, numbers of young American men felt in conflict with the possibility of having to fight in a war that they opposed on moral grounds. Some of the young men literally took *flight* (by airplane, of course) to other countries, such as Sweden and Canada, as an *adjustive reaction* to their frustrations. Many of the early American settlers left their countries of origin for similar reasons.

Will regular flights to the moon be next?

Americans in recent years have tended to be highly mobile. Currently, almost *40 million* of them change their addresses annually. About one-half of the population of the Los Angeles area is reported to move from one place to another each year—all *within* the Los Angeles area. Many Americans also switch jobs amazingly often.

Some of these moves may be related to the psychological reaction of *flight,* a topic so significant to present-day organizational members that chapter 16 will explore it in greater depth.

Conversion

The mind and the body are inextricably related and significantly affect each other. A healthy body tends to facilitate the existence of a healthy mind, while healthy mental attitudes often make for healthier bodies.

psychosomatic

Some bodily disorders, for example, are *psychosomatic* in origin —that is, they are physical symptoms of inner mental conflict. The term *conversion* is used to symbolize *a psychological process whereby emotional frustrations are expressed in bodily symptoms of pain or malfunction.*

conversion

For example, assume that a person whom we'll call Walter Worry, an unusually conscientious employee with your organization, was assigned the responsibility of presenting at a meeting next Monday a detailed forecast of his department's production for the next six months. Let's also assume that Walter's cousins, whom he has not seen for five years, unexpectedly dropped in for the entire weekend on their way to Seattle for their annual vacation.

As a result of the surprise visit, Walter was unable to complete his project on time. Instead of explaining to his boss the actual cause of the

125

incompleted task, Walter developed a painful headache and called in sick on the Monday morning of his scheduled presentation. The pain may have been quite real to Walter, but it could have been caused by his mental frustrations. Many aches and pains can be primarily the result of anxieties.

Were Walter's cousins a pain?

The Uniqueness of Each Individual

Whose needs motivate *them?*

In chapter 2 we discussed the concept of projection; that is, the tendency to attach one's own values to others, something that any manager should consciously attempt to avoid. For example, many managers are naturally inclined to employ motivational techniques that *they* feel will stimulate workers to accomplish specific organizational goals. Some managers overlook, however, that what they themselves feel are important motivators is not as significant as what the *workers* feel motivates them. A manager may explain to employees that the surest way to climb the organizational ladder is to work hard and be dependable. If employees believe this statement and are motivated to want a job with additional responsibility, they will probably apply their energies as conscientiously as the manager hopes. However, if *employees* perceive that the manager's statement is a sham, that promotions come about principally through organizational politics, they may be motivated to use different methods to fulfill their needs. Chapter 9 will discuss some specific methods for improving the attitudes and motivation of employees.

Regardless of the techniques of motivation that managers might prefer, they should continually remind themselves of the uniqueness of each individual within their organizations. To illustrate, assume that you are the manager of a business organization consisting of about ten individuals. Even if all of you were members of the same family, each person would come to the organization with a variety of personal needs. (Some individuals may have traveled farther along Needs Lane than others.)

Why are each person's needs slightly different?

For example, some members of your group might have unusual financial responsibilities and thus be highly motivated to work overtime in order to earn some extra money. Others, however, may feel that their basic needs are fairly well provided for, and be more motivated toward attaining positions with the firm that offer them self-esteem and a sense of personal accomplishment. Still others in the group may feel the need for power, a need that can be satisfied in a variety of ways. For some, the accumulation of vast amounts of wealth satisfies their quest for power. For others, such factors as positions with authority over others may satisfy their needs.

A manager, therefore, would be wise not to lump all individuals into one homogeneous group and assume that a particular motivational factor

Critical: a how it happens all the time.

126

will affect each member of the group in an identical fashion. Each person has a unique set of qualities and, as a result, will respond uniquely to motivational factors.

Summary

In this chapter we discovered the significant relationship between needs and motivation. For purposes of convenience, needs have been categorized as primary and secondary. Needs, however, vary in importance and intensity with the individual and are not mutually exclusive of each other.

An understanding of needs is especially important to managers, who have the vital responsibility of motivating others. Employees and individuals in family and social situations can also benefit from an understanding of needs and motivation concepts.

A need must be felt if it is to motivate. Once a need becomes satisfied, it ceases to motivate. Needs are often merely wants that our culture has convinced us are needs, such as the need for deodorants.

Two major theories of motivation are Maslow's hierarchy- or level-of-needs concept and Herzberg's motivation-maintenance model.

We also examined some of the main types of reactions that individuals may experience in their attempts to adjust to everyday tensions and frustrations. *Adjustive reactions* range from the normal mild kinds to the psychotic extremes.

Managers should guard against the tendency to assume that the same factors will motivate all individuals. Each person in an organization is unique and will thus respond uniquely to specific motivation.

Terms and Concepts to Remember

Basic (primary) needs
Secondary (higher-order) needs
Levels (hierarchy) of needs
Maintenance (hygiene) factors
Motivational factors (satisfiers)
Dissatisfier
Frustration
Adjustive reaction
Compensation
Negativism

Resignation
Repression
Rationalization
Fixation
Obsessive thinking
Displacement
Scapegoating
Flight
Psychosomatic
Conversion

Questions

1. Explain why a need must be felt before it will motivate.
2. What is the distinction between a *want* and a *need*?
3. List the five levels of needs that Maslow indicated exist in human beings.
4. "Needs are not mutually exclusive." Explain.
5. Why is an understanding of motivation concepts especially important to managers in organizations?
6. Explain why, according to Herzberg's two-factor model, maintenance factors do not necessarily motivate workers.
7. Explain the effect of culture on our needs.
8. When a person beomes frustrated, why does he or she tend to experience what is termed *adjustive reactions*?
9. After reviewing the ten adjustive reactions discussed in this chapter, prepare an illustration of each based on your personal observations or experiences.

Other Readings

Dalton, Gene W., and Lawrence, Paul R., eds. *Motivation and Control in Organizations.* Homewood, Ill.: Richard D. Irwin, 1971.

Herzberg, Frederick, *The Management Choice: To Be Efficient and To Be Human.* Homewood, Ill.: Dow Jones-Irwin, 1976.

———. *Work and the Nature of Man.* Cleveland: World Publishing, 1966.

Maslow, Abraham H. *Motivation and Personality.* New York: Harper & Row, 1954.

———. *Toward a Psychology of Being.* Princeton, N.J.: Van Nostrand Reinhold, 1962.

McGregor, Douglas. *The Human Side of Enterprise.* New York: McGraw-Hill, 1960.

Sutermeister, Robert A. *People and Productivity.* New York: McGraw-Hill, 1976.

Vroom, Victor H. *Work and Motivation.* New York: John Wiley and Sons, 1964.

Applications

The Satisfied Sales Representative

The Shifting Sands Mutual Insurance Company is a medium-sized concern situated in Portsmouth, Virginia. Carl Carson, a manager for the Shifting Sands Company, is currently in charge of ten insurance sales representatives whose principal responsibility is to sell all lines of property and casualty insurance to individuals and to business firms.

The sales representatives are paid a guaranteed salary of $800 per month, which is a draw on (is deducted from) future commission sales, and a flat percentage of all new and renewable insurance premiums.

Sammy Sereno, one of the ten sales representatives directly responsible to Carson, has been with Shifting Sands Mutual Insurance for slightly more than fifteen years. During his first ten years, Sereno was highly ambitious and energetic and built up a substantial volume of business, most of which has been renewed automatically each year. Last year, Sereno devoted much of his time to his favorite hobbies, sailing and skin diving, and as a result produced very little new business for the firm. In spite of his current, relatively leisurely life, his net personal income after taxes last year was $31,000. Sereno is married but has no children. He and his wife are seriously considering the adoption of a Vietnamese orphan.

Last week while analyzing the previous year's production figures, Carson noticed that Sereno ranked number ten among the sales representatives in the production of new business. Because of his large volume of renewable sales, however, Sereno ranked third in total earnings.

One of Carson's primary responsibilities is to motivate his representatives into continually acquiring new business, since renewable accounts often do not stay with the company because of the dissolution of customers' businesses, the death of customers, or the accounts moving out of the Portsmouth area and obtaining their insurance elsewhere.

Questions

1. Assuming that you are Carson, how would you attempt to motivate Sereno?
2. What would you do if Sereno said to you, "I am tired of busting my back canvassing my territory for new business"?

A Doctor's Case*

Let me give you a case. At least, I think this is a case.

In my first year in medical school I had an experience which has always stuck with me. One afternoon during an examination, I became aware that two of my classmates were passing pieces of paper back and forth between themselves. I noticed that one would read it, write something on his examination paper, then write something on a piece of paper and pass it back to his friend. During the examination, this happened several times. I was positive that they were cheating.

I was torn by inner conflict in wondering what, if anything, I should do about this situation. It seemed to me that such conduct could not be tolerated in any student. It seemed to me that anyone who would cheat in an examination was not worthy or fit to assume the responsibilities of the medical profession. Also, it seemed to me that it was unfair to the rest of the class that these people should have the advantage of two minds while taking the examination. Of course, I thought, the advantage they would have over the rest of the class wouldn't be much. At most, it probably wouldn't do much more than move them up on the rank list from, say 38th place to 36th, or from 10th to 9th, or something of the sort. But in the awarding of scholarships and prizes, even one place could make a difference. And anyway, it just struck me as unfair to the rest of us. Moreover, cheating seemed to me to be something of a "sin" against the traditions of our school for which I had already developed great loyalty and respect.

I felt something ought to be done. But I couldn't think what. I knew that I simply could not bring myself to report them. I told myself again and again that I *could* be wrong, even though, actually, it was really crystal clear in my mind that they had been exchanging information and that that was *cheating* in anybody's book. But even so, I could not— would not—be a "squealer."

Over the weekend I was home, and I told my father about it. I told him that I felt that something ought to be done but that I didn't know what to do. I told him I couldn't bring myself to "squeal." He agreed with me, both that something ought to be done and that I couldn't, or shouldn't, be a "squealer." He also said he thought the school shouldn't give the kind of examinations where it would be possible for anyone to gain an advantage over the rest by being able to confer surreptitiously with another. He said they were giving the wrong kind of examination. He argued that in real life doctors can and do consult one another. He said they should give examinations in which the students were perfectly free to consult with each other, any medical books, and anything else they thought might be useful before writing their answers. He said he thought that the real measure of a person's ability was how good a judgment that person could come up with after putting his or her own ideas together with any other ideas—some of which might well be conflicting—from available sources.

I said I thought there was a lot in that, but that it really was beside the point, circumstances being what they were. He agreed, but repeated that the school shouldn't give examinations wherein any question of cheating could be involved. He said it wasn't "worthy" of the school to give examinations like that. I said perhaps he was right, but repeated that it didn't help me in this particular situation. We left it at that.

On Monday I was still very much disturbed about this matter, perhaps even more so than at first because I had been "stewing" over it for several days. It seemed to me I was like Hamlet when he couldn't figure out whether "to be or not to be." At lunch I told a couple of my friends about what had been on my mind and asked them what *they* could do. Both seemed to feel strongly that something ought to be done about it but that, "certainly," I couldn't "snitch." One of them asked who the people involved were. I said I felt that I couldn't say. He replied, "Yeah, that's right. I guess you really shouldn't." We talked about it for an hour without getting anywhere.

That afternoon I went to Dr. Griswold, one of my professors in another course, and told him the situation. I didn't mention any names. I asked him if he had any ideas as to what he would do in a similar circumstance. I also told him what my father had said. He was very disturbed that there were students at the school who would cheat. He said they should be "thrown out," and that if he had to vote on it in a faculty meeting he would vote to expel them immediately. But he said that, "of course," I, as their fellow student, couldn't report them. He didn't ask me their names. He agreed with my father about the examinations. He also went on to say that this kind of situation had come up at least once before. He had formed the opinion that if they were going to give examinations of that sort, they ought to either monitor the examination so thoroughly that it would be impossible to cheat undetected, or else have an honor system whereby it would be thoroughly accepted that each student would be honor-bound to report any cheating that came to his or her attention. He said that if they were going to give examinations like that, the school should decide whether it was "going to be fish or fowl," and adopt one system or another and not leave it up in the air. I pointed out that that didn't help me in my problem. He agreed and said it was a "tough one."

That night, the situation seemed to go round and round in my head. And it did all the next morning, too. I happened to run into Dr. Griswold in the hall at noon. He said that he and his wife had had another doctor and his wife in for dinner the night before and that he had told them about the situation I had described to him "without mentioning any names."

He said that the four of them had talked about the case for almost two hours, and that the discussion had gotten ''pretty warm'' at moments. He said that his wife and the other doctor had argued that I should report the cheaters immediately and that I had made a serious mistake in delaying the matter. In fact, the other doctor said he doubted I had the ''right attitude'' since I had even hesitated about reporting the incident. The other doctor's wife had argued that a person in my position really shouldn't pass judgment on others or ''feel any holier than anyone else.'' Dr. Griswold laughed, and said, ''So there you are.'' The idea that *I* might be showing the wrong attitude by *not* reporting these people bothered me deeply. But so did the comment of the other doctor's wife about being ''holier'' than someone else. I wondered if I was being ''stuffy,'' ''self-righteous,'' or quixotic.

That afternoon, I went to Dean Parker and told him about this situation without mentioning any names—not even which examination had been involved. I told him that I felt kind of foolish bringing such a problem to him, but I felt that an important issue was involved. I also told him about my conversations with my father, my friends, and ''one of the professors,'' whom I did not name. He listened very quietly and attentively. When I got through he said that he thought it was serious, all right. He said that if the matter was brought to him officially, he would call the people in and tell them he thought such conduct was outrageous and completely unworthy, and that they had better think things over and ''search their hearts'' to decide whether they were up to the responsibilities they would assume as doctors. He said that, as far as he was concerned, he would probably hesitate to expel them, since he felt that everyone deserves a second chance, but that this breach of ethics should, at least, be brought to the attention of and profoundly impressed upon these men. He went on to say that he was quite sure that most of the faculty, especially the younger members, would vote to expel these people forthwith. I asked him if he thought I should report the two to him officially. He said, ''No—I don't think so. I don't really see how you could. I don't think I could.'' He asked me if I had considered just going to these people myself and telling them that I had seen what they had done and ask them if they thought it was right. I said I hadn't.

My talk with Dean Parker wound up with his suggesting that, if I wanted to, I might talk it over with Dr. Sorrel, one of the members of the faculty who had come to be sort of an informal personal counselor to students. I knew Dr. Sorrel slightly. I thanked him for talking it over with me and said that I'd think about it some more.

Questions

1. How do you feel about the way the student reacted to what he observed between the two other students during the examination?

2. Evaluate the advice of each of the concerned student's ''advisors.''

3. If you had been the disturbed medical student, what would you have done about the situation?

Moe Graduates

Moe Tivait was a senior in high school when he began working for the Peach Company. The work was seasonal, beginning just prior to the harvest and ending in early December. For six years Moe was called back each season to work in the factory side of the business. Each year the plant superintendent put Moe on a different job, often with different crews and even occasionally assigning him to do one-person tasks. Moe's activities included driving small trucks and fork lifts, operating conveyor units, feeding the processing hoppers, fumigating, and performing numerous general labor tasks.

Moe was well liked by the plant superintendent, and the production supervisors generally sought him for their crews. His co-workers found him amiable, hard working, and a credit to any crew. Moe's work did not go unrewarded, and by the fourth year he was at the top of the laborer's pay scale for seasonal workers.

Moe started college during his second year at the Peach Company. During the off-season he attended day classes, and during the harvest season he attended night college. Only a few co-workers knew of his academic pursuits since he rarely discussed his personal activities with his supervisors.

Late in November of Moe's sixth season with the Peach Company, the plant superintendent asked him if he would like to work full time. By then, Moe could handle nearly any production job in the factory. He knew all the procedures for moving the raw product in and the packaged product out, he was extremely proficient on operating and repairing production equipment, and he enjoyed offering suggestions to improve production. The superintendent knew Moe had been married the previous Christmas and he was afraid he might lose Moe to another employer.

As Moe mulled over the superintendent's offer, he thought about his experience and long career with the Peach Company, the degree in environmental sciences he would receive in January, and the baby he and his wife were expecting in late spring. Moe needed to review his goals in light of this offer from the Peach Company.

Questions

1. Relating your answer to Maslow's concepts, what was the motivational pattern displayed by Moe over the six-year period?
2. What motivational factors should the plant superintendent consider in convincing Moe to accept his offer?
3. What should be the superintendent's response if Moe tells him that he wants a better job than he has had during the past six years?

We Have Got to Get Organized Around Here!

When you finish this chapter, you should be able to:

1. **Give a general definition** of the term **organization.**
2. **Explain** the four major levels of the organizational pyramid.
3. **Describe** the difference between delegating authority and assigning responsibility.
4. **Restate** in your own words the differences among line, staff, and functional authority.
5. **List and describe** at least four significant principles of organization.
6. **Contrast** tall with flat organizations.
7. **Explain** what determines the optimum number of persons who should report to one manager.

> If you don't know where you are going,
> you will end up somewhere else.
>
> —Laurence J. Peter

Assume that you and about ten of your friends decide that you've about had it; the pressures of everyday urban life have finally gotten to you. You have concluded that working for an organization isn't even for the birds. All of you are going to hang it all up and form a hassle-free commune somewhere.

A Communard Experience

One of the members of your group finds a choice piece of fertile virgin land for sale at a fairly good price in southern Oregon. Wow—does that ever sound great to you and your tribe! All of you are ecstatic with glee. No more are you going to be "organizational people," as your poor fathers have been, or as you were when you slaved away all day long in that dingy and somber concrete and steel building downtown.

You and your friends raise the necessary money, put your toothbrushes and a few other personal objects into your backpacks, and start toward your new commune life. Ah, at last freedom from organizational conformity and stress!

Where Did All Those Hostile People Come From?

One of your first experiences with your non-organization "organization" is not too unlike a situation in which your company once found itself. Do you remember when that disgruntled group picketed in front of your building frantically waving signs that asserted that the company you were working for was making gigantic profits yet showing no concern for what it was doing to the environment? Now, of all things, some of *your* new neighbors have begun protesting vehemently against the invasion into their community of those "unkempt punks."

A commune with a public relations problem?

You now have an organizational public relations problem not much different from the problems that many large business firms periodically experience. What happened to that hassle-free experience? Your goals are quite important to each of you so, after considerable face-to-face contact, sincere attempts at communication, and a bit of compromise with your neighbors, your group's image begins to improve and the hassles diminish.

136

But We Wanted to Get Away from Structure!

Is any organization likely to remain leaderless?

Originally your plan was to be a leaderless organization in which everyone "did his own thing." But those darned dishes have been moldily sitting in that dirty sink for two and a half weeks, and you are getting sick and tired of scraping hardened granola off plates before you can reuse them.

Even more important, all of your friends had previously promised that they would pitch in and do their fair share in fulfilling the basic needs of all the group. However, there's one dude, Ellsworth, who says that he doesn't know beans about growing carrots. He insists that we ought to grow grass instead so that we can have a place to lie around in the sun and chew gum. His hierarchy of needs seems to be a bit different from yours!

Are You Feeling the Point?

The purpose of the previous illustration was not to knock community living (*chacun à son goût!*), but to stress that wherever there are two or more persons there also exists an organization, regardless of what it may be called. The communal little organization might survive adequately, and its members may even be contented with the absence of structure. However, the chances are that for most people in our society, and especially for those who want what they believe to be a better life, greater satisfaction of needs and goals is likely to be achieved when a reasonable amount of organizational predictability exists.

The Purpose of Organizations

Are organizations good or bad?

Organizations are not necessarily good or bad in themselves, even though in recent years numerous popular books have been written to emphasize some of the less favorable aspects of organizations. *Up the Organization*, for example, a best-selling book of the early 1970s, was written by Robert Townsend, formerly a top executive with the Avis Corporation. Perhaps the title of his book expresses the attitude that many persons have today toward organizations. But are organizations in general necessarily deserving of attack and criticism? Or shouldn't such attitudes be directed toward the leaders who are insensitive to the human needs of individuals both within and outside of their organizations?

Like It or Not, Back to the Straight World!

Since the focus of this chapter is on concepts of organization, we had better develop an understanding of the term *organization*. In order to achieve its goals more effectively, any organization should have four major characteristics:

1. *Purpose* and *objectives*
2. *Coordination* of people
3. *Specialization* of activities
4. *Hierarchy* of authority

organization

These factors can be combined into the definition of what we shall refer to as an *organization*, which is a *group of individuals coordinated into different levels of authority and segments of specialization for the purpose of achieving the goals and objectives of the organization.*

Let's attempt to clarify our definition. Organizations are formed for what *purpose?* Generally to achieve certain *goals and objectives.* Without a purpose, in effect, there is no organization. *People* are also necessary for an organization to exist. Ghost towns became uninhabited because they were no longer able to attract and hold people. Personnel should be *coordinated* for effectiveness, which ordinarily requires a *hierarchy of authority*, or leadership. *Specialization*, although sometimes the cause of human relations problems (see chapter 9), often permits a more efficient accomplishment of organizational goals.

Isn't a commune an organization?

Returning to the hypothetical example of your southern Oregon commune, you probably would have quickly discovered that the goals of the group would be accomplished far more effectively and efficiently with some sort of *coordination and specialization* of its necessary activities. Those in your group with more ability or experience would tend to coordinate and influence others in a fashion not particularly unlike that of managers in the various levels of any organization.

Let's Start a Business

Assume that you have decided to start your own business, a print shop specializing in the printing of business forms. You have had considerable experience as a journeyman printer and have decided that now is the time to take the big step and start your own concern. So you buy a printing press, rent a little shop off Main Street, obtain the necessary business licenses, hang out your shingle, and you find yourself in business.

Originally you had hoped that you could run the business by yourself, somewhat informally, and have your spouse come in on Tuesdays and Thursdays to help keep the records straight. Business has been fair, but you discover that you are not really utilizing your printing press as fully as you might each day. However, you cannot seem to find the time to leave the shop in order to drum up additional customers.

Specialization and Coordination Needed

Specialization wanted.

You decide that your principal problem is that you need a salesperson out in the field to generate more business. So you place a want ad in the local newspaper and soon thereafter hire a bright young graduate of a local college to sell for you. The person, however, is almost too energetic. She brings in so much new business that you are unable to handle it all on one printing press. You buy another press, and you now need another person to run it.

Time passes and your business has boomed. You now have three salespersons who have continually been bringing in large orders. No longer can you handle everything in your cramped little shop, so you lease additional space on the third floor of the building next door.

Why is coordination of activities necessary?

Can you envisage some of the organizational problems that are developing? The formal organization is expanding haphazardly, as it does in so many firms that start small but grow rapidly. Usually such fast growing firms discover the need for reorganization after their growing pains signal the necessity for drastic changes in the structure of the organization.

In chapter 4 we examined the nature of formal and informal groups and discussed why they exist. The formal organization, as you should recall, is essential if goals and objectives are to be attained in an orderly and predictable manner. Let's turn now to some additional characteristics of the formal organization.

Hierarchy of Formal Organizations

hierarchy

In any organization there is what can be termed a *hierarchy*, a term that refers to the *various levels of authority in an organization*, ranging from the board of directors to the operating workers. In order to comprehend organizational structure and authority relationships, an understanding of the hierarchical arrangement is essential.

Operative Employees

pyramid
operating employees

The formal organization structure can be made clearer by portraying it in the form of a *pyramid*. As you can observe from figure 6–1, at the base of the pyramid are the *operating employees*, the workers. All the people in organizations are technically workers or employees, but the distinguishing factor at this level of the organization is that operative employees do not supervise other employees.

First Line Supervisors

first line management

Moving up the pyramid we find the *first line managers*, usually referred to as supervisors or foremen. Their positions customarily require both a technical knowledge of their jobs and skill in human relations since they have direct authority over the operative employees. Highly developed conceptual skills are helpful, but not essential, for this level of management.

Middle Management

middle management

The next level of the pyramid portrays *middle management*, consisting of superintendents, plant managers, and heads of departments. Individuals at this level sometimes literally feel caught in the middle, both pushed and

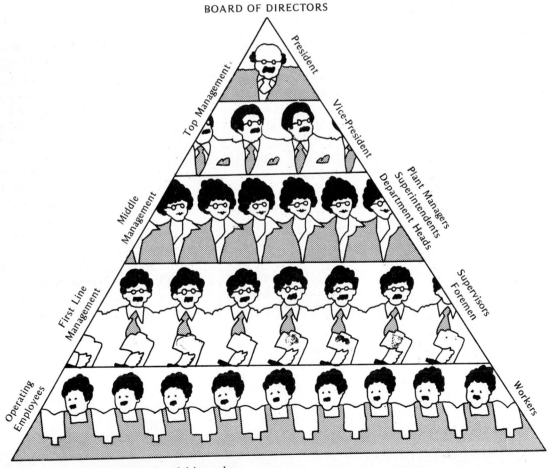

BOARD OF DIRECTORS

Figure 6–1. The organizational hierarchy

pulled by other managers on each side of them. Middle managers, for example, generally do not determine organizational policies or actually perform the operative work. However, they are responsible for seeing that the policies developed by top management are carried out. Leadership abilities and communication skills are especially important at this level of management.

Top Management and the Board of Directors

top management

At the apex of the pyramid is *top management*, which includes the senior executives, vice presidents, and the president. Top management constitutes the *administrative level*, which determines the objectives and basic policies of the organization. Conceptual skill is of paramount importance at this level.

board of directors

The principal purpose of the *board of directors* is to act in the interest of the stockholders (the owners of a corporation) who elected them. The board members influence overall policy since they select top management. In some instances key executives also serve on the board. In public institutions, such as colleges and universities, this level is customarily referred to as the *board of trustees*, and in school districts as the *board of education* or *school board*. Boards of trustees and school boards are elected to represent the communities that they have been chosen to serve.

Organizational Authority and Responsibility

How is an *organization chart* like a roadmap?

Organization charts can be defined as formal documents that indicate the chain of command and the titles that have been assigned to the managers. Organization charts are somewhat like road maps, since both are guides to official relationships. Road maps indicate, for example, the relationship of roads and bridges to specific territorial locations. Organization charts indicate people's locations or *positions* in the hierarchy and their *relationships* within a formal organization. Both provide a means of visualizing important aspects of a whole situation.

Is a roadmap the same as the territory it represents?

Just as road maps may not present an accurate picture of the territory at all times (bridges are sometimes washed out), so may the *actual* relationships in an organization vary from the formal. Therefore, both road maps and organization charts are merely *guides* to official relationships. Charts especially aid us in determining which of the basic types of *organizational authority structures* a specific entity has adopted. Before we discuss the principal authority structures, we should clearly understand the meaning of *authority* and how it relates to the concept of *responsibility*.

Authority and Responsibility

authority

Authority can be defined as *the right of individuals in an organization to make decisions, act, and direct others to act.* Authority, however, is ineffective without the *ability* to exercise it. A person who has been assigned specific authority but lacks the necessary leadership skills will find considerable difficulty in motivating followers. A person may have the necessary authority to give orders, but his or her authority will not guarantee that the orders will be carried out.

responsibility

Authority generally goes hand in hand with *responsibility*, the latter defined as an *obligation or duty that employees have been directed to carry out by someone with authority over them.*

The Distinction between Authority and Responsibility

What is the difference between *assigning* responsibility and *delegating* authority?

There is what at first seems to be a confusing distinction between authority and responsibility. Try to understand the distinction, which is this: *Authority* is something that can be *fully delegated* (given or entrusted to another), but responsibility can be only *partially delegated*. More precisely, *responsibility* can be *assigned to*, *or shared with*, someone else, but the *ultimate* responsibility *remains* with the person who has done the assigning.

Do captains get stuck when ships run aground?

For example, on an aircraft carrier many persons *share* the captain's responsibility for ensuring that the objectives of the ship and the Navy are achieved. Nevertheless, even when the captain is comfortably asleep in his cabin, he retains the *ultimate* responsibility for the actions of his crew. If the ship runs aground, those persons who were piloting the vessel at the time of the mishap are responsible, but the captain too is responsible, for he has merely shared part of his responsibility with others.

142

In private organizations the presidents of firms may not be fully aware of some of the negligence of their key executives, but they still retain the ultimate responsibility for the actions of subordinates that relate to company operations. A supervisor may have assigned responsibility to his or her operative workers for carrying out a particular task, but the supervisor continues to be responsible for the activities within the department.

Restated, authority is *delegated*, or given, to others; responsibility customarily is *assigned to*, or *shared with*, subordinates. Office managers may have the responsibility to make certain purchases for their departments within the specified limits of their entrusted authority. However, a problem sometimes develops when persons are assigned certain responsibilities but not delegated sufficient authority to carry out their duties effectively.

Organizational Authority Structures

There is no single type of formal authority structure that all firms use. Organizations usually employ a modification of the several basic forms, among which are:

1. Line authority.
2. Line and staff authority.
3. Functional authority.

A brief discussion of the advantages and disadvantages of each follows:

Line Authority

line authority

Of the major forms of organization, *line authority* is the simplest, and in its pure form is usually found among smaller organizations. Sometimes called the military type of structure, authority runs from top to bottom (down the chain of command), and responsibility runs from bottom to top (up the chain). An oversimplified example of the pure line organization is illustrated in figure 6–2.

Authority flows downward, responsibility flows upward.

Ms. Gonzales is first in command and has direct line *authority* over Mr. Steinberg, who thus is directly *responsible*, or accountable, to Ms. Gonzales. Mr. Steinberg in turn has direct authority over Ms. Smith, Mr. Jones, and Mrs. Johnson, the three workers who are directly accountable to Mr. Steinberg. *Authority flows downward* through the organization and *responsibility flows upward*. Each person in the organizational hierarchy is responsible only to one boss. The advantages of the pure line form are that it:

1. Is simple and easy to establish.
2. Eliminates doubt about responsibility and authority.
3. Is flexible and permits speedy decision making.

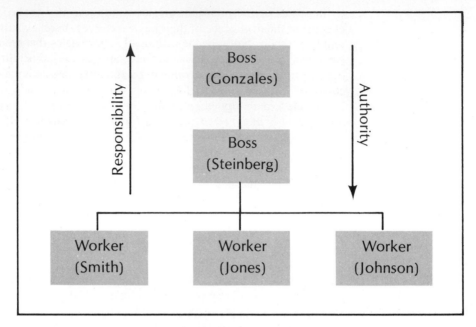

Figure 6–2. Line authority structure.

Some of the disadvantages are that it:

1. Overworks top managers with minor details because they have to approve subordinates' activities.
2. Does not use skilled specialists, who are often needed in organizations.
3. Inhibits initiative because of the fear of dissapproval from higher level managers.

Why wouldn't pure line be used for large organizations?

Most large organizations, however, cannot be managed effectively in a pure line authority structure. Rapid technological changes, as well as the need for breadth and depth of knowledge of legal, financial, and labor-management problems, have necessitated the development of a service function usually referred to as *staff authority*.

staff authority

Line and Staff Authority

line and staff authority

Modern organizations customarily combine *line and staff authority*. Staff members ordinarily (although there are numerous exceptions) do not have direct authority over the line members. Because of their technical or professional knowledge, staff members commonly provide *assistance* or *advice* to the line members, which helps to free line managers from details either not directly related to daily operations or requiring specialized skills and knowledge.

Departments that are regularly classified as staff are personnel, advertising, and legal. Usually small companies begin operations as pure line organizations and add staff members as the organization grows. A simplified example of a line and staff organization chart can be viewed in figure 6–3. Staff activities are often designated by the use of a dotted line. In the simplified chart in figure 6–3, you can observe a staff specialist supplying assistance directly to the president. The staff member might provide service for or advice about activities such as planning, research, or the determination of executive manpower needs. The staff specialist serving the general manager might be in charge of the purchasing or personnel departments, both of which assist line operations. A personnel manager, for example, customarily would not be directly in charge of the operative employees, the workers, but would be responsible for assuring that personnel needs are met. He or she may conduct training programs

What is the purpose of a staff function?

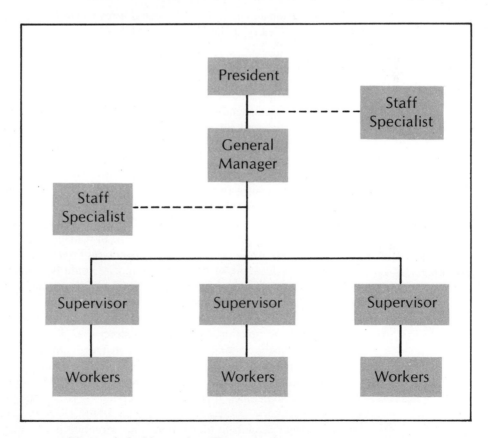

Figure 6–3. Line and staff organization

for company personnel as well as provide counseling and other services. Personnel managers, however, within their own departments, would be empowered with direct line authority over their immediate subordinates.

The major advantages of the line and staff type of organization are that:

1. The staff is a source of technical and specialized information.
2. It takes advantage of the specialization of labor.
3. It relieves line managers of specialized detail work.
4. It combines the advantages of the line authority with the flexibility of staff members who can cut across department lines.

Among the disadvantages are that:

1. Staff specialists may be resented by line managers because of their position and influence.
2. Staff members can cause friction if they attempt to exercise direct authority over line personnel.
3. Confusion and delay can be created if responsibilities of line and staff are not clearly spelled out.

Functional Authority

functional authority

The third major type of structure that many organizations use, either temporarily or permanently, is *functional authority*. The basic difference between the line and staff structure and the functional is that in the latter form the *staff specialists exercise direct authority over some line department activities.*

When might functional authority be used?

An example of functional authority could be found in the case of a personnel manager (whose function is ordinarily staff) who conducts training programs. The trainees technically are assigned to other departments, but during the temporary training sessions the personnel manager might exercise direct authority over them. In management literature, this type of relationship is referred to as *functional authority.*

Another example of functional authority could be found in the manager of an accounting department, also generally a staff position. The chief accountant ordinarily would not exercise line authority over sales personnel. In some firms, however, the accounting manager may be delegated the functional authority to direct the sales personnel to deal with delinquent customer accounts, for instance, collection. In usual organizational practice, many departments that are officially designated as staff or advisory actually exercise direct authority over some aspects of the line. Sometimes this functional authority is a result of unwritten policy.

Pros and cons?

A major advantage of the functional structure is that employees can benefit from the knowledge of specialists in different fields. However, human relations problems associated with "serving two masters" frequently develop. Consequently, they should be employed with caution because of the tendencies for rivalries to develop among departments and for managers to "pass the buck" where a functional authority arrangement exists.

Organization Chart Forms

Is this horizontal jive, or for real?

In general, most organization charts are presented in a *vertical* fashion, which means that the chart is prepared to display the various levels in the organization along with their vertical relationships in the chain of command (see figure 6–2). Occasionally, however, organization charts are presented in a *horizontal* fashion, in which all organizational levels are shown arranged from left to right. Some managers feel that, since we normally read from left to right, horizontal charts are easier to read.

On horizontal charts everyone, from the president to the operative employees, is portrayed on the same level (see figure 6–4). From a psychological viewpoint, people who would have been placed at the bottom of the hierarchy on traditional charts may not feel that they are the "lowly workers."

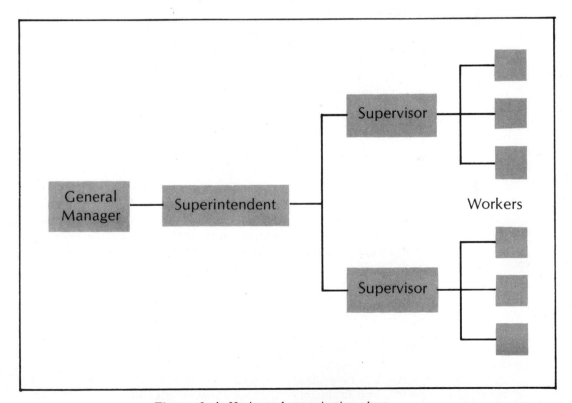

Figure 6–4. Horizontal organization chart

A Few Principles of Organization

Although the study of human relations, unlike economics, is not ordinarily loaded with principles, there are a few important organizational concepts that are generally included in any text on management. Some of them will be discussed here—the scalar principle, unity versus dual command, span of control, and tall versus flat organizations—and others will be discussed in chapter 8.

The Scalar Principle

scalar principle

The *scalar principle* is related to the chain of command and asserts that *authority and responsibility in an organization should flow in a clear, unbroken line from the point of ultimate authority* (the boss at the top) *to the workers at the bottom of the hierarchy*. Rarely should this chain be broken.

What problem can develop from ignoring the scalar principle?

For example, assume that a worker, Bill, has a complaint about a fellow employee but, instead of mentioning it to you, his line supervisor, he leapfrogs (bypasses) the chain of authority and complains directly to your boss. Any direct action taken by your boss would tend to usurp the authority delegated to you and probably reduce your effectiveness with your departmental personnel in the future. In general, therefore, communication should follow official channels, or problems related to our next principle, the *unity of command*, are quite likely to occur.

The Unity of Command

unity of command

The principle of the *unity of command* simply means that *no subordinate shall be responsible to more than one superior*, principally because the orders from one may conflict with the orders from another and thus place the subordinate in a difficult and awkward situation.

Why is it awkward to serve two masters?

Have you ever had to "serve two masters," that is, have you ever had one boss who regularly gave you orders to perform specific tasks and another boss in the same organization who often gave you conflicting orders? Such arrangements place subordinates in unnecessarily uncomfortable positions. When you find yourself on the receiving end of conflicting orders, often the most effective approach, where possible, is to ask your direct superior what he or she believes you should do. Even if you are directly and equally accountable to both bosses, you might be able to resolve the problem by discussing your plight with each of them.

dual command

Dual command is the term generally used to denote a situation whereby *one subordinate is accountable to more than one superior*, a condition which should be avoided wherever possible.

Span of Control

Have you ever been attempting to study when a few friends came in to see you? At such times it becomes difficult to carry out your plans. Just imagine if you were highly popular and had friends wandering into your house about every fifteen minutes during the time that you allot for studying. Would you get much homework done?

span of control

If you understand the schoolwork problem, you can probably readily understand a concept termed the *span of control*, which refers to the number of subordinates that one manager can supervise directly, and may also be called the *span of management* or the *span of supervision*. The principle asserts that *the larger the number of subordinates reporting to one manager, the harder it is for him or her to supervise effectively*.

Any manager has only so much available time and can attend to a limited number of activities during a given period. How many persons should report or be responsible to one manager is debatable and depends principally upon the *type of organizational structure*, the *supervisor*, his or her *employees*, and the *nature of the work itself*.

Tall versus Flat Organization Structure

tall vs. flat

Closely related to the span of control principle is the concept of *tall* and *flat* organizations. Ordinarily when a *narrower span of control* (when few individuals report to one manager) is desirable, out of necessity the organizational hierarchy will be taller. See figures 6–5 and 6–6 for examples of tall and flat organizations. The two charts illustrate the organizational structures of the Kaiser Aluminum and Chemical Corporation before and after a change to a flatter structure, a move customarily not too common for large organizations.[1]

According to the chief executive of Kaiser Corporation, Cornell C. Maier, the major advantage of the change to a flatter structure is in decision making, which he feels currently takes places much faster and with fewer delays than when the company had a tall organization. There are now fewer levels in the organizational chain of command through which communication must flow.

Ordinarily, however, a major disadvantage of a change to a flat organization is the substantial increase that develops in the span of control. To offset this problem partially, ten top management jobs in Kaiser were eliminated. In addition, salaried employment was cut by 17 percent, and administrative overhead dropped $15 million in one year.

One cannot say with certainty that one structure is always better than the other because so many variables have to be taken into account. In tall

---

[1]"Kaiser Aluminum Flattens its Layers of Brass," *Business Week*, 24 February 1973, pp. 81–84.

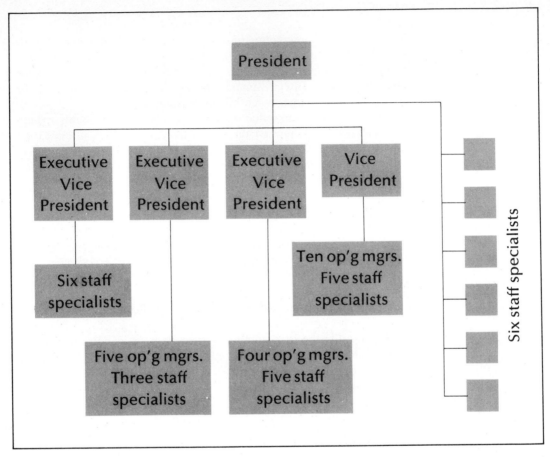

Figure 6–5. Kaiser's tall organization

structures each manager works with fewer people and therefore may be able to supervise them more effectively. However, the chain of command has more links and thus there is the potential problem of distorted communication. In flat organizations managers usually have more persons accountable to them. However, managers who have learned to delegate effectively are often able to handle a broader span of control.

Some studies indicate that flat structures are usually preferred by managers of smaller organizations. In large organizations with a flat structure and a broad span of control (many persons reporting to the same manager), managers often have difficulty in getting to see their own bosses, a problem much less common in smaller organizations. Managers of large companies, however, tend to prefer tall organizations because they usually offer more opportunities for promotion than do flat organizations.

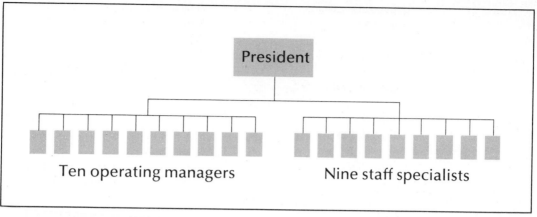

Figure 6–6. Kaiser's flat organization

Summary

The purpose of this chapter has been to highlight some of the more important concepts of organization. Although often criticized, organizations are not in themselves necessarily good or bad. Organizations and organizing are necessary for the accomplishment of goals in an orderly and predictable manner. The attempts to eliminate structure entirely would tend to result in *dis*organization.

In most organizations there is a hierarchy, or different levels of authority, which is often illustrated by the use of organization charts.

Responsibility accompanied by authority enables organizational personnel to make decisions more effectively. Authority may be line, staff, or functional in nature. Structure may be tall or flat; the latter often facilitates communication since there are fewer layers through which messages must pass.

A number of principles related to organizations have been developed. In this chapter we discussed the scalar principle, the unity of command, and the span of control. Additional organizational principals and concepts will be discussed in later chapters.

Terms And Concepts To Remember

Organization
Hierarchy
Organizational pyramid
Operating employees

First line management
Middle management
Top management
Board of directors

Organization charts   Scalar principle
Authority   Unity of command
Responsibility   Dual command
Line authority   Span of control
Staff authority   Tall versus flat organizations
Functional authority

Questions

1. Specialization of activities is said to be a characteristic of effective organizations. Can you think of any negative humanistic implications resulting from a high degree of specialization?
2. Assume you have confronted someone who believes that organizational members would be better off in unstructured situations. Attempt to convince the person of the necessity of formal organizations.
3. Why do middle managers sometimes feel that their positions are awkward?
4. How might a key executive also serving as a member of the board of directors be in a situation of conflicting interest?
5. Explain what is meant by the statement, "Organization charts are somewhat like road maps."
6. Why do organizations tend to add staff members as they increase in size?
7. What human relations problems do you expect might develop in organizations with functional authority situations?
8. Why is it considered an abuse of sound management concepts for a person to be responsible to more than one boss?
9. What would influence how broad your optimum span of control might be in relation to your subordinates?

Other Readings

Ivancevich, John M.; Szilagyi, Andrew D., Jr., and Wallace, Marc J., Jr. *Organizational Behavior and Performance*. Santa Monica, Calif.: Goodyear Publishing, 1977.

Kast, Fremont E., and Rosenzweig, James E. *Organization and Management: A Systems Approach*. New York: McGraw-Hill, 1970.

Leavitt, Harold J.; Dill, William R.; and Eyring, Henry B. *The Organizational World*. New York: Harcourt Brace Jovanovich, 1973.

Lundgren, Earl F. *Organizational Management–Systems and Process*. San Francisco: Canfield Press, 1974.

Luthans, Fred. *Contemporary Readings in Organizational Behavior*. New York: McGraw-Hill, 1972.

Magnuson, Karl O. *Organizational Design, Development and Behavior.*
Glenview, Ill.: Scott, Foresman, 1977.

Applications

Hot Line to the Top

My name is Cary Scrant. I am a college student studying business administration at a local community college. Every summer since I was
fifteen years old I have worked at the Brilliant Color Company, a pro-
ducer of fluorescent materials. I am directly accountable to both the
production manager and the traffic manager and feel that I get along very
well with both. I think that I am well liked and accepted by my fellow
workers. I also happen to be the son of one of the partners.

Since the relocation of the plant from Oakland to Richmond, California, there has been a decrease in the morale due mostly to the attitude of
the production manager, Tom Mixer. He rules production with an "iron
hand" without any use of the participative technique of management. His
leadership is clearly autocratic. Mr. Mixer seems to resent any suggestions and has thus caused production to become less efficient. As a result,
I have heard an increasing number of complaints from my fellow employees in the paper and cardboard processing division of the plant. The
other employees seem to feel that since I am the son of one of the
partners, I should be able to get some type of action.

I have had numerous conversations in the past with my father on the
various aspects of the company. My father welcomes these discussions
and respects my ideas and suggestions. I have always been interested in
the company, but my interest seems to be more intense now. I see the
inefficiencies of the plant and can tell my father a fair amount about it
during our discussions. I don't accept any information from my fellow
employees as fact. If I don't already have first-hand knowledge of it, I
check it out. I'm aware of the efforts of management to resolve problems
and, on many occasions, have defended company action and policy.

The general manager and the production manager are beginning to
feel a certain amount of pressure from the top. I was recently called in to
the general manager's office, along with the production manager. The
general manager came directly to the point. He doesn't like me to talk to
my father about the problems in the plant. He feels that neither he nor the
production manager can be effective leaders if the employees have a hot
line to the top.

I explained to them that I observe a lot of waste and inefficiency in the
plant and that the money that the company makes provides the roof over
my head, the clothes on my back, my food, and the funds for my education. I know, but I didn't mention it, that I will probably be employed by

this company in the future and don't want my future livelihood jeopardized by the inefficiencies of the production manager.

The general manager receives information given to him by the production manager. He is not aware of everything that goes on in production; he has a laboratory, an office, and a sales force to oversee. Thus the time he devotes to production is limited by his present span of control.

Questions

1. What appears to be the problem in this case? Is there more than one?
2. What should be done about this situation? By whom?
3. Has Cary made any inferences not based upon fact? If so, what are they?

A Cola in the Face is Worth. . . .

Employees of the Larson Manufacturing Company are allowed to take their morning breaks at their own discretion. After workers buy beverages and snacks from the machines in the foyer just outside the production area, they are supposed to consume them at their work places rather than congregate around the snack machines.

During his morning break, Jack Shea bought a cola drink and a Twinkie, and then stood near the machine drinking and eating them. Judy Mills, one of five supervisors assigned to the production area, noticed Shea and approached him saying, "You bought your stuff. Now get back to work!" Since Shea worked for another supervisor rather than for Mills, he felt justified in continuing to stand there sipping his cola and munching on his Twinkie.

Mills came by again and spoke sharply. "I said get back to work! Now get going! Do you hear?" Shea became so upset at Mills's remarks that he waved the cola bottle forward and splashed the drink into her face.

Questions

1. If you were Mills, what would you do now? Why?
2. Do you think Mills has the right to give orders to a worker she does not supervise? Explain.

7

Techniques of Leadership

Okay, People, Follow Me . . . I Said Follow Me! Aw Come On, *Please* Follow Me?

When you finish this chapter, you should be able to:

1. **Restate** in your own words the difference between leadership and management.
2. **List** at least five traits that are said to be common among effective leaders.
3. **Summarize** the differences between positive and negative leaders.
4. **Contrast** the three major styles of leadership.
5. **Name** the three essential determinants of the "best" style of leadership.
6. **Contrast** X, Y, and Derived X theories of managerial attitudes.
7. **Describe** some of the major gains to be derived from the MBO process of management.
8. **Identify** the three skills that are necessary for effective management.
9. **Summarize** four ways by which managers can improve their leadership skills.
10. **Discuss** the need for a healthy growth atmosphere in organizations.

> The manager does have power *over*
> people,
> but has to use that power
> with a skill which approaches artistry
> to have power *with* people.
> —Robert N. Hilkert

> Employees react to management's be-
> havior and not to its protestations.
> —Saul W. Gellerman

Assume that you are placed in a room with five persons who were chosen at random to work on the solution of a particular problem. An interesting phenomenon would probably unfold. If your group is typical of many, you would soon discover the emergence of an *informal leader*, a person who would most likely be able to influence the other members of the group in certain ways. Your group, therefore, is an organization from which a leader has evolved.

Why do organizations develop leaders? Organizations tend to develop *leaders*, that is, people who influence others. Can you imagine how difficult the fulfillment of organizational goals would be if there were not specified individuals with the authority and responsibility to plan, organize, direct, and control their activities?

The Function and Characteristics of Leadership

Is there a simple definition of *leadership*? Perhaps we had better attach a meaning to the term *leadership*, which has no simple definition applicable to all situations. As you will shortly discover, there are a variety of leadership styles that may be applied effectively to different situations.

Situational Thinking Revisited

A person should alter his or her leadership style to fit a particular situation. A leader's conduct during an emergency, for example, might vary substantially from his or her conduct during normal working conditions. Furthermore, leaders may sometimes use *positive* and at other times

158

negative techniques of leadership. Effective leaders may find that in some situations an *autocratic* form of direction is most effective and in other situations that *participative* or even *free-rein* approaches are useful. Some leaders are designated as such by the *formal* organization; others develop their influence over members of their groups naturally and *informally* because of such characteristics as age, seniority, knowledge, education, and popularity. Informal leaders, for example, emerged on college campuses all over the United States during the turbulent 1960s.

Leadership Defined

Is leadership an antisocial activity?

Now let's try a more formal definition of the term *leadership*, which has been described by Huse and Bowditch as "the effort to influence or change the behavior of others in order to accomplish organizational, individual, or personal goals."[1] Such a definition might strike you at first as being somewhat Orwellian, or negative, but think carefully about your own behavior with close friends or with your parents. In order to accomplish some of *your own* goals, don't you customarily try to *influence or change* their behavior in some manner? Basically, the attempt to influence behavior is what leadership is all about. Your goals don't have to be invidious or negative when leadership techniques are being employed.

The Difference Between Leadership and Management

leadership

management

Although not necessarily obvious on the surface, there is a significant difference in meaning between the terms *leadership* and *management*, although they frequently are used interchangeably. *Leadership* is a type of activity that deals *directly* with people and their *behavior*; it is only one aspect of management. *Management*, a broader concept, *includes* the activity of *leadership*, but in addition may be *nonbehavioral* and involves functions that do not directly or immediately affect others.

What is the difference between *leading* and *managing* Igor?

Perhaps a couple of very basic illustrations will make the distinction clearer. Assume, for example, that your handsome German shepherd, Igor, has again escaped from your front yard and run down the block in hot pursuit of his favorite redhead—the neighbor's slender Irish setter. You loudly screech, "Heeeeere, Igor! Come on home, Igor!" Your *direct* interaction with Igor would be an example of a behavioral leadership function; that is, you are attempting to influence his behavior immediately.

Now let's assume that you are deeply concerned about Igor's frequent disappearances, sometimes for hours at a time, so you decide to restrict at least part of his extracurricular activities. You start *planning* a gate

[1]Edgar F. Huse and James L. Bowditch, *Behavior in Organizations: A Systems Approach to Managing* (Reading, Mass.: Addison-Wesley, 1973), p. 145.

designed to prevent his escaping from the yard. This activity is an example of *management conduct*. You engaged in a function (planning) that doesn't immediately or directly affect your faithless dog's behavior until later. But if your best friend, Igor, is an adroit jumper, he may create additional management problems for you! Try, if you will, to relate these examples to the organizational world of work.

Let's leave our canine illustration now and start examining some of the leadership aspects of organizations.

Formal Leadership

Where do formal leaders come from?

A person may be promoted or transferred to a position of formal leadership from *within* an organization, or may be recruited specifically for the particular position from a source *outside* of the organization. To insure the future availability of leaders from within the organization, management development, or succession, programs are often provided.

As previously mentioned, the formal leadership of an organization can generally be discovered by looking at a company's *organization chart,* which illustrates the chain of command and shows the titles that have been officially assigned to managers.

What Makes People Leaders?

What does a leader need to be a leader?

Neither the titles that some individuals have been assigned nor their positions on formal organization charts are what make some persons leaders. In order to function as leaders, they must have followers. Leaders will be able to lead only when they can effectively influence people *over extended periods of time*. Many famous titular heads of countries have fallen or have been forced to resign when they lost their ability to influence others effectively, and especially when they lost the confidence of their public.

Even in military organizations, where the formal organization can be extremely significant, one can find numerous examples of designated leaders who lost their ability to influence their subordinates effectively. A second lieutenant, for example, can shout "Chaaarge!" at the top of his voice as he rushes frantically to the top of a hill, but the gold-plated bars on his neatly laundered battle dress do not guarantee that his men will follow; sometimes they don't!

Do Effective Leaders Have Anything in Common?

It's risky business to assert that effective leaders have common traits or characteristics. Different kinds of work situations often require different kinds of leaders. Also, we can see important leaders who apparently lack the characteristics thought to be essential for effectively leading or

160

**What tends
to influence
the specific
traits that are
desirable
in leaders?**

influencing others. As a result, there is much debate over whether leaders do tend to have a standard set of traits.

Yet, regardless of the great debate, there do seem to be certain traits that are likely to assist individuals in leading others more capably. We will not go into a lengthy discussion of the traits, but instead list those that frequently appear in leaders who have achieved favorable results:

1. Intelligence
2. Ability to communicate and listen
3. A strong desire to achieve
4. Many interests and sociability
5. Positive and sincere attitudes toward subordinates
6. Self-confidence
7. Enthusiasm
8. Self-discipline
9. Manners
10. Emotional stability

An important point to keep in mind, however, is that most leadership traits are not inborn; they can be learned and developed.

Leadership Attitudes

In chapter 2, in the section on perception, we presented some simple perceptual tests. How we perceive drawings and photographs, however, is often far less hazardous than how we perceive human beings. If you were a manager, how would you perceive the people who work with you?

Positive versus Negative Leaders

Some managers tend to perceive their subordinates in quite positive or favorable ways and others in negative or suspicious ways. Would you be what could be called an X-rated or a Y-rated manager? Which of the two sets of beliefs listed below seems to fit your conceptual scheme?[2]

Theory (Group) X

1. Typical individuals basically dislike work and will avoid it whenever they can.

**A bit negative,
wouldn't you say?**

2. Because most people dislike work, they have to be pushed, closely supervised, and threatened with punishment to get them to help achieve the objectives of organizations.
3. Most people basically are lazy, have little ambition, prefer to avoid responsibility, and desire security as a major goal.

[2]This concept was originally developed by Douglas McGregor, late Professor of Industrial Management at Massachusetts Institute of Technology. See *The Human Side of Enterprise* (New York: McGraw-Hill, 1960).

4. The typical worker is self-centered and has little concern for organizational goals.

Theory (Group) Y

1. Most people find work as natural as play or rest and develop an attitude toward work related to their experiences with it.

Are you positive?

2. People don't have to be threatened with punishment to be motivated toward assisting an organization to accomplish its goals. They will be somewhat self-directed when they are able to relate to the objectives of the organization.
3. Within a favorable human relations climate, the average person learns not only to accept but also to seek responsibility.
4. A large, not small, part of our working force has the ability to exercise imagination and creativity on the job.

X and Y Labels

What is all this X and Y stuff?

Don't be confused by the letters *X* and *Y*, which are merely labels that Professor McGregor assigned to two theories or general ways in which workers may be perceived by managers. Theory X, as you may have discerned, takes a somewhat pessimistic view of humanity. Theory Y, by contrast, begins with the premise that workers will do far more than is expected of them if treated like human beings and permitted to experience personal satisfaction on the job. Theory Y does *not* represent the extreme of the back-slapping school manager who bends over backwards to be regarded as a nice guy.

X-rated = the traditional approach

Y-rated = the modern approach

If your set of beliefs falls into Theory X, you tend to fit into the pattern of the more *traditional manager*. Theory Y, however, is the result of newer and more *positive assumptions* that have developed in recent years. An increasing number of managers have discarded the traditional attitudes. Since your beliefs significantly influence the way you work with and through other people, an understanding of the two views is important.

Derived X Theory

Derived X

Many managers believe (or at least hope!) that their approach to leadership is the ''correct'' one. Many managers are sincerely interested in adopting a more positive stance in their managerial activities, but, unfortunately, their previous experiences have caused them to develop an attitude that we'll term *Derived X,* or the *I've-been-burned theory*. The following illustration should make this theory clear: A single person has fallen deeply in love with a close acquaintance, but soon thereafter is abandoned and deeply hurt by the person. The ditched individual may have had optimistic and positive attitudes about his or her suitor, but if such disappointing experiences recur regularly, the individual may *shift* to a Theory X position in any future relationships.

The same holds true for managers. For example, a manager might try to maintain optimistic and positive attitudes toward subordinates but be "burned" in the process. The following is a list of attitudes that can be derived from negative experiences with employees:

The I've-been-burned Theory (Derived X)

You people are deriving me X!

1. I want to feel that people are conscientious and find work a natural activity, but I've been burned too many times by some of my employees.
2. I've given my subordinates the chance to make decisions and to assume responsibility, but I've been burned too many times. They've simply taken advantage of me.
3. I've tried to create an atmosphere of growth and development for my subordinates by giving them the freedom to make mistakes and to fail, but I've been burned too many times. They haven't grown and developed; they've merely made mistakes and failed.
4. I've tried to get workers to participate in planning activities for achieving organizational goals, but I've been burned too many times. They're more interested in paydays than in accomplishing organizational goals.

If you find yourself shifting from a Y position to Derived X, you could probably benefit from an attempt to analyze your situation thoroughly. Could your shifting attitude possibly be caused by preset notions about your subordinates? Are you truly concerned about your employees and actually trying to do something for them, or is your concern merely lip service? Remember that you're likely to be judged more by your behavior than by your words.

Of course, a manager must be realistic. You're likely to be burned occasionally. And there undoubtedly are some workers who are not self-directed and self-controlled. Some workers do seem to prefer security over responsibility. There are also employees who prefer to seek satisfaction during their leisure time and who merely look to their jobs as a means to a non work-related end. But in spite of these realities, try to retain a certain degree of vulnerability—to be realistic in your feelings, but vulnerable in your behavior.

You must have a certain amount of trust in subordinates; you can't reasonably search all workers as they leave the premises each day. Few people want to work in an atmosphere of suspicion. A Derived X set of attitudes could cause the very conditions you are trying to avoid by creating a negative challenge for the workers—a self-fulfilling prophesy. If distrusted, workers might be motivated to see what they can get away with, since human behavior is often the result of the expectations of others.

Traditional Leadership

What problems do negative leaders have?

negative leadership

Have you ever had a boss who was a negative leader? He or she is the type of person who attempts to motivate you through fear, and feels that people must be *forced* to cooperate and produce, mainly because, "People are just no damn good!" Managers who practice the more traditional, *negative leadership* approach toward their subordinates tend to engage in excessively close supervision and find difficulty in delegating work. As a result, much of their time is expended on "putting out fires," so to speak, and in checking the work of subordinates, instead of on the necessary and usual management functions of planning, organizing, directing, and controlling.

Fear and Motivation

What are some of the results of fear?

Workers who must operate in an aura of fear may be productive in the short run, but over the longer run their morale is likely to be adversely affected, to the predictable detriment of the quantity and quality of their output. Often subordinates who work under negative leaders devote much of their time to trying to protect themselves from the boss by keeping unnecessary records in order to prove later that "It wasn't my mistake, boss!" Workers on the receiving end of negative motivation may appear to be cooperative while often searching for the opportunity to "put one over" on their supervisors. Turnover ratios of company personnel tend to be considerably higher in organizations where the climate is filled with tension and fear, thus substantially increasing the training and operative costs of the entity.

Modern Management

positive leadership

Modern managers have learned that a more effective approach results from the application of more positive techniques of leadership. *Positive leaders,* for example, assume that most people basically want to do good work if they are given the opportunity to see the reasons for their efforts. They attempt to increase, rather than decrease, the satisfaction of their subordinates. Positive leaders attempt to explain why a job is to be done rather than to coerce a person into doing it. Effective leaders soon learn that a positive human relations approach results in the expenditure of even less time, since their subordinates feel that they can use their initiative without the fear of failure and the need for covering up mistakes.

You might be productive for both a positive and a negative leader, but from whom would you be likely to get the most job satisfaction? For whom would you rather work over the long run? When you become a leader, will you recall these concepts? Keep in mind that concepts not applied are quickly forgotten.

Styles of Leadership

The categories of positive and negative leadership attitudes constitute one of the classifications of leadership. Another relates leadership styles to the philosophy of the leaders and distinguishes three styles: autocratic, participative, and free rein.

As a potential leader in organizational situations, you may already have recognized some of the value in encouraging subordinates to participate in making some of the decisions that affect the achievement of the goals of your organization. However, you probably find that your approach must, at times, be decisive and direct and that you cannot, for various reasons, afford the time that the participative approach to leadership requires.

A Major Problem

Is there a "best" style of leadership?

A problem faced by many leaders is that of balancing the two values of participation and decisiveness. What sort of a leader do you prefer when you are subordinate to someone else? One who *tells* you what to do? One who *asks* for your opinions and advice? Or one who *presents you with a task* and permits you to perform the job *without direct supervision*?

There is no one approach to leadership that neatly fits every situation. Before we can decide when to use a particular style of leadership, we should explore some of the major characteristics of the three principal forms.

Autocratic Style

"I'm the boss! You do what I say!"

Persons who employ *autocratic* or *authoritarian* styles of leadership could be termed *tellers*. Autocratic leaders usually feel that they know what they want and tend to express those wants as direct orders to their subordinates. Autocratic leaders usually keep decisions and controls to themselves. In a sense, their subordinates are protected from making bad decisions, since autocratic leaders have assumed full responsibility for decision making.

In order to be successful, autocratic leaders must have a broad and diversified background. Autocratic leaders usually structure the entire work situation for their workers who merely do what they are told, that is, follow orders. This form of leadership is looked upon as somewhat negative because followers frequently lack adequate information about their functions and fear using their own initiative in their work. Furthermore, individual growth is far more difficult to attain within an autocratic framework.

Participative Style

Another style of leadership is termed the *participative* or *democratic* approach. Individual members of a group who take part personally in the decision-making process often have, as a result, a far greater commitment to the objectives and goals of the organization.

"What are *your* ideas on this project?"

The participative approach, however, does not necessarily assume that leaders make no decisions. On the contrary, leaders should understand in advance what the objectives of the organization are in order to draw upon the specific knowledge of the group. Often the combined knowledge and experience of the members of a group exceed that of the leader. Furthermore, problems worked on collectively often give birth to new ideas, created as a result of the interpersonal exchange.

For example, assume that you are the manager in an organization contemplating a change in a particular production process. Human beings tend to resist change, even when a new situation is easier or more efficient. There is, however, no labor law that requires that you, a manager, must do any more than merely notify the workers of their new duties as a result of the change. If you do follow such a direct, nonparticipative approach, what might be the reaction of the workers? In many industrial situations where change is forced upon others, the equilibrium of the group members is so extensively upset that excessive conflict has developed, made manifest by such activities as wildcat strikes, boycotts, slowdowns, and so on. Might there not be more effective ways to develop group commitment to organizational objectives?

How do you deal with change?

Effective managers using the participative approach will customarily meet the workers affected by the change and inform them fully of the problems, needs, and objectives of the organization. Then the participative manager will ask for the group's ideas about implementing the change.

Human beings in general like to feel that their ideas are of value. Quite frequently, the ideas developed by the group will be similar to (or even better than!) the manager's. An extremely important result of a participative approach is that workers who feel their ideas are being used are generally more committed to the decisions. There is less likelihood that employees will feel that the changes are being shoved down their throats.

Does a participative leader lose control over the group?

Some managers hesitate to use the participative style for fear that control over their followers will be lost. However, participation by workers often eliminates feelings of hostility and opposition and, instead, creates a climate of cooperative attitudes that tends to *enhance* managers' influence over their subordinates. Often managers wish to exercise a power over their employees that they don't really have. Through participation, managers do give up some of their authority, but they gain far more control by using positive forces within the group.

Free-Rein Style

"Here's the task; see you next Wednesday."

Another approach to leadership is the *free-rein* or *laissez-faire* technique, which is, in a sense, the *absence* of direct leadership. By this approach, a task is ordinarily presented to the group, which establishes its own goals and works out its own techniques for accomplishing those goals within the framework of organizational policy. The leader acts principally as a liaison between outside sources and the group and ascertains that necessary resources are available to the group.

Evaluation of Leadership Techniques

What determines the "best" style of leadership?

Which technique of leadership is the best? The answer to this question depends on three important factors: the *leader*, the *followers*, and, most significantly, the *situation*. Let's look at some of the principal advantages and disadvantages of each style.

Autocratic Cons and Pros

Why does the autocratic style tend to be negative?

The autocratic approach tends to be a negative style of leadership that can not only create problems of both morale and production in the long run but also fail to develop the workers' commitment to the objectives of the organization.

However, in some situations the manager appears to have no choice but to apply the autocratic approach. For example, during an emergency

167

When might you use the autocratic approach?

or crisis, there is rarely sufficient time to assemble the group for a question and answer session. If the building were burning, it is doubtful that an effective manager would say to his or her subordinates, "People, we have a problem. The entire second floor of our factory is engulfed in flames. The ceiling in this room should collapse within five minutes. What are your suggestions regarding the resolution of this problem?" Instead, the manager would probably shout, "Hey! The building is on fire! Everybody get the hell out of here right now!" It is doubtful that even so autocratic an approach would evoke much resistance from employees.

The autocratic approach might be used during an emergency occasioned by the breakdown of machinery with which the manager is familiar. Time being extremely important in such situations, the manager might well use a direct approach to leadership.

Assumptions of the Participative Approach

What assumptions does the participative approach make?

The participative approach tends to be extremely effective in numerous situations. Workers like to feel that their ideas are important and tend to feel considerably more committed to changes in which they have participated. Workers also develop a greater feeling of self-esteem. However, this approach necessitates some important assumptions. For example, there is the assumption of a considerable *commonality of interest* between the managers and their employees.[3]

The participative approach also assumes that the workers have the *necessary knowledge and skill* to participate in the decision-making process. If knowledge and skill are lacking, managers may find themselves in the position of either being bound by bad decisions or overriding the decisions of the group, thus detracting from the participative approach.

What problems can the participative approach create?

Another potential problem with the participative approach is that group members whose ideas have been rejected may feel alienated. The approach may also encourage the workers to expect to participate in all future decisions, regardless of complexity, an expectation that management may not be able to satisfy. Or if the workers feel that they are being "used" or manipulated, they may use the power of the group against the management. Participation may also take considerable amounts of time, which can be a source of frustration to an impatient management.

---

[3]In any group there may be some individuals who refuse to relate to their jobs, especially those who perceive their positions merely as means to other more satisfying ends. They thus prefer not to expend any energy on participative decision making. Furthermore, employees in the organization must be receptive to the participative approach. Some workers might perceive the managers as ill-qualified if they have to consult with the "lowly workers."

The Applicability of a Free-Rein Approach

When is the free-rein approach applicable?

In some instances a free-rein approach to leadership could degenerate into chaos. In others, the absence of direct leadership is appropriate. For example, the director of a science laboratory or medical clinic does not have to be involved in every decision made by the scientists or doctors. Such professionals usually have the knowledge and skill to accomplish their tasks without direct supervision. The director might present a task to a scientist who would decide how to accomplish the organizational goals.

Free rein may be found in education. A dean seldom tells professors how to perform their jobs. The dean usually tells them what subjects they are to teach; the methods of carrying out the objectives of the institution are generally decided by the professors themselves.

As you may determine from our discussion, the style of leadership can vary with the *occasion*, as well as with the *types of leaders* and *followers*. Most important, however, is that effective leaders will *alter their own styles to fit the needs of a particular situation*. As you may recall, the term for this sort of an approach is *situational thinking*.

Want Results? Try MBO

Many employees fail to live up to the expectations of their bosses. Why is this? Frequently, it is because employees feel left in the dark; they're not the least bit clear as to what their managers expect from them. We've seen in chapter 3 that ineffective communication can cause organizational problems and conflict. And for a manager to communicate organizational objectives to employees so that the employees understand and accept them is far from simple.

management by objectives

To overcome some of these difficulties, an approach related to participative management—termed *management by objectives (MBO)*—is used by many modern managers. Sometimes referred to as *results management*, MBO's major focus is on involving managers and their subordinates *jointly* in developing specific *goals and objectives*. Naturally, estimates of future results must fit into the overall scheme of the organization's goals and objectives.

Now just what is it we want to accomplish?

Establishing objectives mutually, of course, isn't enough. A formalized MBO approach also involves developing specific *plans* for accomplishing the goals, which are either agreed upon and accepted by the manager or modified by mutual agreement between the manager and his or her subordinates. The expected results that are agreed upon then become a guide for future employee performance.

What's our plan?

The MBO process requires that the manager provide employees with periodic feedback. The manager should meet regularly with employees to

Let's take a look at how we're doing.

appraise them of whether progress has been made and if objectives need *modifying.* The sequence of MBO activities is given in figure 7–1. One of the key advantages of MBO is that it creates a situation in which employees tend to feel greater involvement with their work. This participative approach to management also helps employees develop more positive attitudes toward their jobs since they are able to participate in decision making that affects them directly and personally. Of course, MBO is unlikely to succeed in a climate of distrust or when a manager fails to recognize and consider subordinates' needs in relation to the established objectives.

Establish objectives.

Decide on specific tasks, resources, and time frame necessary to achieve objectives.

Review and appraise actual results obtained by subordinate. Modify activities if necessary.

Figure 7–1. The sequence of activities involved with MBO.

When applying the MBO process, a major challenge for the manager is to make certain that employees understand what constitutes realistic objectives. A vague objective such as, "I will work harder during the forthcoming year" or "I will perform better on my job," would certainly be a desirable goal, but hardly specific enough to meet the following basic requirements for sound objectives suggested by Massie and Douglas. They suggest that objectives must:

Do your objectives meet these guidelines?

1. Be measurable and usually quantitative
2. Be specific
3. Identify expected results
4. Fall within the power of the individual manager or unit (not allow buck passing)

170

5. Be realistic and obtainable
6. Clearly state time limits for completion[4]

Leadership as a Skill

Some people seem to have a natural knack for leading others, but fortunately good leaders are not born that way. Effective leadership, like good listening habits, is an activity that is usually developed.

Skill and Knowledge Necessary

A competent manager requires skill and knowledge, neither of which is inborn; they are developed and acquired. For example, assume you work in the sales department of an office equipment manufacturing company and aspire to be a manager. What skills might you need to acquire?

What skills does a manager need?

In general, there are three skills that you and any individuals with managerial aspirations should attempt to develop: technical skills, skills in human relations, and conceptual skills. Now let's see how the three skills relate to your personal desires to become a manager.

Technical Skill

technical knowledge

As a potential manager, you should have the *knowledge* and *ability* necessary to perform the particular task or type of activity related to your job. As a typewriter salesperson, for example, you should have the technical knowledge that enables you to decide which types of equipment are best suited for the specific needs of your customers.

Human Relations Skill

working with and through others

If you become a supervisor or manager with an office equipment firm, technical skills continue to be useful, but become less important than the behavioral skill of being able to *work effectively with and through people*. We already have discussed a number of attributes that are essential for competent managers, such as perception, communication, listening, empathy, and motivation.

For example, proficient managers are more likely to perceive subtle changes in the behavior of their employees, changes that can cause serious problems if not dealt with immediately. Moreover, effective managers are able to communicate both orally and in writing with fewer misunderstandings.

[4]Joseph L. Massie and John Douglas, *Managing: A Contemporary Introduction* (Englewood Cliffs, N.J.: Prentice-Hall, 1977), pp. 280–281.

Conceptual Skill

conceptual skill

A third significant skill that becomes increasingly important as individuals ascend the organizational hierarchy is *conceptual skill*, which term denotes the abilities to analyze, plan, and coordinate the overall operations of an organization and its personnel.

In summary, therefore, human relations skills are important, regardless of your level in an organization. As you rise, however, technical skills become less, and conceptual skills more, important.

The Development of Managerial Skills

How can you develop managerial skills?

Skill in management doesn't usually develop by accident; it can be acquired—by trial and error, formal education, management development programs, and supplemental reading.

Trial and Error

Should skill be developed by chance?

As with any skill, managerial skills can be developed with ordinary practice and through *trial and error* on the job. Although many highly-skilled managers achieved their positions and developed their abilities in such random fashions, more systematic approaches are currently being used. Let's turn to some other ways in which leadership skill can be developed far more rapidly and with much less happenstance.

Formal Education

Formalized education can make your experiences more meaningful and your trials less filled with error. Courses in human relations, management, business, and the liberal arts can frequently enable individuals to advance more rapidly in organizations.

How permanent is education?

A factor to remember, however, is that formal education can become outdated rapidly. Some scholars contend that the knowledge acquired from a formal education tends to become obsolescent within seven years. Therefore, in one sense, a person never really becomes an ''educated'' individual; he or she remains a person ''pursuing an education.'' Regardless of the validity of such estimates of obsolescence, change in our society *is* occurring so rapidly that many people have become overwhelmed by it. In chapter 10 we will explore in some depth the problems that rapid change can bring to members of organizations.

Management Development Programs

The major burden for the development of managerial skills rests on the individual organizational members themselves. However, well-organized companies usually have programs designed to assist and accelerate the development of the skills of those with apparent managerial potential.

**What do you do
when there's no one
to take a manager's place?**

Some firms have discovered the hard way that they had failed to groom anyone for unexpectedly vacated managerial positions. Other more farsighted firms have initiated formal company programs to develop managers.

**Should managers come
from within or without?**

Alfred P. Sloan, Jr., while head of General Motors, held the philosophy that a primary duty of any executive is to develop a successor, preferably one more capable than himself. Numerous organizations subscribe to Sloan's philosophy, although there are notable exceptions. Recently many large companies have acquired the reputations of enlisting the service of executive "headhunters" who raid other corporations in order to fill top level executive positions for their clients. However, these are exceptions, not the rule, nor are the majority of managerial and supervisory positions top level in nature. Consequently, the policy of internal management development programs continues to retain considerable merit.

For example, the SAFECO Insurance Company of Seattle conducts a program by which individuals throughout the company are selected to attend a home office management development course. Individuals are first asked if they are interested in attending the course and told that their attendance does not guarantee them future management positions. Usually, however, future managers are chosen from those who have attended. The program attempts to educate the trainees in current managerial and human relations concepts. Its major purpose is to enable the company to develop human resources for the future, rather than to be caught with their organizational pants down by not having individuals ready for vacated managerial positions.

Supplemental Reading

**Read any
good books lately?**

One way for managers to maintain their acquired educations is to continue *reading regularly* after their formal training and classroom education have ceased. Some organizations today even provide their managers with "reading breaks," said to be far more healthful than coffee and cigarette breaks! Publications such as *Business Week*, *The Wall Street Journal*, and *Fortune* frequently present case histories of other firms, knowledge of which can often assist you in your own organizational activities. Each year numerous books on business and economics are published. Well-rounded managers, however, will attempt to supplement their acquired education by reading books other than those related only to business.

The Need for a Growth Atmosphere

Employees tend to function more effectively when their own managers provide a healthy atmosphere for growth. To develop into managers,

173

freedom to fail

individuals must first learn to make decisions. The opportunity for decision making by subordinates in some organizations is rare, especially in those where employees do not have the *freedom to fail*. Certainly, employees should not make excessive amounts of mistakes, but some employees seldom feel free to make decisions because of the consequences of mistakes.

Some firms do realize that errors will be made but, if employees are to develop managerial skills, they must be permitted to make decisions on their own. In a healthy atmosphere of growth, employees are given responsibility and a reasonable amount of freedom to carry out that responsibility.

Managers, in a sense, are teachers. One of their chief responsibilities is to educate and assist others. If managers want to encourage initiative and decision making in their employees, they should be cautious when handling the mistakes made by conscientious employees.

Conclusions

Management is still far more of an art than a science. Lawrence Appley, while president of the American Management Association, asserted, "Management is the accomplishment of results through the efforts of other people."

Managers, therefore, should acquire the answers to two significant questions: *What activities* are necessary and desirable for the accomplishment of organizational goals, and *by whom* are these goals to be accomplished? The style of leadership that leaders choose in particular circumstances largely govern the success of their future efforts.

Summary

The term *leadership* has no catch-all meaning, but can be defined as the ability to influence the behavior of others in order to accomplish specific results.

Management, which includes the activity of leadership, is a broader concept and may include *nonbehavioral* as well as *behavioral* activities. Leadership *directly affects* the *behavior* of individuals in organizations.

Leaders are not truly leaders unless they have both *followers* and the *ability* to influence people over extended periods of time.

Although there is not complete agreement, some writers contend that there are specific traits apparently common to many effective leaders.

Leaders may be classified according to their attitudes toward subordinates: *positive* or *negative*; or by their style of leadership: *autocratic*, *participative*, or *free rein*. The best type of leadership depends upon three major factors: the *leader*, the *followers*, and the *situation* itself.

A formalized managerial procedure used by many organizations today is *management by objectives* (MBO), a technique that tends to result in greater commitment toward organizational goals.

To be effective, managers need three major skills: *technical*, *human relations*, and *conceptual*. Managerial skills can be developed through *happenstance*, *formal education*, *management development programs*, and *supplemental reading*.

Managers, in one sense, are educators, and therefore have the responsibility to groom others for leadership. Individuals tend to develop leadership traits more rapidly in an atmosphere that gives them a reasonable amount of freedom to carry out their assigned responsibilities.

Terms and Concepts to Remember

Leadership

Management

Theory X

Theory Y

Derived X

Negative leadership

Positive leadership

Autocratic

Participative

Free rein

Management by objectives (MBO)

Freedom to fail

Questions

1. How would you define the term *leadership*?
2. What is the major distinction between *leadership* and *management*?
3. What two factors are essential if a leader is truly to be a leader?
4. What are some of the traits ostensibly common to effective leaders?
5. Explain the significance of McGregor's *X* and *Y* theories.
6. What tends to cause a person to become "Derived X"? How might this condition be avoided?
7. What are some of the probable consequences of workers operating in an aura of fear?
8. Describe the circumstances in which the three major styles of leadership might be used effectively. Describe some situations to which they might not be applicable.
9. What are human relations skills? Why are they important for managers at all levels?
10. What are some of the principal gains to be derived from the MBO process of management?
11. Why do technical skills become less important as a person rises in the organizational hierarchy?
12. Describe four ways in which managerial skills can be developed and improved.

Other Readings

Drucker, Peter F. *People and Performance: The Best of Peter Drucker on Management*. New York: Harper & Row, 1977.

Dunn, J. D., Stephens, Elvis, and Kelly, J. Roland. *Management Essentials: Resources*. New York: McGraw-Hill, 1973.

Haimann, Theodore, and Hilgert, Raymond L. *Supervision: Concepts and Practices of Management*. Chicago: South-Western, 1977.

Huse, Edgar F., and Bowditch, James L. *Behavior in Organizations: A Systems Approach to Managing*. Reading, Mass.: Addison-Wesley, 1973.

Russell, Bertrand. *Power*. New York: W. W. Norton, 1966.

Sisk, Henry L. *Management and Organizations*, 3d ed. Chicago: South-Western, 1977.

Applications

What's Charlie's Complaint?

John Zamora is a dock supervisor for a large freight line. Charlie Williams works for John as a dockworker. One morning, in an attempt to discourage what John felt was too much "goofing off" by Charlie at work, John made a comment about Charlie being lazy to one of Charlie's co-workers, Jimmy Paige. In fact, John really criticized Charlie for being a regular "goof off." Jimmy and Charlie are good friends, and Jimmy told Charlie what John had said.

Later that afternoon, around 2:30 P.M., John was watching Charlie and the rest of the crew on the dock. Charlie appeared to be taking it easy again. However, at one point he seemed to be having some difficulty with a particularly bulky piece of freight. John happened to be walking by at this time and gave Charlie a hand putting the piece on a cart since no one else was close by. John then returned to the office for most of the remainder of the afternoon.

The next morning Charlie filed a grievance because his supervisor, John, had performed work reserved for union members.

Questions

1. What appears to be the problem in this case?
2. Why do you think Charlie filed a grievance? Do you feel he has grounds for a grievance?
3. What could have been done to prevent this problem from happening?

The Merritt Boiler Case

Charlie Cashew, the plant manager of the Merritt Aviation Assembly Corporation of San Jose, California, had reason to suspect that one of the firm's boilers was defective and should be inspected immediately. However, the company was busy with Saturday overtime production and, as a result, neither a boiler repair person nor an insurance company inspector would be available until Monday.

Cashew directed his immediate subordinate, Freddy Filbert, to ask two men in his department to crawl into the boiler to check it. Filbert asked Pete Kahn and Nathan McNutt, both lathe operators, to enter the boiler opening, a space barely large enough for a medium-sized man to crawl through.

Kahn and McNutt strenuously objected to being told to perform the task, arguing that it was beyond the scope of their duties and was extremely dangerous. In fact, they flatly refused and asked to see Cashew, the plant manager.

Filbert first telephoned Cashew and then went with Kahn and McNutt to Cashew's desk, where the following discussion ensued:

> *Cashew:* What in hell's with you two prima donnas? I understand you didn't follow Filbert's order to inspect the boiler.
> *Kahn:* That's not our job; we're lathe operators, not monkeys. Furthermore, it's too darned risky. Those boilers get awfully hot when they're fired up.
> *Cashew:* There's no danger. And nobody's going to turn on the boiler while you are in there.
> *Kahn:* How do we know that? Besides, there's not much air in those things. What if we fainted?
> *Cashew:* Fainted? That won't happen, but if it did somebody could get you out.
> *Kahn:* That's what you say. But I'm telling you right now, we're not going into that stuffy tin can!
> *Cashew:* Listen, Kahn. You and McNutt are going into that boiler whether you like it or not. And to prove that this company isn't run by chickens, I'm going to go in first. If you don't follow me, you two are through with this company. And in addition, for all that backtalk you gave me, even if you do come with me you both have earned unpaid holidays for three days starting tomorrow!

Questions

1. Define the problem.
2. Evaluate the solution pursued by Cashew.

3. How would you have handled the problem if you had been Cashew? Filbert?
4. Should a manager prove to subordinates that he or she is "not chicken"?

Management by Whose Objectives?

Andy Goren is director of human resources for Lester & Darby, Certified Public Accountants. L&D was experiencing a high rate of staff turnover. Resignations were frequent among high achievers, accountants who were no more than two or three years into their careers. Through exit interviews, Andy heard these sample statements:

1. "I never know what is expected of me."
2. "No one ever tells me if my work is good or bad."
3. "When I have a problem and want help, partners do not listen."
4. "Partners only worry about chargeable time (billable client services)."
5. "I want more personal opportunities to grow."
6. "I don't think anyone knows what this firm's objectives are."
7. "The partner in charge is a hard-X leader."
8. "L&D does not have a communications problem. They simply don't have communications!"
9. "Partners meet to discuss everything, real participative style, but we never get decisions."

There were no complaints about salaries, promotions, or the quality of training seminars.

Andy met with Ken Booker, the partner in charge, to review his findings and recommendations. Andy proposed that the firm adopt management by objectives (MBO). Ken reluctantly agreed to a trial MBO program. He said he feared that if young accountants were given a chance to set their own goals, they would "forego profit and bankrupt the firm with their fun and games."

The MBO program was kicked off at a three-day partners' meeting. The partners explored firm objectives for auditing, tax services, and data processing consultation. The three-day debate about the firm's objectives was regarded by all partners as their most successful meeting ever. At the conclusion of the meeting each partner was given a list of six or seven accountants. The partner would serve as a sort of homeroom teacher, a counselor to the accountant. With guidance from a partner, each accountant would set his or her objectives (MBO's) for one year.

An announcement went out to the staff extolling the merits of MBO. The promise was clear that every effort would be made by the partners to create an environment that nurtured individual growth. A partner would meet with each staff member, one-on-one, to communicate what was expected of each person and to set MBO's.

Ken looked over his list of counselees. For his first counseling session he selected Sharon Chapman, a four-year experienced audit supervisor. Sharon held an MBA from Stanford University, had passed the CPA examination, and consistently received high performance ratings from all partners. Ken felt sure that Sharon would understand MBO and this would be an easy first experience at goal setting.

Ken and Sharon held a brief first meeting. Ken explained how the program would work, the advantages to the firm, and what would be expected of Sharon. A second meeting was scheduled to review Sharon's goals.

For the second goal-setting meeting, Sharon prepared her MBO's on a page as shown below. The handwritten entries are Ken's changes. Ken said, "With only 1,300 hours of client work, you will not earn your salary. At this stage in your career you must spend your time on client auditing because you need to develop your technical skills. A few years from now you'll be able to spend time with client prospects and personnel activities. We're not interested in nonprofit volunteering." The meeting ended when Ken had completed his changes to Sharon's MBO's.

Annual MBO Plan

Activities	Hours	Ken's goals for Sharon
Chargeable Client Services	1300	*1850*
• Estimate time to complete client jobs.		
• Hold performance interviews with subordinate accountants at the end of each audit.		
New Client Development	200	*0*
• Entertain one client prospect per week.		
Civic Activities	100	*0*
• Volunteer one day per month to CPA Society's Minority Business Service.		
Campus Recruiting	100	*10*
• Schedule 6 days of campus interviews.		
• Schedule 52 hours of interviews during student office visits.		
Instructor at Staff Training School	40	*40*
• Teach classes on inventories and CPA ethics.		

Attend Professional Seminars	80	*80*
• Attend CPA Society Personnel Seminar in May.		
• Attend Auditing Through Computers Seminar in August.		
• Attend Tax Reform Act Seminar in October.		
Professional Reading	100	*100*
• Read two technical books.		
Personal (holidays, vacations, etc.)	200	*160*
• In July raft the Colorado River with my husband.		
	2000	*2240*

Questions

1. Does Ken appear to be an X-rated or a Y-rated manager? What has influenced your judgment?

2. Do you think MBO could solve the turnover problem? Why or why not?

3. Is self-fulfilling prophecy a problem in this case? Explain.

4. Is it important that Sharon is an economic (profitable) unit for her firm? Explain.

5. If you were Andy, what would be your advice to Sharon? To Ken?

6. Which goals do you think Sharon will achieve? Why?

When you finish this chapter, you should be able to:

1. **Summarize** some of the principal problems that supervisors experience both with themselves and with others in organizations.
2. **Recall** the importance of the delegation process to managers.
3. **Recognize** a major purpose of disciplinary action.
4. **Describe** how rules should be enforced for greater effectiveness.
5. **Identify** the problems that can develop when a person has responsibility without the accompanying authority.
6. **Restate** in your own words at least five ways in which managers can reduce the frequency of their problems.

Now that I'm almost up the ladder
I should, no doubt, be feeling gladder.
It *is* quite fine, the view and such,
If just it didn't shake so much.
—Richard Armour

One of the tests of leadership is the
the ability to recognize a problem
before it becomes an emergency.
—Arnold H. Glasow

A manager once asserted, "You've got to learn to live with troubles. When there are no troubles, then there's no business!" There is a certain element of truth in that statement and one could even apply it to public organizations by substituting the word "activity" for "business."

Unfortunately, troubles and problems are all too prevalent in the organizational world. Yet, as we already have learned, a better understanding of the human side of organizations can assist individuals in anticipating and preventing many problems.

For us to assume, however, that all human problems *will* be anticipated and prevented is probably too much to expect at the present state of organizational development. Consequently, this chapter is going to attempt to transport you through a maze of reality called "troubles," a journey well known and traveled by most organizational members. We shall look at some of the more common difficulties that you might encounter with yourself or others if you find yourself in a leadership role in an organization. Even if you do not have managerial aspirations, it is to be hoped that you will profit by a greater awareness of some of the troubles experienced by others.

The problems to be discussed are divided into three types. First we deal with some of the more common troubles of individuals *themselves,* problems that significantly affect the organizations of which the individuals are a part. Then we discuss some of the more common difficulties that supervisors and managers experience with *other members* of their groups. The chapter concludes with some specific suggestions for *developing more effective leadership in organizations.*

Problems with One's Self

Problems of Individualism

Can I be me or must I be he?

One of the difficulties besetting managers and non-managers is that of reconciling the necessity of *being one's self* with that of being an effective *team member* of an organization. Organizations, like people, have philosophies, and organizational members are expected to subscribe, in general, to the philosophies of the organizations for which they work. Robert N. Hilkert, a banker, expresses a fairly common attitude toward organizational philosophy.

> Our decisions are contained within the framework of our philosophy. By "our philosophy" I mean that of the institution we serve and that which is our own, *provided that our personal philosophy does not for long conflict with that of the institution which we serve.* If we cannot live with the philosophy of our employer, and if we cannot bring him around to ours, then our days in that organization are numbered. We must decide whether to leave before we are requested to do so.[1]

At first glance, Mr. Hilkert's philosophy may seem somewhat crass. However, regardless of your personal reaction to his words, it is important that you recognize that organizations, as do people, differ considerably in mentality. Before accepting a position with a particular organization, you should attempt to "know thyself" *and* "thy organization." Otherwise, you may soon discover that philosophically the relationship is incompatible.

The likelihood that you will approve of everything about a particular organization is slight. For example, if your standards of dress and hair style are liberal—far more liberal than those of your organization—what do you do? You might try to change the organization's standards, but you may discover that some standards in organizations are changed slowly and that your efforts are largely unappreciated.

Is being a rebel always worth it?

You next might ask yourself some important questions. In general, do I like my job? Does it ordinarily satisfy my basic and my higher-order needs? Do the opportunities for advancement that I desire exist? Will I necessarily find a better job elsewhere? If you feel that the advantages of your job outweigh the disadvantages, perhaps you can adjust your standards to those of the organization.

---

[1]From an address delivered by Robert N. Hilkert, while First Vice President of the Federal Reserve Bank of Philadelphia, at the Annual Convention of the American Institute of Banking, May 30, 1961, in Seattle, Washington (emphasis added).

185

The question of organizational ethics that differ from yours is another topic altogether and will be discussed in chapter 16.

Admitting Errors

Are managers human?

Managers shouldn't make mistakes, should they? If you agreed, you have crowned managers with glistening golden haloes (untarnished!). Managers, too, are human and will make mistakes occasionally, although naturally they cannot afford to err excessively. Managers also have egos and, like most persons, may be embarrassed when they make errors of judgment. Some managers will become excessively defensive and try either to cover up their mistakes or to "pass the buck." However, as a sign on the late President Harry S. Truman's desk stated: "The buck stops here."

Should managers know everything?

Leaders will generally earn far more respect by admitting when they are wrong or do not know something. Attempts at concealment generally fail in the long term. However, some employees are mentally set to believe that their managers should know everything. For them, perhaps, exposure to the realities of human fallibility would be more beneficial in the long run.

Wants Beyond Capabilities

Could you fly to the moon?

Not everyone has the aptitude to become a neurosurgeon. The desire to pursue a particular profession is usually not sufficient in itself. Let's take a look at the hypothetical case of a young man named Bob whose father happens to be a well-known neurosurgeon. Bob and his family have for some time assumed that he would follow in Dad's footsteps. Although bright in many ways, Bob unfortunately lacks the aptitude and abilities of a surgeon. Bob, however, refuses to recognize his limitations and, having the "right connections," has been accepted by a medical school. Bob is highly motivated, a factor that sometimes offsets lesser ability, but in his case motivation fails to get him through medical school. He flunks out.

What has occurred in Bob's case is a problem of motivation and needs that sometimes develops in individuals whose aspirations are excessively high in relation to their capabilities. Although many management skills can be developed, not everyone, for example, has the capabilities to direct and coordinate a division of a large corporation. Frustration often results when a person fails to "know thyself" sufficiently and believes that he or she has capabilities that do not exist.

The Problem of "Making It"

**After you've
"made it," then what?**

An additional problem related to self sometimes develops after individuals have accomplished long sought goals. For years individuals may have strived to achieve their present positions and on reaching them discover, to their dismay, that they are frustrated. Why? Do you remember our stroll down Needs Lane in chapter 5? After the second cheeseburger and french fries, your hunger need was satisfied and, we learned, a satisfied need ceases to motivate. In other words, no longer does the motivation exist for the pursuit of a particular goal once you have achieved it. Perhaps the person at the head of a large corporation doesn't feel as successful as many people might imagine. The manager's goal, once attained, may not offer precisely the satisfactions expected. A reevaluation of one's present situation and future goals then becomes desirable.

On Becoming "Peter Principled"

Another related problem can develop for some persons with fairly strong higher-order needs. Take, for example, John, who has performed well in every position that he has held in a particular firm. If he has done a reasonable job, the chances are good that he will be promoted to a higher level. Can you see what could occur? John has performed admirably in position A. As a result he is promoted to position B. After an outstanding and conscientious performance in position B, John is promoted to position C. But—alas! He now discovers that he is grappling for his very existence in position C. He finds that he cannot perform as well as he did in his previous positions, so he is likely to remain in position C indefinitely.

**Did John get
too high on the job?**

Peter Principle

John has become the victim of what Laurence Peter termed the *Peter Principle*, which he defined as "the tendency in a hierarchy for employees to rise to their level of incompetence."[2] Professor Peter contends that the validity of his principle is proven by the profusion of poor leadership in organizations today. Whether Peter's conclusions are as universal as he claims can be debated. Nonetheless, there are numerous examples of persons in organizations who might admit, at least to themselves, that they have become "Peter Principled."

**You mean . . .
become
"unprincipled"?**

Who knows? Perhaps one day you will be promoted to a position in which you feel incompetent. If so, what should you do? Flee? Resign? Try to avoid your boss and your subordinates? Or couldn't you pursue a more positive approach and attempt to become un-Peter Principled? First,

[2]Laurence J. Peter, *The Peter Prescription* (New York: William Morrow, 1972), p. 11.

you might try to discover what your deficiencies actually are, and then develop a plan for overcoming them. And perhaps your only deficiency is a temporary feeling of uncertainty about your ability to perform your new job, which is quite a normal feeling when faced with new challenges. You certainly needn't be destined for a life of mediocrity solely because of a promotion.

The Law of Parkinson

Have you ever noticed before embarking on a vacation or business trip that you were concerned about not having enough time to pack your luggage? If you have taken trips regularly, you may have noticed that the preparations for them tend to expand to fill the available time. In other words, if you have three days to prepare, you may spend much of those three days getting ready, whereas if you have only half an hour advance notice you still manage to pack.

Have you ever been amazed at how fast you readied yourself for work or school on mornings on which you overslept? Some persons ordinarily allow about two hours in which to ready themselves, yet twenty minutes will suffice when they oversleep.

Parkinson's Law

Can you actually have less time when you have more time?

The point of the above examples is expressed by C. Northcote Parkinson as *Parkinson's Law*: that *work expands to fill the time available for its completion.* [3] Although individuals differ, many persons work far more efficiently when they are pressed for time. When individuals have excessive amounts of time, they often find less important tasks to do. According to an old adage with a grain or two of truth in it, "If you want something done soon, then give the task to a busy person."

Parkinson also contended, tongue-in-cheek although painfully close to the truth, that managers make work for one another by hiring more and more assistants each year, even when normal workloads are declining.

An intelligent use of time, accompanied by adequate planning and the establishment of objectives, can enable you to break Parkinson's Law, not only with impunity, but also with the rewards of accomplishment. However, you must be willing to overcome some of your deep-seated habits in order to combat "Parkinson's peril."

K's Law

Let's assume that you are really a well-organized person. You are well aware of the pitfalls of Parkinson's law, so you carefully plan your activities right down to the minute, the hour, the day, the week, and even to the month and quarter. You don't look for additional work to fill any gaps in your time; in fact, you feel that you don't even have any time gaps.

[3]C. Northcote Parkinson, *Parkinson's Law* (Cambridge, Mass: The Riverside Press, 1957), pp. 2–12.

But you may find that your sophisticated and highly developed state of organization doesn't really matter. Additional activities, tasks, responsibilities, and interruptions seem to gravitate toward you. This particular stumbling block is termed *Kossen's Law (K's Law)* and is defined in this manner: *Regardless of your state of organization, new tasks and interruptions will seek you out, thereby expanding your responsibilities, commitments, and work load.* As a poster produced by *Supervisory Management* magazine wryly depicts:

Kossen's Law

Management is a series of Interruptions Interrupted by Interruptions

Source: Reprinted by permission of the publisher of *Supervisory Management.* © 1976 by AMACOM, a division of the American Management Association.

189

I know you're in there. I can hear you thinking!

There are ways, however, to break Kossen's Law. One method is to develop a periodic, *closed-door, no-incoming-telephone-calls-please policy.* This approach runs the risk of irritating people who want to talk to you. However, such problems can be minimized if you make your intentions clear and yourself accessible at specified times.

Here's what you might do if you are asked to take on a responsibility that you know cannot be worked comfortably into your already crammed schedule: Be honest with the person. Point out that you would sincerely like to help, but that your present schedule will prevent you from doing a satisfactory job on the project. You could also indicate that, rather than do a lousy job, you would rather not take on any additional responsibilities at this time.

How to break the law.

In some instances, you might maintain a better personal image with the requester if you indicate that you would like to give the request some careful consideration first before deciding. Then, within two or three days, contact the requester and indicate that your present schedule doesn't allow you to take on any additional responsibilities. Don't let too much time elapse, however, between the request and your response. If you do, you might begin to develop guilt feelings that could interfere with your normal working activities.

The Principle of Exception

There is nothing particularly wrong with being a firefighter, but the job descriptions of most managers do not call for the putting out of fires as one of their principal activities. Nonetheless, managers who have not developed the ability to delegate discover that much of their time is spent on routine matters that should have been assigned to others.

exception principle

The managerial concept termed the *exception principle* has often been abused by "firefighter managers." The exception principle means that *regular, recurring activities and decisions should routinely be delegated to and handled by subordinates and that unusual nonrecurring decisions should be referred to a higher level.* Some managers, apparently unaware of the exception principle, find themselves running from one crisis to another because they failed to spend enough time on the more important managerial functions of planning, coordinating, and controlling.

Problems of Delegation

delegation

Closely related to the exception principle is the problem of *delegating work.* In small organizations, *delegation* is less essential (sometimes not even possible), but in larger organizations delegation is necessary if managers and supervisors are to perform their assigned responsibilities

effectively. Not only does delegation relieve managers of certain activities, but also it tends to enrich their subordinates' jobs. Delegated tasks and added responsibilities help develop subordinates for advancement.

Why aren't some supervisors able to delegate work?

Numerous managers find it difficult to assign responsibilities to others. These are sometimes the types of leaders who tend to look upon subordinates negatively (the X or Derived X approach), have little faith in their workers, and feel that "if you want something done right, you've gotta do it yourself!"

In some cases managers who cannot delegate may actually lack confidence in themselves, fearing that they are giving something away that rightfully belongs to them. Often these are the managers who spend the last two hours each day in the office trying to determine what work they are going to take home that evening. Sometimes persons who are afraid to delegate fear that their subordinates will "show them up" by doing better jobs than they could. Delegation, however, like management by exception, is essential for managers who want to be free for other more important managerial functions.

The Problems of the Boot Ensign

There is a situation in the military that has a parallel in civilian organizations, one that could be called " the problems of the boot ensign." In the United States Navy, a boot ensign is a person who has completed officers' training school and recently arrived at his first assignment quite inexperienced. However, because of his rank in the formal hierarchy, the newly commissioned officer sometimes finds himself in an awkward situation. He has authority over enlisted men who not only are much older but who usually have been in the military considerably longer, in some cases between fifteen and twenty-five years, while the ensign may have served for a matter of months. A problem arises when the young officer starts exercising his authority without drawing on the background and experience of his noncommissioned subordinates who, as a result, tend to resent him deeply. Effective leadership becomes difficult under such circumstances.

How can a "green" leader gain the respect of subordinates?

A similar type of problem can develop in civilian organizations when young college graduates are placed in positions of authority over older persons and do not utilize the experience of their subordinates. If you ever find yourself in a situation where you are supervising others much older or with more experience than yourself, you will usually be more effective *after* you have earned their respect. A participative approach can be effective in such circumstances. Attempts to effect significant changes in the organization before you gain the confidence of the group will often meet with stiff resistance. Your subordinates will tend to be far more cooperative with you if you manage to help satisfy their needs for self-esteem and identity by participation.

The Problem of Paternalism

paternalism

A style of leadership that is no longer common, but prevails nonetheless, is the paternalistic approach. *Paternalism*, a term with derogatory connotations, indicates the type of management that *overdoes its apparent concern for the welfare of employees*.

For example, several years ago there was in the Midwest a factory manager who had read about the link between smoking cigarettes and the incidence of cancer. He responded like a protective father, deciding that it would be better for his employees if they did not smoke. So the following Monday, the manager sent a notice through the plant: "Commencing immediately, smoking is prohibited in this factory."

Do employees want to be fathered at work?

What do you think happened? Would the workers really appreciate the manager's concern? Or would they resent the arbitrary withdrawal of their custom and privilege? Resent it they did, and everybody walked out until the manager backed down and canceled his new rule.

When you become a manager, guard against the tendency to act like an overprotective father. Siblings don't always appreciate the good intentions of their paters.

Supervisory Problems

In this section we discuss some of the more common troubles that many supervisors have with their subordinates, among them the difficulties surrounding the firing of employees, the problems of taking disciplinary action, the enforcing of rules, the problems of responsibility without authority, psychological distance, role expectation, and differing aspirations of subordinates.

Firing

Firing employees is one of the most painful chores managers may ever have to face, one that taxes their human relations skills to the utmost. So difficult is the firing of employees that some managers have eliminated the word *firing* from their vocabularies and in its place substituted less emotional words such as *dehiring* or *termination*. But no matter what

193

they call it, managers must at times face the unpleasant task of firing employees.

Employees should be dismissed only as a last resort after other reasonable efforts at correction or discipline, such as oral warnings or suspensions, have failed. Some traditional managers feel that if a person has done something serious enough to warrant discipline, he or she should be fired. A more constructive and modern approach is that the *situation* should be corrected rather than the *person* punished.

Why is correction more desirable than punishment?

There are occasions when employees must be dismissed, especially during economic recessions when the staff has to be reduced in order to cut costs.

There is no simple way to fire employees, but there are some useful tips that can make dismissals somewhat easier on people:

1. *Come directly to the point.* Don't beat around the bush and be so tactful that the employee doesn't really understand your intentions.

Ready, aim, fire!

2. *Timing* is extremely important. The bad news will probably be less disastrous if presented to the employee late in the working day. To save the employee unnecessary embarrassment, be certain that other employees do not overhear you. Related to the question of proper timing is the individual's personal situation. Can your decision be postponed in the event of a serious family illness? Can your decision be timed to avoid sentimental holidays, such as Christmas?

3. *Let the employee know why* he or she is being dismissed. The dismissal may be the result of cost-cutting measures rather than the employee's own action. By informing the employee of the reason, you will help eliminate the feelings of self-doubt that often result from a dismissal. An employee fired for a negative reason can benefit by knowing what types of behavior should be avoided in the future.

4. *Don't encourage retaliation* during the termination interview by losing your temper, even if the employee becomes belligerent. Angry employees will occasionally attempt to get revenge against you or the organization.

5. *Terminate the employment as soon as possible* after the decision to fire has been made. Often, even if two weeks notice is mandatory, immediate dismissal with two weeks' salary paid in advance is preferable to retaining the employee for the two weeks. Employees are frequently not very productive during their last days with an organization and, if disgruntled about the firing, can sow the seeds of discontent among other employees.

Disciplinary Action

disciplinary action

Another source of "trouble" for leaders is in situations requiring *disciplinary action,* which is *a means of negative motivation, or penalties, applied to employees who fail to meet organizational standards.* The majority of employees follow rules and regulations as expected. Occasionally, however, some employees do not and thus require disciplinary action of some sort.

Positively-oriented managers generally feel that discipline should not punish but instead be corrective and constructive. Since you, the potential manager, should be concerned that the situation returns to normal as rapidly as possible, your disciplinary action should deal with the *specific rule infraction* rather than with the employee in general.

Rules

rules

Rules relate to disciplinary action and can be defined as guiding statements of what action and conduct is or is not to be performed. An illustration of a rule is, "Coffee breaks are to be not in excess of fifteen minutes and are to begin at 10:15 A.M. and 2:15 P.M. daily."

Should rules be inflexible?

Should a rule be treated as something *inflexible* or as a *guide* to performance? An organization attempting to maintain a favorable human relations climate would be likely to treat each person as an individual and therefore be reasonably flexible in enforcing rules. For example, some employees are consistently late, or absent after paydays and weekends; others are customarily dependable and conscientious. In reality, many managers relate the enforcement of rules to the overall past behavior of their employees.

Rules, however, should continually be re-evaluated to ascertain whether they are applicable to changing organizational conditions. Employees tend to lose respect for rules that either seem illogical and out of date or are not enforced. Also, rules must be communicated to and understood by the employees. Rules should always be enforced equitably, promptly, and consistently or they will lose their effectiveness.

For example, assume that a firm has a company parking lot with special places nearer to the plant for executives of the organization. For the past six months, about ten operative employees have parked regularly in the reserved spaces, but nothing has ever been said to them by management. On one particularly dreary rainy Monday morning, an executive arrived at the parking lot a bit late and could not find a parking space near the plant. He became enraged at the prospect of becoming soaked by the downpour, and discovered that two of the reserved spaces were filled by workers' cars. He determined who they were and suspended them for two days without pay for the infraction of the rules.

The punished pair could become hostile for a number of reasons and might even submit a grievance to their shop steward or union. The rules hadn't been enforced previously so the workers had reason to believe that the rule, in effect, didn't exist. Also, the punished individuals were only two of about ten persons who had used the executive spaces during the

(handwritten margin notes) "Hot Stove Theory of Discipline" — immediate — impersonal — consistent — Forewarning — Progressive — oral warning — "written" — suspension — termination

past six months, yet the others were not disciplined. Was it fair suddenly to enforce the rule without advance notice after it had been ignored for six months? Morale problems could develop from what might seem like an insignificant event.

The San Francisco Employers Council has developed a useful checklist of questions for supervisors to ask themselves before taking disciplinary action against employees for infractions of rules.

1. Do I know the facts?
2. Is the employee getting the same penalty others have gotten for the same offense?
3. Is the rule that has been violated a reasonable one?
4. Did the employee know the rule?
5. Have proper preliminary procedures been followed?
6. In appropriate cases, has the employee been warned in writing and given lesser penalties, according to past practice or work rules? (This doesn't apply to major violations of which there is absolute proof.)
7. Am I being fair and impartial? Or am I reacting against the employee because he has challenged my authority?
8. What is the employee's past disciplinary record and length of service?
9. Does the employee have a reasonable excuse for violating the rule?
10. Can the employee's guilt be proved by direct objective evidence—or only by circumstantial evidence?
11. Does the company have a past record of strict rule enforcement? If not, were employees notified of management's intention to crack down on violations of this type?

Responsibility Without Authority

Some managers find themselves in "trouble" when they have been assigned responsibility without authority, an inordinately awkward position for a leader.

Why is responsibility without authority undesirable? For example, assume that you are the personnel director of an organization and have been assigned the responsibility to develop and administer a new training program for employees. You are responsible for the program's success, but you have been delegated no authority to order the materials necessary for your program. Excessive amounts of your time might be expended on trying to persuade "the powers that be" of the necessity of such normal expenditures. Your job could have been made much easier and more efficient if you had been delegated ample authority along with a clear indication of its limits.

Another problem of responsibility without authority can arise for department heads who are responsible for the profitable operations of their sections, but have not been delegated the authority to select their staff. In well-managed organizations, supervisors or foremen would not necessarily recruit personnel for their departments, but they would customarily have the authority to accept or reject anyone chosen for their sections by the personnel department. When supervisors are placed in the position of being responsible for personnel whom they did not originally choose, their morale and attitudes are likely to be affected adversely.

Psychological Distance

psychological distance

A situation that some leaders find difficult is that of determining how friendly or close they should be to their subordinates. *Psychological distance* is the term used to denote the *mental attitudes of supervisors toward their subordinates from the standpoint of the closeness of the working relationship*. The greater the psychological distance, the more remote the managers are from their employees.

For example, believing that "familiarity breeds contempt," some managers avoid becoming close to their employees, contending that too much closeness leads to loss of respect and control. Other leaders try extremely hard to be "one of the gang" with their subordinates. Still others attempt to strike some sort of a balance between the two extremes.

Which approach seems best? There is not complete agreement, but the more modern approach to management suggests that a minimum (but not its complete elimination) of psychological distance is the most effective. The important factor is that supervisors should be genuinely interested in their personnel.

Why do some leaders feel that distance begets respect?

Managers who are not afraid to get to know their subordinates as human beings and who are seen as human beings themselves actually tend to gain respect and control. Managers who are willing to be close to their employees must be careful that all their subordinates are treated fairly and without favoritism. Managers will lose a substantial degree of effectiveness if they develop the reputation that all an employee needs to obtain special favors is to be "a friend of the boss." To be close to subordinates requires a reasonable amount of confidence, not only in one's self but also in one's subordinates.

A parallel can be found in the United States Navy, which has both seagoing divisions and air force squadrons. The official policy of the Navy, in general, has been that officers should not fraternize with or become particularly close to enlisted personnel. On Navy ships, for example, there have been special areas designated "Officers' Country," in which enlisted personnel are forbidden. Even gangways, or exits from ships, have been segregated.

In the Navy air force, however, the officers, many of whom are pilots, seem to favor less psychological distance from their personnel. One of the principal reasons given is that an airplane's ability to fly successfully is greatly dependent upon the mechanical service of their subordinates. Many officers state that they are able to fly with a greater feeling of security when they treat enlisted personnel as human beings. Maybe managers in civilian organizations should behave more as though their own lives depended on the activities of their subordinates.

Supervisors should guard against appearing to be excessively familiar, which can sometimes lead to problems when discipline is to be administered or less pleasant tasks assigned. Excessive remoteness, on the other hand, can create artificial barriers between management and workers and result in less effective interaction and communication. Once again, leaders should attempt to use *situational thinking* and develop the ability to know which approach enables them to accomplish specific organizational goals.

Role Expectation

role expectation

We've already discussed how people tend to assume different roles in different situations. Problems often arise when managers have one set of expectations of their leadership roles and followers have another. A concept related to this problem is termed *role expectation*, which simply is *the way in which individuals are mentally set to perceive the behavior of others*.

What can you do when your employees' role expectations differ from yours?

Relating this concept to *psychological distance*, organizational leaders may subscribe to the philosophy that they will be more effective by minimizing the psychological distance between their workers and themselves. However, if the role expectation of the workers is such that they expect their boss to keep his or her distance, attempts at closeness may not only be difficult but also impossible. Psychological distance relates to feelings of trust and, if a group of workers has a deep-seated distrust of authority, managers will find it difficult to foster closeness and participation. In such an atmosphere situational thinking and sensitivity become important.

Shouldn't rules affect the boss, too?

Role expectation can likewise create problems when workers feel that rules should apply not only to themselves but also to their bosses. For example, workers would probably feel that a rule against smoking in a company auditorium should apply to everyone. If managers smoke in the room but workers cannot, the disregard for organizational rules can create role conflict and discontent among the workers who will feel that rules are being applied against them in a discriminating fashion.

Aspirations Differ

Doesn't everyone want to lead?

Managers, too, are sometimes guilty of unrealistic role expectations. For example, some managers are surprised when an employee refuses an offer of promotion to a supervisory or management position, but not

198

everyone wants to, or necessarily should, be a manager. Jim, for example, had worked for fourteen years in a branch office of a large bank. He knew the technical aspects of his job better than most employees and had a personal style with the public that fostered the company's image. Each time promotional opportunities arose, Jim turned them down. Some of his fellow workers had difficulty in understanding him. Think back, however, upon the motivational concepts discussed in chapter 5. Each individual, as you may recollect, has different needs. Only Jim himself really knew why he did not want a promotion. Perhaps he was confident in his present position and felt as though he would lose some of his feelings of security. Regardless of his own personal motives, if Jim has performed his job satisfactorily, is there any particular reason for not permitting him to remain in the position?

Suggestions for Reducing Troubles

Reams of literature have been distributed to supervisors and managers about methods of making their leadership more effective. Some of the advice may sound like the ''ten easy steps'' approach to successful leadership. But if managers were seriously to consider and apply some of the suggestions, idealistic though they may sound, to their daily activities, they might well reduce their supervisory problems. In the remaining section, therefore, we shall make some suggestions about eliminating some supervisory problems and maintaining a more favorable human relations climate in the organization.

Are there any dangers in trying to know employees better?

1. *Know Your Personnel*. Leaders must work with and through people. An adequate understanding of your subordinates, not only of their behavior on the job, but also of their private lives and backgrounds, may help your efforts to motivate them. However, any personal information you have about employees should be confidential. For example, if you develop the undesirable reputation of being an organizational gossip, you will probably find difficulty in learning any useful information about your subordinates.

Also remember that each worker is different; a complimentary remark that would please one person might make no impression on, or even be displeasing to, another. Nor can all persons withstand criticism to the same extent. An improved understanding of your personnel can make situational thinking far easier.

How can you get subordinates to want to do things?

2. *Help Your People Want to Do Things*. We have already discussed the various methods for motivating employees. You can attempt to force personnel to do the things you want, but such coercion will usually work against you in the long run. Effective managers will generally try more positive techniques of leadership in order to motivate employees to *want* to perform their assigned tasks. A participative approach often motivates

employees constructively. Subordinates are frequently far more motivated and committed to carry out plans that they themselves have helped to establish.

What are the
reasons for praising
in public and
criticizing in private?

3. *Praise Often and in Public.* Have you ever heard the statement, "The boss never tells me how well I've done, but she sure lets me know when I've goofed!" Workers need positive feedback to help them maintain their motivation and morale. This is a suggestion easily overlooked during the many hectic pressures of a normal workday. Don't delude yourself into believing that your subordinates are necessarily contented simply because they have not heard any criticism from you about their performance. Observe the effects that *sincere* compliments, especially paid in public, can have on subordinates. The results are sometimes astounding.

Why are
some managers
afraid to be human?

4. *Be Sincerely Interested in Subordinates.* The key advice here is to *be human.* Don't be afraid to use first names and to be called by your first name. Your name does not determine how loyal your subordinates are to you, but your *actions* will. Be genuinely sincere when you ask subordinates about their health and families; they can often perceive when you are asking more from habit than from interest. The occasional luncheon together can often enable you to know your employees better and provide you with the opportunity to express a greater interest in them as human beings. However, be careful in your efforts to be friendly that you do not appear to be showing favoritism to certain employees.

How do you
gain by sharing
responsibility?

5. *Don't Be Afraid to Share Responsibility.* We've already discussed how the inability to delegate prevents managers from having ample time for thinking and planning. Furthermore, the sharing of responsibility helps to develop and prepare subordinates for more responsible positions.

Is any job perfect?

6. *Accentuate the Positive.* The boss or the subordinate who continually complains about almost everything is usually unpleasant company. Almost any job has its good and bad aspects, but when you focus on the favorable sides your entire job tends to seem more enjoyable. A positive approach also is advisable when you are establishing rules for employees. Instead of saying, "Do not operate machinery without face masks," you might evoke a better response by saying, "Save your eyes from injury. Wear face masks when operating machinery."

How do you
want to be followed?

7. *Lead as You Want to Be Followed.* People tend to follow as they are led. Leaders should set examples for their subordinates. Supervisors who distribute sloppily prepared memos, maintain messy work areas, are continually late for work, and break company rules are, in a sense, inviting their employees to do the same. Leaders set the tone for the individuals whom they supervise.

Why do most
people want
to know the reasons?

8. *Tell People Why Things Are to Be Done.* Most people want to know the reason for changes and activities that affect them personally. Not only does such information reduce the chance of rumors developing, but also it may enable more useful contributions to flow from the subor-

dinates to supervisors. Employees are sometimes able to build construc- tively on information received from supervisors.

Why are mild complaints beneficial?

9. *Don't Fear Gripes.* Don't be afraid of relatively mild complaints from your employees; often they serve as a safety valve and help to prevent more serious eruptions later. Unfortunately, there is a tendency for some employees to complain regardless of the conditions. As one manager wryly exclaimed, "You could give some people a sack full of gold, and they would complain about the condition of the sack!" Be alert, however, for complaints that may be valid and could lead to serious difficulties in the future if not recognized and resolved immediately.

Why is dignity important to many workers?

10. *Treat Subordinates with Dignity.* The master-slave relationship has, we hope, been laid to rest in our culture. The United Nations has proclaimed that all the workers in the world are entitled to be treated with respect and human dignity. Not only is such advice both reasonable and humane, but also its practice tends to foster loyalty, reduce turnover, and enable employees to feel that their jobs are important—factors beneficial to both employees and the organization.

Summary

The purpose of this chapter has been to illustrate some of the more typical problems that leaders in organizations regularly face as a part of their daily activities.

We initially discussed two broad catagories of leadership problems: those that leaders have with *themselves*, and those that leaders experience with *others*. Finally, we offered some specific *suggestions* for developing more effective leadership in organizations.

Out of necessity our investigation has not included every possible leadership problem, but instead has attempted to stress the need for sensitivity and greater awareness on the part of leaders if they are to be successful in reducing the severity and frequency of their organizational problems.

The next chapter continues along a similar vein with its primary focus on what managers can do to deal more effectively with the problem of *employee morale* in organizations.

Terms and Concepts to Remember

Peter Principle
Parkinson's Law
Kossen's Law (K's Law)
Exception Principle
Delegation

Paternalism
Disciplinary action
Rules
Psychological distance
Role expectation

Questions

1. Why do most managers tend to prefer to hire personnel who subscribe to the overall philosophies of their organization? What are the potential dangers to organizations that encourage excessive conformity among employees?
2. Why do many leaders tend to find it difficult to admit mistakes?
3. How can a person successfully "break" Parkinson's Law?
4. Describe Kossen's Law. How might its implications be avoided?
5. Why is the delegation process so important for managers to learn?
6. What would be the difference between a paternalistic management and one that had a sincere desire to develop a healthy human relations climate?
7. Why should employees be fired only as a last resort?
8. What are some arguments favoring and opposing flexibility in the application of rules?
9. Why does a manager with responsibility but little authority find it difficult to function effectively?
10. Should all managers maintain about the same pychological distance from their employees? Explain.

Other Readings

Capwell, Theodore. *How to Run Any Organization*. Hinsdale, Ill.: Dryden Press, 1976.

Kohn, Mervin. *Dynamic Managing*. Menlo Park, Calif.: Cummings Publishing, 1977.

Leavitt, Harold J. *Managerial Psychology*. Chicago: The University of Chicago Press, 1964.

Massie, Joseph L., and Douglas, John. *Managing: A Contemporary Introduction*. Englewood Cliffs, N.J.: Prentice-Hall, 1977.

Peter, Laurence J. *The Peter Prescription: How to Make Things Go Right*. New York: William Morrow, 1972.

Todes, Jay L.; McKinney, John; and Ferguson, Wendel, Jr. *Management and Motivation: An Introduction to Supervision*. New York: Harper & Row, 1977.

Applications

The Warehouse Order-Filling Problem

The Totlers Toy Company has a warehouse in Midway, Washington, on a lot approximately the size of a typical city block. Thirty-five persons are employed to fill orders on the day shift, and twenty-three work on the swing shift.

The employees have been assigned specialized duties in the particular sections of the warehouse in which they work. A number of problems have developed in recent months. For example, almost every day some sections are extremely overloaded with work, while employees in other sections are standing around with little to do.

When the workload becomes excessive in some sections, employees tend to become harried and tense, a situation that has resulted in a fairly high number of complaints from customers. On numerous occasions, shipments have been delivered with incorrect quantities and unordered items.

Questions

1. If you were the warehouse manager of the Totlers Toy Company, what would you do in order to resolve the problems?
2. What style of leadership would you apply? Why?

If Only There Were More Hours in the Day

At precisely 7:30 A.M. on a damp and dreary Monday morning in February, George Gains, operations chief of the Beaumont City Fire Department, drove his compact car out of the garage of his comfortable lakefront home. The automatic garage door swung shut and George headed toward the administrative offices of the Beaumont City Fire Department. The trip to the office took about 30 minutes and gave George the opportunity to map out his daily activities mentally with few interruptions.

George has worked for the Beaumont City Fire Department since shortly after graduation from high school. Although he never attended college, George was a good student, enjoyed reading, and was able to pass civil service promotional examinations with relative ease. George also seemed to get the right breaks on his way up the organization. Early retirements occurred in each of the positions he was interested in assuming. As a result, his rise in the organization was meteoric. At age 31, he was the youngest person ever to hold the second-in-command, assistant to-the-chief position with the department.

George felt good this morning. He had completed a briefcase full of paperwork last night at home and thought, "Today is going to be the day I get a lot done that I've been wanting to do for a long time." His mind began to sort out the day's work, attempting to establish priorities and goals.

"Oh, oh," he thought out loud to himself. He suddenly remembered that he hadn't yet worked out a specific plan for developing a first-line management program for fire station captains and lieutenants. George's boss, Chief Bryson, had asked him last Wednesday afternoon if anything specific had been developed yet. The training program for first-line managers was one that George himself, while battalion chief in the training division, had proposed to the former operations chief, Franklin Hill. Hill retired before anything was done with the recommendation. George's boss, Chief Bryson, agreed that the concept and implementation of management training was long overdue, but a year had already slipped by, and George had still done little in the way of formulating specific plans. George realized this was one of the projects he should work on today.

A traffic light suddenly changed from green to red, and George's thoughts momentarily left his work. As the light turned green, his mind and automobile shifted back into gear. He thought about another project that he had not started yet—the development of an improved appraisal system for probationary employees. Changes in fire fighting equipment and methods, along with public relations demands, had rendered the old system obsolete. His thoughts focused on a few more projects that required planning, and he felt that "Today's gonna be the day, for sure, that I get those projects out of the way."

Suddenly George realized that he was approaching the parking garage below the building in which he worked. As he left the elevator and walked toward his office, he met Alice Brown, battalion chief of the training division, and sensed something was wrong.

"What's wrong, Alice?" asked George. "You look like something's bothering you."

"It is," responded Alice. "Glenna, my new typist, hasn't come in, and she didn't show up Friday either."

"Did she notify you?" asked George.

"I haven't heard a thing from her," answered Alice.

George was visibly upset and said, "Those young people fresh out of school these days just aren't dependable. Well, why don't you have Edna in Personnel give Glenna a call?"

"Okay," replied Alice, "but could you possibly get me a typist for today? I have three reports that have to be submitted to Chief Bryson by tomorrow morning."

"I'll get back to you within the hour," responded George.

As George continued toward his desk, he saw his assistant, Bobby Bruner. "Good morning, Bobby," greeted George.

"Oh—hi, boss," answered Bobby. "I'm glad to see you. I have those budgetary reports ready to be sent to the battalion chiefs and engine company captains. I checked them twice on the calculator for accuracy. Should I mail them out now?"

"Not yet," advised George. "I want to check the figures once more myself just to make sure that there are no mistakes. I'd be embarrassed if they went out of here with any errors."

George left Bobby and called Personnel to see if they could find a typist for Alice. He then began his usual morning routine. He telephoned each battalion chief to see if they had any personnel, equipment, or budgetary problems. Then he began his morning inspection of the office. He helped a clerk find a storage place for an older typewriter, detailed two typists who had run out of work, helped another typist move the position of her desk because of the glare from a nearby window, cleared away several boxes of office forms from an aisle, and answered a telephone that was ringing on an unattended desk.

George then returned to his own desk and started approving vacation schedules that had been submitted by all fire house captains for the fire house personnel. George always made the final decision in the event of conflict.

The phone rang. George answered it and talked with Captain Franks from Engine Company 6 who wanted permission to switch shifts with one of his lieutenants. George agreed to the change, and then realized that he was five minutes late for a staff meeting that he himself had arranged for this morning.

After the meeting, George returned to his desk, looked at his watch, and realized that it was lunchtime. ''Where did the morning go?'' he asked himself.

After lunch, George began again. His afternoon went something like this:

1. Two more tours through the office.
2. A telephone call from his son who wanted to know if he could go to a movie this evening.
3. A telephone call from a firefighter who had been injured in an automobile accident and required hospitalization.
4. Reviewing copies of talks given by members of the Fire Service Speakers' Bureau.
5. Two meetings with battalion chiefs regarding personnel problems.
6. Approving requisitions for supplies from the various fire stations.

It was now late in the afternoon and George was exhausted. It was time to head for home again. After two interruptions on the way to the building garage, George entered his car and pulled out into the rush hour traffic. As he drove home, he asked himself, ''Where did my day go? I didn't do anything on the projects I thought about this morning on the way to work. Am I really a manager—or merely a messenger? If only there were more hours in the day, I know that I could accomplish some of the longer-range goals that I've been thinking about for some time. If I only had the time. . . . ''

Questions

1. George seems to feel that he doesn't have enough time to accomplish his goals. Do you agree? Explain.
2. If you were George, what might you do to accomplish more of your longer-range managerial goals and objectives?

9 Nobody Gives a Damn About Us

Problems of Morale in Organizations

When you finish this chapter, you should be able to:

1. **List and describe** the principal factors that influence morale.
2. **Recognize** the major warning signs of poor morale.
3. **Explain** the relationship between morale and productivity.
4. **Describe** the various methods for measuring or evaluating morale.
5. **Name** at least five ways in which jobs can be made more satisfying.

Nothing is really work unless you
would rather be doing
something else.
—James M. Barrie

Like every man of sense and good
feeling, I abominate work.
—Aldous Huxley

The year, 1936. The film, a classic satire on assembly-line work entitled *Modern Times*. When a dehumanized Charlie Chaplin went mad—when he left his factory work station after monotonously tightening pairs of bolts hour after hour and then tried to tighten the supervisor's nose, fire hydrants, and the buttons on women's dresses—industrialists didn't laugh at what they saw. Instead, they reacted defensively.

Although much progress seems to have been made, and many managers have achieved a high degree of enlightenment and sophistication in the area of industrial relations since the 1930s, organizational strife and conflict continue. Almost one-half of all strikes in the United States during 1976, for example, resulted from issues other than wages. And most of these non-monetary disputes were concerned with such factors as plant administration, general working conditions, and job security.

"Blue-collar blues," "tight-white-collar of dissatisfaction," "worker alienation," "the Charlie Chaplin twitch." These have been some of the catch phrases of recent years, representing what is believed to be the proliferation of dissatisfaction among workers toward their jobs.

Morale in Organizations

Organizational literature abounds these days with articles on the heightened managerial concern to make jobs less dull. A steadily increasing number of organizations are experimenting with programs of job enlargement, job enrichment, industrial democracy, team approaches, flexible working hours, planned time off, and a host of others designed to improve workers' satisfaction and attitudes toward their jobs and thus improve organizational productivity.

Morale Defined

morale

Morale is an elusive thing, not easy to define, control, or measure, but exerting a strong influence over the human relations climate in organizations. *Morale* refers to employees' *attitudes* toward either their employing organizations in general or toward specific job factors, such as supervision, fellow employees, and financial incentives. It can also relate to the *individual* or to the *group* of which he or she is a part. For our purposes, we shall define morale as *the atmosphere created by the attitudes of the members of an organization.* It is influenced by how they perceive the organization and its objectives in relation to themselves.

What is this thing called "morale"?

In this chapter we shall, by design, focus first on the negative—that is, on poor morale—in the hope of assisting you to develop a greater sensitivity toward the problem. Initially we shall examine *the factors that influence morale*, then look at some of the principal *warning signs of low morale,* and then take a more positive approach by presenting some of the *current techniques* adopted by organizations in the United States and abroad to enrich jobs and improve morale.

Factors Affecting Morale

The attitudes of employees are significantly influenced by the ways in which they perceive a number of important factors, such as:

1. The organization itself
2. Their own activities, both on and off the job
3. The nature of their work
4. Their fellow workers
5. Their superiors
6. Their concept of self
7. The satisfaction of their needs

The Organization

How might the organization affect morale?

The organization itself influences workers' attitudes toward their jobs. For instance, in situations where the workers have had little opportunity to participate in establishing organizational objectives, the goals may seem distant and unreal. The public reputation of the organization, especially an unfavorable reputation, can adversely affect the attitudes of employees. Can you think of any other ways in which the organization can influence employees' morale?

Employees' Activities

Could marital spats affect morale on the job?

Workers are the product of their *total environments*. The workers' relationships with their families and friends can significantly influence their behavior and attitudes on the job. Most organizations feel that employees should have the right to their own personal lives. However, when their activities off the job affect their performance on the job, managers should have both the responsibility and the prerogative to discuss such activities with employees. Some organizations offer employee counseling, ranging from marital to drug abuse, to help with problems.

The Nature of Work

What, in addition to money, do people want from their jobs?

Historically, work has tended to become increasingly specialized and routinized while the worker has become progressively better educated. Many behavioral scientists contend that workers' current economic security and education have led them to expect considerably more than just material prosperity from their work.

Many types of jobs, however, seem to contribute toward boredom, obsessive thinking, and alienation. An occupational psychologist, Dr. Norman Wilson, of Britain's National Institute of Industrial Psychology, feels that there are certain *work characteristics* that tend to create stress for the employee. He lists:

1. Forced, uniform pacing (assembly-line operations moving at a constant speed).
2. Repetition and short time cycles (repeating the same simple task over and over).
3. Large impersonal organizational structures (the feeling of being merely a number rather than a person).
4. Organizational goals that from the shop floor appear vague and unattainable (a lack of understanding of organizational goals).[1]

Fellow Workers

How are workers influenced by their associates?

The emergent, or informal, system in an organization can also significantly affect morale. Assume, for example, that you are a worker whose previous attitude toward company policies has generally been favorable. However, as a member of a group, your attitude toward a working condition could be swayed by the collective action of your cohorts or union. A condition that formerly did not disturb you may suddenly have adverse effects on your morale because of the influence and pressures of the group.

[1]"Assembly Line Blues Hit Britain," *Oakland Tribune*, 16 June 1973, p. 7-E.

Leadership

Who has the main responsibility to maintain morale?

Management sets the tone and has the primary responsibility for establishing a healthy organizational climate. Consequently, the *actions of management* exert a strong influence over the morale of the work force. High rates of turnover, for example, often indicate ineffective leadership. The latter portion of this chapter examines some of the ways in which management can maintain or improve morale.

Concept of Self

The *self-concept* of workers (that is, how they perceive themselves) also tends to influence their attitudes toward organizational environments. For example, individuals who lack self-confidence or who suffer from poor physical or mental health frequently develop morale problems.

Personal Needs

When might a paycheck influence morale?

How workers' *personal needs* are satisfied can significantly influence their morale. Paychecks and fringe benefits, for example, satisfy personal needs. Although increases in pay do not necessarily motivate employees to increase productivity, paychecks nonetheless can be a source of morale problems, especially when compared with the paychecks of other employees doing similar work or those of workers in other firms within the same industry. Employees can become disgruntled when they feel that their paychecks are not in line with the "going industry rates" or are not keeping up with rising prices.

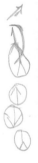

Attitudes, Morale, and Productivity

Changing Attitudes

What causes attitudes to change?

We have concluded that morale is related to attitudes. Managers should recognize, however, that attitudes and, therefore, morale factors change. What may be of prime importance to individuals today may be secondarily important tomorrow.

Strikes provide illustrations of a change in attitudes. During some periods, they occur more frequently for *security reasons*. For example, better pensions were the main issue in the 1973 strike by ten thousand rubber workers against B. F. Goodrich Company. A United Rubber Workers' poll found that 36.4 percent of the rank and file felt that improved pensions were the key issue; 32 percent wanted higher pay. However, the galloping inflation of the mid-1970s caused the pendulum to swing back toward higher wages as one of the key issues relating to employee morale.

Morale and Productivity

Generally speaking, there tends to be a positive relationship between high productivity and high morale. Under conditions of poor morale, favorable output is difficult to sustain for long. Profits are usually adversely affected when poor morale reduces productivity. Lower profits can mean fewer wage gains in the future. A full and cumulative circle, in effect, can occur, since wages can affect morale.

High morale, however, does not necessarily cause high productivity; it is merely one, albeit an important, influence on total output. For example, a group of workers could be happy in the social relationships that they had developed on the job, but they may be so busy clowning around that their productivity is low. Their morale may be high because of the *lack* of effective leadership. Consequently, for high morale to favorably affect productivity, it must be accompanied by reasonable managerial direction and control. Furthermore, a group that lacks cohesiveness will probably lack high productivity.

What is essential for high morale to stimulate productivity?

Warning Signs of Low Morale

Morale in organizations is something that managers frequently take for granted, as most Americans until recently took their supply of natural resources. Morale is often not noticed unless it is poor or until something has gone amiss. Frequently, by the time management recognizes the deterioration of morale, it is faced with crises as rapid in their onslaught as was the sudden awareness of the energy crisis in 1973. Deep organizational scars have sometimes been left when inadequate attention was paid to the warning signs of deteriorating morale.

Is morale there if you don't notice it?

Perceptive managers are continually on the lookout for clues to the state of morale. Among the more significant warning signs of low morale are *absenteeism, tardiness, high turnover, strikes and sabotage*, and *lack of pride in work*.

Absenteeism

What causes high absenteeism?

If a person enjoys certain sports, he or she will often exert the effort necessary to participate in them. If workers enjoy their jobs, they will usually exert the effort necessary to do what is expected of them. However, the nature of work, as well as the workers themselves, is changing. Some types of industries have developed severe morale problems, which are evidenced by high rates of *absenteeism*.

This problem has been especially acute in the automobile industry. According to Edward Cole, while president of General Motors Corporation, "Some GM plants see as much as 20 percent absenteeism on certain Mondays and Fridays. We have to staff for the absentees, and as a result our total costs go up, and productivity per work hour goes down."[2] The problem of absenteeism has become so acute in the automobile manufacturing industry that, as a means of discouraging it, some observers have proposed that those who do show up for work get an extra reward through a "bonus hours" plan. Under this proposal, workers who put in a given number of days without being absent would be given an extra day off.

Which are the "popular" days for absenteeism?

Absenteeism on certain days is indicative of employees' negative attitudes toward their work. Mondays, Fridays, before and after holidays, and the day following paydays tend to be the most common days for absenteeism. If as a manager you ever discover abnormally high absenteeism on these days or, for that matter, on any day, an investigation of the causes of the absences would be in order.

Tardiness

Did slaves in the cottonfields worry about punctuality?

Excessive *tardiness*, like absenteeism, is a warning sign of low morale. Workers who dread their jobs are not often eager to arrive early or even on time, whereas those who derive substantial satisfaction from their jobs will often arrive on the job early.

High Turnover

turnover rate

In every organization some employees leave and others are hired. When the *turnover rate* —that is, the amount of movement of employees in and out of an organization—begins to rise abnormally, another warning sign

[2]"America's Lead in World Technology Diminishing," *Oakland Tribune*, 20 May 1973, p. 43.

of poor morale could be flashing before the eyes of management. A formula suggested by the U.S. Department of Labor for computing turnover rates is:

$$\frac{\text{Number of separations during the month}}{\text{Total number of employees at midmonth}} \times \ 100 = \text{Turnover rate}$$

If there were 30 separations during a particular month, and if the number of employees at midmonth was 400, the rate of turnover would be:

$$\frac{30}{400} \times \ 100 \ = \ 7.5\%$$

High turnover is costly because of the need to train inexperienced new personnel, plus the added expense of fringe benefits and the additional paperwork associated with hiring new employees.

Some managers may feel that morale is always satisfactory when turnover ratios are low. However, turnover ratios tend to be low during periods of economic recessions when jobs are scarce. When economic conditions return to normal, disgruntled employees often begin to seek employment elsewhere. Ratios and costs then begin to rise.

When does low turnover not indicate high morale?

Strikes and Sabotage

Strikes and sabotage are examples in the extreme of discontent in the work force and are costly in human and economic terms. According to the United States Department of Labor, during 1976, not a particularly unusual year, there were 5,600 strikes amounting to 38 million workdays. The trend may be worsening. Although lower than the four-year high reached in 1974, time away from work due to strikes in mid-1977 was at its highest level since 1971.

During the 1970s, the automobile industry was singled out by some social critics as a prime culprit in the area of job satisfaction. The industry experienced high rates of absenteeism and frequent recalls of defective cars. Many behavioral scientists believe that the principal problem related to the *nature of work* (assembly-line techniques) prevalent in the auto industry: work has been broken down into *simple, specialized,* and *repetitive tasks* to increase efficiency.

How does the nature of work affect morale?

General Motors Corporation Truck and Coach Division attempted an experiment during the early months of 1973 using *teams of workers* to assemble motor homes. The experiment was short-lived, however, because the management believed that it was too slow to meet GM's standards of production. The chairman of the board of directors of General Motors Corporation, Richard C. Gerstenberg, contended that the plight of the worker in the auto industry was "magnified by political leaders, union officials, and social critics."[3]

Lack of Pride in Work

What has caused an "I-don't-give-a-damn" attitude in the United States?

Few discontented workers will find it easy to take pride in their work. An attitude that may be expressed as "I don't give a damn" seems to have emerged in the United States. Observe, for instance, the manner in which so many persons carelessly open their car doors so that they bang against other automobiles, especially yours! Look at the litter and garbage lining our streets and highways. Observe the cigarettes that are extinguished on linoleum floors in public buildings. Some social observers contend that attitude is naturally transferred to the workplace, and especially to those organizations where the opportunities for job satisfaction are lacking.

The problem of job dissatisfaction knows no bounds. Any type of job, industry, or country can be inflicted with the malady. For example, in May 1973, at Chrysler Corporation's British subsidiary, six hundred automobile workers on one shift were sent home early and forfeited one and a half hours pay because of shoddy work on the assembly line. According to management, the assembly line had to be stopped because of poor workmanship five times during one shift, and two out of three cars were being rejected. The dispute grew into a major strike costing Chrysler more than fourteen thousand cars and considerable goodwill.

Chrysler's British subsidiary has been plagued with severe labor troubles and, according to some critics, with unimaginative management. Its market share dropped from 12.3 percent to less than 7 percent in eight years. John J. Riccardo, chairperson of Chrysler Corporation, has hinted that he might even be happy to see British unions follow through with their threats to "occupy the factory and man the gates" if Chrysler decides to shut down its British operations.[4]

The British government, in turn, has ordered a study to try to determine how jobs could be made more satisfying for workers on assembly lines. Great Britain has been plagued with industrial strife. Workers have been known to cheer vociferously when assembly lines broke down. There have even been occasional outbreaks of sabotage, intended to stop the assembly lines. In the United States, Senator Edward M. Kennedy introduced a bill to authorize the Health, Education and Welfare Department (HEW) and the Department of Labor to make a thorough study of workers' discontent.

Who's affected by the tight-white-collar blues?

The *tight-white-collar blues* is another current catchphrase. Assembly-line workers are not the only victims of the morale malaise; white-collar

---

[3]"Wanted: Ways to Make the Job Less Dull," *Business Week*, 12 May 1973, p. 147.

[4]"Chrysler and Britain Steer a Rough Course," *Business Week*, 17 November 1975, p. 52.

workers and executives have also been affected. In fact, over the past three decades, the trend has been moving toward a larger proportion of days off the job in *non*manufacturing areas than in manuacturing.

Further evidence of the growing disenchantment of white-collar workers was reported in an American Management Association survey, which indicated that of 2,821 executives questioned, 52 percent of supervisory managers "found their work, at best, unsatisfying." The study found that 30 percent of the executives believed that business activities have adversely affected their health in the last five years. And nearly 50 percent of them have changed, or have contemplated changing, their occupations since 1967.[5]

We've seen that the problem of morale in organizations is serious and can have dire effects on our nation's productivity. The United States, traditionally the world leader in growth in productivity (output) per work hour, fell dramatically in this area during the early 1970s to a position near the bottom of the list of advanced nations.[6] During the second half of the decade, productivity improved dramatically in the United States, but continued to sag in Canada. There is no simple explanation for these changes, but the attitudes of the workers, that is, their morale, could be significant. If we are going to compete effectively for world markets, we have to develop innovative solutions to the problems of the discontented worker in the United States.

Evaluating Morale

Management, in order to improve morale, must first attempt to discover what is causing poor morale. In the following section, we discuss some of the ways in which management can measure and evaluate morale.

Statistical Evaluation

absenteeism and turnover records

One way to measure morale is to evaluate actual results. *Absenteeism and turnover records* can provide useful information. For example, assume that between 1975 and 1980, the absenteeism rate in your organization rose from 2 percent to 7 percent. Taken alone, these figures would not be absolute proof that morale had deteriorated. Combined with other techniques of evaluation, however, the statistics could give you a fair indication of morale trends and the potentiality of problems.

[5]"'White-collar Blues' Turn up in a New Study of Businessmen's Job Attitudes," *The Wall Street Journal,* 29 May 1973, p. 1.
[6]"America's Lead in World Technology Diminishing," *op. cit.,* p. 43.

Employee Counselors

How might
employee counselors
measure morale?

In some organizations there are *employee counselors* whose principal function is to assist employees with their problems and complaints. For example, Xerox Corporation employs a person whose title is Employee Relations Manager to act as a company ombudsman with whom employees, it is hoped, can feel free to discuss their problems in confidence.

Counselors are in the position to discover morale problems early. A snag can arise, however, if management regards the counselor as a source of information and the word gets out that he or she is a "lap-dog" or spy of management. Counselors quickly lose effectiveness when employees distrust them.

Observation and Listening

What might a sudden
change in the behavior
of an employee indicate?

Another approach to uncovering what is bothering workers is so obvious that it is often overlooked: *observation and listening*. An alert management can usually perceive when personnel are behaving differently. A sudden change in the behavior of a particular employee is often a clue that something might be worrying him or her. For example, perhaps the employee doesn't hear you when you speak and periodically appears to be in a fog. Perhaps the employee has started drinking on the job, or seems irritable much of the time. An increase in the frequency of accidents may also be a sign of a morale problem.

Far too frequently managers do not even listen to the response after they have asked their employees how things are going. We've already discussed the importance of removing one's "earmuffs" in order to be a more effective listener. One of the most effective means of discovering why employees are discontented is to *ask them*, and then *listen* carefully to the answers.

Regular Buzz or Gripe Sessions

What is the pur-
pose of buzz sessions?

If management has established a climate of trust and open communication, a fairly effective means of determining what is disturbing the employees can be the regular use of *buzz* or *gripe sessions*. Some organizations allocate specific times each week—say, Fridays from 9:00 to 9:30 A.M.—for meetings during which employees are given the opportunity to air their complaints. Much can be learned about the employees' attitudes from the use of this technique when the psychlogical distance between management and the workers is not excessive. A feeling of mutual trust is essential.

Morale Surveys

Morale surveys are used by some managers to explore in greater depth specific attitudes and opinions of employees. Various names have been attached to such surveys, including *attitude, opinion*, and *employee* surveys. In general, there are two types of morale surveys: *interviews* and *questionnaires*.

Interviews. In chapter 4 we discussed some of the more common techniques of interviewing, two of which closely relate to employee attitudes: *interviews with current employees and exit interviews*.

The process of *interviewing current employees* about their attitudes has its shortcomings. Employees who fear possible reprisals tend to conceal their real opinions and, instead, answer questions according to what they think the boss would like to hear.

The *exit interview* explores the attitudes of employees who leave the organization. This approach also has its limitations since some employees fear that honesty may cost them a favorable letter of recommendation. The interview approach, however, does have the advantage over questionnaires of permitting greater sensitivity and interaction to responses.

Questionnaires. A second and more widely used method of surveying attitude is by the use of *questionnaires*. Of the two principal types, one is termed *descriptive* and asks open-ended questions; the other, referred to as an *objective survey*, is more common because it is simpler and costs less to administer to large groups.

The following are some specific suggestions about the use of surveys:

**What are some
"tips" on the
use of surveys?**

1. Efforts should be made to *create a positive* and *trusting attitude among employees* toward the survey.
2. The survey should have the *active support of top management*.
3. *Questions should be carefully framed* so as to avoid any built-in biases of management.
4. In order to obtain more candid answers, *identification* of the respondent *should not be required*. Management should be more interested in *what* the attitudes are than in *whose* attitudes they are.
5. For best results employees should *learn of the results* of the survey as soon as possible.
6. *Management action*, based on the survey results, should be taken.
7. *Comparisons* of data from year to year should be made to ensure that progress toward improvements is being made.

**Why is the supervisor
a key person in
administering surveys?**

Attitude surveys can be a useful management tool when conducted properly and regularly. If improperly administered, surveys can cause employees to feel suspicious or distrustful of management and not answer the questions candidly. A final important point: Supervisors must be instructed about the purpose and value of surveys. Since supervisors will be administering the surveys, they can make or break the efforts.

Greater Concerns Over Employee Morale

Are employees like robots; that is, mere mechanical objects, whose only human trait is caring for their paycheck? Traditional managerial views seem to lean in that direction. But such beliefs are shortsighted and often serve to hinder the accomplishment of organizational goals. We learned in chapter 5 that the need for self-esteem—a feeling of self-worth as a human being—exists in most people. Without such a feeling, many employees become bored, disgruntled, alienated, and sometimes even destructive.

Can jobs be made more satisfying? Many modern managers believe so. A section later in this chapter discusses several methods that have been used by increasing numbers of companies throughout the industrial world to improve the workplace.

Work in America

Elliot Richardson, while Secretary of Health, Education and Welfare, initiated an important and controversial study entitled "Work in America," the results of which were released in December 1972. The purpose of the project was to investigate the changing work ethic in America, the extent of job dissatisfaction, and the means to allay the increasing unrest that had begun to move from the nation's campuses to business and governmental organizations.

The study concluded that significant numbers of American workers are dissatisfied with the quality of their lives and that dull, repetitive, seemingly meaningless tasks, offering little challenge or autonomy, are causing discontent among workers at all occupational levels.

What have been some symptoms of *alienation* among workers?

Workers in America, the report asserts, feel alienated from their jobs, and these feelings tend to result in the increased frequency of alcohol and drug abuse, mental illness, shoddy work, pilferage, and sabotage. The report concluded that job enrichment is the wave of the future. The future, apparently, is upon us already, for the list of organizations experimenting with job enrichment techniques is growing rapidly. Some of the more active organizations in this field have been General Foods, Dow Chemical Company, Polaroid, Volvo, Saab, Virginia Bell System, and Hewlett-Packard.

Concern for the Human Element

Many jobs have been designed with little consideration for their demoralizing effects on the individuals who have to perform them. Workers today, however, want to be recognized as individuals, not regarded as automatons. They want to enjoy a sense of belonging rather than suffer a sense of alienation. The elimination of monotony on jobs is not as dif-

219

What are the major purposes of job enrichment?

ficult as some more traditional managers apparently want to believe. New styles of thinking, however, are necessary for programs to succeed. Managers who resist new efforts on the grounds that employees are treated too much like spoiled children should attempt to recognize that the prime aim of such programs is to make the *total organization more efficient*, not solely to provide greater satisfaction to the workers.

Suggestions for Improving Jobs

Earlier you learned that monotony on the job can result in boredom, obsessive thinking, and reduced productivity. Technology in the United States and elsewhere has developed to an extent that has created numerous problems for managers and workers in organizations. An increasing number of firms have responded with more positive approaches to the human problems developing from a high degree of specialization. Let's now examine briefly some suggestions that managers might consider when they are modifying work environments in their organizations.

Create Whole Jobs

job enlargement

Job enlargement is the process of *increasing*, rather than decreasing, *the complexity of the job* in order to appeal to the higher-order needs of workers. There is a belief current among some managers that by providing workers with the opportunity to make greater use of their minds and skills they are more able to help satisfy their need for self-esteem and dignity.

whole job concept

Sometimes referred to as the *whole job concept*, this technique suggests that you, as the manager, attempt to give workers more complete, or whole jobs, to perform. The technique has a greater chance of success if you draw on employees' suggestions when trying to introduce greater challenge into jobs. Try to develop an environment in which employees are able not only to be actively involved in their jobs, but also to participate in both planning and then evaluating the results of their efforts. An example of job enlargement would be to allow a person on an assembly line to perform more than one specialized function.

Job Enrichment

job enrichment

Job enrichment is another approach to reducing employee discontent, one that can take a variety of forms. Job enrichment frequently involves greater use of factors that are intended to *motivate* the worker rather than only to *maintain* a satisfied feeling toward the job. (Remember Herzberg's motivation-maintenance model?) Basically, job enrichment is a form of *changing or improving* a job so that a worker is likely to be

220

more motivated. It provides the employee with the opportunity for greater recognition, advancement, growth, and responsibility, thus helping to overcome some of the principal causes of worker alienation. An example of job enrichment would be to allow secretaries to sign their own outgoing letters and be responsible for content and quality.

Not all attempts at job enlargement and job enrichment are successful. The ways in which new programs are introduced are as important as the programs themselves. Problems can develop with programs that are poorly introduced or ill-timed as a result of differing perceptions of organizational members. For instance, top management may initiate a program that it perceives as one that will satisfy and motivate the workers. However, if the employees perceive the change as a management gimmick, the program is unlikely to succeed. Nor are all workers alike; some may not respond to programs on which others may thrive.

industrial democracy

Many of the suggestions that follow are variations of job enlargement or job enrichment, sometimes referred to as forms of *industrial democracy*.

Build Responsibility into Jobs

risk decisions

Don't be afraid to allow your subordinates to make *risk decisions*. Delegation, as we have learned, can aid employees in their growth and development as well as freeing you, the manager, for other tasks.

Modify the Work Environment

teams

This suggestion is a broad one and could be applied together with all our suggestions for improving jobs. Wherever possible, *teams* or *work groups* should be used. Smaller groups tend to be more cohesive than larger ones. Team members are usually more productive when they can participate in choosing compatible workmates for their group. With effective leadership, teams tend to improve work standards and accept new processes more readily.

social contact

Workers generally prefer some degree of *social contact* with other employees. The opportunity for conversation, therefore, tends to enhance morale, especially on repetitive jobs that do not require much mental concentration.

music

Music can be an effective morale builder in some circumstances, but the captive audience—the workers—should participate in determining the types of music that are to be played.

rest and exercise breaks

Regular rest breaks have been known for some time to have beneficial effects on productivity. Some firms have recently introduced voluntary *exercise breaks*, which can be a healthful source of enjoyment, especially for workers whose jobs do not require much in the way of physical exertion.

Flex Your Working Hours

flexitime

Can you imagine showing up for work at almost any time you want plus being able to leave your job early or late, depending on your own personal desires? This concept, known by a variety of names, including *flexitime* and *flexible working hours,* is not a pie-in-the-sky idea. It already exists in many firms throughout the world. The variable working hour concept was first introduced by a West German aerospace firm in 1967. By 1978, more than 100 U.S. corporations and some 70,000 government employees were on flexitime working arrangements.

Bascially, flexibility wipes out the 9-to-5 syndrome faced by many employees and enables workers to enjoy hours that more closely match their personal life styles. Workers still must work a preestablished number of hours—say, 40 hours per week, or 80 hours over a two-week period. But the major difference between flexitime and a conventional system of work hours is that under the former, employees have the freedom to choose, within certain limitations, what times they begin and quit their jobs each day.

What good is it?

What are the benefits of flexitime? For one thing, it reduces traffic congestion in crowded urban areas, which in itself makes going to and returning from a job less hectic for the worker. But the benefits are more far-reaching than a mere alteration in traffic patterns. Individuals under flexitime can take care of family and other personal affairs more easily; this tends to reduce absenteeism in organizations. For example, employees with children can arrange their hours to coincide with babysitting or school requirements. Furthermore, those employees who are "morning people" can start work at a time when they are likely to be more productive.

Hey! How come I gotta stay?

Flexitime is not without shortcomings, however. Some firms have found that flexitime requires a more elaborate system for keeping track of employee working hours, thus tending to increase administrative costs. Some supervisors have also complained that coordinating employees who start at varying times is more difficult. And morale problems could increase—rather than decrease—in organizations where some employees are *not* permitted to participate in the program due to the nature of their jobs. In general, however, many firms, including Hewlett Packard, Control Data, and Metropolitan Life, have found that flexitime has improved morale, increased productivity, and given employees a greater sense of control over their own lives.

Try Two for the Price of One

job sharing (twinning)

Another novel idea that has begun to catch on in some occupations is a practice referred to as *job sharing* or *twinning.* Under this sytem, two

222

workers divide one full-time job. Not only are the hours split in half, but so are salary and fringe benefits.

Those who especially favor the twinning concept are mothers and fathers who want income plus more time to spend with their families or other interests. Others who lean toward job sharing include older people who want to retire gradually, those with physical limitations, and students.

Surprise! You have just given a berth to twins!

Although twinning has the drawback of doubling an employer's training and personnel costs, the overall benefits seem to outweigh any disadvantages. For one thing, employers can more easily achieve affirmative action hiring goals by tapping labor markets previously unaccessible. Another major advantage, according to some studies, is that part-time workers tend to approach their work with far more energy and enthusiasm, and tend to put in more than a half day's work in a half day's time.[7] Absenteeism also tends to be less since one of the "twins" can cover for the other in the event of illness or other reasons for being absent.

Although still not a common organizational hiring practice, twinning has become increasingly prevalent in such fields as teaching, library and lab work, the professions, and in government. Some states, such as Wisconsin and Massachusetts, encourage twinning among government employees.

Rotate Jobs

job rotation

Job rotation helps reduce boredom. However, certain employees, especially those who have been with the company for a long time, may resist being placed in less pleasant jobs.

[7]"Two for the Price of One," *Time,* 3 May 1976, p. 68.

entry-level position

"up for grabs"

jobs for the handicapped

Sometimes an unpleasant job is made an *entry-level position*. Employees can be told that the job is monotonous, but temporary. Another possibility is to put *dull jobs* "up for grabs" each day. Sleepy or hungover workers may even prefer a day on a job not requiring much use of their minds. Another possibility is that *physically* or *mentally handicapped persons* might be given simple jobs. For example, deaf *individuals* hired as mail handlers can be effective workers and are not distracted by their environments.

Imaginative managers can develop many more innovations to make jobs more interesting, including temporary transfers and special projects. However, job enrichment to be successful must have the support of top management and likewise be accepted by workers at all levels. Considerable education of supervisors and employees is essential if programs are to succeed. Stumbling blocks exist when supervisors fear that such programs may threaten their decision-making authority. Programs viewed by employees as deceptive management schemes designed solely to increase their workloads are also unlikely to succeed. A *climate of trust and understanding is essential* for the effective use of morale-building techniques.

trust is essential

Current Industrial Programs

Why is "our business is different" a negative attitude?

Let us now examine a few of the specific programs that have been tried, some with outstanding success. Managers who are reluctant to change tend to react to examples of new programs with the cliché, "Our business is different." Although every business *is* different, a closed mind often prevents management from recognizing significant similarities. A more constructive approach might be to ask, "In what way is our business similar?" Examine some of the examples that follow and consider ways in which these approaches might be modified for your particular industry.

Volvo and Saab

The automobile industry in Sweden before the 1970s had been suffering considerably from labor difficulties. Many workers did not enjoy industrial jobs. One-third of them left every year, and absenteeism rates were especially high. Management discovered that assembly-line jobs were just too dull so, after some serious experimentation, significant organizational changes were made during the early 1970s.

Volvo, a Swedish firm manufacturing automobiles, aircraft, and heavy equipment, completed two new automobile plants in 1974. They cost about 10 percent more than the usual factory because of a new concept in the automobile industry: they were designed for people. The new factories, for example, have different styles of interiors. One has

Are Swedes spoiled, intelligent—or both?

five hexagon-shaped buildings constructed to please workers. Working spaces have been painted with bright colors and large windows provide natural lighting.

How do *worker teams* tend to enhance morale?

For the purpose of enriching jobs, each worker, instead of performing a single repetitive task, is a part of a *worker group*, or *team*, which is responsible for its own part of the automobile, such as the gear box, the brake system, or the steering mechanism. On some teams each member changes jobs every day to reduce monotony. Two workers in the Volvo plant have even been placed on the twelve-person board of directors. In the company's Göteborg headquarters, most private offices have been replaced by open work areas to facilitate greater contact between white-collar and executive personnel.

At Saab, another Swedish automobile manufacturer, teams are now making decisions that foremen used to make, such as when to schedule rest breaks and whether to work a little faster in the morning so that they can rest in the afternoon. At Saab's automobile engine factory near Stockholm, for example, individual teams perform the whole assembly of each engine, and the group is personally responsible for its own work. The managements at both Volvo and Saab have been enthusiastic about the results thus far. Saab made its work teams a selling point in the United States with their advertisement, ''Bored people build bad cars. That's why we're doing away with the assembly line.'' (See figure 9–1.)

Bell System

The Bell System in Virginia conducted experiments that, instead of involving assembly-line workers, were concerned with clerks, telephone operators, and installers. One of the major changes related to telephone installers, who previously had been members of a pool. Each installer was put in charge of *all the work for a specific area*. Morale of the workers is reported to have risen substantially as a result.

Telephone operators within the Bell System used to behave like robots; the standard way of doing everything allowed little room for individuality. When anything unusual or interesting happened, the employees had to turn callers over to their supervisors, many of whom paraded anxiously behind the operators. The company changed conditions so that now there is only one supervisor in each section whose primary job is to assist operators with calls they cannot handle. According to Bell management, service has improved, turnover and absenteeism have dropped, and the morale of the operators has risen.

Gaines Dog Food

Industrial democracy, another name for job enrichment, started in 1971 at the Topeka, Kansas, factory of the Gaines Dog Food Company. The

Bored people build bad cars. That's why we're doing away with the assembly line.

Working on an assembly line is monotonous. And boring. And after a while, some people begin not to care about their jobs anymore. So the quality of the product often suffers.

That's why, at Saab, we're replacing the assembly line with assembly teams. Groups

of just three or four people who are responsible for a particular assembly process from start to finish.

Each team makes its own decisions about who does what and when. And each team member can even do the entire assembly singlehandedly. The result: people are more involved. They care more. So there's less absenteeism, less turnover. And we have more experienced people on the job.

We're building our new 2-liter engines this way. And the doors to our Saab 99. And we're planning to use this same system to build other parts of our car as well.

It's a slower, more costly system, but we realize that the best machines and materials in the world don't mean a thing, if the person building the car doesn't care.

Saab. It's what a car should be.

There are more than 300 Saab dealers nationwide. For the name and address of the one nearest you call 800-243-6000 toll free. In Connecticut, call 1-800-882-6500.

Figure 9-1. Saab's job enrichment selling campaign in the United States.

firm, like Volvo and Saab, uses the team approach. The team members set up their own job and work rotation assignments. The workers determine quality control, maintain the machinery that they themselves operate, and share the unpleasant tasks.

When a job within a group becomes vacant, the team members interview every new applicant. There are usually between six and seventeen persons on a team. When personnel problems occur, the team holds meetings to work out solutions. The team leader's principal purpose is to motivate and direct rather than to supervise so that he is more like a member than a leader. Psychological distance is at a minimum. During the first two years of the experiment, production rose by 30 percent and turnover was favorably low. The firm, in order to enhance morale, even allows reasonable amounts of horseplay.

Summary

During the present decade, workers have attained *higher educational levels* and managers have displayed *increased awareness and concern* for the morale of their workers.

Morale, a condition related to the attitudes of employees, can be influenced by factors both *on and off the job*. Managers should continually be on the lookout for the *warning signs of poor morale* in order to prevent the deterioration of a healthy organizational climate. Among the more important signs of worsening morale are: *higher rates of absenteeism, tardiness, turnover, strikes and sabotage*, and *lack of pride in work*.

Morale can be measured and evaluated in ways ranging from *informal observation* to *formal morale surveys*.

Rapidly expanding numbers of organizations have in recent years initiated new programs of *job enlargement* and *job enrichment,* sometimes called *industrial democracy*. In general, workers seem to develop greater feelings of satisfaction when their jobs *avoid monotony* and offer some degree of *challenge. Teams* or *work groups, job rotation, social contact, music, rest* or *exercise breaks* can help relieve some of the boredom and prevent low morale. Flexible working hours and job sharing are fairly recent innovations intended to make work more enjoyable.

Essential to the success of any or all of the programs that may be developed is an *acceptance* by both the workers and the management along with a *climate of trust and understanding* between them.

In the next chapter, we turn to a topic that can also exert significant influence on morale: the problem of administering change and its effects on the equilibrium of organizational members.

Terms and Concepts to Remember

Morale	Questionnaires
Turnover rate	Descriptive surveys
Morale surveys	Objective surveys
Interviews	Worker alienation

Job enlargement	Flexitime
Whole job concept	Job sharing (twinning)
Job enrichment	Job rotation
Industrial democracy	

Questions

1. What are some possible exceptions to the generalization that productivity tends to follow morale?
2. Explain the following statement: ''Employee perception tends to influence morale.''
3. What major job characteristics seem to contribute toward boredom and alienation among workers?
4. What are some suggestions that you might offer to a young supervisor about to conduct his or her first interview?
5. Assume that you have been assigned the responsibility to develop a highly enriched job in your particular field. What changes would you be likely to make?
6. What are the key factors to consider when administering morale surveys?
7. Critically evaluate the following statement: ''All individuals in organizations would prefer to have their jobs enriched.''

Other Readings

Ford, Robert N. *Motivation Through Work Itself*. New York: American Management Association, 1969.

Garson, Barbara, *All the Livelong Day: The Meaning and Demeaning of Routine Work*. Garden City, N.Y.: Doubleday, 1975.

Montagu, Ashley. *The Humanization of Man*. New York: Grove Press, 1962.

Suojanen, Waino W. et al, eds. *Perspectives on Job Enrichment and Productivity*. Atlanta: Publishing Services Division, Georgia State University, 1975.

Sutermeister, Robert A. *People and Productivity*, 2d ed. New York: McGraw-Hill, 1969.

Torbert, William, and Rogers, Malcolm P. *Being for the Most Part Puppets: Interactions Among Men's Labor, Leisure, and Politics*. Cambridge, Mass.: Schenkman, 1973.

Widick, B. J. *Auto Work and Its Discontents*. Baltimore: Johns Hopkins University Press, 1976.

Applications

The Dull Letters Case

The Cowboy's Fund Insurance Company, a large organization in Bangor, Maine, has a stenographic pool consisting of more than forty persons. Many of the company's letters are of a technical nature, dealing with such matters as subrogation, reinsurance, and co-insurance clauses. Most of the stenographers are not highly versed in the complexities of insurance jargon. In an attempt to improve efficiency, management established a system of standardized paragraphs covering nearly every topic about which customers or agents might enquire.

The stenographers new duties include reading the customers' questions and then inserting the "proper" paragraphs into formal letters with standardized styles for opening and closing. The letters are then turned over to the supervisor for signature.

Absenteeism and turnover in the stenographic pool have been considerably higher than in any other department. The atmosphere among the employees appears to be extremely tense. Some employees frequently burst into heated arguments. Customers regularly complain about errors in their correspondence.

Questions

1. What appears to be the main problem?
2. Assume that you have been requested to improve productivity, accuracy, and morale among the employees. What specific changes would you make? How would you introduce the changes?

The Fifty Percent Tellers

Penny Nichols is a teller at the shopping center branch of the Inanout Bank. There are nine tellers, eleven operations workers, and five management employees at the branch. The tellers are considered to have more responsibility than operations workers and thus are on a higher salary scale. Except during the peak transaction hours, only three tellers are stationed at the customer windows. When Penny and the other tellers are not doing window duty, they perform a myriad of random tasks as assigned by one of the managers. Most of these tasks involve assisting the operations workers and include working the safety deposit vault, handling various types of correspondence, check processing, and inter-bank transactions. In this branch approximately 50 percent of each teller's work day is spent performing teller duties.

Recently during a rest break, Penny and her teller co-workers were discussing the random tasks they are directed to perform. They noted that the managers have no apparent system for assigning random tasks. They also noted that the operations employees often resented their assistance. Further, some tellers felt the random tasks were assigned just to keep them busy. Penny related their feelings to one of the managers, who said he would discuss it with the other managers.

Questions

1. Does the branch have a morale problem? Explain your answer.
2. What should the managers do about the feelings as revealed by Penny?
3. What should Penny and the other tellers do next?

When you finish this chapter, you should be able to:

1. **Explain** the importance for managers to anticipate the need for change before crises arise.
2. **List and describe** the major causes of employee resistance to change.
3. **Restate** in your own words at least seven suggestions for managing change more effectively.
4. **Support,** with illustrations, an argument in favor of the need for increased social change by corporations.

Time changes everything except something within us which is always surprised by change.
—Thomas Hardy

Change alone does not beget progress, but without change there can be no progress.
—Anonymous

"You know, you just get familiar with one process, and then those white-collar turkeys upstairs up and change it on you. Shoooot! I think they're just tryin' to play games with our minds!"

Attitudes like this one are not particularly uncommon among workers in organizations. The introduction and administration of change is probably one of the most *difficult* tasks managers must face, since employees, regardless of their positions or educations, tend to resist alterations in their work environment.

However, the administration of change is probably one of the most *important* tasks managers face, since conditions in the world of work seldom remain static. The sage Greek philosopher, Heraclitus, once said, "There is nothing permanent except change." He went on to declare, "You should not step twice into the same river." One of his wise Greek friends, Cratylus, added, "And you could not step even *once* into the same river!" These are fairly abstruse remarks, so reread them if they didn't make sense immediately.

How do the words of Heraclitus and Cratylus relate to the world of work?

In this chapter we will expose you to some of the principal problems associated with organizational modification. The chapter is divided into four major sections:

1. The effects of change.
2. The natural resistance to change.
3. The effective management of change.
4. The need for social change.

The Effects of Change

Unfortunately, change often occurs only *after* management recognizes that conditions are in a state of crisis. A more rational and usually far less costly approach is for leaders to attempt to anticipate the need for change and to develop creative innovations *before* serious problems evolve.

The Need for Anticipation

Why should management attempt to anticipate the need for change?

Far too frequently, managers in organizations have not set aside the necessary time for analyzing changing conditions or attitudes, and have suddenly found themselves right in the middle of severe complications. Managers, as we have already noted, must learn to delegate routine matters so that they can utilize more of their time for planning necessary changes. The conditions discussed in the previous chapter as being symptoms of poor morale, such as high turnover or absenteeism, can often be anticipated and prevented before their occurrence.

As a result of the lack of innovative management, some firms run into serious financial difficulties. Whenever possible, the need to change with the times (or even before!) should be anticipated, and management should attempt to implement these changes before the crisis stage is reached.

For example, automobile manufacturers, such as Hudson, Packard, and Studebaker, failed to keep pace with changing public tastes after World War II, and as a result no longer produce automobiles in the United States. With the exception of American Motors Corporation, automobile manufacturers in the United States were slow to recognize the public's inclination toward smaller cars. Consequently, for several years, firms from Europe and Japan carved gigantic slices out of the American market.

Much of the racial strife that took place in the streets and institutions of America during the 1960s could have been anticipated and prevented—a few national leaders tried, and failed—if relevant and humane changes related to the *causes* of unrest had been made before the explosive release of tensions. Instead, the lack of foresight by those charged with managing our society resulted in brutal loss of life and excessive destruction of property.

Another example: the words of numerous scientists and oil company executives had fallen on deaf ears long before the fourth Arab-Israeli conflict, the Yom Kippur War of 1973, because Americans refused to believe that the supply of the world's natural resources was limited. Suddenly, however, in late 1973 when gasoline stations started displaying signs declaring "Out of gas," Americans quickly had to change many of their habits and values. Once again, change did not take place until after we had entered the crisis stage.

The Rip Van Winkle Effect

Try to imagine that you had fallen asleep between the years 1969 and 1979. Upon awakening and observing the changes that had occurred since you originally assumed a Rip Van Winkle posture, you would probably feel alien and shocked by what you saw. During those ten years,

235

however, the rest of the world did not doze. On the contrary, numerous changes took place: people's appearance, values, peace "breaking out" in Vietnam, Arab states assuming a dominant position in international economic affairs, the United States dropping to sixth place among the world's nations in per capita income, availability of resources, "creeping metrication" (gradual switchover to metric system), galloping inflation, music styles, radically different climate on college campuses, and the digital watch, CB transceiver, and electronic TV game crazes.

future shock

In a sense we have all been subjected to the Rip Van Winkle effect. Change has occurred so rapidly in our society that our ability to cope with it has not kept pace with the changes. Such was the theme of a best-selling book by Alvin Toffler, *Future Shock*, a term that has become part of the American language. Toffler defined it as "...the dizzying disorientation brought on by the premature arrival of the future."[1] He feels that future shock may well be the most important disease of tomorrow. Have you been vaccinated yet?

The Natural Resistance to Change

Why learn about the concept of change?

Regardless of our attitude toward change, the likelihood of our having any success in attempting to prevent it is negligible. A safe prediction is that change *will* continue to take place all around us in the future. Perhaps more rational than the attempt to prevent the unpreventable, therefore, would be the attempt to learn more about change so that we can deal more adequately with its effects.

Why do so many individuals tend to fear and resist alterations in their environments? In the next section we attempt to answer this question by examining some of the more common attitudes and conditions that often retard or obstruct the introduction of change, including:

1. Personal attitudes.
2. Training and environment.
3. Financial reasons.
4. Alterations in one's social life.
5. Habit.
6. Natural fear of the unknown.
7. Fear of change.
8. Myths.

Personal Attitudes

Change affects different people in different ways. How individuals respond to particular changes is significantly influenced by their *personal*

[1]Alvin Toffler, *Future Shock* (New York: Bantam Books, Random House, 1970), p. 11.

attitudes. Some individuals seem to thrive on change while others react negatively to the mildest modification even when the change is beneficial. In general, people tend to operate in a state of equilibrium. When this equilibrium is upset, as in the case of a change in their working environment, there is a *natural tendency to resist such change*.

For example, before 1972, the attitude of many American people toward China was exceedingly unfavorable. Accurate information about the people of China was largely unavailable in the United States. Many Americans assumed that most Chinese people walked around with pigtails dangling from their heads, chipped front teeth protruding from their sinister mouths, and rags sloppily wrapped around their swollen dirty feet.

Then, in 1971, there was a ping that was heard around the world: the sound of a table tennis game. An American Ping-Pong team had been invited to participate in a tournament in China. The publicity surrounding this game helped to shape new attitudes among Americans. Shortly thereafter, in February 1972, former President Nixon made an official visit to China, one that received extensive worldwide television coverage, and almost overnight Americans began to learn more about present-day China than ever before. A seemingly insignificant event, therefore—a Ping-Pong game—had substantially affected the perception of the American people, whose attitudes changed with amazing rapidity. Similar changes in American attitudes toward Cuba began to take place in 1977 as the Carter administration attempted to break down the long-standing barriers that resulted from years of little communication and exchange between the United States and Cuba.

Sometimes individuals balk at change because they do not want to exert what they feel to be the *extra effort* necessary to learn new things. For example, a boss might want to surprise his or her secretary with a new and modern electric typewriter. The secretary, however, may be enraged upon discovering that the old familiar manual typewriter is gone.

Sales representatives whose firms have developed new items designed to assist their customers are sometimes startled at the discouraging response they receive from their accounts. Some employees even perceive changes as threats to the security of their jobs or as added burdens to their "already over-burdened workloads."

Training and Environment

Other significant influences on either the receptiveness or resistance to change among individuals relate to their backgrounds. Parental influence, for example, is often considerable. Some child psychologists contend that the first six years of a person's life determine much of what follows; these are the highly formative years. It follows, therefore, that the *religious and educational training* of young children would also tend to influence their attitudes toward new and different experiences. Training and environment influence perception, which in turn affects people's attitudes toward any change they may confront.

Among the attitudes that were changed by former President Nixon's visit to China was that of the Americans toward Chinese medical practices. Acupuncture, the Chinese practice of inserting special needles into the body to cure disease or relieve pain, had previously been denounced by the American medical profession as something approaching witchery. Suddenly acupuncture became the new rage in medical journals. Clinics specializing in needlework began to spring up throughout America. Both *training and environment*, as you readily can see, substantially influence a person's response to change. *Leadership*, too, is a part of the environment of employees and can likewise influence attitudes.

training and environment

leadership

Financial Reasons

Why might changes appear to threaten the pocketbook?

Workers may not work for bread alone, but a major cause of their resistance to change is the fear of losing their *jobs*, their primary source of *income*. For example, workers, when new and more efficient processes are introduced, sometimes perceive the changes as threats to their jobs. In some instances, workers feel so threatened by the changes that they attempt to sabotage the process or product. Many such feelings are unfounded, however, and can be placated if the change is introduced with greater sensitivity by managers. More effective ways to introduce and manage change will be discussed later in this chapter.

Alterations in One's Social Life

A result of change that is easily overlooked by management is its effect on the social lives of employees. Even college instructors can be affected. For example, assume that you are a member of the business department of a college and have been an instructor of accounting for ten years. One semester, the head of your department decides to rotate teaching responsibilities among the various instructors in order to "enrich" their jobs. You are assigned to teach three sections of bookkeeping rather than your usual accounting for the forthcoming school year.

Some instructors might welcome the change. However, many of your personal friends are CPAs, and you perceive the change as a reduction of your status. Sometimes seemingly insignificant changes can affect the self-esteem of employees or their standing with their co-workers, families, and friends. A person's *self-image* can be threatened by certain changes.

Some organizational changes require that employees move to a different community. Such uprooting of one's family can influence the worker's morale. Children must transfer to new schools, and the entire family must leave its friends behind and cultivate new acquaintances. To some, such situations are exciting and challenging; to others, they are threatening.

Should talking be permitted during working hours?

Other types of changes can break up established patterns of *social interaction* or *conversation* on the job. A change from bench-work to assembly-line production, for example, might have the effect of eliminating the informal communications system among the employees. Such a change might be resented by some workers.

Habit

Have you ever tried to quit smoking?

Do you ever feel you're in a rut? Do you travel to work or school in precisely the same way each day, after hurriedly devouring a breakfast identical to the one you ate yesterday morning? Habits seem to make life less threatening and more comfortable. Things always seem to have been better ''in the good old days.'' Sometimes, however, we become so accustomed to doing things in a particular manner that we fail to recognize that there may be better ways.

For example, many organizations require their field personnel to submit regular written reports to their managers. In time new forms are developed that may partially overlap or even duplicate other forms. The coincidence sometimes goes unnoticed. Employees who question their superiors about the necessity of such duplication may be told, ''Well, we've always done it that way.'' Even when forms or processes are changed and improved, there is often a resistance to the new—the old way usually seems more comfortable and predictable.

**How many
prunes in a kilo?**

Habit also works on a national level. Americans, for example, are experiencing the effects of change as a result of the passage by Congress in August 1972 of the Metric Conversion Act, which calls for a gradual conversion to the metric system over a ten-year period. Although most of the world already uses the simpler and more logical metric system, such a change will require a massive educational push. Persons accustomed to thinking in terms of inches, feet, and yards, instead of in centimeters, meters and kilometers, have already suggested that the change must be communist conspired! Other have blamed the capitalists who ''are going to force us to buy a liter of paint for the price of a quart!'' (which may not be too painful since a liter is slightly larger than a quart!).

Many American firms have already begun to use the metric system, so their employees have had to learn some new ''new math.'' General Motors Corporation and Ford Motor Company, for example, started a gradual shift to the metric system in 1973. The American drug industry and medical profession have long been on the metric system.

Natural Fear of the Unknown

**Why do people
tend to fear
the unknown?**

Fear of the unknown is probably one of the basic causes of resistance to change. Change begets uncertainty, an uncomfortable situation to say the least. And uncertainty sometimes begets pressure to prevent change. Carefully read the words of warning by David McCord Wright from *Democracy and Progress:*

> From freedom and science
>   came rapid growth and change.
> From rapid growth and change
>   came insecurity.
> From insecurity
>   came demands which ended growth.
> Ending growth and change
>   ended science and freedom.

Workers often fear change because they do not understand how the change might affect them; they fear, quite naturally, the unknown.

Insurance companies have capitalized on the public's fear of the unknown and its desire to reduce uncertainty. When you buy a house, for example, you have suddenly acquired a risk. There is the chance, or fear, that your house may be destroyed by fire or some other peril. The payment of a *certain* number of dollars—the insurance premium—transfers the burden of the risk to the insurance company. In the event of fire, you are reimbursed for roughly the amount of your loss. You have reduced the fear of uncertainty.

Similarly, the manufacture of devices to prevent crime and to detect smoke and fires became growth industries during the 1970s because of prevalent fears of the unknown. American society had changed drastically. So intense was the desire for security that many families barred the windows on their houses and installed expensive and complex electronic alarms costing thousands of dollars. During the cold war of the 1950s, a mild American panic caused some families to buy underground atomic bomb shelters—some of them with picture windows!

Fear of Change

Is fear frightening?

The *fear* of change can sometimes be as upsetting as the change itself. For example, in organizations rumors of layoffs could cause premature resignations or other types of undesirable behavior. People frequently react more to what they *feel* the effects of the change will be than to the change itself.

While editor of a ship's newspaper, a young sailor once started a near panic by publishing a special April Fools' Day issue. Each article began with exaggerated statements about imminent changes and ended with the statement that the columns were false. Apparently many readers didn't glance at more than the first few paragraphs. One article, for example, falsely reported that the ship, which ordinarily seldom left its berth at New London, Connecticut, was to change its home port to Reykjavik, Iceland. Although few men were acquainted with Reykjavik, near panic ensued. Some individuals went so far as to cancel their weddings. One fellow was in tears after reading the article.

Franklin D. Roosevelt touched on this type of reaction in his inaugural address in 1933 when, referring to the numerous and recent bank failures, he asserted, "We have nothing to fear but fear itself."

The Effect of Myths

Do myths make life easier or more difficult?

Superstitious beliefs or myths can cause resistance to change in some individuals. For example, workers who believe that a particular ethnic group is naturally lazy or smells different may resist any moves to integrate *any* members of that group into the work force. In the late 1960s, Washington state construction workers from Seattle and Tacoma marched on the state capitol in Olympia in protest against the hiring of black trainees on public projects—all the while sporting tiny American flags on their hard hats.

Another example of blind faith existed in a large printing plant bindery where a worker operating a large paper-cutting machine refused to use the safety feature designed to protect the operator's fingers. The man argued that he had faith that God would watch over him and protect him while he was operating the machine and therefore, did not have to use the feature. One day the cutter amputated his right hand.

The late John F. Kennedy skillfully summarized the concept of belief in myths when he declared:

> The great enemy of the truth is very often not the lie
> —deliberate, contrived and dishonest—but the myth
> —persistent, persuasive, and unrealistic. Too often we
> hold fast to the cliches of our forebears. We subject all facts
> to a prefabricated set of interpretations. We enjoy the
> comfort of opinion without the discomfort of thought.[2]

The Effective Introduction of Change

**How can change
be introduced
more effectively?**

managing change

Now let us turn to the crux of the matter, the way in which change can be introduced more effectively. We have already learned that most individuals tend to have a natural resistance toward change. Therefore, the *manner in which managers introduce change*, regardless of how ideal it might be, *largely determines the success of their efforts*. By applying some basic concepts, managers can improve their track records. Some important considerations for leaders to keep in mind when introducing change are as follows:

1. The change must be useful.
2. The manager should be empathetic.
3. The change must be communicated.
4. Employees should participate where possible.
5. The benefits should be stressed.
6. Timing should be considered.
7. Change should be gradual.

The Change Must Be Useful

utility

Any leader attempting to introduce change into the organizational environment should make special efforts to see that the affected individuals understand its utility. Workers who see no valid reason for a new situation will tend to resist it. They may feel that the change occurred ''just for the sake of change,'' rather than for any logical reason.

---

[2]From a commencement address at Yale University on June 11, 1962.

242

The Manager Should Be Empathetic

A manager's perception of change in a particular work situation is not as important as the workers' perception of it. Managers should strive to employ *empathy* by asking themselves, ''How might my subordinates see and react to this change?''

The Change Must Be Communicated

In chapter 3 we discussed methods for ensuring more effective communication throughout organizations. As we discovered, any modification of the work environment tends to upset the equilibrium of those affected. Consequently, *clear and effective communication* of any change and its probable effects is essential if the work force is to accept it. Many changes are likely to be naturally resisted, but if changes are not understood, the chance of resistance increases considerably.

clear and effective communication

For example, assume that sales in your organization have been outstanding during the past three years and are expected to continue at similar brisk rates. Your plant, situated at New Bedford, Massachusetts, is currently operating at the limit of its capacity. Output, however, has not been able to keep pace with current and anticipated demand.

You and the other managers of the organization decide to open another plant in Oakland, California, thus having production and marketing operations close to two major population centers. Since the expansion doesn't directly affect workers at the New Bedford plant, no official notification or announcement is made to the employees there.

However, rumors start flying through the New Bedford plant. The employees believe that the real purpose of the new Oakland plant is to *replace* the existing facility, not merely to supplement it. Morale rapidly takes a nosedive, and the union representatives call for a strike. Considerable damage is done to the morale of the employees before the true facts of the move are made known.

The illustration may seem exaggerated but, for example, in 1971, Firestone Tire and Rubber Company proposed to the local United Rubber Workers' Union in Akron, Ohio, that a group of employees work a five-day, forty-hour week. Until then, the employees had been working the industry's traditional six-hour day, six-day work week, which was originally instituted by management during the depression as a device to spread the work. The workers rejected the company's proposal, so Firestone moved its operations to a new plant in Tennessee.[3]

You can see, therefore, that when the reasons for impending change are not made clear by management, distorted interpretations of its pur-

[3]''Joining to Save Jobs in Akron,'' *Business Week*, 12 February 1972, p. 44.

pose and effect can easily be made. Resistance often develops because the employees misunderstand.

Employee Participation

participation

Perhaps you can now see how many of the concepts discussed in previous chapters can be applied to the problems of administering change. In chapter 7, for example, on styles of leadership, we suggested that a participative approach can effectively be used to develop support for organizational plans and objectives. When one has to make changes, the use of *participation* can especially be helpful because of its tendency to achieve greater commitment on the part of the participants. Employees tend to be more anxious to see self-imposed innovations succeed than those that appear to be forced upon them.

You may have learned that in mathematics the whole of an object is *equal* to the sum of its parts. In human relationships, however, the whole is often *greater* than the sum of its parts. Ideas developed by the *entire group* (the supervisor and his or her workers) working together are frequently *more effective* and *creative* than those developed by one-person rule.

How does "getting it off your chest" help?

Managers should encourage subordinates to air their complaints and feelings about proposed changes. Changes generally seem much less threatening when employees can discuss them openly.

Benefits Should Be Stressed

Hey, boss— what's in it for me?

"What's in it for me?" may sound like a selfish remark, but is likely to be on the minds of workers about to be subjected to organizational change. A new process, for example, may be useful because it reduces labor, but how are the persons who previously had been providing the labor likely to be better off? Might they not perceive the labor-saving process as a threat to their economic security? Do you recall Maslow's *security* need in the levels-of-needs concept? To optimize the acceptance of change, managers should try hard to reveal how the *persons affected by the change may benefit*.

The Problem of Timing

When is the best time to introduce change?

The question of *timing* is as important in managerial activities as in athletics. Leaders should attempt to choose a good time for the initiation of any change. There is no one perfect time to introduce a modification into the work environment, and the best time is likely to be influenced by:

1. The current human relations climate in the organization
2. The nature of the change itself
3. The type of industry

Too Much Too Soon

Why is gradual change usually more acceptable?

We've already discussed the concept of *future shock,* the problem of change that occurs more rapidly than people's ability to absorb and cope with it. The concept can be applied to organizations as well. *Gradual change* is more likely to be accepted than excessively rapid change. Individuals seem to need ample time to become accustomed to new situations. Managers should guard against the tendency to introduce too much change too fast for employees to absorb and accept.

The Need for Social Change

How has management's role changed?

social change

Historically, the managers of many organizations have refused to engage in another important area of change—*social change*—until *after* their backs were, so to speak, up against the corporate wall. In chapter 17 we will explore in more depth the topic of organizational responsibility toward society. In any chapter on change, however, there should be some mention of the need for management to recognize its changing role in relation to society as a whole.

One example of changing attitudes could be observed in a recent Salaried Employees Quarterly Report, in which the president of Dow Chemical Company, E. B. Barnes, made an official statement that he would have been unlikely to have made in the 1960s. He stated, "We have dedicated ourselves to providing equal opportunity for all employees. Any supervisor who supervises minority or women employees who cannot count at year-end on having developed some of them for promotion has not done his job."

Organizational Responsibility

preventive action

There are many areas in which management has continued to lag behind the need for social change, such as in hiring the handicapped and the aging, or in showing greater concern for the environment. Change *after* a crisis has occurred usually is far more costly to organizations than *preventive action* taken before the onset of a problem.

Private organizations that are slow to recognize the need for change in their attitudes toward social responsibility are, in effect, extending an invitation to the federal government to expand its involvement in the private sector. Corporate leaders should favor voluntary rather than compulsory action on their part.

Summary

Change affects different individuals in different ways, but in general most people tend to feel a natural resistance to change.

There is a continual need for managers to be sensitive to the desirability of innovation before conditions in the organization deteriorate to the crisis stage.

Individuals tend to resist change for numerous reasons. An alert and cautious management should attempt to familiarize itself with the major causes of resistance in order to manage change more effectively and beneficially for both management and workers.

The smoothness (or friction) with which managers introduce change is influenced significantly by their awareness and application of specific behavioral concepts. For example, the use of employee participation in planning changes tends to achieve greater commitment on the part of the participants.

Private organizations are responsible not only to their owners (the stockholders), employees, and customers, but also to society in general. Although substantial social change continues to be necessary, many corporations have in recent years displayed increasing social concern, especially in such areas as the hiring of minorities.

A private sector that refuses to recognize its responsibilities to the general public will probably witness increased involvement in its affairs by the federal government.

Terms and Concepts to Remember

Future shock   Managing change
Natural resistance to change   Social change

Questions

1. How does the concept of future shock relate to organizational change?
2. How do personal attitudes influence attempts by managers to introduce change?

3. List some of your own experiences that might cause you to resist certain types of change.
4. How would your attitude toward a new labor-saving process differ if you were working part- instead of full-time?
5. What sort of changes in your job might affect your self-esteem and the esteem in which your family and friends hold you?
6. Why are habits once established so difficult to break?
7. What causes some people to hold steadfastly to myths?
8. Assume that you are a manager in a firm that plans to move to a new building in the suburbs. Outline some major considerations for effecting this change with a minimum of friction among employees.
9 Do you feel that private organizations should pay the costs of social change? Explain your position.
10. Why might some workers view as threatening a sudden enlargement of their jobs?

Other Readings

Dalton, Gene W.; Lawrence, Paul R.; Greiner, Larry E. *Organizational Change and Development*. Homewood, Ill.: Irwin-Dorsey Press, 1970.

Davis, Keith. *Human Behavior at Work*. 5th ed. New York: McGraw-Hill, 1977.

Fabun, Don. *Dimensions of Change*. Beverly Hills, Calif.: Glencoe Press, 1971.

Leavitt, Harold J. *Managerial Psychology*. 3d ed. Chicago: University of Chicago Press, 1972.

Schon, Donald A. *Technology and Change*. New York: Delacorte Press, 1967.

Toffler, Alvin. *Future Shock*. New York: Bantam Books by arrangement with Random House, 1970.

Applications

The Station Harry Print Shop

In Oakland, California, is a printing plant that prints letterheads, business cards, office forms, and other miscellaneous items for sale to business organizations on the west coast.

The shop is a combined lithography and printing shop with approximately eighty workers assigned to the plant. The plant is one of five division plants situated in various parts of the United States.

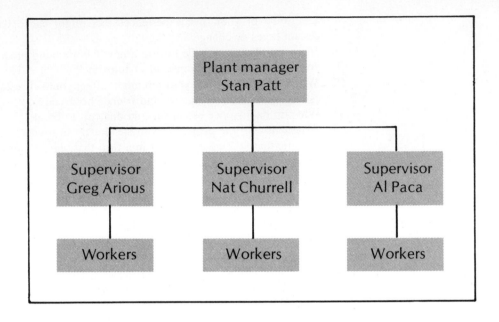

Organization of plant. On this page is an organizational chart of the Oakland plant at the time a particular problem developed.

In charge of the entire plant in 1978 was Stan Patt. Assisting him in the management of the plant were three supervisors: Greg Arious, in charge of the Letterpress Department; Nat Churrell, in charge of the Bindery Department; and Al Paca, in charge of the Lithography Department.

Waste and pilferage. Probably as a result of a free-rein type of leadership climate in this organization, there was considerable waste and pilferage of materials. A large number of the workers were known to be running small businesses during their spare time by printing office forms, letterheads, and other forms for local merchants at low cost and with company supplies.

The working hours of the print shop were from 8:00 A.M. until 12:00 noon, and from 1:00 P.M. until 4:00 P.M. Most of the workers, however, were ready to depart for lunch by 11:30 A.M. and nearly all of them had cleaned their machines and were ready to leave by 3:30 P.M.

Excessive costs. Operating costs of the plant became so outrageous that officials in the home office became aware of the excessive waste. A manager from the Atlantic division, Mr. Rip A. Sunder, was transferred to the Oakland plant to take remedial action. Sunder was known among home office officials as a "trouble shooter" or "efficiency expert." He came in as Stan Patt's immediate superior.

Sunder could readily observe the excessive waste of materials and time that was going on in the shop. Consequently, he decided to administer a number of changes in order to improve the efficiency of the plant.

The administration of change. The major changes made by the end of Sunder's first week were that:

1. The lunch hour was shortened to thirty minutes so that the workers were not permitted to leave until 12:30 P.M.
2. The workers could not begin to clean up their machines until 3:50 P.M.
3. Materials had to be checked out in the name of the user. For example, if a press operator had to run a printing job requiring 4,500 impressions, he or she was allowed to check out 4,505 sheets of paper. If more was needed because of problems or damage to some sheets, the operator had to sign a form and give a reason.

Effects on morale. The morale of the workers changed considerably within two weeks. They continually grumbled about the new working conditions and stated regularly that they felt Sunder did not know what he was doing. The behavior of the workers began to change markedly. For example, one of the usual jobs in the bindery was that of collating the pages. Approximately fifteen workers would walk round and round a large rectangular table on which were spread the printed pages to be gathered into books or pamphlets. The job of gathering the pages was monotonous and repetitive, and previously the workers had engaged in idle conversation to help pass the time.

About three weeks after Sunder's arrival, the workers started spontaneously shrieking and catcalling as they walked around the table. They then began to imitate various jungle animals and birds, dogs, cows, and any other animal that came to mind. One man began to use roller skates in his journey around the table. Although morale had apparently become worse as the days passed, productivity rose to an unprecedented level.

Additional unrest. Joe Kerr, an informal leader in the Bindery Department, decided that some sort of action must be taken to embarrass Sunder. One afternoon, during a lull in the jungle calls, Kerr shouted to the other bindery workers, "Hey, we don't have to put up with this stuff. Let's plan a wildcat strike." Informally, the workers agreed. However, a number of the married workers were unable to convince their spouses of the merits of the plan.

Mr. Forallus requested to assist. Morale became progressively worse in the plant. Frequent arguments began to break out among the workers and occasional fist fights developed. Productivity started to decline. These developments became known to Mr. Ben E. Fishel, who was in charge of the home office. Fishel decided to request assistance from Harmon E. Forallus, a graduate of the Harvard School of Business, who was directed to report to the plant in order to attempt to resolve the conflict. The initial action taken by Forallus was to call a meeting of all print shop personnel including Mr. Sunder.

> *Forallus:* My name is Harmon E. Forallus, and I've called this meeting because I've heard of some extremely serious problems developing in this division. In all my days in the printing business—ever since my graduation from Harvard—I've never heard of a print shop being run like this one.
>
> I've been informed by various sources that the morale in this plant is extremely low. There is no excuse for a condition like this to develop. Mr. Sunder, aren't you aware that there is a positive relationship between morale and productivity? If you continue to cause morale to be low, what do you think is going to happen to the productivity of your shop? (Mr. Sunder's head began to quiver nervously, his left cheek suddenly developing a tic).
>
> Sunder, this is no way to run a print shop. These men are human beings. Don't you realize that? Unless you can enlist their cooperation, you are never going to have a smooth and effective organization here. There have to be some changes, Sunder. I am going to be assigned to this plant for approximately two months and I want to see some results! Do you understand?

> *Sunder:* (Still twitching) Yes, Mr. Forallus.

Sunder's reaction. Some of the men later expressed concern for the treatment Sunder received during the meeting. Others believed that such action was long overdue.

The following day Sunder suspended all of the changes that he had made. Morale soon rose to a relatively high level again, and the workers once more became unconcerned with waste.

About a week later, Mr. Sunder cut off his right index finger while operating an electric band saw at home.

Questions

1. What is your reaction to the actions taken by Sunder and Forallus?
2. What better approaches might both individuals have taken?

The New Broom Case

It was one year ago when Chan C. Lore accepted the leadership of the sprawling Capitol City College District. Chan formerly headed a smaller district in a neighboring state where he successfully kept within his budget while providing excellent academic services to the community.

Chan's former college district consisted of a single college with various off-campus sites. Chan's new position in Capitol City required him to administer three colleges, four campuses, and a number of off-campus sites. The Capitol City District has been functioning on a decentralized basis since its inception fourteen years ago. Evening college is considered a separate facility, independent of the day college.

Chan recently received district board approval to reorganize the entire college district. He is taking advantage of the numerous retirements and resignations that occurred recently to restructure each college, placing his personnel selections into key positions. New positions have been established and staffed from both inside and outside the district. Chan has combined the day and evening colleges, apparently in order to deal more effectively with personnel who are trying to form a union.

The new centralization of the district will create a greater supervisory control of instructor assignments and appraisals. In the past, instructors have had personal contact, on almost a daily basis, with a coordinator in their discipline. The coordinator worked at the direction of the department chairperson. Now, under the reorganization, both the coordinator and the department chairperson positions have been abolished. The chairperson has been replaced by an area dean with responsibilities in several departments, and the coordinators appears to be a thing of the past.

The general structure of the reorganization has been announced, but details and future plans are a matter of conjecture. Area deans, associate deans, assistant deans, and other administrators are still "feeling their way" and are apparently not privy to the master plan. The faculty has recently learned of the changes and, in general, they strongly oppose the plans for reorganization.

Questions

1. In your opinion, why didn't Chan C. Lore announce more details or plans concerning his plans for reorganization?
2. What do you feel are the principal reasons why many of the instructors are resisting the changes?
3. At this late date, how can Chan C. Lore gain acceptance of the change and attempt to raise the morale of the instructors?

three

Constraints on Organizational Behavior

When you finish this chapter, you should be able to:
1. **Identify** the major reasons for the development of unions.
2. **Recognize** why some employees **do,** and others **do not,** choose to join unions.
3. **Contrast** the reasons for the passage of the Wagner and Taft-Hartley Acts.
4. **Explain** how some managers tend to perceive unions.
5. **Describe** some of the past non-human relations reactions to unionism.
6. **Give** a general definition of collective bargaining.
7. **Describe** a typical grievance procedure process.
8. **Restate** the purposes of mediation and arbitration.

Wherever we find competing self-interests,
we find the possibility of conflict.
It was out of such conflict
that the trade union movement was born.
And it was to resolve
the issues such conflict produces
that collective bargaining was developed.
—AFL-CIO statement on unions

"Which side are you on, boys? Which side are you on?" These are words from a tune which was chanted many years ago by avid and enthusiastic supporters of the labor union movement. The song, never quite one of the "disco favorites," is rarely heard these days, but its philosophical melody lingers on in the tendency for organizational members to identify exclusively with either management or labor—an unwholesome attitude denoting that each is on opposite sides of an economic fence.

However, all organizational members are just that—*members of organizations*—and, if the needs of both management *and* labor are not integrated with each other's, both, in all likelihood, will find themselves far worse off. Labor strife can be costly for all parties involved.

Regardless of your own attitudes toward either management or labor, both groups are quite likely to be with us for a considerable time. As a result, an understanding of the purposes and functions of labor organizations is essential, especially if you are—or intend to be—a manager who must deal with union members and officials.

The purpose of this chapter, therefore, is to present some background information designed to assist you in understanding the labor movement. In addition, we shall examine some of the principal reasons that some organizational members *do* and others *don't* join unions, and then discuss two key laws dealing with management and labor that significantly affect the human side of organizations. Finally, we shall explore some of the previous non-human relations approaches to unionism, and conclude by examining the collective bargaining process and the grievance procedures typically employed by management and union members.

The Extent of Unionism

We discussed formal and informal work organizations in earlier chapters. We also examined the importance of needs satisfaction to the individual

**Why did
unions develop?** employee. Unfortunately, the needs of many organizational members have often gone unsatisfied in the past and, as a result, workers have created a second organization—one *within* the primary organization— with which managers must deal. Secondary organizations—known as *unions*—basically have emerged as a result of the unsatisfied needs and wants of workers.

What Is a Union?

union defined A *union* may be defined as *an association of workers that has as its major objective the improvement of conditions relating to employment.* "Conditions," one of the words in our definition, can represent anything from higher wages to a day off with pay on an employee's birthday.

**In what way
are union and
business or-
ganizations similar?** The purpose and goals of both business *and* labor organizations are probably more *similar* than different. For example, both groups consist of individuals coordinated for the purpose of *maximizing returns* and *minimizing losses*. The returns with which directors and managers of corporations are concerned are *profits,* while the returns to union members consist of *wages and benefits*, which are dependent on profits. Both the managers of corporations and the officials of unions will fail to maintain their positions of leadership and influence unless each continues to satisfy the felt needs and desires of those to whom they are primarily responsible.

**What can result
from strife
between manage-
ment and labor?** History cites numerous examples of clashes between management and labor that have been excessively costly, not only in terms of economic resources but sometimes in terms of lives lost. Substantial production was lost in 1946, for example, during which *113 million workdays* were lost because of strikes. In more recent times, the number of strikes grew annually from 1960 until 1970. This annual growth saw the number of work stoppages rise from 3,300 in 1960 to 5,700 in 1970 before declining to 5,010 in 1972. Against the backdrop of the energy crunch that started in 1973, and with high unemployment and prices increasing more rapidly than the wages of many workers, economic issues once again have risen to the forefront of union demands. Inflation typically brings about greater concern among the rank and file about wages and tends to create additional human relations problems for managers. As evidence, there were 5,600 strikes in 1976, over half resulting from wage disputes.

Scope of Present-day Unionism

**Why is "only 25 per-
cent" not insignificant?** In 1977, there were approximately 24 million union members in the United States, which was only about *25 percent* of the total labor force. But "only 25 percent" is not insignificant, since virtually all employees in basic industries, such as steel, aluminum, railroads, and rubber, are unionized. There have been slight declines in the total union membership of workers in the *manufacturing* and *construction* industries, which is not

particularly surprising in light of technological labor-saving techniques that have been developed in recent decades.

A current trend, however, is the increase in the numbers of union members in *nonmanufacturing* industries. *White-collar workers,* such as clerical, technical, and professional workers, joined unions in record numbers during portions of the 1970s. *Agricultural workers, government employees,* and *women* have also accounted for much of the recent growth in union membership. The implication is that managers of the future will continue to need an understanding of workers' organizations along with an awareness of effective human relations techniques that can be followed in dealing with members of union organizations.

Employee Associations

A number of persons who tend not to identify with the labor movement *per se* belong, instead, to groups called *employee associations*, which, in many instances, perform virtually the same functions as unions. Employee associations have often been formed by persons, such as white-collar workers and teachers, who may have certain philosophical objec-

tions to being identified as members of union organizations. The general philosophy of both employee associations and unions—needs satisfaction—is similar, although some associations do not engage in formal collective bargaining; instead, they may be concerned primarily with welfare and recreation.

The trend during the 1970s has been for employee associations, especially those in public employment, to expand their collective bargaining activities, and in many cases they have been successful in competing with unions for the right to represent public employees on such matters as hiring policies, disciplinary practices and other administrative rulings. Although still relatively new, in 1977 public employee associations had nearly 3 million members—making them an increasingly significant element of labor relations.

Why Workers Join Unions

There is no single reason why 24 million persons in today's work force have joined unions. Some of the more common reasons are:

1. To secure certain types of employment
2. To prevent inhumane treatment of workers
3. To enhance employment situations
4. To attain more power

Let's take a brief look at each of these reasons

To Secure Employment

Some individuals join unions because they have no other choice; membership is a requirement for regular employment in certain types of occupations, such as in the printing or construction trades. Although legally no one has to be a member of a union at the time of hiring (such *closed shops* are now technically illegal), in many instances the only manner in which he or she can obtain employment is through a union hiring hall. In other cases, a person must join a union within a specified time, usually between sixty and ninety days after being hired, a situation known as a *union shop*.

Old-time union members sometimes have become upset with younger members who believe that union dues should not have to be paid in order that jobs may be held. The older members contend that the younger workers are not aware of the struggles that were necessary for the attainment of present wages, benefits, and working conditions, that they are only interested in "slot-machine unionism," since they "don't do much more than pay dues and grumble."

In some instances, there exists what is known as an *agency shop*. This means that the employee is not required to join a union but must pay regular dues and fees because he or she receives the benefits of labor–management contract negotiations.

To Prevent Inhumane Treatment of Workers

Greater awareness of human relations techniques by management, as we already have learned, is relatively new. There is a fair chance that unions would never have achieved their importance had the human relations movement begun about the same time as the industrial revolution. Instead, however, workers used to be regarded as things of not much greater value than pieces of leather, things that had no rights, that could either work at their own risk or look elsewhere for employment. Managers of yesteryear tended to have a "love-it-or-leave-it" attitude toward workers and their jobs.

Working hours were long and conditions often hazardous. Fringe benefits and job security were unknown. Many factories were unaffectionately termed "sweatshops," places where workers frequently were treated with little humane concern. If workers were injured on the job —even due to the negligence of the employer—courts usually would rule against the worker by applying the "assumption of risk doctrine," which meant that employees worked at their *own* risk. Workmen's compensation laws were unknown before the 1930s.

Many workers felt that the only way in which such inhumane treatment could be overcome was through the development of collective action made possible by unions. Workers, however, underwent years of

closed shops *illeg.*

union shop *legal*

agency shop

just cause

How does the way workers are treated influence their attitudes toward unions?

arduous struggle before attaining many of the ''rights'' that seem commonplace today. But even though considerable progress has been made in the area of industrial management, a sizeable proportion of the work stoppages in 1976 were human relations oriented, and included issues of plant administration (25 percent), job security (5 percent), and miscellaneous working conditions (4 percent).

To Enhance Employment Situations

How do unions satisfy higher-order needs?

The needs of workers seldom remain static or satisfied. We have learned that as one need—such as economic—becomes reasonably satisfied, other needs, such as social, safety, or self-esteem, become increasingly important. Many workers believe that only through membership in unions will they be able to accomplish gains in such areas as enhanced working conditions and increased welfare and security benefits.

To Attain More Power

How do workers gain power through union membership?

Individually, many workers contend, a person wields little in the way of bargaining power with employers. If an individual lathe operator, for example, were to withhold services (attempt a solo strike), his or her employer would probably find an immediate replacement. A greater balance of bargaining power tends to develop, however, when most of the workers under union direction collectively threaten to withhold their services from their employer. This need or desire for greater power on the part of some workers is what motivates them into becoming union members.

Why Workers Don't Join Unions

Three out of every four persons in the labor force do not belong to unions. Let's look now at some of the reasons why some persons choose not to join employee organizations.

No Felt Need—Identification with Management

Why have white-collar workers tended not to identify with labor unions?

Certain individuals *perceive their situations to be better* than they would be if they were represented by unions. In the past, white-collar workers have tended not to identify with ''labor.'' The *route to management positions* has usually been through white-collar jobs, a condition that has often induced office workers to feel that their joining a union would put them on the other side of the fence from management and thus reduce their chances for advancement to more responsible positions. It has customarily been easier for white-collar workers to relate to management since they usually dress like the boss rather than like the workers in the plant. This identification with management may be changing, however, since a trend is indicated in the rising number of white-collar workers joining unions.

Cultural Backgrounds

cultural backgrounds

Some persons tend not to relate to unions because of their *cultural backgrounds*. Perhaps they were raised in a family atmosphere, or worked in business situations, that strongly opposed the labor movement.

Satisfied Basic Needs

satisfied basic needs

Other employees feel that their *basic needs are reasonably well-satisfied*—they live in middle- and upper middle-class neighborhoods—and do not identify with the so-called "struggle of the working class."

Attitudes change, however, and occasionally persons who previously shunned unions for various reasons decide to become members. Among the conditions that at times have caused some workers to change their minds about unions are: organizational changes that seem threatening, layoffs, pay cuts, rapid inflation that diminishes the real value of paychecks, and peer pressure.

Key Management-Labor Legislation

It is beyond the scope of this book to discuss labor-management legislation or history in any detail. Nonetheless, managers and union officials should attempt to familiarize themselves with important legislation affecting labor relations, especially the *Wagner* (1935) and the *Taft-Hartley* (1947) Acts, along with some of the attitudes toward the labor movement that preceded these acts. The following section, therefore, is intended to provide you with a brief synopsis of labor history.

Pre-1930s Repression

Before the 1930s, American employers made few efforts to update their ideas of industrial and human relations. Workers had virtually no voice in influencing their working conditions, wages, hours, and benefits. Managers of the period probably would not have predicted that one day their successors would sincerely be concerned with such concepts as job enrichment, morale, positive motivation, and effective communication.

repression phase   The period preceding the 1930s is sometimes called the "repression phase" of the labor movement. Since most judges came from wealthy, propertied backgrounds, they tended to represent the establishment of the times. Union leaders argued that some of the rights of the establishment should belong to the working class. The courts, however, didn't agree, and customarily ruled against labor unions.

As is frequently the situation during healthy economic periods, union membership declined during the prosperous 1920s. The pendulum swung to a more favorable side for unions during the Great Depression of the 1930s, a period during which unemployment was exceedingly high, at times approaching 25 percent of the labor force. Sentiment, as a result of this difficult period, shifted toward the working people.

The Supportive 1930s

Before the depression of the 1930s, various attempts to provide workers with the right to bargain collectively with their employers had been thwarted by the courts, which generally ruled supportive labor legislation to be unconstitutional. In 1935 an act referred to as the *Magna Carta of organized labor* was passed, resulting in a period that could be termed the
Wagner Act of 1935   *supportive phase*. Popularly known as the *Wagner Act*, but officially called the *National Labor Relations Act of 1935*, the legislation, in effect, virtually ordered management to stop interfering with the efforts of unions to organize workers. The act was so sweeping in its coverage and intent that it required managers to re-evaluate their approach to industrial relations.

The heart of the Wagner Act is Section 7, which conveys the basic philosophy of the act.

> Employees shall have the right to self-organization, to form, join, or assist labor organizations, to bargain collectively through representatives of their own choosing, and to engage in concerted activities for the purpose of collective bargaining or other mutual aid or protection.

National Labor Relations Board   The *National Labor Relations Board* was given the responsibility of carrying out the provisions of the act.

The Restrictive 1940s

A pendulum seldom remains in one position, nor do industrial relations generally remain static for long. A prodigious shift in public sentiment
Why did the pendulum swing away from unions in 1946?   away from unions resulted from the numerous work stoppages that occurred in 1946. A wave of strikes in that year resulted in time lost amounting to 113 million workdays. Major industries, such as coal and public

utilities, were paralyzed during parts of 1946, which significantly influenced the attitude of the general public toward labor unions.

After the congressional elections of November 1946, those who were elected sensed public sentiment to favor restrictive labor legislation. So

Taft-Hartley Act

on June 23, 1947, over President Truman's veto, the *Taft-Hartley Act,* officially termed the *Labor Management Relations Act of 1946,* became law. Union people referred to it unaffectionately as the "Slave Labor Relations Act."

By its key provisions, the Taft-Hartley Act:

1. Enabled the United States Attorney General to request an eighty-day court injunction (so-called "cooling off" period) to prevent strikes that "imperil the national health and safety."
2. Outlawed the closed shop, secondary boycotts, sympathy strikes, and jurisdictional strikes.
3. Outlawed featherbedding (an employer's having to pay for services not performed).
4. Prevented the charging of excessive initiation fees or dues.
5. Prevented the refusal of labor to bargain in good faith with management.
6. Permitted states to outlaw union-shop contracts, which require workers to join a union (states can pass so-called "right-to-work" laws).

The Wagner and Taft-Hartley Acts are not the only laws with which responsible organizational members should be acquainted, but they are two of the most significant affecting labor relations.

Management Perception of Unions

If you were a manager, how might you perceive unions and their activities in relation to your responsibilities with an organization? Naturally each manager would tend to view unions somewhat differently, depending on his or her own experiences, background, and attitudes. Let's look now at some of the more typical ways in which some managers perceive employee groups.

Threat to Decision-Making Prerogatives

competition for rights

Some managers tend to perceive unions as a form of competition; that is, they feel that union officials are attempting to take away some of the *rights of managers to make decisions.* In a sense, this attitude of we-versus-them does not make for a healthy organizational climate and tends to make contract renegotiation time exceedingly difficulty.

263

Reduction of Efficiency and Productivity

deterrent to efficiency and productivity

Management sometimes perceives unions as a *deterrent to efficiency and productivity*. Managers sometimes feel that unions have been too successful in establishing work rules that have tended to restrict output and thereby increase production costs. Some union contracts have restricted, for instance, the width of paint brushes, so that houses take more strokes and more time to be painted.

featherbedding

Jobs have changed and sometimes require fewer persons, but some unions have demanded that workers who are no longer needed continue to be included as a part of a worker group. The practice of a union's requiring an employer to pay for labor not performed has been termed *featherbedding* and has been declared an unfair practice by the Taft-Hartley Act. Featherbedding continues, however, in various subtle ways in some industries.

Splitting Employees' Loyalty

division of company loyalties

Managers sometimes feel that unions have tended to *divide employees' loyalties* to the primary organization. Employees, for example, are directly responsible to their supervisors in the formal organization, but may bypass them during disputes by communicating directly with shop stewards or union officials. Managers, therefore, sometimes feel that unions tend to complicate the formal organizational structure by introducing "outsiders" into the decision-making process.

Let's now look at certain obstacles that some managers have attempted in previous eras to throw in front of the labor movement.

The Non-Human Relations Approach to Unionism

Before the supportive 1930s, workers found it difficult to form unions, not only because of the unsympathetic attitudes of the courts, but also because of some of the vicious anti-union techniques of management. Among the more common non-human relations approaches were: firing "labor agitators," blacklisting, locking out workers, and requiring yellowdog contracts. A brief summary of these techniques follows.

Firing "Labor Agitators"

firing troublemakers

Fairly often, before the general acceptance of collective bargaining as an industrial way of life, management would dismiss employees who attempted to organize other workers. Such employees generally were branded as ''troublemakers,'' or ''labor agitators,'' and often found difficulty obtaining employment elsewhere since they were placed on the management *blacklist*.

MEDIATION)
ARBITRATION - BINDING

Blacklisting

blacklists

Managers, in order to discourage workers from attempting to form labor organizations, generally placed the names of such ''troublemakers'' on lists referred to as *blacklists*. Managers typically would exchange their lists with managers from other firms in order to prevent union organizers from obtaining employment. Since unemployment insurance was nonexistent at the time, such an approach tended to discourage many would-be organizers from actively supporting the labor movement.

Lockout

lockout

Another approach used to combat the threat of unions was the company *lockout*, which in one sense is a strike called by management. When workers collectively threatened to withhold their services, or made what was believed to be excessive demands, management could merely lock the doors of the plant and not let the workers return to work until they rescinded their requests. The workers seldom had ''staying power'' (economic resources) equivalent to the company's and thus would be unable to remain away from work for long. The lockout, therefore, served as an effective—although counterproductive—means of crushing the demands of workers' groups.

SUNSHINE

Yellowdog Contracts

yellowdog contract

Another pre-1930s approach was to require newly-hired employees to sign a statement that they agreed, as a condition of employment, not to join a union. The ''agreement'' was referred to as a *yellowdog contract*, but was later outlawed by the Norris-LaGuardia Act of 1932.

Paternalism and company unions may be included in a list of management attempts to discourage unionism. However, as we have seen, many of the techniques have since become history and are no longer considered acceptable by most present-day managers.

Collective Bargaining

Lives have been lost and valuable property destroyed in the past when workers were attempting to achieve the right to engage in collective bargaining with their employers. Until passage of the Wagner Act in 1935, most legislation favoring collective bargaining was declared unconstitutional by the courts.

Today, however, there is little question that conflict arising over the right to bargain collectively is basically a thing of the past. As a result of law and custom, there have developed procedures, accepted by management and labor, for collective bargaining.

Individuals whose awareness and frames of reference are limited to what they view on the evening news might be surprised to learn that most collective bargaining agreements (contracts) are developed in an aura of mature, peaceful negotiation, rather than through the violent strife often observed on the news media. There are approximately 150,000 collective agreements in the United States today. Of these, 147,000 were successfully negotiated without any work stoppage taking place. Since smoothly negotiated contracts are seldom newsworthy, however, the bulk of publicity has naturally been heaped upon the conflict situations.

Purpose of Collective Bargaining

What is collective bargaining?

Collective bargaining is the process of negotiation between representatives of management and of labor for the purpose of establishing a written agreement with a minimum of conflict. The negotiators attempt to reach agreement on wages, working conditions, and other matters of their choosing. The written contract is legally binding on both the employer and the employees.

Both sides are expected to approach the bargaining sessions in "good faith" after each has engaged in extensive research into the strengths and weaknesses of the other's bargaining position.

The Necessity for Compromise

How might each side gain by an attitude of compromise?

Few agreements between labor and management are reached without a fair amount of give and take on the part of the participants. Generally, each side initially approaches the bargaining table with certain generalized demands. Subsequent sessions usually find the representatives presenting a more detailed schedule of demands including certain minor items that can be traded away later if necessary.

A Continual Process

Why is negotiation really a continual process?

Although formal negotiations customarily take place only once a year, or possibly every two or three years, managers should recognize that the bargaining process is not terminated after the formal contract has been drawn up by the lawyers and signed by the representatives. Interpretation of the terms of the contract usually takes place year-round.

The contract, remember, is merely a set of symbols, and although the wording should be as understandable as possible, the contract has been prepared by humans and thus must be interpreted by humans, not all of whom perceive the same symbols in precisely the same way.

Do all people read a contract in the same way?

Grievances occasionally result from different interpretations of the contract and, as we have learned, the cost of some types of conflict can be excessive. Some work stoppages, for example, not only have cost the adversary parties millions of dollars in sales and profits and thousands of dollars in wages, but also have sometimes hit the public directly in the form of strikes that cause garbage to pile up on the streets, transportation systems to be disrupted, burials temporarily made impossible, mail prevented from being delivered, and air travel plans interfered with.

Management representatives must strive to communicate effectively the intended meaning of the contract to other managers, supervisors, and foremen. Union representatives have similar responsibilities to communicate the terms of the contract to the rank and file union members if the agreement is to be accepted readily. Rejection of negotiated agreements by rank and file members used to be rare, but has become more common in recent years. During some years, for example, as many as one out of every seven negotiated agreements was rejected by union members, possibly implying less than desirable communications between union officials and union members.

Boulwarism—Past and Present

What might be a union reaction to "Boulwarism"?

Until 1973, General Electric Company employed a bargaining technique with union representatives referred to as "Boulwarism"—which meant that the management representatives would make an offer that *they* felt was fair and leave virtually no room for negotiation. The technique was named for Lemuel Boulware, who was for a long time the company's industrial relations manager.

The approach was similar to styles of negotiation prevalent during the 1930s and proved excessively costly for General Electric in 1960, during which the approach backfired and resulted in a 100-day work stoppage by some 150,000 production workers. It appears, however, that Boulwarism was given a decent burial in May 1973, when General Electric executives updated their bargaining style by displaying a willingness to bargain more flexibly.

Modern management negotiators have learned that the hard-line Boulwaristic approach is generally far less effective than skillful bargaining techniques and a willingness to be flexible.

Grievance Systems

What is a *grievance*?

Included as a part of most labor-management agreements are specific procedures for the handling of grievances, or disputes. *Grievances are feelings, sometimes real, sometimes imagined, that employees may develop toward their employment situations.* Disputes over the interpretation of contracts, for example, can erupt at any time, although carefully worded and clearly communicated agreements can lessen the frequency of such grievances. Nonetheless, the opportunity for employees to assert their individuality through the mechanism of the *grievance system* can enhance industrial relations substantially by providing a safety valve for tensions arising in disputes between management and workers.

Grievance Procedures

grievance procedure

Grievances can be handled on an informal basis. Generally, however, a specific *grievance procedure* is incorporated into the formal contract between labor and management. This process provides a means for equitably analyzing alleged, and correcting actual, wrongs felt by organizational members.

Fair and consistent methods of supervision can lessen the frequency and intensity of complaints and formal grievances. Even in the best-managed companies, however, there will probably be occasions on which workers feel that they have been treated wrongly by their managers.

**What can
an employee
do if he feels
wrongly disciplined?**

An employee disciplined for smoking in an area designated ''no smoking'' would have a grievance if he or she had seen managers regularly smoking in the restricted area. Through formal grievance procedures, the employee who feels wronged has an official mechanism for challenging unfair or inconsistent assertions of authority.

Grievance procedures are not standardized in all contracts between labor and management, but they follow a similar pattern of between three and six steps.

Grievance Procedure Steps

The written agreement that results from collective bargaining between management and labor representatives ordinarily will spell out the specific steps or procedures to be followed when either an employee or employer has a complaint.

Take a careful look at the following example of a formal grievance procedure actually used by one industry. If you were a manager or union official, you would be expected to understand the process. Read the agreement, and see if you could explain it to other employees.

Section XIX   Grievance Procedures

A. The parties to the Agreement agree that for all differences, misunderstandings, or disputes which arise between Company and Union in regard to wages, working conditions or other conditions of employment, discharge or any other dispute, an earnest effort shall be made to settle any differences immediately as follows:

*supervisor
and union steward*

Step 1. In the event of any disagreement or dispute between Company and any worker, or Union, the matter shall be taken up with the supervisor by the Union Steward within twenty-four (24) hours after the existence of such a dipute is discovered.

*union and
company representatives*

Step 2. In the event that such dispute cannot be settled within one work day, the matter shall be taken up by a Union representative with Company's representative.

submitted in writing

Step 3. If the matter is not settled under Step 2 within two (2) work days, the matter in dispute shall be reduced to writing and submitted to Company's designated representative and a Union representative.

to arbitration

Step 4. If the parties have not resolved a dispute arising out of the interpretation of this agreement within seven (7) days, the matter shall be submitted to an arbitrator selected by Union and Company. If they cannot agree on an arbitrator, one will be chosen by the Federal Mediation and Conciliation Service, whose decision on the matter shall be final and binding on both parties.

grievance committee

B. A grievance committee of five (5) workers shall be established by the Union; said committee may participate at any step of the grievance. If the Company requests a meeting of this committee during working hours, Company shall pay the members for their time at their hourly rate or average piece rate.

specific disputes

C. Any disputes arising between Union and Company under Sections I (Recognition), XXV (Strikes, Boycotts, and Lockouts), II (Union Security) or IV (Hiring) shall be taken up directly by Company's representative and Union's representative and shall proceed immediately to arbitration, if said persons cannot resolve the dispute within five (5) days.

payment of arbitrator

D. All testimony taken at arbitration hearings shall be taken under oath, reported and transcribed. The arbitrator's fees and expenses shall be assessed as a part of his award against the losing party as he shall determine the same.

Arbitration and Mediation

You may have observed in step 4 of the grievance agreement that when the parties are unable to resolve the dispute within a specified number of days they may then submit the complaint to *arbitration*. An *arbitrator* is a "disinterested third party," someone not directly affiliated with the company or union, who has been chosen to act as judge in the dispute and to make a decision *binding* on both parties involved in a conflict.

In some instances, *mediation* may be used instead of arbitration. A *mediator* performs a function similar to that of an arbitrator, but his or her role is more one of attempting to *bring together* the two sides involved in a dispute in an effort to effect a *compromise*. The mediator, however, has *no binding authority* but can only suggest solutions to the dispute.

What is the major difference between an arbitrator and a mediator?

Frequent Grievances—A Warning Sign

Grievances are less likely to occur within organizations that have established healthy human relations climates similar to those we have already discussed. Organizations that have leaders with a sincere interest in understanding the motives, feelings, and sentiments of their employees usually discover that most disputes can be resolved before the first step in a grievance procedure needs to be taken.

What might a high grievance rate indicate?

Companies that experience excessively high grievance rates—say, *more than about 15 grievances per 100 employees within one year*—should recognize such situations as potential warning signs of a deteriorating or unhealthy human relations climate. Such a condition necessitates careful analysis and probable remedial action by management.

The Need for Mature Leadership

Strife and conflict between management and labor have usually been harmful for all parties involved—including the general public. For example, the threat of a strike in a particular industry can induce the buyers of the product to stockpile the material and possibly look for sources in other countries to assure a stable supply. Irregular domestic purchasing by customers generally creates an unstable employment situation when buyers decide to exhaust their hedged purchases before placing new orders. (Hedge buying and its effects are illustrated in the Application section at the end of the chapter.)

The establishment of such groups as *labor-industry human relations committees,* which communicate on a continual—not merely annual—basis, can assist management and labor in resolving potential disputes before the contracts are due to be renegotiated.

What is needed with increasing frequency is more mature leadership on the part of both groups. When an atmosphere of open communication and mutual trust can be established, both parties should discover that they will gain far more than they will risk.

Summary

Unions, the outgrowth of workers' unsatisfied needs, are secondary forces that alter the formal structure of organizations. Employee associations, often performing functions similar to unions, are becoming increasingly more significant—especially in public employment.

Workers have a variety of motives for joining unions: Sometimes there is no other way to secure a particular job. Additional reasons include the desire to prevent unfair treatment of workers, to enhance employment situations, and to attain more power than can usually be acquired by individuals. Some persons do not relate to unionism and tend to perceive that their own employment situations are enhanced by not being union members.

Two legislative acts of special significance to the labor movement are the Wagner (prolabor) and Taft-Hartley (promanagement) Acts.

A major concern of the labor union movement has been the attainment of the right to bargain collectively for the purpose of improving working conditions and benefits. Management and union representatives should approach the bargaining table with attitudes of good faith and with a flexible and sincere willingness to compromise.

Grievance systems are customarily established during contract negotiations and provide a systematized means for the equitable resolution of disputes between management and workers. When conflicts cannot be resolved within a specified number of days, complaints may be submitted to and settled by arbitration, during which a third party determines the outcome of the dispute.

High grievance rates, a sign of an unhealthy human relations climate, are less likely to develop in industries where both management and labor representatives display a sincere desire to communicate on a continual basis.

Terms and Concepts to Remember

Union	Blacklisting
Employee association	Lockout
Closed shop	Yellowdog contract
Union shop	Collective bargaining
Agency shop	Grievance
Wagner Act	Grievance procedure
National Labor Relations Board	Arbitration
Taft-Hartley Act	Meditation
Featherbedding	

Questions

1. If business and labor organizations have similar goals, as indicated in the chapter, why do they sometimes conflict?
2. Is the fact that union membership is only about 25 percent of the total labor force conclusive evidence that unions lack significance in America? Explain.
3. Why do some persons prefer to identify with employee associations rather than with unions?
4. In cases where labor has not been successful in negotiating for a *union shop,* why might union officials favor the *agency shop* as a reasonable compromise?
5. What sort of economic climates led to the passage of the Wagner (1935) and Taft-Hartley (1947) Acts?
6. Explain the following sentence: "Collective bargaining is really a continual—not a once-a-year—process."
7. In what way is "Boulwarism" not actually *collective* bargaining?
8. What is the principal difference between *arbitration* and *mediation*?

Other Readings

The American Worker. Washington, D.C.: U.S. Department of Labor, 1976.

Best, Fred, ed. *The Future of Work*. Englewood Cliffs, N.J.: Prentice-Hall, 1974.

Brody, David, ed. *The American Labor Movement*. New York: Harper & Row, 1971.

Cohen, Sanford. *Labor in the United States*. 4th ed. Columbus, Ohio: Charles E. Merrill, 1975.

Reynolds, Lloyd G. *Labor Economics and Labor Relations*. 6th ed. Englewood Cliffs, N.J.: Prentice-Hall, 1974.

Applications

Crises Bargaining and Hedge Buying

For many years the steel industry had regularly experienced what is termed "crises bargaining" during the periodic renegotiation by labor and management of its collective bargaining agreements. Generally, before each series of bargaining sessions there was the threat of prolonged strikes.

Customers of the major steel firms were well aware of how crippling strikes could cut off their future supplies of materials. As a result, many customers engaged in "hedge buying," that is, stockpiling steel products during the six or eight months prior to the beginning of the negotiating sessions for the new contracts.

A vivid example of the problem occurred in 1971, during which the industry ran at top volume to fill stockpiling orders. That year also witnessed steel imports from foreign sources rising to their highest level in history.

Contrary to customers' expectations, however, there was no strike in 1971. Customers lived off their stockpiles during the rest of the year after the collective bargaining agreement was signed, and, as a result, one hundred thousand steelworkers were laid off, some for as long as eight months, and more than forty thousand jobs were completely eliminated. Steel companies estimated that they lost sales worth approximately $80 million in 1971.

Question

Assume that you are a negotiator for the United Steel Workers Union and that you would like to avoid crises bargaining in the future because of the extreme economic hardship that it places on your members. What proposals would you make to your fellow union officials and to management representatives in order to avoid such discord in the future?

Let's Organize

The Kramer Co. assembles and distributes a nationally advertised brand of lawn mowers and a successful, but less well-known, golf cart. Two years ago a new plant was opened in Austin, Texas. The site was selected because there was an ideal vacant plant and a number of available workers who were unsympathetic to unions. Shift work was available and many university students worked full time because the pay was good.

In the first two years of operation, sales increased and the plant expanded to employ 450 people. Unions became interested in organizing the new plant, and the Teamsters began to pass out literature at the plant gate. The first organizing meeting was so sparsely attended, however, that the union dropped its campaign. Rumor circulated that employees were "turned off" by national press and TV coverage of alleged misuse of pension funds by top union leaders.

The avowed policy of management was to prevent unionization. Management stepped up its campaign of "union avoidance." The Kramer Co.'s personnel practices included:

1. Plant wages that were above average for the area. A merit system was implemented to reward better workers, and management hoped that supervisory merit ratings of assembly workers were impartial.
2. All open jobs to be posted in a job bidding system. From the workers who signed the bid sheet, jobs were assigned on the basis of seniority plus ability to do the open job.
3. Overtime that was voluntary. Some workers who wanted lots of money could work 20–30 hours per week overtime; other workers refused overtime.
4. The attempt to assure fair treatment. No employee was to be discharged before the plant manager conducted a "fact finding" study.
5. Making every effort to avoid class distinctions. For example, ensured benefits were the same for all the employees—there were no reserved parking privileges, etc.
6. Management participation with hourly employees on teams in softball and bowling leagues.

To the surprise of management, they received a mailgram from the Allied Industrial Workers Union announcing the names of twenty-six employee union organizers. Top management first believed there was a mistake. Soon they discovered that organizing meetings were being held at a nearby motel. Management's mood shifted from disbelief to disappointment. After all, had they not provided good jobs and good pay to 450 people?

Charlie Charge, shipping supervisor, informed Art Able, plant manager, that an employee in his crew had punched the time card for Delbert Drew, one of the announced union organizers. Quite by accident, Charlie had noticed that all the workers were clocked in, but in fact Delbert was not at work. A half hour later Delbert arrived at work, and when confronted by Charlie, Delbert admitted that his pal Eddie had punched his time card because Eddie knew Delbert had overslept. Learning of these facts, Art said, "Delbert is a trouble maker and both employees are to be fired."

Delbert and Eddie filed an unfair labor charge with the National Labor Relations Board, stating that they were fired for union organizing. They reported that Charlie knew workers in his crew punched each other's clock cards regularly, and no employee had ever been disciplined. Management had rules listing reasons for discharge. One rule concerned "Falsification of Company Records." Management reasoned that a false punch on the clock card could result in payment for time not worked.

An underground newspaper published an interview with Delbert. Questioning was pro-union. Delbert's responses alleged "favoritism" and "lack of impartiality" in wages, hours of work, and promotions. Management decided not to answer the criticisms.

The NLRB Administrative Law Judge heard both sides of this unfair labor dispute. On findings of fact, he ruled that Delbert and Eddie were discharged for union organizing activities, which is an unfair labor practice. Delbert and Eddie were ordered reinstated to their jobs with back pay.

Questions

1. Do you agree or disagree with the ruling to reinstate Delbert and Eddie? Why?
2. What is your opinion of the company's "union avoidance" policy?
3. Would you recommend a grievance procedure? Why or why not?
4. Why might assembly workers who are well paid and have opportunities to bid for better jobs feel a need to organize unions?
5. After Art learned the "facts," what alternatives might he have considered?
6. If you were a union organizer, what employee needs would you focus on to win worker support for your union?

When you finish this chapter, you should be able to:
1. **Contrast** the difference between prejudice and discrimination.
2. **Recognize** the nature of prejudice.
3. **List** the major causes of progress for minorities during the past two decades.
4. **Describe** the need for self-identity among minorities.
5. **Explain** how the attitudes of whites have for many years tended to retard the progress of minorities.
6. **List** some of the major ways in which government and business can improve the chances for equity in employment opportunities in American society.

> With a little understanding,
> the manager will be able to deal
> with minority people as people, not as
> minorities.
>
> —Robert M. Fulmer

If someone were to ask if you were prejudiced, how would *you* respond? Regardless of your answer, the chances are that you have some prejudices; virtually everybody does.

All prejudices are not necessarily harmful, however. Some of your prejudices may be quite reasonable, excusable, even justifiable. Perhaps they are merely directed toward such things as certain types of food or drink. Assume, for example, that every time you eat an egg prepared in any manner you become excessively sick. Although you are not personally acquainted with every egg on the earth, your past experience with the little oval objects has been such that your generalized antipathy toward eggs is not particularly unreasonable.

Prejudice against food and drink is one thing; prejudice against human beings is, however, quite another, and is frequently beset by erratic emotion, economic discrimination, and sometimes even senseless and bloody violence.

different treatment group

In this chapter we shall explore some of the principal human relations problems concerned with persons who receive *different treatment* for reasons unrelated to their employment situations. "Different treatment" is a politer way of saying "discrimination." Some individuals are treated differently principally because they are a part of a special group. In our diverse society there remains considerable prejudice and discrimination toward groups whose common bond has been an accident called birth.

In the first part of this chapter, we shall investigate the *nature of prejudice* and *discrimination* and discuss groups that tend to be on the receiving end of both. We shall then examine the *quest for self-identity* among minorities, and evaluate a few of the "pacifiers" that have been employed by some organizations. We shall conclude with some specific recommendations for managers who are concerned with *equal employment opportunity* or *affirmative action programs,* along with a topic of current concern—the problem of "reverse discrimination."

The concepts presented in this chapter apply to basically any member of a group that receives different treatment because of factors beyond his or her control. In subsequent chapters we will explore human relations problems related to women, older employees, and those with physical and mental limitations.

The topic of discrimination is in itself an emotional one. Your own background and experiences will influence your perception of the material covered in this chapter. Now let us turn to the nature of prejudice by first developing definitions of the terms *prejudice* and *discrimination* for our use in this section.

The Nature of Prejudice and Discrimination

prejudice is internal

discrimination is external

Are you ever likely to have *all* the facts?

Prejudice is basically an *internal* phenomenon and relates to an attitude of *prejudging*, or *the making of judgments based on insufficient evidence*. If you understand and are reasonably well acquainted with something or someone, in effect you are not *pre*judging.

Discrimination is the *result* of prejudice and is *external*. It is an action directed either *against or in favor of something or someone*.

In many of our daily activities we tend to make prejudgments about situations and people. In the real world of work, decisions must be made or organizations could not function. The pressures of time often do not permit the exploration of all available evidence. However, when we make judgments based on less than complete data, we should leave a margin for error in case the results differ from our expectations. We should at least attempt to withhold our judgments until after we have examined the best available evidence.

Prejudice—An Acquired Habit

How do we acquire prejudice?

According to most studies, prejudice directed against other human beings is a *learned response* and not one inborn in individuals. Parents are believed to be the major teachers of prejudice. Yet, by words and actions, parents can also teach their children to grow up in harmony with people of different races and backgrounds.

As children grow older, they tend to be influenced by their peers. The earliest years, however, are the most significant, according to Dr. Ner Littner, a child psychologist in Chicago, who contends that, "the first six years set the pattern for the child's life." Dr. Littner feels that if adults use prejudice as a means of solving their own personal problems, they will have learned it from their parents or whoever raised them.[1]

---

[1]"How Youngsters Are Taught to Be Bigots," *San Francisco Sunday Examiner and Chronicle*, 19 October 1969, p. 15.

Prejudice in Favor of a Group

**How might you
be "burned"
by prejudice
in favor of someone?**

Prejudice is not always directed *against* others; it can *favor* a particular group. For example, there are certain types of national clubs or groups whose members regard one another as "brothers" or "sisters," even when they do not even know one another. In some instances the "brothers" have little in common other than their club affiliation, which creates a type of prejudgment in favor of some other individuals.

Sometimes people who either possess the same types of sports cars, are members of the same faith, or who have attended the same universities, develop positive prejudgments about each other. These prejudices, too, may well be inaccurate, and personnel managers should guard against succumbing to the "old-school-tie" form of prejudice, as well as to negative prejudice, when interviewing applicants for positions.

Preventive Prejudice

*preventive
prejudice*

**How might preventive
prejudice apply to
your own work situation?**

Some persons engage in an activity that could be termed *preventive prejudice*, which means that they *prejudge the intentions of others and thus attack them on the basis of an often unfounded belief that they plan to attack first.* For example, during the Korean Conflict, some persons argued that the United States should attack China first, before China's "inevitable" attack on the United States. There was no evidence at the time that China intended to invade Long Beach, California, or any other part of North America; nevertheless, an attitude of preventive prejudice prevailed. General Douglas MacArthur was fired as head of the military forces in Korea by President Truman because of the former's attitude of preventive prejudice toward China.

The "Oppressed Majority"

Who is on the receiving end of discrimination in America? One could semantically argue that there really is no such thing as prejudice against a minority in the United States since, collectively, those discriminated against add up to a majority.

The symbols of minority and majority, however, are not as important as the fact that numerous persons in American society are discriminated against in employment as a result of the prejudiced attitudes of some members of organizations.

Who are the "oppressed majority"?

The list of groups on the short end of the employment stick is appalingly long and includes the poor, blacks, Hispanics, Asian, Eskimo and Native Americans, women, the aging, the physically and mentally limited, the obese, homosexuals, and—to a lesser extent—those who belong to certain religions.

Job opportunities for some of the "oppressed majority," however, have improved noticeably in recent decades. Rather than focus on statistics, which frequently do not reveal the entire story, we shall review some of the reasons for the expanded minority opportunities.

Causes of Expanded Opportunities

The sixties could be regarded as a decade of *future shock*, a period filled with one mind-jarring event after another. Among the more significant historical happenings during the period were:

The freedom rides in the South—1961.

The passage of the Manpower Development and Training Act—1962.

The civil rights march on Washington, D.C.—1963.

The assassination of President John F. Kennedy—1963.

The passage of the Equal Pay Act—1963.

The passage of the Civil Rights Act—1964.

The assassination of Malcolm X—1965.

The race riots in Watts—1965.

Racial violence in Detroit—1967.

The passage of the Age Discrimination in Employment Act—1967.

The assassination of the Reverend Martin Luther King, Jr.—1968.

The assassination of the presidential candidate Robert Kennedy—1968.

The demonstrations at the Democratic Convention in Chicago—1968.

What caused the gains of the sixties?

These events are believed by many social observers to have helped set the tone for the increased gains and improved employment opportunities for special employment groups during the seventies. The cliché, ''Time cures all ills,'' had little to do with the improvements. Instead, as we can observe in retrospect, numerous pressures were building up in American society. *No one event* can be given full credit for being *the cause* of the expanding opportunities; instead, a combination of situations operated in a cumulative fashion to influence employment patterns for minorities. Among the more significant forces at work: new legislation, higher educational attainment, protests and demonstrations, guilt and fear, government pressure, and changing hiring practices. Let's briefly examine them.

Laws

legislation

Congress passed some significant laws during the 1960s. The Manpower Development and Training Act of 1962 permitted many individuals to acquire occupational training for the first time. The Civil Rights Act of 1964, with its provisions for equal employment opportunities—Title VII—*prohibited employers, labor unions, and employment agencies from discriminating against persons on the basis of color, religion, sex, or national origin.*

Title VII, Civil Rights Act

What can laws do?

Legislation, of course, cannot alter the feelings of hatred that some individuals might have for others, but it can help to create a climate that makes the unfair treatment of human beings more difficult.

Education

educational level

The *educational level* of white and nonwhite youth had risen. More students were challenging the traditional views of the establishment on a wide variety of subjects ranging from war to environment to racism.

Protests and Demonstrations

protests and demonstrations

Militant *protests and demonstrations* played no small part in the changes of the decade. Although many managers of firms denied that they would alter their hiring practices under pressure or duress, one could readily observe during the sixties and seventies vast changes in the hiring practices of organizations of all types.

Guilt and Fear

guilt and fear

Other possible causes of the rapid changes in the situations of minorities are felt to be both the *guilt* of some persons for the past inhumane treatment of minorities and the *fear* of others that they had more to lose by not initiating fairer employment practices.

Government Pressure

government pressure

The various levels of government spend billions of dollars annually. Many businessmen and women have discovered that to obtain public contracts they must follow equal employment opportunity guidelines. The *government,* consequently, had put *pressure* on many companies to hire minorities.

Fairer Employment Practices

affirmative action programs

And finally, increasing numbers of firms began *affirmative action programs*; that is, they began to hire more equitable numbers of minorities and women by controlling their intake of new employees.

There is little argument that considerable progress was made during the sixties and seventies by groups that have traditionally been treated differently. But if you were a minority person right now, how would *you* answer the question, "Are you satisfied?" Few persons, regardless of their color, sex, or ethnic origin, desire to remain static; they feel that there is usually room for improvement.

Would *you* be satisfied?

Managers, in order to increase their effectiveness, should attempt to develop a better understanding of the feelings and sentiments of minority employees. Why is it, for example, that many individuals have developed a strong sense of pride in their "roots," ethnic origin, or sex? How have attitudes of some white persons influenced the employment opportunities for minorities? Let's now examine some of the factors that have affected the organizational behavior and employment situations of those on the receiving end of prejudice and discrimination.

The Need for Self-Identity

Should blacks try to forget their color?

S. I. Hayakawa, politician, semanticist, and former president of San Francisco State College, has contended that blacks will be able to achieve a greater sanity if they can forget, as far as possible, their color. Hayakawa has suggested, "If you are a biochemist and this is foremost in your self-image, you will expect to be treated as just another biochemist; the self-fulfilling prophesy will operate, and people will in all likelihood treat you as just another biochemist. If you are a parent and expect to be treated as just another parent at a P.T.A. meeting, people will in all likelihood treat you as just another parent, learning meanwhile, that the problems of Negro parents are no different from those of white parents. But if you are a biochemist or a parent and expect to be treated as a Negro, people are going to treat you as a Negro—whatever that means to them.''[2]

Have blacks and most other nonwhites in America ever been permitted to forget their color? Could they forget *even if they wanted to?* Is it reasonable to assume that the white social and business associates of blacks, for example, truly ignore color any more than a person ignores the fact that another individual has a foreign accent or that an automobile is blue, green, white, or black? Individuals need not necessarily see something good or bad when they perceive an object with color, but they *are* likely to see color.

Is white America "color blind"?

Is the economic or sociological position of nonwhites necessarily enhanced by their attempting to forget color? Can they really forget? Hayakawa seems to be ignoring the realities of recent years when minorities have striven to achieve a long-overdue self-identity and a collective pride in the color of their skins. White America does not happen to be "color blind" in its perception of race, so why should blacks and other minorities attempt to forget the unforgettable?

Some of *My* Best Friends . . . .

Would you mind living next to blacks if you were black?

Apparently unknown to numerous whites, however, is that most blacks do not necessarily desire to live in white neighborhoods. Paul Cobb, while a director for Oakland Citizens Committee for Urban Renewal, once explained, ''We black people don't mind living next door to a black family. Some of *our* best friends *really* are blacks! But what we do mind is the lack of opportunity to obtain *decent housing* and *decent job opportunities.*''

Stereotyped Attitudes—Past and Present

Although attitudes have changed substantially in the past two decades, many people still tend to stereotype minorities, sometimes unknowingly. Part of the problem may stem from words having different meanings for different people. For example, some people seem unaware that certain words are offensive to minorities. The world *boy* is disliked by most

---

[2]S. I. Hayakawa, *Symbol, Status, and Personality* (New York: Harcourt, Brace and World, 1963), pp. 77–78.

**"Hey, man—
don't call me boy!"**

blacks. "What's in a word?" you might ask. Well, if you or your ancestors had been slaves and were called "boy" by "the Man"—the so-called Master—regardless of your age, you also might display some sensitivity toward the word. Words are important, and even more important is the feeling of self-respect that most people desire.

Progress . . . but . . . .

We all like to hear that progress has been made in the area of understanding people's needs. Yet, examples of insensitivity continue to surface all around us. For example, while commerce secretary with the Nixon Administration, Maurice H. Stans publicly professed surprise that American blacks were offended by his reference to Africans as "boys." Another member of former president Nixon's cabinet, Earl Butz, while agriculture secretary, was driven from office after having been quoted making racial slurs. And in April of 1977, Billy Carter, brother of President Jimmy Carter, made the following comment to a black city council candidate in Oakland, California: "Well, I hate to say it, but we all have a nigger in the woodpile somewhere."

**Stepping on toes
with a foot in the mouth!**

The Problems of Employment—Are All "Those People" Really That Way?

Minorities have always experienced unemployment and poverty rates substantially higher than the rates for white males. Too frequently, the non-white has not been able to acquire the skill or training for many jobs; to some employers this has been "proof" that the nonwhite lacks the intelligence and ambition of a white person.

**Why haven't
some minorities
acquired skills
and training?**

In some cases, nonwhites *have* lacked ambition and initiative. But before a white person says, "See, I told you so," he or she should try to figure out the cause. Imagine if you and members of your cultural group had been the victims of overt discrimination for hundreds of years—what would your attitudes be likely to be? For centuries, some cultures have been oppressed by overtly discriminating laws, social institutions, behavior patterns, living conditions, distribution of political power, figures and forms of speech, and cultural viewpoints and habits. Even thought patterns have forced blacks, Puerto Ricans, Mexican Americans, Asian Americans, Native Americans, and others into positions of inferiority and subordination.

**There but
for fate
go I.**

Some employers have felt that they couldn't afford to take the economic risks associated with hiring minorities. Their comments have sometimes resembled the following: "Personally, of course, I'm not prejudiced. I certainly don't have anything against hiring any of those

285

people, especially if I could get a good one, but what would my employees or customers think? It's just too risky."

Why is bigotry costly?

Numerous business people have discovered, however, that the risk of bigotry is economically more costly than the risk of racial tolerance. Race riots in the United States, arising out of prolonged frustration, have cost the business community millions upon millions of dollars and, of no lesser importance, lives have often been lost. On some occasions, businesses have been forced to close their doors because insurance has become unobtainable in their "high-risk" communities.

At Least It Was Out in the Open—Overt Discrimination

Although a bloody Civil War was supposed to have abolished that "peculiar institution" called slavery, most *overtly* racist laws and institutions continued for more than 100 years after it ended. Even long after World War II, there existed in the United States legally segregated schools, neighborhoods that excluded nonwhites and Jews, laws prohibiting interracial marriages, and the custom of separate—but *unequal*— public facilities like bus seats, toilets, and restaurant, hotel, and motel accommodations. Even the right to vote continued to be denied to many people.

overt discrimination

Much progress has been made during the past two decades in eradicating legal forms of *overt discrimination*. Most Americans probably agree that deliberate subordination of any minority is improper. Yet, at the beginning of 1977, there was still only one woman and no blacks holding the position of chief executive officer in America's largest 500 industrial corporations. According to a Korn/Ferry International survey of 370 major companies, minority membership on corporate boards actually declined to 13.1 percent in 1976, after a big leap from 10.7 percent in 1974 to 15.1 percent in 1975.[3] "It takes time," consoles the well-meaning nonminority. "I haven't got that much time!" harangues the impatient minority who feels discriminated against.

Sure, but in the long run, we'll all be dead!

The Problems of Institutional Subordination

With the history of oppression experienced by most minorities, it is quite incredible that so many members of special employment groups have advanced as rapidly as they have in recent years. Nevertheless, for many people, the road to opportunity continues to be cluttered and obstructed with subtle—but real—barriers. Discrimination may not be as overt as in the past, but considerable racism still exists in the form of *institutional subordination*. Instead of using color or sex as the basis for making dis-

institutional subordination

[3]"The Changing Fashion in Company Directors," *Business Week,* 14 March 1977, p. 32.

criminatory decisions, other "clear and reasonable" bases related to the proposed activity or right are often used.

Most civil rights groups favor, as do employers, hiring individuals based on their merits and qualifications. Unfortunately, however, there are institutions that succeed in disguising the fact that discrimination continues to exist. For example, assume that an employer needs workers to fill jobs requiring advanced electrical skills. The employer, let's also assume, wants to hire people who are qualified electricians regardless of color or sex.

What happens, though, if the local electricians' union has never admitted blacks, Mexican Americans, women, Vietnamese or other minorities in the past? In such instances, the employer may not be prejudiced, but the very nature of the institution—in this case, a union that has not encouraged minorities to join—perpetuates discrimination. Employers who carefully examine their recruitment policies may discover that unknowingly they have indirectly contributed to institutional subordination.

Quasi Attempts at Equity

pacification

Until relatively recently, much of the employment of minorities has been of the nature of *pacification;* that is, hiring one or two persons for highly visible positions and placing limitations on advancement for the purpose of placating critics of an organization's employment practices. Let's now take a brief look at some of these techniques.

Token Placement

token placement

Some employers apparently attempted to assuage their consciences by engaging in what is sometimes referred to as *token placement,* the assigning of a few, carefully selected minority group workers to highly visible situations and operations and making few or no subsequent additions. Dick Gregory has a joke about the window-dressing (sometimes called "storefront nigger") approach. He stated that he "walked down the street one day and saw a big sign advertising Hertz-Rent-A-Negro!"

Double Standards

special job assignments

job ceilings

Double standards of selection, grievance handling, and discharge operate very often to the disadvantage of minorities. For example, *special job assignments*, which prevent one's exposure to promotional channels, have been common practices of such subtlety as to defy detection. These sometimes serve to justify the existence of *job ceilings* above which minority workers may not be promoted.

job floors   In some instances, *job floors* are established below which minority workers are not employed. These tend to be established in times of crisis, such as a chronic shortage of scientists and technicians, when skilled non-whites are unhesitatingly hired, but the needs of minority job seekers with lower skills are ignored.

"Messin' Around" with Affirmative Action

Years of prejudicial attitudes and discriminatory practices in employment are not easy to eradicate, even with legislation, when management itself is not fully sold on the need to hire minorities. Not surprisingly, affirmative action programs have either been resisted by some firms or misused as justification for certain types of activities. For example, according to a workbook on affirmative action prepared by the National Education Association, some organizations have employed practices that have served to discredit the entire concept of affirmative action. These include:

Disaffirming actions aren't required.

1. The use of affirmative action requirements as an excuse for not employing or promoting white males whom the employer did not want to employ or promote in any case.
2. The confusion of goals with quotas in discussing affirmative action and in attempting to implement it.
3. The playing off of women and minorities against each other—a divide-and-conquer technique (whether conscious or unconscious) that serves to defeat the purposes of affirmative action.
4. The appointment of unqualified or underqualified women and minorities either to promote the reverse discrimination myth or simply as a misguided attempt to comply with federal requirements.[4]

Neglect Can Be Costly

There must be the sincere effort on the part of employers to avoid conditions that will work to the detriment of either the minority people hired or to the organization itself. The lack of positive action can sometimes be costly for organizations. For example, in August 1973, Federal Judge Sam C. Pointer, Jr., ordered the United States Steel Company and three union locals to pay $200,000 to 61 black workers who, in the judge's estimation, might have earned that much if a fair promotion system had been in effect. Black workers at the company's operations near Birmingham, Alabama, had earlier taken the company and several union locals to court.

In other cases employers have hired minorities for specific jobs, failed to train them adequately for the positions, and then fired them for

4 "Affirmative Action: What It's Really All About," *NEA Advocate,* March 1977, p. 5.

incompetence. United States District Judge John Feikens of Detroit, in a case involving Ford Motor Company, indicated that equal employment opportunity requires the *training* as well as the hiring of minorities. And in January 1977, the Children's Medical Hospital Center in Oakland, California, received a court order requiring that a $500,000 training fund be established for minority employees. The fund is intended to support educational training of minority service workers and licensed vocational nurses. An additional $10,000, plus $28,000 litigation costs, was ordered to be paid to the ten persons who won the lawsuit against the hospital.

Positive Proposals

Is there any *one* best answer?

We have learned from our study of perception that not everyone perceives problems in precisely the same fashion. Especially on as chronic and sensitive a matter as minority employment practices there are likely to be various opinions about the "best" solutions. The suggestions made in the following section should *not* be regarded as *the utopian answers* to a complex problem. Instead, it is hoped that such suggestions can serve as a basis on which responsible members of organizations can apply imagination and creativity in order to establish their own constructive policies.

Government Responsibilities

What can the government do?

Government, without excessively encroaching on what some believe to be the prerogatives of the organization, has broad and multifold responsibilities relating to the creation of improved job opportunities for minorities. The federal government can assist the private sector by:

1. Enforcing *equitable legislation* to help maintain the tone established for the elimination of unfair treatment of all persons in employment.
2. Providing the *resources* for training programs.
3. Offering *tax incentives* to employers who cooperate in programs designed to reduce minority unemployment.
4. Developing strong and clear *standards* for affirmative action programs to be met by any employer with contracts involving public funds.
5. Being *less involved with rhetoric* and more concerned with specific positive action.

Business Responsibilities

Progressive managers can do much to correct the inequities of the past. Regardless of the programs chosen by a particular organization, they must have the full backing of top company officials, who have to be willing to commit the company's resources to the programs. Employers can assist by:

1. *Establishing affirmative action programs.*
2. *Actively recruiting, hiring, and training minorities* to turn them into a work force with·skills comparable to those of whites, in order to build on the progress of the past two decades.
3. *Establishing clear policies* by top management, which are *communicated* to organizational personnel responsible for carrying out the program.
4. *Providing training programs for supervisory personnel* that are designed to help them overcome their prejudices and stereotypes.
5. Helping minority college graduates *overcome their apparent reluctance* to commit themselves to *business careers.*
6. *Avoiding making a fetish out of employment tests*, which are often geared to the backgrounds and performance of white, middle-class employees, who possess knowledge gained through experiences many minorities have never had. Frequently tests are not directly related to the job for which a person may be applying. When tests are used, they should be only a *part* of the entire selection process.

The importance of two factors—*adequate selection* and *training procedures* for minorities (and for that matter any employee!)—should be stressed. One of the surest ways to destroy faith in affirmative action programs is to assume, before active recruiting, that no qualified minorities exist and so hire an unqualified, untrained minority member. Regardless of the personal attitudes or biases of specific managers, affirmative action programs are likely to continue as a way of organizational life far into the future. Much more constructive than attempting to stop the unstoppable or using such programs as scapegoats is to figure out ways in which fair employment practices can be made a basic and integral part of the overall selection and employment process. And especially important to the success of such programs is the willing support of supervisors and existing employees.

How to sabotage an affirmative action program.

Problems of Supervision

The supervisory level is of key importance in implementing an equal employment opportunity program. Bass and Barrett aptly expressed it: "While the top levels of management are committed to a more liberal policy in terms of hiring the disadvantaged, the supervisor on the shop floor is *least committed* to this plan, but is the man who will be *most important* in implementing a program of this sort."[5]

[5]Bernard M. Bass and Gerald V. Barrett, *Man, Work, and Organizations* (Boston: Allyn and Bacon, 1972), p. 574.

290

Let's examine some typical problems relating to supervisors in organizations that have minority hiring programs.

Mental Set

How do preconceived notions affect the supervision of minorities?

Some supervisors tend to be *mentally set* to perceive characteristics or behavior of minorities and women differently from the way they would see those of white males in the same situations. For example, when some supervisors observe a black on the job, they may be preset to see a "lazy, shiftless" individual who fits their life-long stereotypes. Preset attitudes, unfortunately, can produce an unhealthy atmosphere, one that helps to create the very problems that supervisors are set to see.

The Bending-Over-Backwards Syndrome

Should white supervisors have separate standards for minorities?

Some supervisors who have had little or no experience in managing minorities and are concerned about not conveying a prejudiced attitude are sometimes uncertain about the best approach to follow.

Charles P. Haywood, Deputy Director of the Bay Area Urban League in San Francisco, warns white supervisors "not to feel the need to try to be the symbol of 'white goodness.'" Haywood points out that some well-meaning white supervisors today fall into the "bending-over-backwards syndrome," which he defines as "the reduction of organizational *standards* for minorities."

bending-over-backwards syndrome

Double Standards of Supervision

double standards

The psychologist Dr. Kenneth Clark also warns about *double standards of supervision*, which he contends can be harmful to both minority workers and the organization itself. Whether it be teachers of minority children or supervisors of minority subordinates, Dr. Clark offers some sound advice for anyone in a position of authority:

> They will know that you have different standards for them. They cannot and will not accept condescension although they might exploit it. They will accept only evidence of respect for their humanity, their capacity as human beings, their ability to learn the way people learn, their ability to perform with the same standards by which other people's performances are evaluated. And in respecting these demands, you will be giving not verbal, but genuine acceptance of them as human beings.
>
> They must be provided also with realistic rewards and incentives for meeting single standards of performance and achievement. They cannot be rewarded for double standards which are inferior standards of achievement, and believe that they are being taken seriously. They will accept the same gold medal for clearly inferior work, but they will know that it is a Jim Crow medal whites would not award to whites for the same level of performance.[6]

Preferential Hiring Treatment
—for Whom?

That minorities have been discriminated against unfairly in the past cannot be denied. The question arises, however, whether they should, in some instances, be given *preferential treatment* in hiring until past discrimination has been counteracted.

preferential treatment

The Problems of "Reverse Discrimination"

Has the direction of discrimination in employment begun to turn in recent years? Some observers of the labor market—especially young white males—seem to feel that way. A wry comment commonly heard among some critics during the late 1970s is that "to get a job these days, you have to be a black woman with a Spanish surname"!

[6]Dr. Kenneth Clark, "No Gimmicks, Please, Whitey," *Training in Business and Industry,* November 1968, p. 30.

292

Are complaints of reverse discrimination valid? In a sense they are. For example, as a result of the court ruling previously cited regarding hospital workers, the hospital, in addition to establishing a training fund and paying damages, was also required to carry out the following:

1. Establish an affirmative action committee to look at hospital procedures for the purpose of eliminating the alleged discrimination in hiring and promotion.
2. Develop a recruitment program to solicit applications from black professional, para-professional, and nursing personnel.
3. Hire one black for every two nonblacks until a hiring quota of 15 percent of all professional job categories and 13.9 percent for other categories is reached.
4. Contact all black applicants who applied since January 1, 1975, and weren't hired, and offer them the opportunity to be reconsidered for employment.
5. Give all former employees who were fired because of alleged racial discrimination the chance to reapply.
6. Require the hospital to promote Lawrence Hendley, one of the ten plaintiffs in the case, to a supervisory position.

Equal Employment Opportunity Commission (EEOC)

Title VII of the Civil Rights Act of 1964, and amended by the Equal Employment Act of 1972, established the *Equal Employment Opportunity Commission*. The EEOC, as it is typically called, has the responsibility for regulating employment practices of organizations covered under civil rights acts. Most federal contracts also have clauses requiring "acceptable" proportions of minority employees. Many firms are monitored by the Office of Federal Contract Compliance to ensure that they have adequate minority representation.

Is There a Contradiction Somewhere?

What's your solution?

The solution to the problem of fair employment practices seems a bit fuzzy these days. Current civil rights legislation says that most employers have a legal duty to hire, fire, and promote workers *without regard to color, creed, sex, or age*. The law implies equity for *all* people, not just for minorities. Can an employer meet certain "quotas" (or "guidelines," which is the term generally preferred) without sometimes hiring a lesser qualified minority member over a better qualified white? Is reverse discrimination necessary in the short run in order to attain a more equitable balance of employees in the longer run? Complete agreement on these touchy issues seems highly unlikely in the near future.

Where Do We Go from Here?

Tides Flow In and Tides Flow Out

reverse discrimination

A series of rulings during the late 1970s have been considered setbacks for so-called *reverse-discrimination* practices. A federal judge in 1976 ruled that the City University of New York practiced intentional racial discrimination against whites and Asians when it selected students for a medical school program. Earlier a University of Washington graduate filed suit on grounds that he was rejected solely because he was white. The California Supreme Court, also in 1976, ruled in the highly publicized *Bakke decision* that the special admissions program at the University of California Medical School at Davis was unconstitutional because it granted preferential treatment to minorities at the expense of "better qualified" whites. Many other schools had begun similar programs during the late 1960s. In another decision, AT&T was ordered in June of 1976 to pay damages to a male employee passed over for promotion in favor of a less experienced woman.

A fluttering pendulum?

Bakke decision

Managerial Challenges Ahead

The short run promises to be challenging, but difficult, for professional managers. Not only must they cope with seemingly contradictory legislation, but they must also be able to adapt to the everchanging whims of court rulings. As former U.S. Attorney General Edward H. Levi has stated, "If people examined statutes banning discrimination, executive orders issued pursuant to them, and court rulings interpreting them, they would have a view of a madhouse. The resemblance between the statutes and court decisions would be purely coincidental—and usually there isn't any resemblance."[7] In spite of all these difficulties, however, the concerned manager of today must attempt to deal as effectively as possible with the human problems associated with fair employment practices. Equitable solutions will only be possible after we have shaken off the long-held stereotypes that do not mesh with present-day realities.

Summary

We can barely scratch the surface, in the space of one chapter, of the complex problems that are the result of many years of prejudice and

[7] "Growing Debate 'Reverse Discrimination' Has It Gone Too Far?" *U.S. News & World Report*, 29 March 1976, pp. 26–29.

discrimination toward persons who receive *different treatment for reasons unrelated to their employment situations.*

Although some of the hiring of minorities has been "tokenism" or "window-dressing," many previously skeptical companies have learned that their fears were unfounded. Not only have their minority employees been, in most cases, satisfactory workers, but also other employees, through increased exposure to minority workers, have found that much of their prejudice had been based upon ignorance and a lack of understanding.

The "principle of rising expectations" applies significantly to minority Americans who now expect to share in the economic fruits of the so-called "American Dream." They observe various and attractive goods and services in abundance advertised for consumption, and feel that they deserve their rightful share.

The word *prejudice* means to *pre*judge. A prejudgment is usually an attitude based upon insufficient facts, or no facts at all. As white Americans learn more about the similarities, as well as the differences, between minority Americans and themselves, many fears and uncertainties should become allayed. Likewise, minority Americans must prepare themselves for the opportunities that are continually opening up.

More fortunate Americans must strive to improve the lot of those less fortunate than themselves. Violence, turbulence, and unrest are likely to exist in the United States if there are groups who feel that they have been put down. No group will continue indefinitely to accept oppression without reaction or revolt. The longer such sociological infection is permitted to fester, the more difficulty Americans are likely to find in their attempts to resolve the serious problems.

The late president, John F. Kennedy, in an address to Latin American officials, made a statement that relates to our own domestic situation: "Those who make peaceful revolutions impossible, make violent revolution inevitable."

Terms And Concepts to Remember

Different treatment group
Prejudice
Discrimination
Preventive prejudice
Title VII, Civil Rights Act
Affirmative action programs
Overt discrimination
Institutional subordination
Pacification
Token placement

Special job assignments
Job ceilings
Job floors
Bending-over-backwards syndrome
Preferential treatment
Equal Employment Opportunity
    Commission (EEOC)
Reverse discrimination
Bakke decision

Questions

1. What seem to be the principal causes of the development of prejudice? How can the prejudicial attitudes be changed?
2. What were the major causes of the increased economic gains for nonwhites during the 1960s and 1970s?
3. In what ways may tokenism actually be beneficial in the long run in helping to develop a more healthy organizational climate?
4. Why are many members of minority groups still not fully satisfied with the "tremendous progress they have made during the past two decades"?
5. Do you feel that nonwhites should attempt to forget their color? Why or why not?
6. Why have many individuals in recent years developed a strong sense of pride in their "roots," ethnic origin, or sex?
7. What are some other solutions to the problems of equal employment opportunity programs that you feel would be beneficial, but were not mentioned in the text?
8. Why is the supervisor one of the key persons in determining the success or failure of a minority hiring program?
9. Assume that you oppose "preferential hiring" treatment on the grounds that it is discrimination in reverse. What other means would you employ to offset the inequities of past unfair employment practices?

Other Readings

Burma, John H. *Mexican-Americans in the United States—A Reader.* Cambridge, Mass.: Schenkman, 1970.

"Growing Debate 'Reverse Discrimination' Has It Gone Too Far?" *U.S. News & World Report,* 29 March 1976, pp. 26–29.

"How to File a Complaint Against Unlawful Job Discrimination." Washington, D.C.: Equal Employment Opportunity Commission, 1970.

"Know Your Employment Rights." Washington, D.C.: Manpower Administration, United States Department of Labor, 1970.

Racism in America and How to Combat It. The U.S. Commission on Civil Rights. Clearing House Publication, Urban Series No. 1. Washington, D.C.: Superintendent of Documents, U.S. Government Printing Office, 1970.

"Social Issues: A Long, Hard Trail for Operation Navajo." *Business Week,* 19 May 1973, pp. 104–105.

The Supervisor's EEO Handbook—A Guide to Federal Antidiscrimination Laws and Regulations. New York: Executive Enterprises Publications, 1974.

Young, Jared J. *Discrimination, Income, Human Capital Investment, and Asian-Americans.* San Francisco: R & R Research Associates, 1977.

Applications

The Unacceptable Letter

The Cambio Cash Register Company adopted an affirmative action hiring program about six months ago. The program was somewhat casually introduced to supervisors during one of their regular bi-monthly staff meetings.

Thomas Tart, an energetic, highly meticulous supervisor in the Accounts Department, felt that he was not a particularly prejudiced person, but he was not completely enthusiastic about the prospect of hiring minorities for his department. Nonetheless, "as a loyal company man," he felt that he had to go along with the new program.

Tart hired as one of his secretaries a young black woman, Mary Johnson, a recent graduate of a local community college. Mary Johnson had not previously worked in an office. Her experience was limited to the secretarial training she had received while in college. Tart was a demanding and particular boss, not only with Mary, but with all of his subordinates.

About two weeks after Mary was hired, Tart asked her to prepare a letter to send to one of the firm's major customers. Tart had previously told Mary what style of correspondence he favored.

Mary prepared the letter and handed it to Tart, who examined the item carefully. The letter was neatly prepared, but in a different style. Tart was upset and curtly exclaimed, "When I ask you to prepare a letter in a particular way, you damned well better do it that way!"

Mary became angry at Tart's remarks. She immediately went to Tart's superior and complained that her supervisor was prejudiced against blacks.

Questions

1. What seems to be the problem in this case?
2. Assume that you are Tart's boss. What would you do about the problem?
3. How might the frequency of similar situations be lessened?

Equal Opportunities—with a Nudge from the Judge

A large retail chain store and eight local unions were charged with discrimination against blacks, Spanish-surnamed Americans, and females. The alleged discriminatory practices were in the areas of hiring, testing, training, intimidation and harrassment, causing constructive discharges, reprisals, segregated job classifications, and failure to promote. To avoid costly litigation, the parties entered into a consent decree. The twenty-four page consent decree set forth details for eliminating discriminatory employment practices. The following statements are quoted from the consent decree:

- In the event of any conflict between the provisions of this Consent Decree and a provision of any collective bargaining agreement between the Company and any local unions, the provisions of this Consent Degree shall prevail.
- Nothing provided in this Consent Decree shall require the Company to hire, promote, transfer or retain unqualified employees.
- The Company shall continue its training of interviewers to standardize the hiring process, eliminate discriminatory practices, if any, and educate interviewers as to the equal employment opportunity policy.
- The Company commits itself to make all reasonable efforts to maintain no less than 4.1% black, 9.1% Spanish-surnamed American, and 39.3% female employees enrolled in its Retail Management Training Program (RMTP) at all times.
- Supervisory personnel performing evaluations shall receive specialized instruction in nondiscriminatory, objective performance of such evaluations.
- Until such time as the goals set forth in the Appendix have been achieved . . . the company will place special emphasis upon promotion of black, Spanish-surnamed American, and female employees.
- Before final discipline is imposed, the employee will be afforded the right to present his or her position regarding the alleged misconduct.
- The Company shall commit and direct all levels of management . . . to give increased support to the . . . equal opportunity policy.
- The Company, through its management personnel, shall participate actively in minority and female community affairs.
- Store management and other supervisory personnel shall be informed that failure to support and implement the Company's equal employment opportunity policy will subject these individuals to disciplinary action, up to and including discharge.
- To any charging party who receives a final award of backpay, the master (Court appointee who hears individual claims for hiring,

reinstatement, and/or backpay) may also award to said charging party reasonable attorneys' fees incurred in resolution of his or her claim.

- As part of its review of compliance . . . the EEOC may inspect premises, examine witnesses, and copy documents. For a period of five years, the Company will submit quarterly statistical reports of progress to the EEOC.

Questions

1. Do you feel the terms of this consent decree will further the cause of equal employment opportunities? Explain.
2. The consent decree has directed the company to make all reasonable efforts to maintain minimum percentages of minorities and females enrolled in its Retail Management Training Program. Do you believe that these are realistic goals? Explain.
3. What about reverse discrimination?
4. In what ways could charges of "reverse discrimination" result from the above consent decree?
5. Would you want the responsibilities of a store manager? a personnel manager? Chief legal counsel? Why or why not?

When you finish this chapter, you should be able to:

1. **Contrast** the employment opportunities for men with those of women.
2. **Describe** the long-term changes in female participation in the work force.
3. **Present,** with illustrations, an argument against the traditional mythological generalities about women.
4. **Summarize** the major effects of institutions and home environments on the perpetuation of unfavorable treatment toward women.
5. **Explain** why in many instances it is both impossible and undesirable for a "woman's place to be in the home."
6. **Summarize** some possible solutions to the problem of discrimination based on sex.
7. **Restate** some of the major problems and potential solutions to the difficulties faced by women managers.

Wherever women work, progress is coming—but slowly. Often it seems like half a step backward for every step forward.

—Claire Safran

No person should be denied equal rights because of the shape of her skin.

—Pat Paulsen

Men, put yourself into a pair of women's shoes. If you were a woman, here's what you would be confronting:

You and other women amount to *more* than 50 percent of the population, but when you are hired for jobs, historically you have been hired for the *less remunerative occupations,* the so-called women's jobs.

If you were an "average" full-time female worker, you would earn slightly less than *60 percent* of what a full-time male worker does, according to the United States Bureau of Labor Statistics. In 1975, for example, the median income for women was $7,700, for men, $13,100.

If you were a *woman* with a *college degree,* your income would tend to be no better than *male high school graduates'.*

If you were a woman, perhaps you would know that, in 1923, a group of militant suffragettes, after long-awaited success in obtaining for women the basic right to vote, presented a bill to Congress designed to make women first-class citizens under the Constitution. You might also know that the bill was sent to the House Judiciary Committee where it remained in hiding for *forty-nine years*, until finally passed by Congress in 1972. Known as the Equal Rights Amendment (ERA), the bill requires ratification before March 1979 by three-quarters of the states to become law.

If you were a woman, men, you might know that *Title VII* of the Civil Rights Act of 1964 also applies to you, a woman, and that the act created an Equal Employment Opportunities Commission (EEOC), to help reduce discrimination against women and nonwhites.

But . . . the beat goes on, and women continue to be barred from numerous jobs.

How do those shoes feel now? Those shoes that you are wearing, made out of genuine empathy, are probably beginning to hurt your feet, aren't they, men? Here's another tragic note that should put a tender blister on your big toe: The *lowest pay of men* begins about where *women's highest pay leaves off*, even though in some jobs women are more productive than men.

302

Happy reunion?

So how would *you* feel at a ten-year class reunion knowing that you—even if holding a well-paying "woman's job"—are making less than most of your male classmates?

Take off your unmasculine shoes now, men, relax your feet, tense up your minds a bit, and let's try to find out a few more things about how women have been treated in the *past* and how they might be treated in the *future*. And, women—wipe those smug looks off *your* faces. Unconsciously, you may be more guilty of "sexism" toward *women* than are some men.

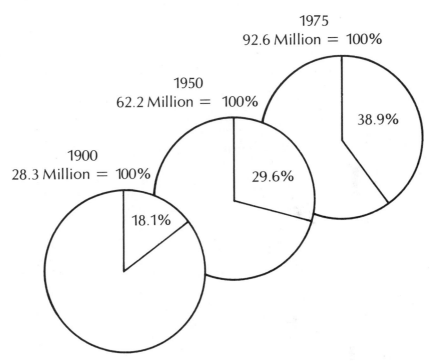

Figure 13–1. Proportion of women in the labor force. Source: Department of Commerce.

The Female Labor Force

Long-term Changes in the Female Labor Force

What has been the secular trend for women in the work force?

The trend since 1900 for women joining the work force has been steadily upwards. In 1900, there were only about *5 million women* in the civilian labor force, which was only about *18 percent* of all workers (see figure 13–1), and only about *20 percent* of the total female working-age population in the United States at the time.

Between 1950 and 1975, however, the number of women in the civilian labor force jumped by *18 million* to *36 million,* which was almost *40 percent* of all workers and about *46 percent* of all women of working age. Between 1950 and 1975, the number of women in the labor force about *doubled.* In contrast, the number of men in the labor force grew at a much slower rate, gaining *25 percent* over the same period.

Spurred on by changing social values and attitudes, economic considerations, and the influence of governmental action, we can see that women have become a real and significant part of the labor force, currently constituting about two-fifths of the civilian labor force. Higher educational attainment, rising divorce rates resulting in more women becoming heads of households, decline in the birth rate, and the high costs of maintaining a household are all likely to encourage the trend toward greater female participation in the work force. Consequently, in our concern with the human side of organizations, we should not, as has traditionally been the case, overlook women as a significant and integral part of today's organizations.

The Changing Age Groups

Why are there now *more* married women in the work force?

Contrary to some popular beliefs, all women in the work force are not shapely young twenty-year-olds planning to work just until they "find a man" or "get pregnant." Before 1940, the typical woman worker *was* young and single, but since 1940, older married women have joined the ranks of working women in increasing numbers. For example, the number of married women in the labor force increased by 17 million between 1940 and 1975, while the number of single women in the market expanded by 1.7 million. In terms of participation rates, less than 15 percent of married women were workers in 1940, but by 1960, this had increased to 30 percent. Since 1960, there has been a big jump in *all* groups under 65, with the most dramatic changes occurring among *married women.* About 45 percent of all married women were in the work force in 1975. Prior to the 1960s, the bulk of the increase was concentrated among mothers of school-age children. But, starting in the early 1960s, the emphasis shifted to mothers of preschool children.

The Unnatural Superiority of Man

What does the Bible feel about women?

Do you feel that it is somewhat of an inborn or natural phenomenon for men to feel superior to women? After all, even the Holy Bible implies that woman, taken out of man, is of lesser value than man. In Leviticus, 27:1–4, we can read:

The Lord spoke to Moses saying: Speak to the Israelite people and say to them: When a man explicitly vows to the Lord the equivalent for a human being, the following scales shall apply: If it is a male from 20 to 60 years of age, the equivalent is 50 shekels of silver by the sanctuary weight; if it is female, the equivalent is 30 shekels.

The teachings of the Bible have, apparently, been carefully followed, since the total money earnings of women have traditionally hovered around 60 percent of the total income of men.

Two German Philosophers

Is it kosher to be a chauvinist pig?

One of the most famous of all German philosophers, Fredrich Wilhelm Nietzsche, lent support to the Bible's view when he proclaimed: "God created woman. In the act he brought boredom to an end—and also many other things. Woman was the second mistake of God."

Even before Nietzsche, another German philosopher, Arthur Schopenhauer, attempted to convince the world of the natural superiority of man by declaring: "It is only the man whose intellect is clouded by his sexual impulse that could give the name of the fair sex to that undersized, narrow-shouldered, broad-hipped, and short-legged race."

Have many men changed their attitudes much since Nietzsche, Schopenhauer, and others were overtly displaying what might have been some of their own inner insecurities? Some have. Have you?

A Wartime "Holiday"

Is prejudice toward women *inborn*?

We haven't yet answered our question about whether it is *natural* for men to be prejudiced in their views of women. Such attitudes, if they are inborn, seemed to have taken a holiday during World War II when there were tremendous shortages of labor and unemployment rates of less than 2 percent. In fact, labor was so scarce in 1942 that almost anyone, regardless of sex or color, could obtain a job in previously impenetrable fields. The changed attitude was typified by a popular song of the day about Rose, the homemaker, who became known as "Rosie the Riveter."

Why the return to "normal" after WW II?

Perhaps the experience of the 1940s tended to prove that if American society really wants to eliminate job discrimination it can, that prejudice toward women is not necessarily inborn but more socialized in nature. After the war, however, attitudes and employment conditions for women once again returned to "normal."

305

A Widening Differential?

*Equal Pay
Act of 1963*

In spite of legislation stipulating equal pay for equal work regardless of sex (the *Equal Pay Act of 1963),* a substantial amount of discrimination against women remains. The gap between the incomes of men and women has actually widened in recent decades. Although the income of full-time, year-round working women rose from $2,827 in 1956 to $7,719 in 1975, their income as a percentage of men's earnings actually *declined* from *63 percent* to *59 percent* over the same period. A break-down by occupation groups reveals the same pattern (see figure 13–2)—women's share of total earnings declined in almost every category. Female clerical workers suffered the sharpest drop in earnings relative to men during the period, declining from *68 percent* to *62 percent* of men's incomes. The relation of female to male income in the same occupations ranged from a high of *66 percent* for the professional group to a low of *39 percent* in sales.

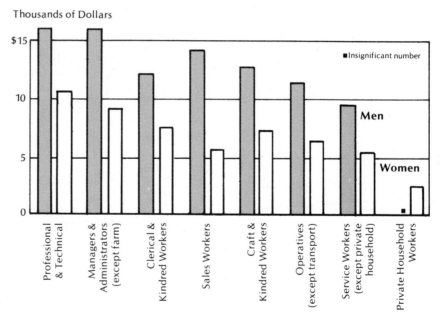

Figure 13–2. Median earnings of selected occupational groups by sex, 1975. Source: The Conference Board.

Attitudes and Myths About Women

A discussion of prejudice disturbs some people. Do you remember how we learned in chapter 2 on perception that individuals tend to believe that which they are *set* to believe? What we have been *taught* influences our perception. There is also a human tendency for prejudiced persons to turn a deaf ear to anything that may prove them wrong.

We now are going to discuss briefly some of the *preset notions, myths,* and *generalities about women.* Whether you are a man *or* a woman (women's attitudes are also influenced by their culture), think seriously about these generalities. Try not to react defensively. Don't worry, our conclusions will not parasitically attach themselves to your brain if you do not want to accept them. But at least examine the myths carefully and give them and our conclusions some objective thought before accepting or rejecting them.

Women—The Weaker of Which Sex?

The prejudicial attitudes toward women are practically without end. We've all heard many times, often without questioning their validity, attitudes such as: "Marriage and a career don't mix" (why necessarily just for women?); or, "Women are absent from their jobs more than men" (if true, is it due to *women,* or to the *nature of the jobs* that have been open to women?); or, "Women don't stay with an organization long" (is this because of *women* or because women are usually employed at the *lower levels* of the occupational scale with *little prospect for advancement?*); or, "Women are the weaker sex" (yet, they tend to *outlive* men!).[1]

No Myth Shortage

Does mythology provide nourishment for the intellectually underfed?

Paul Samuelson has succinctly summarized some of the *major myths* that many Americans transport in their minds as excess baggage:

Women are built by nature to tend babies in the home. They are emotional. They have monthly ups and downs. They cannot carry heavy weights. They lack self-confidence. Men will not work under a woman. Man-to-man talk will be inhibited by the presence of women. Even women prefer a male physician to a female one. Women lack imagination and creativity. If you mix men and women on the job, they will carry on to the detriment of efficiency and good morals. By the time you have trained a woman, she'll get married and leave you; or have a baby; or alternatively, you won't be able ever to get rid of a woman once you've hired her. If a woman does turn out to be a superlative economic performer, she's not feminine, she's harsh and aggressive with a chip on her shoulder against men and the world (and she's killing her

[1]For a more detailed discussion of these attitudes, see "Toward Job Equality for Women" (Equal Employment Opportunity Commission, 1969), pp. 3–4.

chances of getting married). Women workers, seeking pin money, take bread from the mouths of family breadwinners.[2]

The Influence on Female Roles

Do women prefer to be dominated by men?

Surveys often indicate that most women do *not* relate to or support women's rights movements or groups, and these indications, therefore, are offered as proof that women are not necessarily discriminated against since most are satisfied with their present roles. "Real women," it is often argued, "know what they are and what they really want. They want to be dominated by men."

In 1972, for example, the Institute of Life Insurance in New York published the results of a poll of three thousand young persons, between the ages of fourteen and twenty-five, in seventy-two geographic locations. About three in five agreed that "a woman's place is in the home." However, the poll did admit that the more highly educated respondents tended to reject the statement and that only two in five of the females agreed.[3]

Why might some women be "sexist" toward women?

But let us not forget what tends to influence, or condition, our attitudes. As singer Tiny Tim, a personality not necessarily noted for his philosophical profundity, once said, "You are what you eat." Psychologically, too, our attitudes are conditioned by the nourishment our minds absorb. Women are exposed to some of the same cultural influences as men.

We all are affected by culturalization; that is, society has established "proper" roles for both men and women, and a woman's role traditionally has been defined as secondary to a man's. From birth, many parents get their children hung up in the "pink-and-blue syndrome," where pink equals 60 percent of blue. Parents, the entertainment media, and the printed word have long been involved with the "tracking process." Many women over age 30 today were tracked into roles of near-permanent, or permanent, subordination. They have developed the belief that it is the responsibility of women to be on the sidelines, emotionally cheering on their brave warriors. (We can readily see enduring evidence of such tracking, with female cheerleaders, at football and basketball games.)

Dick, Jane, Janet, and Mark

Are grade school primers "sexist"?

For example, can you remember some of the first primers to which you were exposed? Young children today are exposed to the same stereotypes that have existed for numerous years. Young children's first exposure to

[2]Paul Samuelson, *Economics,* 10th ed. (New York: McGraw-Hill, 1976), p. 790.
[3]"Youth Survey: Woman's Place is in the Home," *San Francisco Sunday Examiner and Chronicle,* 2 January 1972, p. 4, section D.

reading material is likely to have some significant influence on their future values.

For example, in a first-grade reader, adopted by the state of California and used in the public schools throughout the 1970s, appeared the following:

> "Mark! Janet!" said Mother.
> "What is going on here!"
> "She can not skate," said Mark.
> "I can help her.
> I want to help her.
> Look at her, Mother.
> Just look at her.
> She is just like a *girl*.
> She gives up."
>
> "Stop this, Janet," said Mother.
> "Mark IS going to help you.
> He is going to help you now.
> Come on Janet.
> Get up!
> I want to see you skate."
>
> "Now you see," said Mark.
> "Now you can skate.
> But just with me to help you!"

If you were a first grader in a San Francisco school where the above mentioned book, entitled *Around the Corner*,[4] was used in the 1970s, don't you think that your attitude toward little girls might be influenced somewhat by your very first primer?

In another currently used primer called *Around the City*,[5] the following words appear:

> They all jumped into the big box.
> "A train!" one boy said.
> "The box can be a train."
> "Get on the train!" said the boys.

Later:

> The girls went into the box.
> What could the box be now?

---

[4] "Skates for Janet," *Around the Corner* (New York: Harper & Row, 1966), pp. 45–46.
[5] "The Big Box," *Around the City* (New York: Macmillan, 1965), p. 48–53.

The box was not a boat.
It was not a train.
It was not a plane.
The box was a house.
And the girls played house all day.

The above are fairly typical examples of the Dick and Jane or the Janet and Mark elementary school readers in which the boys put down the girls, the mothers are always in their kitchens wearing aprons, the little girls remain indoors playing house while the boys are outside being adventurous.

Attitudes Are Changing

Would Lady Godiva have attracted as much attention had she been a man?

Many high schools have perpetuated stereotypes by not permitting young women to attend classes in automobile mechanics, wood shop, or other trade courses. Many young women have been encouraged, instead, to concentrate on courses in home economics. Even college textbooks for adults in the field of management and human behavior have helped perpetuate the works of Dick and Jane. They have either portrayed women employees as having completely different work characteristics from men, or they continually referred to every manager as "he," such as in " . . . a manager . . . he . . . " Women readers have often found it difficult to identify with the incessant references to males.

But there are some bright signs on the horizon that indicate that such blatant stereotyping of roles is diminishing. Many primary schools, for example, have begun to clean up their acts by trying to select books that avoid the pink-and-blue syndrome. Dr. Benjamin M. Spock, famed author of one of the world's best-selling baby care books, *Baby and Child Care*, was one of the first to "de-he" books. He mended his ways by zealously throwing himself into the job of eliminating sexist references from the 202nd printing of his book.

Many publishers of college textbooks have also seen the writing on the income statement. Recognizing that sexist books will be more difficult to sell on college campuses, most publishers have either begun to require or, at least, to urge their authors to "de-he" their new or revised editions. Another sign of the changing times: American Telephone and Telegraph Company has promoted its current attitude toward women in its advertising. (See figure 13–3).

Many of the changes now taking place will take some time, however, to work their way through the system, since views long held are not easy to change.

The Part Played by the Home Environment

How does the family influence male and female roles? The entire blame for the stereotyping of males and females cannot be placed on the doorsteps of the educational system; the family also exerts a strong influence. For example, at home girls are usually taught to play with dolls while boys play with guns and tools. As Marilyn Power Goldberg asserts:

> Women are taught from the time they are children to play a serving role, to be docile and submissive, get what they want by being coy instead of aggressive. They are socialized to expect that they will spend their lives as housewives and mothers—for toys they are given the tools of their trade: dolls, tea sets, frilly dresses, and so on. They are never encouraged to think in terms of a career, unless it be one which is an extension of the serving, subordinate role in the family, such as nursing or being a secretary. As they grow they learn that it is unfeminine and therefore abhorrent to be self-assertive or to compete with men. Thus most women mature with the understanding that their primary role is that of housewife and mother and that, while they may by chance work, their contribution will be merely supplemental and temporary; they will not have a career. This is true despite the fact that most women who work are essential to support themselves and their families.[6]

[6]Marilyn Power Goldberg, *The Economic Exploitation of Women* (Andover, Mass.: Warner Modular Publications, 1973), p. 2.

Figure 13–3. AT & T advertisement promoting women executive theme.

Institutional Sexism

What are some unfair ways of screening women from "men's" jobs?

Some organizations have used as a part of their hiring process employment tests that tend to screen out women. Although every job in the Pacific Telephone Company is now, as required by law, open to anyone without regard to sex, in the past an applicant for the position of framer, *institutional sexism*

for example, had to be able to lift sixty pounds. Rarely did any framers ever have to lift anything weighing that much. In a sense, therefore, the lifting requirement was a form of *institutional sexism,* something akin to the institutional subordination concept discussed in the previous chapter.

S Stands for Sham?

Would you believe— "Sam" Porter?

Sylvia Porter, a famous business columnist, admits that she had to use her initials instead of her first name for about eight years of her career because, "Editors at most New York dailies and the Associated Press weren't ready for a female financial writer." [7]

"Women's Jobs" Earn Less

Why do women earn less than men?

"Women's jobs"

Frances Blau Weisskoff points out the lack of logic in the statement that "women earn less because they are in 'lower-paying occupations.'" Weiskoff feels that instead the statement should be that "women earn less because they are in 'women's jobs'." [8] By women's jobs is meant those that in the past have been, with few exceptions, the only ones open to women: bookkeeping, stenography, office work, telephone operations, school teaching, cashiering, and waiting tables in coffee shops.

Look at figure 13–4 to see what Weisskoff means. Although occupational opportunities for women have improved, women workers remain highly concentrated in a small group of occupations. Over *11.5 million* worked as clerks in 1975, an increase of more than *7 million* since 1950, and accounted for over *one-third* of all employed women. An additional 22 percent worked in the service industries and as household workers. While growth rates were the fastest in the professional and technical categories—the total rose from 1.8 million in 1950 to 5.3 million in 1975—the raw statistics do not tell the whole story. The concentration was greatest at the primary and secondary teaching level (40 percent). Representation of women in professions such as law, engineering, and medicine remains at low levels, even though their number continues to expand.

**He: You're getting a divorce?
She: No, my client is.
He: You're the secretary?
She: No, I'm the lawyer.
He: You're the *lawyer*?**

The future does look a bit brighter for women in the professions, however. Although only 5 to 7 percent of American lawyers were women in 1975, the number of women in the nation's law schools climbed from 7.6 percent of total enrollment in 1960 to 9.3 percent in 1971 and to 20 percent in 1975. Nearly one-fourth of the nation's incoming medical students were women, up from 13 percent in 1972. Graduate business schools have experienced comparable gains, which suggests that many more women will be holding high-paying jobs in the future.

[7] "Women in Employment," *The Wall Street Journal,* 24 March 1972, p. 1.
[8] Frances Blau Weisskoff, "'Women's Place' in the Labor Market," *The Second Crisis of Economic Theory* (Morristown, N.J.: General Learning Press, 1972), p. 165.

313

A Woman's Place

Just where *is* a woman's place?

As you may have noticed, the title of this chapter borrowed a portion of the cliché, "A woman's place is in the home." Take an informal survey on the topic of a "woman's place" among almost any group of men and you are likely to discover that some of them will quite vehemently defend what they believe to be the validity of the cliché.

Male Resistance and Female Mental Health

As we have learned, however, the secular trend for female entry into the work force has been upward, while the male mood of resistance has fallen. In fact, one survey showed that *half* of the men questioned would not object if their wives took jobs, which is felt to be a substantial improvement over past attitudes.[9]

What effect does a mother's working have on her children?

Apparently, larger numbers of women no longer believe that a child's healthy development and survival are dependent on a full-time mother. In fact, many women feel that both the child and she will be mentally *more healthy* by having a regular exposure to a variety of people and environments. Apparently there is some female agreement since more than half of all mothers in the United States who have children in school also hold jobs, as do over one in three mothers with children under six years of age. (See figure 13–5).

Should the woman have the right to decide if she wants to work?

Perhaps the decision about the situation of "a woman's place" should rest with the woman. What does *she* prefer and where will *she* get the most psychic satisfaction? Regardless of women's feelings, many men

[9]"A Woman's Place is on the Job," *Time,* 26 July 1971, p. 56.

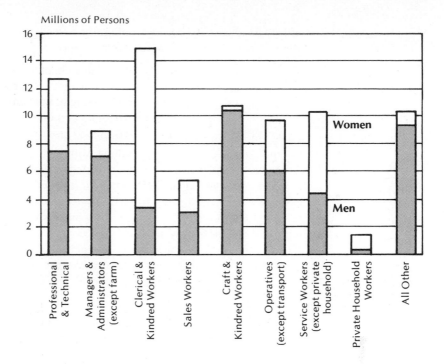

Millions of Persons

Figure 13–4. Occupation of employed persons (annual average) by sex, 1975.
Source: The Conference Board.

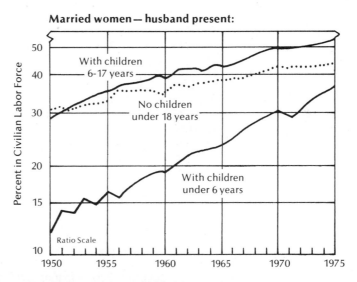

Figure 13–5. Labor force participation rates of married women by presence and age of children, 1950–1975.
Source: The Conference Board.

still contend that their wives belong at home. Many of the same men often wonder why their wives seem so discontented with their lives at home.

More Education

How might education influence a "house-spouse's" attitude?

Today, more women complete high school and college and find less satisfaction "dusting and kaffeeklatching with the 'girls' all day." Nearly *three-quarters* of women workers have high school diplomas today compared to only *one-half* in 1952. Over *40 percent* of all college graduates now are women, and many of them want to put their education to work. In 1975, for example, over *50 percent* of all women with high school diplomas and nearly *64 percent* with college degrees were employed. (See figure 13–6). Perhaps the traditional male attitude contributes significantly to the excessively high divorce rate (about one out of three marriages) in the United States.

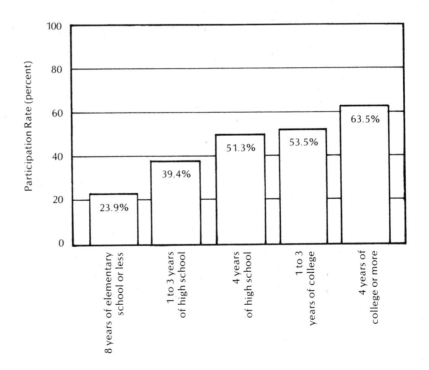

Figure 13–6. Labor force participation rates of women by years of school completed, 1975. Source: U.S. Department of Labor.

Statistical Discrimination

Is high turnover related to the employees' sex?

If you are a business person, you certainly have the right to argue that you are not a social worker—you naturally have to select people who you feel will benefit the organization the most. You also know from experience that "women's jobs" tend to have higher turnover and absenteeism rates than do other jobs in your organization; so you may feel that placing a woman in a responsible "man's job" would be too much of a risk for the company. After all, in managerial jobs you want people who are going to remain with the company for a while.

statistical discrimination

That sort of reasoning might make one guilty of applying what is termed *statistical discrimination*, which is *the making of prejudgments about a person's potential performance in a higher-level job based upon statistical results in a lower-level job.*

Why is turnover higher on "women's jobs"?

For example, it *is* true that "women's jobs" tend to have high turnover rates, but we have already asked whether this is due to the *nature of women* OR to the *job itself*. Higher turnover might occur because such skills as typing and shorthand are easily *transferred* from one organization to another. Another factor is that "women's jobs" tend to provide *less* satisfaction of higher-order needs than do many "men's jobs." Jobs open to women in the past have often been dead-end, with scant opportunity for advancement.

Employers who engage in statistical discrimination are, in a sense, applying the fallacy of composition. They may have had bad experience with women in jobs that tend naturally to have high turnover rates, and thus transfer this experience to other situations. However, is it really likely that turnover would be as high among *women managers* as it is among *clerk typists*? Perhaps we should realistically search for ways in which specific jobs can be *enriched* rather than statistically discriminate against women who want positions with greater responsibility and opportunity for advancement.

Turnover in "Men's Jobs"

One factor often overlooked is the relatively high turnover rates of *all* workers in organizations. For example, a comprehensive survey of career-switching by the U.S. Department of Labor indicated that of the total work force, individuals have held their jobs for an average of only *4.2 years,* and that nearly *a third* of all American workers change their careers over a five-year period. According to the study, only *47 percent* of men and *40 percent* of women with jobs in 1965 had the same occupation in 1970. Furthermore, the turnover of men is not as low as some would like to believe. Another Department of Labor report indicated that

317

the average 20-year-old *man* could be expected to change jobs about six or seven times during his working lifetime.

Possible Solutions to the Problem of Discrimination Based on Sex

How can the problem of sexism be resolved?

As with any chronic problem, there seldom are any simple solutions that will quickly right all past wrongs. However, the sincere acceptance and application of a variety of approaches can have the effect of exerting steady pressure in order to ensure that all human beings in our society are able to obtain their fair share of the fruits of the American system. The following discussion of possible solutions is by no means complete, but serves as an illustration of some of the changes that might be made to help alleviate past problems.

Legislation

Can laws influence attitudes?

"You can't legislate morality," is a comment that has been often made by some persons and, as we have already mentioned, they are probably right. However, laws *can* help to create a *different moral climate*. For example, before the passage of civil rights legislation, some business people stated that they weren't prejudiced, but if they served "nigras" in their restaurants or motels, their regular customers would stop patronizing their establishments. After the passage of civil rights laws, some of the same persons were saying that they were glad their competitors had to serve Negroes so that no one business person would have to stick his or her neck out.

At a recent conference on women's rights held at Merritt College, Oakland, California, James Hitchcock, staff manager of the Equal Employment Opportunity Department of the Pacific Telephone and Telegraph Company, when asked what caused the telephone company to change its policy toward women, candidly and without hesitation replied, "The law." He was then asked, "Why not before?" His answer: "Most managers were men." Legislation, therefore, may be a partial solution to the problem of women's rights.

Equal Pay Act of 1963

In 1963, Congress approved a law—the *Equal Pay Act*—forbidding sex discrimination in wage scales, and attempting to guarantee that women doing the same work as men would be paid the same.[10] The following year, 1964, the significant *Title VII* of the Civil Rights Act of 1964 made its first appearance and applied equally to women as it did to

---

[10]The Equal Pay Act applied, however, only to employers covered by the Fair Labor Standards Act of 1938, and did not apply to women in administrative, professional, or executive positions.

Title VII

ethnic minorities.[11] Title VII, as you may recall from the previous chapter,

> prohibits discrimination because of race, color, religion, sex or national origin, in hiring, upgrading and all other conditions of employment.

Executive Orders and guidelines

Since 1964, there have been occasional *Executive Orders* along with Equal Employment Opportunity Commission (EEOC) *guidelines* disseminated to ensure compliance with the Civil Rights Act. Currently, for example, if a woman believes that she has been discriminated against in an employment situation on the basis of sex, she may file a charge with the EEOC. Employers, employment agencies, and labor organizations are prohibited by law from punishing any woman because she has filed charges or spoken out against any employment practices made unlawful by Title VII.

The Twenty-seventh Amendment

In 1972, Congress passed the Twenty-seventh Amendment to the Constitution (ERA), which specifically stresses that equality of rights shall not be denied or abridged on account of sex. The amendment becomes a part of the Constitution if three-fourths of the country's state legislatures ratify it.

Labor Union Assistance

What has been the labor movement's attitude toward women?

Union organizations have historically improved working standards for many persons, but have done little to foster improved opportunities for women. Often unions have either barred women from membership in certain trades and occupations or perpetuated wage discrimination. For example, in the lithographic trade there were in the past contracts negotiated by the union that called for about a 15-percent difference between the wages of women and men—*for the same type of work.*

Over 4 million women belong to labor unions, but in a recent year only 38 held office in their union at the national level. Stated differently, 21 percent of union members are women, but 93 percent of the union leaders are men. No woman has sat on the National Executive Board of the AFL-CIO; no woman has headed any international union; few women have held elective or appointive offices in an international union; few women have sat on boards of state federations of labor; few women have headed local unions; and few unions have bargained for issues of special concern to women, such as child care, maternity leave, or job rights.

There are signs of change, however, with greater numbers of women union members anxious to have "Rosie the riveter" give way to Rosie

---

[11]In 1964, opponents of the Civil Rights Act of 1964 amended the job discrimination clause on the basis of *sex* as well as race or national origin. Specifically *excluded* from the act, however, were employees of educational institutions and of state or local governments, both categories occupied largely by women.

the international vice-president, Rosie the shop steward, and Rosie the president of the local. As partial evidence of such attitudes, in March 1974 over 3,200 trade union women convened in Chicago for the founding conference of the Coalition of Labor Union Women (CLUW) to work within the union structure to better the position of working women in America.

Revision of "Protective" Standards and Laws

How have "pro-tective" standards restricted women?

There have been some organizations with standards, and states with laws, that served to discriminate against women. One example is a rule that prevented a woman from acquiring a job that required her to lift more than fifty pounds, even if she were capable and wanted the job. Some "protective" laws have restricted women's participation in the labor market; laws, for example, that prohibited a woman from working the same number of hours a week as a man. Such laws, which were intended to assist the "weaker sex," in effect, relegated them to poorly paid jobs in segregated categories and barred them from much upward mobility.

Day-care Centers for Children

Almost 40 percent of all working women are their families' *sole wage earners* or earn the *bulk* of the family income, according to the Institute for Social Research at the University of Michigan, which made a study during the early 1970s. Over *35 percent* of working mothers in 1975 had preschool children, which tends to create a situation in which the mother often nets little, if anything, after the payment of transportation, clothing, and child-care costs. (See figure 13–5.)

Is there a need for day-care centers?

A number of concerned individuals and groups, including the National Organization for Women (NOW), feel that a national network of high-quality child-care centers should be made available to all citizens on the same basis as public schools, parks, and libraries.

day-care center

Adequate numbers of low-cost *day-care centers* are not yet available in the United States. Many husbands feel that there is no reason for their wives to work if they net little income after expenses. Yet some psychiatrists contend that working may be more economically sound than paying couch fees for therapy. Often the opportunity for a working wife to be around other people during the day enhances her family relationship. The wife doesn't have to be the sole family member listening to "how things went at the office today."

Should a woman work if she nets little income?

The need for day-care centers is not limited solely to the children of working married women. In 1975, for example, there were 7.5 million mothers who were either unmarried, separated, widowed, or divorced and living alone with their children; that is, they were the principal means of their families' support.

Paid Maternity Leave

maternity leave

Another goal of the National Organization for Women, and already in existence in some countries, is a system of paid *maternity leave*. Such a program could be incorporated into social security or employee benefits, and could be defined as a *medically-related work interruption*. The concept should not seem so new or radical if you think about the employment contracts that already allow benefits for work interruption due to illness or accident.

Is an appendectomy more deserving of a paid leave than childbirth?

Having made a study of its own staff of 1,560 persons, 60 percent of them women, the Federal Reserve Bank of Boston calculated that paid maternity leave "would have a negligible impact on overall wage costs and will not price young women workers out of jobs."[12]

Should men be eligible for maternity leave?

parental leave

Even if maternity leave were not paid for, many women feel that they should have the right to return within a reasonable time to their jobs after childbirth without the loss of seniority or other accrued benefits. Something that now may seem radical, but probably will not in time, is "parental leave" for *both sexes*, so that the husband can provide assistance to his wife immediately before and after their child is born.

Problems of the Woman Manager

Based on the long-held stereotypes of women in the world of work, it shouldn't come as too much of a surprise to learn that only a small proportion of organizational managers are women. Accurate figures are hard to come by, but some estimates indicate that women today total about 15 percent of first-line management, 5 percent of middle management, and only 1 percent of top management. The ranks of women first-line and middle managers, although still relatively slight, have increased dramatically in recent decades. Predictions are that their proportion is likely to swell during the forthcoming two decades.

The Managerial Woman

Why try for nothing?

"Effective management favors no gender," to coin a cliché. Unfortunately, however, culturalization and selection processes for managerial positions have traditionally favored the male. As a result, many women seldom aspired to managerial positions in the past. After all, why aspire to a position only to be disappointed by the realities of hiring and promo-

[12]*The Wall Street Journal*, 13 May 1973, p. 1.

tional practices? As we've indicated, however, "times—they are a chan-gin'."

To be effective managers, women needn't "act like a man." But they do need to "act like a manager." The concepts of management and lead-ership previously discussed apply to any manager regardless of sex. Woman managers do, however, confront some situations and problems that tend to be unique because of their sex. These problems can be clas-sified as relating to her *subordinates,* her *peers,* and her own *bosses.*

"Yes, Sir, Ms. Callahan"—Dealing with Subordinates

As a woman supervisor, don't be preset to perceive problems with your subordinates as being caused solely because you are a woman. Often problems related to your sex will never arise unless you search too long and hard for them and thus create a self-fulfilling prophesy. Paranoia can be counterproductive. However, be prepared to deal with any problems that do arise.

Problems with Male Subordinates

As a female manager, you may find some males resent being held ac-countable to a woman. In some instances, either consciously or subcon-sciously, they might try to make you look bad, bypass your authority, or even give you the silent treatment. What can you do if confronted in such a way by a subordinate? As with any problem, try to discover what the problem really is. Talk openly with your subordinate and ask him to level with you. Remember that it takes time for any new manager to gain the respect of subordinates, so try to be patient and understanding of their attitudes. Don't be afraid to exert your authority, but try wherever possi-ble to draw on the input and participation of all your subordinates in order to gain their confidence, respect, and commitment. Also remember the concepts of change discussed in chapter 10. Your presence may represent a radical departure from the established order of things. Try, above all, to be firm, fair, and friendly in your dealings with subordinates.

Why might a male resent a female boss?

Problems with Female Subordinates

How can a woman boss gain the confidence of her subordinates?

Many women employees firmly believe that they prefer male managers over females. This attitude shouldn't surprise us either, since men man-agers have, until relatively recently, been the only type they've been fa-miliar with. As a result, women who blindly accept the traditional pink-and-blue syndrome may—like their male counterparts—resent the pres-ence of a female superior. Some women subordinates feel that it lowers their own status to have to take orders from another woman. Once again, try to get such problems out into the open and discuss them frankly. Use the participative leadership style where possible and attempt to serve as a role model for women subordinates to emulate. Perhaps you can help them realize that their own chances for future advancement as women will probably hinge on your successes or failures. Be sure to attempt to understand why your subordinates feel the way they do. Your problems should be lessened if you display a genuine concern for their feelings and needs.

Peers and their Effect

Should women managers receive special treatment?

Females and males have certain responsibilities toward each other in any organization if goals are to be accomplished with minimum difficulty. Some male managers feel that the woman manager expects special treatment, which should not be the case. Of course, the male manager should be as supportive or critical of a woman as of a man. Furthermore, the woman should be able to open the door if she gets to it first. Regardless of sex, an important managerial characteristic is courtesy, so should it really be upsetting if a woman holds the door for a man?

Most women managers prefer not to be singled out as women. For example, at meetings, some conference leaders stress the fact that a woman is in the room. As a man, don't say, "Good morning, gentlemen—and lady." Be somewhat casual, and say something like, "Good morning, everyone."

"Shooot! Oops, sorry, lady."

Also, many women would prefer that men not apologize every time they utter a swear word. Most women today have heard the words and are no longer shocked by their sound.

Some men continue to use sexist terms for women, like "birds," "broads," "gals," and "dolls." If, as a woman, these words bother you, let the person who uses them know your feelings. Often the male who has no desire to be offensive doesn't realize that his choice of words offends.

How about the question of who pays the bill when male and female cohorts lunch together? One guideline is for the person who did the inviting to offer to pay. Sometimes, however, older men may insist on paying. If this happens, and you're a woman, you can say that you would like the next outing to be on you.

The great leap forward could be a step backward.

Another peer problem: At a meeting, what should the woman do if asked to perform "secretarial" tasks like recording the discussion or making and serving coffee? One suggestion is that when someone says, "Let's have some coffee," the woman should not jump up, but, instead, merely continue sitting. If silence descends on the meeting, she should look at the person nearest the door.[13] Another suggestion is to say, "Fine, I'll take notes this time, but why don't we rotate it from now

[13]"The Corporate Woman—How to Get Along—and Ahead—in the Office," *Business Week*, 22 March 1976, pp. 107–110.

on?'' Or, ''No thanks, I've already had my quota of coffee this morning—why don't you go ahead and have some.''[14]

Even Lady Bosses Have Bosses

Women who have moved up the ladder sometimes face serious resistance from their male bosses who may have difficulty accepting new female roles. Male bosses, as well as male peers, may perceive women as a new form of competition for the positions on the increasingly narrow managerial pyramid. Or at the other extreme, overzealous bosses may promote women to responsible positions before providing them with adequate training and background—a procedure likely to scuttle a woman's chances of success in management.

How does assertiveness differ from pushiness?

Some less enthusiastic male bosses refuse to develop training programs for woman managers because of established beliefs that the woman will not remain for long on the job (remember *statistical discrimination?*). What can you do about it if you—a woman—are not receiving adequate training and development opportunities on the job? Either you can grin and bear it (that is, do nothing and suffer), you can seek out training and experience on your own, or you can explain to your boss how the organization would benefit from your training. The latter is one of the most advisable approaches. Let your boss know that you plan to remain with the organization, and that you want to advance. Convince him that both he and the organization will benefit by having well-trained personnel such as yourself.

Changed Attitudes

How do narrow attitudes tend to perpetuate the stereotypes?

We have by no means covered every type of problem that women may confront in organizations. The subject is one that is highly volatile and emotion charged. A significant change in the attitudes of both men and women will be necessary if the detrimental effects of sexism are to be eradicated from our society. The continued different interpretation of women's rights from those of men tends to perpetuate the stereotypes, resulting in something of a self-fulfilling prophesy. When a person has little hope of achieving a particular position within an organization, such as that of manager, the person tends, quite naturally, not to identify with the position. For example, few black students even bothered to take business administration courses before there was much possibility of their acquiring jobs with business organizations.

Employers seem to have had a difficult time distinguishing career-oriented women from others; thus, the former have become victims of statistical discrimination. If employer's statistics reflect significantly

[14]''The Three Toughest On-The-Job Problems,'' *A Forthright Guide for Woman Supervisors* (New York: Executive Enterprises Publications, 1974), p. 17.

higher absenteeism for women, it may be because they restrict their employment of women to clerical and other poorly paying jobs and usually employ young women who have had little working experience. Trained women in more responsible and skilled positions are seldom absent more often than men in similar jobs.

Some people feel that there is a *conflict in role* between a woman who desires to have equal job opportunities *and* her door held open or a bus seat offered. Perhaps there *is* a role conflict; values, however, are changing. Many young women today seem far more concerned about "job openers" than "door openers." A modern attitude among many young couples is that whoever is nearest a door opens it. Some women contend that many men who open doors don't necessarily respect women; they open the doors out of habit, not respect. The "problem" of who opens doors is really a side issue and not necessarily related to equal employment opportunities.

Summary

In this chapter we've attempted to explore some territory that traditionally has been avoided by most writers on the subject of human relations. Part of the problem has been that the topic of women and employment tends to be beset with emotion. Times are changing, however, and attitudes should move with the changing times.

Many employers' beliefs are based on tradition and custom. When the typical female employee was younger and less educated, perhaps some of the beliefs were more valid. There has, however, been an increase over the years in the average age of working women, which contributes toward stability of employment. The average working woman in 1975, for example, was thirty-nine years old, married, and working to support completely, or in part, herself and her family. Today a larger proportion of the female working force has more education and different values and responsibilities.

As more firms join the organizations that have started offering women positions with good prospects for advancement, along with training opportunities comparable to those received by men, and the prospect of high pay levels, they are likely to discover that turnover rates will decline.

Ashley Montagu summarized the problem of women succinctly when he remarked:

> What the American woman needs is a great deal of sympathetic understanding. But what the American woman needs quite as much as that is a parallel maturation of the American male.[15]

[15]Ashley Montagu, *The Humanization of Man* (New York: Grove Press, 1962), p. 191.

Terms and Concepts to Remember

Equal Pay Act of 1963
Institutional sexism
"Women's jobs"
Statistical discrimination

Title VII
Day-care centers
Maternity leave
Parental leave

Questions

1. Why, in your opinion, has there been so much resistance to the equal rights amendment to the Constitution?
2. What are the principal myths traditionally assigned to women in our society? What has caused both men and women to accept such generalities?
3. True or false, and explain: The Second World War moratorium on employment discrimination against women is evidence that much prejudice is more *socialized* than *inborn* in nature.
4. Explain the statement, "Women earn less because they are in 'women's jobs'."
5. How would you complete the phrase, "A woman's place is in the…"? What aspects of your background have probably influenced your answer?
6. How has "statistical discrimination" prevented women from attaining more responsible positions in organizations?
7. What have been the principal causes of higher turnover among women employees?
8. What are some major arguments supporting the establishment of more low-cost day-care centers for working mothers? Do you agree with the arguments? Explain.
9. Evaluate the following statement: "Women would make far better managers if they would only learn to think and act like a man."

Other Readings

Butler, Pam. *Self-Assertion Guide for Women: A Guide to Becoming Androgynous.* San Francisco: Canfield Press, 1977.

Chesler, Phyllis, and Goodman, Emily Jane. *Women, Money and Power.* New York: Morrow, 1976.

Hennig, Margaret, and Jardim, Anne. *The Managerial Woman*. New York: Anchor-Doubleday, 1977.

Kreps, Juanita, and Clark, Robert. *Sex, Age, & Work: The Changing Composition of the Labor Force*. Baltimore: Johns Hopkins University Press, 1976.

Levin, James A. *Who Will Raise the Children? New Options for Fathers (and Mothers)*. New York: J. B. Lippincott, 1976.

Marine, Gene. *A Male Guide to Women's Liberation*. New York: Holt, Rinehart and Winston, 1972.

Pomeroy, Sarah. *Goddesses, Whores, Wives & Slaves: Women in Classical Antiquity*. New York: Schocken Books, 1976.

"The Three Toughest On-The-Job Problems." *A Forthright Guide for Women Supervisors*. New York: Executive Enterprises, 1974.

A Working Woman's Guide to Her Job Rights. Washington, D.C.: United States Government Printing Office, 1975.

Applications

Promotion Bypass

Boris Brash is a branch manager whose Portland, Oregon, office has developed a reputation with the company for efficient operations. Recently, a division manager telephoned Brash about a new branch office which was to open within two months in Corvallis. The division manager informed Brash that top management is highly pleased with the way the Portland office has been run in the past and would like him to choose someone from his office to manage the new Corvallis branch.

Brash agreed to find someone and started analyzing his personnel to determine who might make a good manager. He has narrowed the choice down to two persons within his office: Miss Zelda Zealous and Mr. Edgar Eager.

Both Zelda and Edgar are bright young persons in their early thirties. Each has a college degree from a nearby university. Zelda has been with the firm seven years and Edgar five years. Zelda usually seems more effective and tactful when dealing with customers, especially those with complaints, than does Edgar. Both, however, have low absenteeism records, and either one would probably make a satisfactory manager for the new Corvallis office.

Brash is reminded of some of the things that his father, a retired manager, had taught him. He recalls his father telling him that "women, in general, don't make good managers. They have those monthly ups and downs," which certainly would be detrimental to stability in the new office. "Most people prefer male supervisors. Women generally have babies and quit the company; they're not really interested in careers."

Brash wants to be fair. That night he ponders over in his mind which person should be chosen. "Zelda is a good, dependable worker," he muses, "but she probably would become oversensitive in a new managerial role and develop aggressive, pushy female tendencies."

Brash decides to choose Edgar. However, he doesn't want to upset or alienate Zelda, so he plans to invite her to his office tomorrow morning to explain the situation. He intends to tell her that the reason she wasn't chosen for the promotion is because she is the best person the office has, and that the Portland office just can't get along without her.

Questions

1. What sort of problems seem to exist in this case?
2. What do you anticipate might be Zelda's reaction to the reason Brash intends to give her, "Zelda, you weren't chosen for the promotion because you're the best person the office has"?

My Rightful Place

Tom Wack's secretary placed his morning mail on his desk and hurried from his office. Tom had no sooner started to read the top letter when he let out an emotional burst, "Get the attorney on the phone!" Before the lawyer's telephone number could be dialed, new instructions came: "Cancel that call!"

Tom's violent reaction was to a letter from the Ohio Commission on Human Rights, which notified the company of a complaint, reading in part: "Complainant was continuously denied promotions and salary commensurate with her job duties by the Respondents because of her sex. The Respondent company has placed males with less seniority and experience in positions of responsibility over the Complainant and have paid those males salaries far above what the Complainant receives, in addition to perquisites and bonuses inherent in managerial positions."

Tom was hurt deeply. How could Jane Spiegel do this to him? When Tom was hired as a salesperson in 1969, Jane was his secretary. She had three years experience with the company and knew her job very well. During the years, as he moved up the management ladder, he promoted Jane at every opportunity. In fact, Jane was currently "the highest paid broad," as he put it, in his nationwide field distribution network. The only reason she was not higher in the organization was because she refused to relocate to corporate headquarters in Tallahassee, Florida. In 1975, Jane was offered a promotion to become Tom's national sales administrator concurrent with his move to national sales and distribution director. Jane had declined the move because her husband, whom she had recently married, was a bus driver who had eighteen years seniority with the city. She said, "Barney will not be able to find a secure, well-paying job in another city."

One year ago, Tom had promoted Jane to dealer relations coordinator at the Cincinnati distribution warehouse. Last month he considered Jane for promotion to manager in charge of the Cincinnati outlet. Of course, she would have been the only female manager in charge of warehousemen anywhere in the company. Because of the closing last month of the Tulsa warehouse, Jim Hansen was available for reassignment. There was concern that Jim would leave the company if he was assigned to a job in the Florida headquarters. Thus, Jim was transferred, and Jane did not get promoted to the number one job. However, Tom knew she expected that "chance of a lifetime," so he told her the lateral transfer of Jim would be temporary, perhaps six to twelve months. The promise was that when Jim is next promoted, Jane will become manager in charge.

Peter Paulson, director of personnel, examined records and interviewed managers familiar with the Cincinanati situation. Peter's findings were as follows:

	Jane Spiegel's Record	Jim Hansen's Record
Hired	10/10/66 as Clerk Typist @ $475 monthly	2/4/71 as Credit Co-ordinator @ $950 monthly
Education	3 years as education major	BA in business admin.
Age	38 years	31 years
Current status	Promoted to Dealer Relations Coordinator one year ago @ $1525 monthly	Lateral transfer to Manager in Charge one month ago @ $1900 monthly
Latest Performance Evaluations	"Very bright and ready for promotion"	"Excellent results" Manager in Charge, Tulsa
Career Potential	Unwilling to relocate; ultimate potential is Manager in Charge, Cincinnati	Senior marketing and sales potential

Jane talked by telephone to female employees in five cities, telling them of her "suit" against the company and how she "plans to make waves.'' Within a week, five women told their bosses that they would file discrimination complaints if the company agreed to pay Jane ''all the money she wants.''

On a Friday, without requesting an excused absence, Jane was absent all day to review her case with the State EEO Specialist. On that date, the two data entry clerks phoned in ''sick.'' Only Jane and the two trained data entry clerks could efficiently enter orders on the computer so that the warehouse crew could make dealer shipments. Orders were delayed and dealers were angered. When questioned by the manager, all three women said their absences were a ''coincidence.''

Choosing of sides started early. Everyone in the warehouse office seemed to be for Jane or against her. Women who were ''for the company'' stopped speaking to Jane and vice versa. Jane had for many months functioned as second in command. She had been there longer than anyone and knew the ropes better than anyone. Communications problems became so serious that operational efficiencies plummeted, and dealer complaints hit an all time high.

Peter Paulson had placed all managers on notice, especially Jim Hansen and Tom Wack, that every precaution must be taken to assure the claimant-employee, Jane Spiegel, that she will not be harrassed or subjected to reprisal. Under the law, she has that protection.

Jim and Tom met to explore strategies for correcting all operational inefficiencies. They found some problems that were clearly no fault of Jane. However, her attitude had caused serious dealer dissatisfaction. Jim and Tom decided to telephone Peter with this question: ''We know we cannot harrass Jane, but how far can she push us before we can fight back?''

Questions

1. What is the problem in this case?
2. What is your remedy?
3. In the complaint, Jane is arguing that her ''rightful place'' (but for discrimination, where she would have been) is to be promoted and that she receive the salaries, perquisites, and bonuses of managerial positions held by men of like seniority. Do you agree?
4. Should Jane insist that her husband relocate for the sake of her career? Why or why not?
5. Do you feel the men in the warehouse would object to working for a woman manager? Would your answer be different if half the crew were women?
6. Do you feel that women who are subjected to sex discrimination always file complaints? Seldom file complaints? Very rarely file complaints?
7. Does Tom appear to be a male chauvinist? Explain.

14

When you finish this chapter, you should be able to:

1. **Understand** some of the special types of employment problems faced by older and handicapped persons.
2. **Recognize** the traditional prejudicial attitudes toward the aging and handicapped.
3. **Explain** why the problems of the aging are becoming more acute than they were in the past.
4. **Summarize** some of the principal solutions to the problems of aging that have been applied in various societies.
5. **Support** an argument for the hiring of the handicapped.
6. **Identify** the problems associated with managing the handicapped.

> The human being is by nature active
> and when inactive begins to die.
> —Erich Fromm

> To take work away from the worker
> is the cruelest thing society can do.
> —Dr. Harry Weinstein

Someone with visionary foresight once mused, "We're all middle-aged sometime—if we're lucky!" Unfortunately, however, good luck doesn't always accompany middle age, especially when the middle-aged person is out of work. The chances are fairly good that you—the reader of this book—are relatively young. Can you imagine, however, applying for a job and being rejected solely on the grounds that you are forty-five years old and thus "too old to hire"?

Also think about how you might feel if you had previously suffered an industrial accident, or had your right leg blasted off by a land mine while serving in Vietnam, or had been born with an impairment—and people refused to enable you to engage in gainful employment. Would you feel such treatment to be fair?

In the previous two chapters we examined some of the conditions and employment problems of minorities and women. Unfortunately, these are not the only special employment groups in our society. The organizational manager of tomorrow (today?), facing additional social responsibilities and pressure, must understand and be prepared to deal with numerous *special employment groups,* especially since their members are demanding with increasing frequency what they believe to be basic rights in a society that refers to itself as "free."

Why must managers understand *special employment groups?*

In this chapter, therefore, we are going to examine two groups that traditionally have been among the forgotten humans in most studies of organizational behavior: the aging and those with physical or mental limitations, traditionally referred to as the "handicapped."

These two groups by no means complete the list of those that are discriminated against solely because of conditions over which they have little or no control. They do, however, serve to illustrate for the student of human relations the variety of problems with which organizational members are faced in the modern world.

an impairment that limits life activity = handicapped

Employment Problems of the Aging

age bias

Aging is a condition that few of us can avoid experiencing and one most of us would prefer to avoid thinking about. Unfortunately, however, various forms of subtle *age bias* in employment have accompanied the aging process in American society. For reasons that we shall examine, older workers have regularly been discriminated against in the hiring, promotion, and retirement practices of many organizations.

The Variability of the Aging Process

Do all persons age at the same rate?

The term *older worker* is one with little in the way of absolute meaning. If you were to choose thirty people at random, all forty-five years old, you would quickly discover that not all of them have experienced the aging process at the same rate. Some members of your sample would appear trim, agile, youthful-looking, and topped with full heads of their own hair. Others might be plump, muscularly soft, a bit weathered and wrinkled, and sporting heads of hair imported from the Far East. A variety of factors, especially *heredity* and *past dietary* and *health habits,* significantly influence the aging process.

What determines how old is "old"?

The *nature of a particular job* and the *industry* itself also influence how "old" a person is for a specific occupation. Baseball players, for example, are generally considered old if they are in their thirties, while corporate presidents are considered young when they are in their mid-forties.

a "qualified" handicapped person must be hired

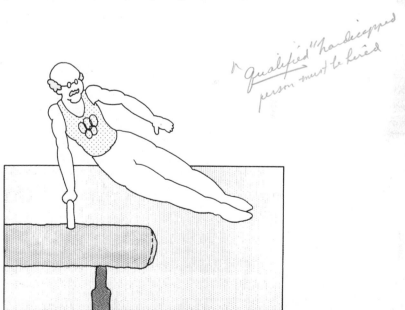

Pops was
still tops
with the Pops
at 82!

Arthur Fiedler, conductor of the Boston Pops Orchestra from 1930 to the late 1970s, is a good example of the variability of the aging process. He finally decided at the ripe age of eighty-two to slow down a bit. So in 1977, Fiedler reduced the number of concerts he was conducting each year from 194 to "only" 164!

The Older Worker Defined

older worker

Recognizing that age is relative, we have arbitrarily decided to define the *older worker* as any person *age forty and over*. The National Advisory Committee for the 1971 White House Conference on Aging arbitrarily chose age forty-five, thus including about four out of ten persons in the labor force. The Age Discrimination in Employment Act of 1967 protects persons over age forty. The age in our definition is not as significant as the specific problems that many individuals experience merely as a result of their own advancing ages.

The Problem of Job Loss for the Aging

There is an expression often uttered by older workers that stresses part of their plight: "Too old to rehire and too young to retire."

How is the
problem of aging
disguised by un-
employment statistics?

The problems of older workers are often disguised by unemployment statistics, which show that unemployment rates tend to *decrease* with age. This condition is not surprising since older persons generally have more *seniority* and thus are usually the last to be laid off. However, once out of work, individuals over forty are likely to remain unemployed much longer than their younger co-workers. In fact, the likelihood of *long-term unemployment* actually tends to increase with age. From the age of forty, many unemployed workers often find job hunting a nightmare.

According to a Ford Foundation study of formerly jobless individuals who were able to secure new jobs, there were *far more increases* than decreases in pay for workers *below the age of thirty-five*. After *age forty*, however, there were more *decreases* than increases in pay among previously unemployed persons. And at *age fifty-five* the chances of finding a higher-paying job became very *slight*.

Should seniority
rights be abolished?

To further aggravate the problem, the advantages of seniority rights for the aging may be succumbing to a recent trend. For example, in January 1973, the United States Department of Labor *struck down the seniority rules* of two major employers, American Telephone and Telegraph Company and Bethlehem Steel Corporation, on the grounds that such rules constituted a major unacceptable barrier to ending job discrimination against blacks, women, and minorities.[1]

---

[1]"The Courts Reinterpret Old-age Discrimination," *Business Week*, 24 February 1976, p. 91.

Why is finding a new job so difficult when you are over age fifty?

Another major problem for older persons, especially those over fifty years old, is that when they lose their jobs, they have difficulty in finding another. A large proportion of workers not covered by employer-sponsored retirement plans face potential financial problems when they retire. They also face personal problems, including loneliness, loss of purpose, housing difficulties, failing health and fear of death.

During the fiscal year ending June, 1974, a total of 1,648 older workers were found by the Labor Department to be underpaid by almost $6.3 million, bringing total back-pay orders since the adoption of the Age Discrimination Act of 1967 to nearly $11 million.

Attitudes Toward Older Workers

The aging find it difficult to secure employment often because of the attitudes of employers. Among the attitudes, that older employees:

1. Cost more in fringe benefits
2. Have fewer years left in which to work
3. Are physically too weak to perform certain jobs
4. Have higher rates of absenteeism

Increased Costs of Fringe Benefits

How might older employees actually reduce operating costs?

An attitude toward the aging often expressed by employers is that operating costs rise when older employees are hired because of the increased expense for health and retirement plans. Not all employers, however, agree that costs necessarily rise; some contend that any increased cost in benefits is more than offset by savings in turnover and training costs.

Fewer Working Years

Why doesn't the younger worker necessarily have more potential years?

Another cause of bias against age is related to the attitude that younger persons potentially have more years remaining with a company; that is, a twenty-five-year-old could potentially be with an organization for forty years, while a person age fifty would ordinarily have fifteen years at the most remaining.

However, as we mentioned in chapter 13 on women employees, a study by the United States Department of Labor indicates that of the total work force, the average time *all individuals* have held their jobs is only *4.2 years*. Other studies indicate that turnover rates are actually *higher among younger workers* than among older workers. Younger workers often feel that they have less to lose by changing jobs, or even careers, early in their working years.

Physically Too Weak

What can be done when an older worker becomes weaker?

Another attitude that has worked to the detriment of older employees is the belief that older workers are physically weaker than younger ones. Although this contention often is true, exceptions are numerous. Many members of society, including medical doctors, tend to try to force the aging into a preconceived role. After all, aren't old people *supposed* to be sick much of the time? There's a story, for example, of the man of 104 who, when he complained of a stiff knee, was told, "After all, you can't expect to be agile," and replied, "My left knee's 104, too, but that doesn't hurt."

reassigned or redesigned

On occasions when an older employee has not had sufficient muscular strength for a specific job, some concerned managers have either *reassigned the person* to a different job within the organization, or *redesigned the job* to enable a physically weaker person to perform it.

Higher Rates of Absenteeism

Is absenteeism only related to bad health?

There is also the belief that older employees have higher rates of absenteeism, another myth refuted by many managers. For example, the absenteeism rate at Hughes Tool Company in Houston, Texas, has averaged about 14 percent, while the rate for older workers has been only around 1 percent.

Factors far more significant than age influence the absence of employees from the job. Young workers are frequently absent for reasons other than those related to illness. An interesting study on absenteeism might be made, if one were inclined, at any afternoon game of the San Francisco Giants to determine the numbers of younger persons who were absent from work for reasons unrelated to their health!

The Changing Nature of Employment

The nature of work has undergone considerable change in recent decades. Educational requirements for today's jobs are often different from those for jobs in the past and, all too frequently, the unemployed person over forty is looking for today's job with yesterday's skills.

Less-Skilled Jobs Diminishing

How does the changing nature of jobs affect the aging?

To a large extent, manual labor has been eliminated by the *greater use of mechanization and automation* in materials handling. As a result, many of the new types of jobs require higher degrees of skill and increased amounts of education.

In general, not only do older individuals tend to have *less education* than do younger workers, but also that education has often become *obsolescent*. In far too many instances, the older workers have contributed to their own demise by *resisting new techniques and processes and refusing to take advantage of training programs* designed to update their knowledge and skills.

The problems of the aging are further aggravated by *changing patterns of employment*, which generally require higher levels of skill, more formal education and training, and knowledge of processes often unknown thirty years ago.

Decline in Self-Employment

Is self-employment the solution?

Because of changing market trends, there is much less likelihood that older persons will be able to take refuge on their own farms or in their own small businesses. Farm population is approaching only *4 percent* of the total population and most of the country's agricultural output is produced by large agri-corporations. The number of small businesses, which are often owned and operated by older individuals, is also likely to continue to decline.

Problems for the Professional Employee

How is the professional employee hit by the aging process?

Older professional employees, such as engineers, scientists, and even managers, may be adversely affected by the new, more advanced technology, not only from the standpoint of obsolescent skills and knowledge, but also psychologically. Imagine, for example, that you are an older executive who, after many years of employment, feels that your higher-order needs, especially those for security and self-esteem, have finally become relatively satisfied. The sudden discovery in your twilight years that the ladder to achievement has been kicked out from under you by the complexities of advancing technology can frequently cause severe mental hardship.

Solutions for Consideration

As with any problem that involves the human side of organizations, essential on the part of those who have the authority to make decisions, both in private and in public enterprise, is the development of a higher degree of *sensitivity and understanding* of the problems of aging employees. Ours has been, and will continue to be in the foreseeable future, a work-oriented society, which in itself can create painful psychological stress on under- and unemployed middle-aged and older persons.

Included among America's long-run goals have been not only full employment and the attainment of a better balance over time between the supply and demand of the work force, but also the rapid placement of all workers in jobs that utilize their abilities. The pressure for fairer treatment of older employees comes at the same time as pressures from youth, women, and minority groups, all of whom are vying for and demanding their fair slice of the American economic pie. Efforts on many fronts will be necessary if a successful melding of the various groups is to be achieved. The solutions, once again, will not be easy and will require cooperation between both private and governmental units in order to establish greater equity for all.

Who wants a piece of the pie?

Now let's examine some recent efforts, both in the United States and abroad, that have been made, with varying degrees of success.[2]

Legislation

Most democratic nations are interested in the effective utilization of their available labor supplies. However, most of the democratic counterparts of the United States, such as West Germany, France, and Sweden, have been far more active in attempting to prevent the unemployment of special groups, such as the aging or the handicapped.

How do *you* feel about government involvement?

One of the major differences between the United States and its western European counterparts has been its attitude toward government involvement and responsibilities. For example, most European nations do not permit the existence of private employment agencies. Another difference is that employers in many European countries generally cannot dismiss a worker without first securing permission from governmental agencies. A revolution in thinking would be necessary before such systems are likely to be accepted in the United States, where the concept of freedom seems to have a different meaning.

The Age Discrimination in Employment Act. There are signs, however, that the attitudes of Americans toward the aging are changing. For example, there is now a federal law designed to protect workers over age forty, entitled the *Age Discrimination in Employment Act of 1967.* As of 1977, an estimated *46 million* of more than 96 million workers in the labor force were covered by the act. The basic provisions of the act are that:

Age Discrimination Act

1. *Private employers* of twenty or more persons, and *federal, state,* and *local governments,* regardless of the number of employees, may no longer refuse to hire qualified workers over forty.

[2]For an excellent and comprehensive discussion of the problems of the aging in the United States and an explatnion of programs in other western nations, see *1971 White House Conference on Aging—Employment, Background, and Issues* (Washington, D.C.: United States Government Printing Office), March 1971.

2. *Employers* may no longer fire employees in this age group because of age alone, or discriminate against them in terms of salary, seniority, and other job conditions.

3. *Employment agencies* may no longer refuse to refer workers in this age group to prospective employers, or no longer may even try to classify them on the basis of age.

4. *Labor unions* with twenty-five or more members may no longer exclude those over age forty from membership or refuse to refer older members to employers simply because of their age.

5. *Help wanted advertisements* may no longer include age specifications.

6. All organizations obligated under the act must post in conspicuous places the rights of employees or union members related to the act. (See figure 14–1 for an example of an approved poster.)

The number of age-bias suits since the passage of the act has grown dramatically. Many feel that this is sufficient evidence that there was a need for legislative protection of older workers. In recent years, an increasing number of suits have involved *groups* of employees, rather than individuals. For example, Standard Oil of California agreed in 1974 to a $2 million settlement for 160 older employees laid off during a reduction-in-force beginning in 1970. Standard Oil was required to reinstate 120 of the laid-off employees.

Training and Counseling Programs

Often in the past, employment services in the United States have done little to guide older persons into training programs because of the belief that they would be difficult to train and place. Also, there is the belief that their training would not be as economically efficient as would the training of younger people who will spend a longer time in the work force. However, studies conducted by the formerly-designated Office of Manpower, Automation, and Training indicate that older workers tend to be readily placed and remain longer in the fields and jobs for which they were trained. By contrast younger workers often move out of the fields for which they were trained.

Unfortunately, there has been little counseling or guidance provided for older persons to lead them to programs that enhance their employability. Government employment services in the United States have tended to stress the quantity rather than the quality of placements and, as a result, have concentrated principally on the younger worker, who is easier to place.

Should there be special training programs for the aging?
Little has been done thus far in America to develop training programs specifically designed for the aging. Yet, the Swedish, West German, French, and Belgian employment services have developed for older

Persons Over 40 Years Note!

The Federal Age Discrimination in Employment Act prohibits arbitrary age discrimination in employment by:

- Private Employers of 20 or more persons
- Federal, State, and Local Governments, without regard to the number of employees in the employing unit
- Employment Agencies serving such employers
- Labor Organizations with 25 or more members

Certain exceptions are provided.

If you feel you have been discriminated against because of age, contact the nearest office of the Wage and Hour Division, U. S. Department of Labor. It is important to contact the Division promptly.

If you wish to bring a court action yourself, you must first notify the Secretary of Labor of your intent to do so. This notice should be filed promptly, but in no event later than *180* days after the alleged unlawful practice occurred.

Questions on State age discrimination laws should be directed to State authorities. These laws may affect the *180* day time limit noted above.

Questions on Federal employment should be directed to the U. S. Civil Service Commission, Washington, D. C. 20415.

U. S. Department of Labor
Employment Standards Administration
Wage and Hour Division

☆ U.S. GOVERNMENT PRINTING OFFICE: 1976 O--207-395

Figure 14–1. An example of an approved poster related to the Age Discrimination in Employment Act.

workers special training courses that are designed so that the trainees can proceed at a pace commensurate with their learning abilities.

Training Allowances

**The unem-
ployed employed?**

To be eligible for training and allowances in Sweden, workers *need not already be unemployed*. The term *unemployed* in Sweden includes individuals who are *likely* to become unemployed some time in the future as a result of changing technology in particular industries. Thus training programs provided *before* unemployment serve as a means of "preventive maintenance."

**Do high allowances
develop malingerers?**

Participation in training programs by the aging is usually impossible, or at least difficult, without some sort of *subsistence allowance*. European compensation during training generally varies from between 70 and 90 percent of previous weekly earnings. In the United States, allowances have customarily amounted to between 35 and 40 percent of previous wages.

Employment Services

Most western European countries have banned private employment agencies on the grounds that their placement practices tend not to foster the social goal of assisting special employment groups, but instead tend to defer solely to the needs of the employer. In the United States, both private and public employment services exist, but neither is national in nature. The American system is composed of fifty-four individual and relatively autonomous systems, with varying philosophies and little communication among themselves regarding the availability of jobs in different regions.

**Would more
coordination
help?**

In European countries and in Canada, any job vacancies must be reported to the public employment agencies. In some countries, such as Italy, the Netherlands, and Israel, the employment services prohibit employers from hiring replacements until the service has had time to recommend suitable candidates, and preference is often given to older workers.

Dismissal of Workers

Older workers have benefited in countries that have restricted the employers' rights to dismiss employees. In the United States, there has been scant limitation placed on decisions of employers in the labor market until recently.

In France, for example, any employer who intends to dismiss an employee must first obtain permission from the employment service.

How does "prior permission" both *give* and *take away* "rights"?

Other countries have similar "prior permission" regulations. In West Germany, dismissal of workers requires sixty days notice. Senior workers cannot be discharged if there are no other jobs available. Older workers with more than twelve years of employment must be given a minimum of six months advance notice before they can be dismissed. If the dismissals are considered "socially unjustifiable," the notices of termination can be blocked.

Job Creation

The difference in approach between western European countries and the United States seems to vary principally in a particular society's willingness to spend money in achieving social goals and in its attitude toward giving up some rights to acquire others. For example, the Swedish philosophy toward unemployment is that jobs shall be created where *employer of last resort* necessary. The government, therefore, assumes the role of the *employer of last resort*, a concept that has not yet gained favor in the United States, except for temporary programs such as the W.P.A. (Works Progress Administration) during the Great Depression of the 1930s.

B. Olsson summarizes the Swedish position toward job creation:

> [Individual assistance] is important in the case of the handicapped and older workers. To this group belong persons (middle aged or elderly) who cannot continue in their own occupation and who without doubt belong to the "partially disabled" group in the proper sense since they are difficult to place in the labor market.[3]

What might be some useful jobs for the elderly in the United States?

The jobs created by the system in Sweden are not merely an exercise in digging holes and then refilling them. Instead, the jobs are often socially useful, such as the clearing and cleaning of parks, lightweight construction on roads and streets, and the provision of guides and library assistants. In some cases, private enterprise is subsidized when members of the "partially disabled" group are employed. In Sweden, public works programs also tend to employ many elderly persons.

Fostering the Mobility of Workers

There is a human tendency to fear the unknown; and many older unemployed workers, for this reason, tend not to seek out potential opportunities in other regions. Sometimes geographical areas or industries decline in their ability to employ workers. Generally, the declining indus-

[3]B. Olsson, "Employment Policy in Sweden," *International Labor Review* 87 (1963):17.

tries have high proportions of older workers who tend to cling to their jobs until the positions are eliminated.

worker mobility

The United States has done little thus far to enhance *worker mobility* from regions that have a surplus of labor to areas that are short of labor. By contrast, the countries of Western Europe, in order to foster increased worker mobility, offer counseling, information on job availability, and mobility subsidies. In Germany and Sweden, for example, a travel allowance is paid, even if a worker has not yet committed him- or herself to accept a job in a different region, but merely wants to examine the situation first.

Some individuals feel that mobility subsidy programs are too costly. In general, however, they tend to reduce net governmental outlays because of the elimination of unemployment compensation and welfare adequate information and counseling, far more workers are usually willing to participate in the programs.[4]

The Need for Adjustment by the Aging

Why is facing the aging process sometimes difficult?

The problems of the aging are further aggravated by the tendency of older people not to adjust readily to the realities of *changed conditions in the job market*. The necessity of having to face the problems of aging is somewhat of a blow to the egos of many. Numerous persons do not want to leave the communities in which they have lived for many years even though the move may be necessary to obtain another job. The possibility of having to accept a job with less pay or prestige can also be mentally painful.

Some older workers not only resist opportunities to be retrained, but also they do not know how to seek jobs effectively. Consequently, in order to offset some of the natural attitudes of the aging, more attention in the future must be paid to the *counseling and guidance* of older employees in order to reduce their potential psychological fears.

Assistance by Private Organizations

Our discussion of possible alternatives and the examination of programs in other countries has concentrated mainly on governmental activities, although private organizations can help considerably in mitigating the problems of the aging.

---

[4]The approaches followed in European countries have not been presented in this text as utopian solutions that American organizations should necessarily adopt *in toto*. However, to ignore or belittle any programs that have not originated in the United States could prevent reasonable attempts to analyze how programs followed in other countries may be modified to suit our own particular needs and problems.

portable pensions

We have already mentioned briefly such aids as *job redesign* and *reassignment*. In addition, pension plans might be modified so they are *portable*; that is, workers would not lose their benefits when they leave a particular company. Instead, benefit credits for retirement would follow the worker from job to job. The lack of portability of most pension plans tends to encourage older workers to cling to their jobs in declining industries rather than encourage them to learn new skills so that they can be employed in other growth industries.

ERISA

vested rights

The Pension Reform Act, known officially as the *Employee Retirement Income Security Act of 1974 (ERISA),* has been a move in the direction of portability by requiring that pension rights be *vested* (permanent) after an employee completes a certain number of years of service. Although most companies had provided some degree of early vesting, until ERISA was enacted, employers were not compelled to provide workers with permanent pension rights. In companies that avoided vested pension rights, employees who were laid off after thirty or forty years of service lost all pension rights. In one celebrated pension catastrophe, when the Studebaker auto factory in South Bend, Indiana, closed in 1963, 4,500 workers under age sixty were able to collect only 15 percent of the benefits they were entitled to after an average twenty-three years of service. Today, the typical pension plan includes full vesting after an employee has worked ten years. Many plans are also required to be insured with the Pension Benefit Guaranty Corporation.

Perhaps changes in attitudes by employers toward the aging are necessary. We sometimes forget that when we were infants, we couldn't have survived without the assistance of people older than ourselves. Some societies, such as those of western Europe and Japan, feel that the younger, more able population is, in a sense, indebted to their elders. Until Americans develop greater sensitivity toward its aging population, older persons will continue to find it extremely difficult to adjust to the problems of growing older.

Retirement—The Need for Greater Flexibility?

mandatory retirement

Many organizations have followed a policy of *mandatory retirement*, that is, the practice of retiring employees at a predetermined age, often sixty-five. Such policies frequently came under attack by individuals concerned with the problems of the aging. Recognizing the variability of the aging process, many organizations have adopted a *flexible retirement* policy, one that permits employees to continue beyond the established retirement age for as long as they are capable of performing their duties.

flexible retirement

Thus far, we have seen some of the difficulties that will have to be faced by many of us. There is another special employment group to which it is even harder for many individuals to relate—the handicapped.

Not Quotas . . . Goals!

Their problems, to be covered in the following section, should also be understood by responsible organizational members.

Problems of the Handicapped

Those with physical and mental limitations, traditionally referred to as the *handicapped,* or *disabled,* are usually given token treatment if any in most texts on organizational behavior. Perhaps little has been written about their employment problems for the same reasons that non-handicapped persons tend not to look at another person's handicap. Have you ever felt self-conscious when your eyes met those of a person whose face was scarred or mutilated? Perhaps we also tend to develop the same uncomfortable feelings when discussing the topic of handicapped persons.

Fortunately for most handicapped persons, their physical or mental limitations or impairments are not quite as visible as are the scars from an accident. However, many employers, for reasons that we shall examine, are afraid to hire the physically or mentally disabled person. Yet, in our society there are numerous individuals who have served in the military during armed conflict and emerged with the loss of limb. For many disabled persons, regardless of the cause of their handicap, entry into the job market has been as difficult as it has been for the minority groups we have already discussed.

Who Are the Handicapped?

Accurate statistics on the number of handicapped persons are scarce. However, estimates by the U.S. Department of Health, Education, and Welfare place the number of handicapped Americans at nearly 50 million. Their unemployment rate is said to be one of the highest of any special employment group, approximately 40 percent among those handicapped who are considered employable.

handicapped defined

When we use the term *handicapped,* just what are we referring to? The U.S. Department of Labor Employment Standards Administration defines a handicapped individual as "any person who has a physical or mental impairment which substantially limits one or more of such person's major life activities, has a record of such impairment, or is regarded as having an impairment." Most handicapped persons, however, are capable of

the qualified handicapped

working and are referred to as *qualified handicapped individuals*. A qualified handicapped individual means a person who is capable of performing a particular job with reasonable accommodation to his or her handicap. Among those considered to be handicapped under the *Rehabilitation Act of 1973* are individuals who are:

1. Visually impaired
2. Deaf
3. Suffering from mental retardation and mental illness
4. Have ambulatory limitations
5. Suffering from alcohol and drug abuse

Causes of Handicaps

Physical and mental limitations can result from a variety of causes, the major ones being:

1. Inborn (congenital)
2. Accidental
3. Disease
4. Birth injuries
5. Cultural or environment deprivation
6. The aging process

Let's now look at some of the traditional beliefs and prejudices about the handicapped and then discuss what might be done to improve their chances for employment.

Common Attitudes Toward the Physically and Mentally Limited

Why don't some employers hire the handicapped?

Employers have given state departments of rehabilitation an assortment of excuses for not hiring the handicapped. Among the more common are that insurance costs will rise, handicapped persons are prone to accidents, and they are offensive to the public. Let's take a look at these reasons.

Increased Insurance Costs

According to Ms. Anna Williams, Placement Specialist of the California State Department of Vocational Rehabilitation, a frequent excuse given by employers for not hiring handicapped persons is that their workmen's compensation insurance premium costs will rise. Insurance rates, however, bear no relationship to the hiring of the handicapped, nor do rates necessarily rise when a disabled employee has an accident on the job that is a result of a previous disability.

Accident Prone

Another common belief about the handicapped is that they are more likely to have accidents than ''normal'' employees. Studies made by the

California Department of Rehabilitation do not support this belief. In fact, the safety records of disabled persons who have been rehabilitated have been as good as or better than those of others.

Handicapped persons tend to be more sensitive to and thus more aware of their limitations, rather like the person who has had a serious automobile accident. And like the person who has *seen* an automobile accident, co-workers will often be more cautious on their own jobs.

Offensive to the Public

Some employers shy away from offering positions to the handicapped for fear that the person's appearance would be offensive to the public. When thinking about the disabled, far too many employers seem to have the image of the armless, legless, wheelchair-ridden invalid. However, there are all sorts and degrees of disability; most are not as severe or as highly visible. Even the severely handicapped are not necessarily a public relations liability. On the contrary, employers who have the reputation for being concerned about people often enjoy an enhanced public image.

Are They Really Handicapped?

The word *handicapped* has unfavorable connotations to many people. Unfortunately, the word often conjures up an image of a wheelchair-ridden person incapable of doing any type of work. In reality, however, most so-called handicapped persons have no desire—or need—to be "charity cases." Frequently they are able and willing workers who have been deprived of opportunity because of misunderstanding and bias. In reality, most individuals whom we consider handicapped are merely persons with *physical or mental limitations*—but not necessarily skill or job limitations. And, in reality, don't we all have physical and mental limitations of some sort?

Don't we all have our limits?

physical or mental limitations

Actually, the number of jobs that require able-bodied persons with unimpaired faculties is declining. Of course, good health, youth, and possession of all limbs and senses is unquestionably desirable. But for many jobs available today, all of these are not essential. Job market demands are changing. Industrial, manual types of jobs are becoming less available, while opportunities in the services, professional, and technical occupations are expanding. For example, 56 percent of those rehabilitated by the California Department of Rehabilitation in a recent year went into clerical, sales, service, professional, technical, or managerial jobs. Such jobs tend to be less demanding physically.

This is not to say that those with limitations cannot handle industrial jobs. In fact, most handicapped people are well-suited for jobs involving their bodies as well as their minds. Thirty-four percent of California's rehabilitated workers have been placed in industrial occupations.

Why Hiring the Handicapped
Is Good Business

"Hire the handicapped—it's good business!" is an old slogan, but it also is a reality. It's good business principally because the handicapped often provide a readily available supply of trained workers, employers' training costs are often reduced, the turnover and absentee rates of handicapped workers tend to be lower than those of others, the handicapped tend to be more efficient on certain jobs, and their presence often elicits favorable responses from co-workers. Let's briefly examine these five reasons.

A Supply of Trained Workers

Employers concerned with assisting the handicapped should contact their state departments of rehabilitation, where they can often locate well-trained workers. These are generally persons who have been evaluated medically, psychologically, and vocationally for the proposed job.

Reduction in Training Costs

Since many departments of rehabilitation also have training facilities, employers often discover that their own training costs are reduced.

Lower Turnover and Absentee Rates

Handicapped persons generally appreciate the opportunity to work. As a result, turnover and absentee rates and, consequently, operating costs tend to be lower among disabled workers since they realize that jobs for them are more difficult to acquire. They also realize that there are often limits on the types of jobs they can perform.

Greater Efficiency

In some cases, handicapped persons may even be more efficient than others on similar jobs. For example, a deaf employee could hold certain types of jobs without being distracted by surrounding noises. Efficiency is, in part, influenced by motivation. Disabled individuals tend to appreciate the opportunity to work and are often highly motivated.

Positive Effects on Co-workers

Some employers have discovered that disabled persons often improve the motivation of *other workers*, who develop a greater appreciation for their *own* situations. The able person may feel, "If a handicapped person can do that sort of work, so can I."

350

Managing the Handicapped

The Need for Selective Placement

selective placement

Selective placement is probably the most important first step in managing the handicapped worker. Selective placement means *matching* the physical abilities of the disabled person with the physical demands of the job. The "matching" process can often be accomplished by redesigning a job so that it is more suitable and safer by what could be a slight change in duties or machine controls, such as changing a lever from right to left hand operation or from hand to foot control (or vice versa).

Maintain a Normal Relationship

How should supervisors treat handicapped workers?

Supervisors are often uncertain about the best approach to take when dealing with handicapped employees. Experienced rehabilitators feel that supervisors should neither overemphasize the handicap nor be over-protective toward the person.

Supervisors should attempt to treat the handicapped employee as they would any other employee. Disabled individuals are generally aware of their own strengths and weaknesses, and generally prefer not to be singled out as something strange or different.

Workers Should Be Open

Handicapped workers should attempt to be natural and honest about their own disabilities. A self-conscious attempt to conceal the condition tends to accentuate it. Rehabilitators generally recommend that the handicapped person attempt to clear the air by explaining what he or she can and cannot do in order to avoid the creation of an exaggerated situation.

A Social Responsibility

One of the stated goals of the United States Congress is *to provide equal employment opportunities for all of its citizens*. Sometimes there is the tendency to overlook the individuals who need the most assistance. Both private and public resources are needed to provide the necessary rehabilitation for handicapped persons so that they, too, may live as full a life as their remaining abilities will permit. The major types of assistance needed by the handicapped include medical examinations and treatment, guidance, counseling, training, and placement.

Much has already been done in Scandinavian countries to enable disabled persons to obtain employment in circumstances as near to normal as possible. To offset the disadvantages of a disability, Austria,

France, Germany, Greece, and Israel have developed official goals for the employment of their handicapped. In many countries, disabled persons are able to obtain employment as vendors of national lottery tickets.

Rehabilitation Act of 1973.

In the United States, the hiring of the handicapped became regulated under the *Rehabilitation Act of 1973* (amended in 1974). The act authorized financial grants to states for vocational rehabilitation services. The act also tells employers with federal contracts over $2,500 the steps they must take to recruit, train, and employ handicapped workers. The regulations further require federal contractors with jobs of $500,000 or more to draw up "affirmative action" plans for seeking out, hiring, and promoting handicapped workers, and to report each year on their results.

physical access

An additional and controversial part of the act (controversial mainly because of the cost of implementing it) is the regulation that requires providing *physical access* for handicapped individuals to public schools, colleges, community health and welfare facilities, and eventually, public transport and housing.

Although in the short run, legislation such as that just discussed placed additional demands on the energies and time of today's managers, the long-run benefits to society as a whole are likely to be substantial. The hiring of the handicapped, for example, can enable another group to participate in the mainstream of American economic activity. Persons previously unemployed can become taxpayers rather than welfare recipients. Probably most important is that the hiring of the handicapped enables *them* to develop a feeling of *contribution and self-respect*. Productive work is usually far more satisfying for the handicapped than enforced idleness.

Summary

In this chapter, we have examined the problems of two additional special employment groups—the *aging* and those with *physical and mental limitations*. No longer can managers afford to overlook the needs and aspirations of groups who formerly were among the "forgotten humans." Government legislation, coupled with a heightened awareness of the social responsibilities of organizations, have substantially changed the traditional approaches to managing human resources.

Older workers, arbitrarily defined as those over age forty, experience difficulty obtaining employment when they lose their jobs. Many of the problems of the aging have been caused by the *prejudices of employers*, their own *resistance to change*, and the *obsolescence of their education and skills*.

The demands of society and the nature of work have changed rapidly in recent years, a situation that necessitates the development of programs designed to assist the aging and the handicapped in maintaining and acquiring employment. New attitudes toward special employment groups are necessary if past inequities in employment practices are to be eradicated.

Terms and Concepts to Remember

The aging
Age bias
Older worker
Reassigned person
Redesigned job
Age Discrimination in
    Employment Act of 1967
Prior permission
Job creation
Employer of last resort
Worker mobility

Employee Retirement Income
    Security Act of 1974 (ERISA)
Vested pension rights
Mandatory versus flexible
    retirement policies
Handicapped
Qualified handicapped
Physical and mental limitations
Selective placement
Rehabilitation Act of 1973
Physical access

Questions

1. What determines how "old" a person is for a specific occupation?
2. Do you feel that there should be *special* legislation and training programs for the aging? Does your own age influence your answer?
3. Since unemployment rates tend to be lower for individuals over age forty than they are for age twenty, what special sorts of employment problems do the aging face?
4. Why have some employers developed prejudices against the aging?
5. In what ways have the actions taken by western European countries to assist their aging differed from the American actions?
6. Which do you feel is more equitable to both the employee and the employer—*mandatory* or *flexible* retirement practices? Why?
7. What are the principal areas affected by the Age Discrimination Act?
8. Do you feel that unemployed older persons should receive training and mobility allowances? Support your answer.
9. What are some of the benefits that tend to result from hiring handicapped individuals?
10. Evaluate the following statement: "You have to be careful when supervising the handicapped. In general, because of their limitations, you can't give handicapped people the same types of tasks you'd give normal people."

Other Readings

Beechel, Jacque. *Interpretation for Handicapped Persons*. Seattle: National Park Service, Pacific Northwest Region, July 1975.

Dickman, Irving R. *Living with Blindness*. New York: American Federation for the Blind, 1972.

Kreps, Juanita M., and Laws, Ralph. *Training and Retraining Older Workers*. New York: National Council on the Aging, 1965.

Miller, Edith, and Bentley, Ernest L. *Listen to the Sounds of Deafness*. Silver Spring, Maryland: National Association of the Deaf, 1970.

1971 White House Conference on Aging—Employment, Background, and Issues. Washington, D.C.: United States Government Printing Office, March 1971.

Working Together: The Key to Jobs for the Handicapped. Washington, D.C.: American Federation of Labor and Congress of Industrial Organizations, June 1973.

Applications

Pruning the Older Branches*

In 1975 a U.S. District Court in Newark, New Jersey, awarded $750,000 to the widow of an Exxon Research and Engineering Company employee who had been forced to retire at age sixty as part of a campaign to prune older, higher-salaried employees from the payroll. The employee, Mr. Rogers, who died of cancer in 1973, went to work for Exxon as a research chemist in 1941 and shared in forty-four patents for inventions to increase the efficiency of Exxon products, according to evidence brought out at the trial.

The court case was initiated by Mrs. Gladys Rogers, the employee's wife. According to trial evidence, Mr. Rogers, a senior research associate, was forced out of the company by being transferred to a job requiring him to be on his feet for several hours. Allegedly, the company's policy was to ease out older, higher-paid executives and replace them with younger men. The jury granted Mrs. Rogers the $750,000 to compensate for the pain and humiliation stemming from age discrimination.

*References: "Exxon Unit Is Found Guilty of Age Bias. Told to Pay $750,000," *The Wall Street Journal*, 6 February 1975, p. 28; "The Courts Reinterpret Old-age Discrimination,' *Business Week*, 24 February 1975, p. 91.

Questions

1. How do you feel about the jury's verdict in the above case?
2. Phasing out older, higher-paid employees can free funds for the hiring of greater numbers of young, lower-paid persons. In your opinion, should a company have the right to engage in the practice of phasing out their older employees before they are age sixty-five? Explain.

The Disabled Woodworker

When Danny Darby was fifteen years old, he had a serious motorcycle accident that required the amputation of his left leg. He was fitted with an artificial appliance that enables him to function nearly as well as anyone under most circumstances. He is currently twenty-two years old and married. Danny enjoys physical activity and spends his weekends bicycle riding and skin diving.

Danny, a high school graduate, learned about a year ago that there was a Department of Rehabilitation near his home where he could obtain assistance and training designed to aid him in preparing for a career job. For a number of years he has had a strong interest in working with wood and was able to obtain training in cabinetmaking through the Department.

About two months ago, the Department obtained a job for Danny with the Madera Cabinet Company. Danny was overjoyed with the opportunity and felt quite fortunate to obtain a job in an area in which he had interests. His major hope, however, was that his co-workers would treat him as they would any other worker.

Unfortunately, Danny's wishes have not come true. Most of his fellow employees seem to feel sorry for him and continually refuse to allow him to carry heavy sections of wood and equipment. Danny has attempted to convey to his co-workers that he can carry whatever they can, but the other employees refuse to heed his requests.

Recently Danny has become quite moody on his job. He sometimes feels that he is being treated as if he were helpless or "some kind of a freak." Danny has started getting into conflict situations with the other employees in areas that do not relate to his disability. Today, Danny has felt especially depressed and believes that he has had it with his job. He has decided that he will tell his foreman, Harry Harmony, that he intends to leave his job with Madera.

Questions

1. What do you feel is the major problem in this case?
2. If you were Harry Harmony, what would you do about the situation?

When you finish this chapter, you should be able to:

1. **Discuss** the changing organizational attitudes toward the problems of alcoholism and drug dependency.
2. **Summarize** the extent of alcohol and drug abuse in the United States.
3. **Recognize** the criteria that indicates the existence of a drinking problem.
4. **Explain** some of the potential causes of alcohol and drug abuse.
5. **Describe** management's responsibilities for establishing and carrying out employee assistance programs.
6. **Explain** the importance of the supervisor's role in influencing the success of the organization's programs.
7. **List** the possible symptoms of alcoholism and drug dependency.

When this Nation became concerned about
drug use among the young,
the public was finally forced
to recognize that adult use of alcohol
. . . is actually the major
drug problem in this country.

—Merlin K. Du Val

In an earlier section we mentioned the cliché, "When there are no problems, then there's no business." Unfortunately, organizational members are discovering that many of today's problems bear little relationship to whether or not there is business activity. Problems seldom discussed around boards of directors' tables ten years ago have become significant and costly today. To illustrate—with increasing frequency are the following remarks being made by some organizational members: "Hey, man—let's go take our joint break." Or "George, how about just one more Harvey Wallbanger before we go back to the office?"

Each of those remarks relates to a major topic of the current chapter, a subject with which more organization policy makers have become concerned: the non-identical twin problems of alcohol and drug abuse among employees. These are relevant human relations concerns that should be of no less importance to managers than are such problems as communication, motivation, and morale. An attitude becoming more prevalent within organizations today relates to the following quotation from the *Management Guide on Alcoholism*, distributed by the Public Relations Department of the Kemper Insurance Group:

> An employee's choice to drink or not drink alcoholic beverages is a personal matter, with which the company is not concerned. On the other hand, the illness of alcoholism and its effect upon work performance are matters of concern to the company.

Our approach in this chapter, therefore, will be to present a general overview of the nature and extent of the problems of alcohol and drug abuse, and then to examine the more successful approaches and guidelines currently being followed by some concerned organizations. Let's now examine how extensive the problems are.

The Extent of the Alcohol Problem

The problems of both alcoholism and drug abuse, regardless of what many persons would prefer to believe, are considerable. Society, both by custom and law, defines what is meant by *drugs*. Some authorities claim that alcohol should be classified as a drug, no less than other types of stimulants, depressants, hallucinogens, and narcotics.

The National Institute on Alcohol Abuse and Alcoholism estimates that nearly *10 million persons* suffer from problems related to alcohol. The most typical stereotype of the alcoholic is the intoxicated derelict staggering clumsily around a dismal skid row street, which is *not* the case since such persons are said to represent only about 3 to 5 percent of all the persons with alcohol-related problems in the United States.

What Constitutes a "Drinking Problem"?

When might drinking be a "problem"?

We should be clear about what generally is meant by a "drinking problem." In all cases related to alcohol abuse, a common factor is the unfavorable effect alcohol has on the *health* or *well-being* of the *drinker*, and on his or her *associates*. According to more detailed information distributed by the National Institute on Alcohol Abuse and Alcoholism, the following are criteria for drinking problems:

1. Anyone who must drink in order to function or to "cope" with life has a severe drinking problem.
2. Anyone who by his own personal definition, or that of his or her family and friends, frequently drinks to a state of intoxication has a drinking problem.
3. Anyone who goes to work intoxicated has a drinking problem.
4. Anyone who is intoxicated while driving a car has a drinking problem.
5. Anyone who sustains a bodily injury that requires medical attention as a consequence of an intoxicated state has a drinking problem.
6. Anyone who comes into conflict with the law as a consequence of an intoxicated state has a drinking problem.
7. Anyone who, under the influence of alcohol, does something he or she avows would never occur without alcohol has a drinking problem.

Alcoholic Defined

alcoholic

A person could experience some isolated examples of such drinking problems without necessarily being an alcoholic. The term *alcoholic* generally refers to the person who *habitually lacks self-control in the use of alcoholic beverages*, or who drinks to the extent that his or her *health is adversely affected*, or that his or her *social or economic functioning is significantly disrupted*.

Drinking Problems Among the Work Force

People drink for a variety of social, cultural, religious, or medical reasons. Approximatly 68 percent of American adults are said to drink at least occasionally. Unfortunately, some persons reach the stage where they feel that they cannot do without alcohol, and many such individuals are employed in industry.

How extensive is the drinking problem?

Estimates of those with drinking problems range from *5 to 9 percent* of the total work force. Studies indicate that there are variations within specific companies ranging from as little as *3 percent* of the employee population to as much as *12 percent*.

the "big hangover"

The alcohol problem is sometimes referred to as the "nation's $25 billion hangover," a conservative estimate of the annual economic drain from the nation, which includes $10 billion in *lost work time* of employed alcoholics, over $8 billion for *health and medical care*, and nearly $7 billion in *property damage, wage losses,* and other costs associated with *traffic accidents*.

The National Council on Alcoholism has gathered the following information on alcoholism in industry:

1. The alcoholic employee is absent two to four times more often than the non-alcoholic.
2. On-the-job accidents for alcoholic employees are two to four times more frequent than for non-alcoholics. Off-the-job accidents are four to six times more numerous.
3. Sickness and accident benefits paid out for alcoholic employees are three times greater than for the average non-alcoholic.
4. The alcoholic employee files four times more grievances than non-alcoholic employees.

Changing Viewpoints toward Alcohol Abuse

Should drinking problems be handled by courts or medical counseling?

treatment legislation

Alcohol abuse in the United States until relatively recently was customarily administered as a criminal act. Although some states had enacted *treatment legislation*, the laws in those states received scant attention and were largely ignored. During 1966, however, some significant court decisions stimulated a radical departure from previously held attitudes.

Hughes Act

National Institute of Alcohol Abuse and Alcoholism

Since 1966, considerable progress has been made in the direction of treatment and rehabilitation. This trend seems likely to continue as a result of the passage of the *Hughes Act* by Congress in 1970, an act that created the *National Institute of Alcohol Abuse and Alcoholism*, whose function is to engage in research and to provide assistance to managers in establishing alcoholism programs.

The laws relating to alcohol abuse have varied from state to state. However, at the National Conference of Commissioners on Uniform

Should alcoholism be a *disease* in one state and a *crime* in another?

State Laws held in Vail, Colorado, in 1971, the commissioners approved and recommended for enactment in all states a uniform alcoholism and intoxication act to encourage treatment rather than criminal prosecution.

The Extent of Drug Abuse

Is drug taking an industrial problem?

How about drugs? Most managers used to believe that the "drug culture" was mostly confined to the college campus or the ghetto. Such is no longer the case, according to one of the largest surveys of the situation ever taken. During the late 1970s, the Conference Board made a study of 222 companies, including 131 manufacturing companies, ranging in size from 250 to 250,000 employees, and determined that *53 percent* of the firms that responded to its questions had discovered drug abuse among

"soft" drugs and "hard" drugs

their employees. The use of *"soft" drugs,* such as amphetamines, is more prevalent than that of *"hard" drugs,* such as heroin. According to the study, most of the companies surveyed were not particularly con-concerned about the use of marijuana by employees unless it affected productivity.

Should there be organizational drug-abuse programs?

Although many organizations have policies to handle the alcoholic, few companies have developed policies to cover the drug addict. Yet, a study made by *Modern Office Procedures* magazine indicated that at least *one in eight employees* has had a drug experience and *one in four job applicants* has experimented with drugs. The problems could worsen in the future. The United States Bureau of Narcotics and Dangerous Drugs has determined that experimentation with heroin and other drugs has now reached down to the seventh-grade level in the schools. One day relatively soon, these students will be applying for jobs in industry and government.

In recent years, it has been estimated that *one out of every forty workers* in the United States uses drugs illegally. According to the National Institute on Drug Abuse, 35 million Americans have used marihuana, and about 15 million are "regular" smokers, puffing a few times a week.

What Is a Drug?

drug defined

A *drug* may be defined as *a substance that has an effect upon the body or mind.* Many substances not usually considered as drugs could be included in this definition, such as alcohol, caffeine, nicotine, cola, pollutants, airplane glue, and household chemicals.

We will concentrate on the types of drugs that can potentially create problems for organizations because of the drugs' capabilities to alter the minds of the users. The abuse of such drugs may also harm the body. The major types of drugs currently being used and abused include:

1. *Cannabis* (marihuana, hashish, and hashish oil).
2. *Hallucinogens* (so-called psychedelics, such as LSD, mescaline, psilocybin, DMT, STP, MDA, and others).
3. *Stimulants* (so-called "uppers," such as cocaine, amphetamine, dextroamphetamine, and methamphetamine, that is, "speed" or "crystals").
4. *Sedatives* or *depressants* (so-called downers, such as barbiturates, that is, "goof balls" or "sleepers").
5. *Narcotics* (opiates, such as opium, morphine, and heroin, that is, "smack").
6. *Miscellaneous* (model airplane glue, gasoline, paint thinners, and others).

Historically, the use of drugs has varied depending principally on availability and custom.

The major problem among office and factory workers appears to center around the abuse of *stimulants* ("uppers") and *sedatives* ("downers"). According to estimates from the National Institute of Mental Health, although millions of people use such drugs safely under the care of physicians, more than five hundred thousand others obtain them from illegal sources and often depend on them to make it through the workday.

Economic Costs of Drugs

What are some of the economic costs of the "nation's long trip"?

We've already revealed the cost of the nation's big hangover—$25 billion. Although accurate cost data derived from what could be referred to as the "nation's long trip" are still scarce, there is ample evidence of the excessive economic costs associated with drug abuse. Drug addiction can become an expensive habit. To support such activities, dependent workers often become *pushers* and sometimes inveigle *fellow employees* into narcotics addiction. Addicts are estimated to be responsible for stealing almost $7 billion in property each year from organizations and individuals. Officials in New York City, where there are an estimated fifty thousand heroin addicts, believe that about *80 percent of the shoplifting* is done by drug users, including some persons employed by the stores.

Costs have also soared as a result of *higher turnover rates* among addicted employees. Since few companies have programs to deal with drug problems, most employees are *fired* when their habits are discovered. For example, Western Electric Company candidly reported that it fired sixty employees and suspended two as a result of eight major drug investigations during a recent year. In a General Motors plant in Los Angeles, undercover police discovered a group of employees selling drugs during the lunch break from a camper in the parking lot. Another example: The Metropolitan Life Insurance Company dismissed more than 100 employees during a single year for using drugs.

public invisibility

Generally, however, most employees with drug problems are not fired specifically for drug use, which, unlike alcohol abuse, has sort of a *public invisibility*. An employee on drugs, for example, can coyly "pop a pill" into his or her mouth unnoticed by the boss and, conversely, the boss could do the same. (Do you remember how you used to slip chewing gum into your mouth in grade school?) Workers with drug problems, therefore, are fired more frequently for the *effects* of their habits, such as *high absenteeism, chronic lateness, sleeping and daydreaming on the job, and theft.*

For what reasons have drug users been fired?

Who Is Affected by the Problem?

Until relatively recently, most managers seemed not to want to recognize that alcohol and drug abuse were human relations problems in need of their attention. When cases did become known, they were often covered up until the employee could no longer function effectively on the job and had to be dismissed, which did little to correct the individual's problem. At long last, however, most authorities recognize that alcoholism and drug addiction are *diseases*, and therefore require treatment as does any disease.

diseases

What sort of conditions sometimes cause the disease?

The problems can beset virtually anyone in an organization. Often some of the best and brightest of employees "catch" the contagious disease of addiction. Especially afflicted are those who feel that the occupational environment is *dispiriting and dehumanizing*. As a result, some employees may feel forced into the escapism of daydreams, drink, and drugs. If efforts at job enrichment are successful, perhaps some of these feelings will be eliminated or reduced.

Others who use alcohol or drugs to excess are those with *financial or health problems*, either theirs or those of members of their family. Some individuals who know that they should stay away from alcohol—persons with ulcers, for example—profusely immerse their damaged surface tissue with straight whiskies hoping to deaden the pain, at least temporarily.

Why is poverty not the sole cause of addiction?

At one time, sociologists believed that if poverty could be eliminated, drug abuse would naturally fade away. This notion was found to be erroneous; *affluent people*, also, are hit by the disease. Read what a Prudential Insurance Company pamphlet says about current drug usage:

> In a world where changes are rapid and yesterday's faiths and values may erode, affluence allows the time and finances to support drug excesses. Loss of goals and drive can be a by-product of affluence. When a person no longer needs to work in order to eat and clothe himself, he may develop problems of leisure. If he has no viable goals, no motivation or drive to create, to study or help others, he may become

Figure 15–1. Alcoholism can hit anyone. Courtesy: National Institute on Alcohol Abuse and Alcoholism.

bored or alienated, and vulnerable to the temptation of using chemical substitutes for productive living.[1]

These words might well apply to the excessive use of alcohol.

Although large urban areas seem to be notorious for the greater availability of drugs, some surveys have discovered that location and the size of the company makes only a minor difference regarding the extent of the problem.

What Causes Excessive Use of Alcohol or Drugs?

peer pressures

Not everyone uses alcohol or drugs for the same reasons. One of the more common reasons is that of *peer pressure*, the desire to be "one of the group." The person who has never smoked a marihuana cigarette, for example, may feel socially compelled to take his or her first puff on a "joint" as it is being passed from person to person. The fear of the group's ostracism or disapproval often motivates some individuals, especially those searching for self-identity or acceptance, to establish their habits.

environmental experiences

escape

Many persons who abuse drugs have had previous *environmental experiences* that have disturbed them. Often they felt rejected or dominated by their parents. Some persons believe that their drug activities can provide them with an *escape* into a group that accepts—rather than rejects—them.

social and business custom

A major difference between the use of drugs and the consumption of alcoholic beverages is that the *latter* has been firmly established in the American culture as a *social and business custom*. Although there are numerous exceptions to the stereotype, business executives are infamous for their lunchtime martinis. And one of the first questions that hosts or hostesses often ask their newly arrived guests is, "What would you like to drink?"

A salient point, therefore, is that society—that is, our culture —strongly influences our tastes and customs. Alcohol and drugs are not the root of the problem; their abuse, however, is an indication of other, deep-seated complications and frustrations.

We have already pointed out how persons who perceive their jobs as being dull or who have personal problems often use drugs and alcohol as an escape mechanism. Some observers feel that *excessive economic security* and *leisure time* are among the paramount causes of abuse. Still others blame the *advertising fraternity*. They cite evidence in statistics that indicate that *one in every six television advertisements* is a promotion for the $6.5 billion "ethical" or "straight drug culture," and over $211 million is spent on such commercials annually.

[1]"Questions and Answers about Drug Abuse," *Prudential Health Series* (Rockville, Maryland: National Clearinghouse for Drug Abuse Information, August 1971), p.6.

Researchers have developed numerous other scholarly theories related to the potential causes of alcoholism. Space limitations preclude our examining them here.[2]

Organizational Approaches to Alcohol and Drug Abuse

treatable diseases

In recent years there has been growing recognition that alcoholism and drug addiction are *treatable diseases*, and that alcoholics and drug addicts need help as does anyone with a malady. There still are some persons—although their numbers are diminishing—who refuse to accept the two ailments as anything other than criminal offenses.

The important point, however, isn't what the problems are called; far more essential is what can be done to assist individuals with such problems. An increasing number of organizations—both private and public—have begun to take an active interest in attempting to reduce the prevalence of the two costly afflictions. For example, according to the National Council on Alcoholism, some 1,200 U.S. employers had some kind of an alcoholism rehabilitation program in 1977.

The Nature of Company Programs

Organizations with established programs have attempted to steer clear of the traditional solutions of either firing the employee with a drinking or drug problem, giving sermons on the evils of excessive consumption of alcohol, or calling in the police to "bust potheads."

What is the nature of current programs?

Instead, modern organizations have been concentrating on *counseling* the employee into seeking treatment, generally with an *outside agency*, while keeping him or her on the job. Although sympathetic understanding of the employee's problem is conveyed, the employee is told that deterioration of work habits, absenteeism, or other troubles created by alcohol or drug abuse will not be tolerated indefinitely. Typical programs, therefore, deal with three principal stages: *detection, treatment,* and *rehabilitation.*

detection, treatment, rehabilitation

The Establishment of Company Programs

Rather than being allowed to develop haphazardly, an alcohol or drug program should have someone specifically assigned to establish and

[2]For a discussion of scholarly theories relating to alcoholism, see "Theories about the Causes of Alcoholism," from the *First Special Report to the U.S. Congress on Alcohol and Health* (The National Institute on Alcohol Abuse and Alcoholism, Rockville, Maryland, December 1971), pp. 61–70.

coordinate it. Individuals with experience in creating undertakings of this nature tend to feel that a new program should not begin with fanfare, but instead be gradually introduced and combined with other ongoing behavioral, medical, and counseling programs.

A Formal Statement of Policy

Why should a company policy be formulated?

Before a program is carried out, however, company management should first establish a formal policy designed to deal consistently with the problems. Apparently because of the illegality of and greater stigma associated with the use of drugs as compared to alcohol, fewer organizations have yet formulated official policies to handle cases of drug dependency.

In firms concerned with both problems, the customary approach has been to employ the same policy for each by substituting the words "drug dependency" for "alcoholism." The Kemper Insurance Group, for example, follows this tack. Since the two policies adopted by Kemper are virtually identical, we have taken the liberty of combining them by placing the words "drug dependency" within brackets following the word "alcoholism." The minor differences between the two policies have been noted.

Kemper Policy on Alcoholism [Drug Dependency]

In accordance with our general personnel policies, whose underlying concept is regard for the employee as an individual as well as a worker:

1. We believe alcoholism, or problem drinking [drug dependency] is an illness and should be treated as such.
2. We believe the majority of employees who develop alcoholism [drug dependency] can be helped to recover and the company should offer appropriate assistance.
3. We believe the decision to seek diagnosis and accept treatment for any suspected illness is the responsibility of the employee. However, continued refusal of an employee to seek treatment when it appears that substandard performance may be caused by any illness is not tolerated. We believe that alcoholism [drug dependency] should not be made an exception to this commonly accepted principle.
4. We believe that it is in the best interest of employees and the company that when alcoholism [drug dependency] is present, it should be diagnosed and treated at the earliest possible stage.
5. [Alcoholism policy only.] We believe that the company's concern for individual drinking practices begins only when they result in unsatisfactory job performance.

6. We believe that confidential handling of the diagnosis and treatment of alcoholism [drug dependency] is essential.

The objective of this policy is to retain employees who may develop alcoholism [drug dependency] by helping them to arrest its further advance before the condition renders them unemployable.

> [Drug policy only.] Employees who develop drug dependencies and addictions, and who are willing to seek and cooperate in treatment, will be given company staff assistance in locating and securing admission to appropriate treatment services available in various communities. Full-time employees covered by health insurance will receive benefits allowable under the plan, consistent with its provisions regarding emotional and alcoholism programs.

The Need for Management Support and Employee Understanding

How can the program be communicated?

The cooperation of all levels of management—especially supervisory—is essential for the success of any employee assistance project. Managers can learn about the programs at *management training or development sessions*. Discussions should not focus exclusively on alcoholism and drugs but should emphasize factors that affect job performance.

Instead of holding special meetings to announce a new program, employees can be notified more subtly and less dramatically at other *normal functions*, such as at safety meetings where some persons with alcohol or drug problems are likely to be present.

Films can be used to disseminate information effectively and can be publicized by notices in the cafeteria. *Literature* can be handed out at *meetings of employees* and placed on *bulletin boards* and *pamphlet racks*. The company *house organ* can be another useful medium for enabling employees to become aware of the services available to employees.

Not all employees with problems will seek counseling on their own. Pacific Telephone Company, for example, feels that their program has done reasonably well with about half of all alcohol and drug cases self-referred; the remainder have been referred by supervisors.

The Stigma of Alcoholism and Drug Programs

How can the stigma of programs be reduced?

The words ''alcoholic'' and ''drug addict'' tend to have disagreeable and frightening connotations to many employees. As a result, company managers involved with the establishment of programs need also to be concerned with semantics when determining what to call their plans. A key problem, therefore, is how to eliminate the stigma of such programs.

As we have already mentioned, the programs should not be considered as something separate and apart from other medical and counseling services. ''When you call something an alcoholic program, you give it the kiss of death," warned James E. Peterson, while employee relations director of the Utah Copper Division of Kennecott Copper Corporation.[3]

Pacific Telephone Company refers to its program as an "Employee Counseling Service," thus not stressing solely the problems of alcohol and drug dependency. Their project includes assistance in a variety of other areas such as self-identity, health, marriage, and financial difficulties. The Firestone Tire and Rubber Company prefers to call its program an "Employee Assistance Program."

Programs are necessary, however, regardless of what they are called. Their success is limited unless positive attitudes exist along with sincere management commitment to the undertaking.

Coverage in Health Insurance Contracts

What is the trend in health insurance contracts? Insurance companies seem to have developed a greater awareness that alcoholism can be treated, for increasing numbers of group insurance contracts now include coverage for alcoholism. In fact, in a recent five-year period, the number of insurance contracts that included coverage for

---

[3]"Kennecott's Approach to Alcoholism," *Business Week,* 4 April 1972, pp. 113–114.

alcohol problems *doubled*. *The Wall Street Journal* quoted a United Auto Workers union official who explained, "Reducing alcoholism problems actually reduces insurance costs since companies won't end up paying for a guy's liver when it goes to hell."[4]

Some companies, such as Kemper, also include coverage for drug-related medical costs in their insurance policies.

Supervisory Responsibilities

How should supervisors handle abuse problems?

Key persons, once again, in the determination of the success or failure of any program are supervisors. Supervisors, however, should *not* attempt to be amateur diagnosticians or counselors, nor become involved in discussing illnesses that they are not qualified to handle. Instead, supervisors should approach alcohol and drug problems as they would any other erratic performance by employees.

Supervisors Should Detect Symptoms

Supervisors, who in effect are monitors of the employees' work, should be trained to recognize the *symptoms* of alcohol and drug problems. Alcohol and drug abuse problems are generally accompanied by *specific changes in work performance and dependability*. If you as a supervisor were to become aware of such changes, you should document in writing all incidents of unsatisfactory behavior. Then you should call in the employee, review the actual record, and inform the person that his or her performance *must be improved*.

After the disciplinary interview is over, you might ask the employee about any personal problems that could be affecting his or her job performance. Whether or not the employee admits to the existence of a problem, he or she could be told that the company has a confidential counseling service that can provide assistance. The employee might initially reject any suggestions to see a counselor, but the idea, nevertheless, has been implanted in the person's head. People sometimes reconsider such advice.

Follow Up Where Necessary

As is frequently the case, the employee may conceal his or her personal alcohol or drug problem, refuse to see a counselor, but promise to improve work performance. The supervisor should continue after this meeting to keep written records of the employee's work performance. Personnel managers generally recommend that information only about job per-

---

[4]"Labor Letter," *The Wall Street Journal,* 17 April 1973, p. 1.

formance, not alcohol or drug use, be included in the employees' records.

If the deficiencies continue, a second meeting becomes necessary and the supervisor may need to use a more direct approach, perhaps something like:

> Pete, you promised me that your performance would improve. Instead it has continued to deteriorate. I've shown you specifically what I mean. You and I both know that such performance cannot continue. Consequently, I'm going to send you to see our company counselor (or doctor), and unless you and the counselor work out your problem, I'm afraid your job is going to be in serious jeopardy.

The above approach may appear, at first glance, to be harsh and cold, but experienced supervisors have found that the desire by the employee to hold his or her job is one of the most effective motivational tools.

Supervisory Guidelines

Let's summarize some *specific guidelines* for supervisors to follow when they suspect an employee has an alcohol or drug problem.

Never—repeat, *never*, accuse an employee of using drugs or being an alcoholic. If you do, you may open yourself and the company to a slander or defamation of character lawsuit.

Do not attempt to diagnose the employee's problem. This function should be performed by a company specialist qualified in such matters.

Do not discuss drinking or drug problems with the employee; instead, focus on *job deficiencies* and *corrective action*.

Do attempt to learn to recognize the symptoms of alcohol or drug abuse.

Do follow up after an employee both begins and completes rehabilitation to ascertain that he or she is following prescribed recommendations.

Do not dismiss a previously satisfactory employee for deteriorating performance before giving the employee ample opportunity to seek assistance.

Recognizing Symptoms

Pinpointing the specific symptoms of alcohol and drug abuse problems is not a simple task. A supervisor's main responsibility, therefore, should not necessarily be that of uncovering evidence of dependency on alcohol and drugs but instead be that of observing declining job performance.

Yet, there are certain behavioral patterns that some excessive users of alcohol and drugs display. Let's start with alcohol.

Signs of Alcoholism

signs of alcohol problems

The *signs of alcoholism*, unfortunately, do not always become manifest until the middle or late stages of the problem. The earlier that treatment begins, naturally, the easier it will be. The following are some of the more common signs and symptoms of alcoholism:

> The need to drink before facing certain situations.
>
> Frequent drinking and intoxication.
>
> Steady increases in the amount of alcohol consumed.
>
> Drinking alone.
>
> Early morning drinking.
>
> Absenteeism, especially on Monday mornings and after holidays.
>
> Frequent denial of drinking.
>
> Family quarrels and disruptions over drinking.
>
> The occurrence of blackouts.
>
> Poorly explained lapses in fulfilling responsibilities.
>
> Decline in work performance.
>
> Occasional sloppy personal appearance on the job.
>
> Hangovers on the job.
>
> Occasional automobile accidents or moving violations off the job.
>
> Hand tremors.
>
> Occasional complaints from customers of the company.

In effect, anything that results in declining performance on the job could be a warning sign of a drinking problem.

Signs of Drug Dependency

signs of drug dependencies

Drug dependencies also produce observable changes in employees' work performance. The signals, however, are not always obvious. Some managers have mistaken an employee's euphoric appearance for the "look of love." Some of the symptoms associated with alcoholism could also relate to drug dependency. Other warning signs relating to drug use are:

> Anxiety reactions and states of panic.
>
> Accidents due to impaired judgment and distorted perceptions of space or time.
>
> Attitudes of paranoia, or excessive suspicion of others.

Mental confusion, loss of contact with reality, and lapses of memory.

Indifferent, apathetic, and sometimes compulsive behavior.

Dilated pupils, a flushed face, and a feeling of being chilly.

Occasional convulsions.

A deterioration of values.

Falling asleep on the job, that is, drowsiness.

Abscesses, needle marks, and "tracks" (discolorations along the course of veins in the arms and legs).

The regular wearing of dark sunglasses indoors (to protect dilated pupils).

An unhealthy appearance because of poor diet and personal neglect.

What can influence the symptoms? No one person would necessarily have all or any of these symptoms. And a supervisor should guard against assuming that the presence of one or more symptoms is conclusive proof of alcohol or drug abuse. Symptoms will likewise vary with the *stage of alcoholism* and the *type of drug used*, as well as with the *experience of the drug user*. Samples of employees' urine have indicated the taking of certain drugs in quantities that would kill less experienced users, yet the users went undetected until examined medically.

The Urinalysis Debate

Some organizations feel that urinalysis is effective in determining which employees have drinking or drug problems, while others feel that such approaches are incompatible with their basic philosophies. The United States Bureau of Narcotics and Dangerous Drugs warns there have been established in recent years many disreputable firms offering cheap, but inconclusive, analyses, and there always is the danger of encroaching on the civil rights of employees by methods that might be construed as accusatory.

Treatment and Recovery Services

Where does treatment generally take place? The *treatment* of alcoholism and drug addiction is generally not the function of the employer. Instead, the coordinator of a program generally maintains *local consultants* or recommends *community resources* to the willing employee. *Alcoholics Anonymous* is reputed to be one of the best sources of therapy for the alcoholic, as are *Al-Anon* groups for families of alcoholics. For persons in need of drug therapy, there are various public and private nonprofit organizations whose services are available throughout the United States, especially in the larger urban areas. For example, the Illinois Drug Abuse Program provides separate vocational assistance and detoxification services. There are numerous "half-way houses" which are designed to assist present and past addicts.

Summary

This chapter has provided a relatively brief overview of the broad, complex, and changing problems of alcoholism and drug abuse. Troubles that previously were believed to be the exclusive domain of the ghetto or college campus have spread to all segments of society. As a result, employers have begun to recognize the need for action in areas that until recently were largely ignored.

No longer are the non-identical twin problems of alcoholism and drug addiction looked upon solely as the responsibility of the courts; both are now recognized by most authorities as *diseases* that are "caught" by individuals either influenced by their peers or attempting to reduce the stress and tensions of their environment.

A number of concerned managers have developed organizational policies and programs designed to deal with the problem drinkers on their payrolls. Fewer firms, however, have developed policies and programs for drug-dependent employees; but an increasing number of organizations, such as the Kemper Insurance Group, have begun to recognize that when a drug epidemic is raging, business cannot expect to remain immune.

The key ingredients of any successful organizational program attempting to control drinking and drug problems are:

1. Knowledge of the need
2. Top management commitment
3. Workable disciplinary procedures
4. Effective referral process
5. Follow-up procedures

Terms and Concepts to Remember

Drinking problem
Alcoholism
The "big hangover"
Treatment legislation
Hughes Act of 1970
Drugs

The "nation's long trip"
Public invisibility
Peer pressures
Treatable disease
Signs of alcoholism
Signs of drug dependency

Questions

1. What was meant by the following statement made in the Kemper *Management Guide on Alcoholism?* "An employee's choice to drink or not drink alcoholic beverages is a personal matter, with which the

company is not concerned." Do you agree with its intent? Should the same reasoning apply toward drug use? Explain.

2. What are the major types of drugs currently being used and abused? Which kinds are most prevalent among employees?

3. Why is it desirable for organizations to establish official alcohol and drug abuse policies and programs?

4. What is meant by the statement: "Drug use has sort of a public invisibility"?

5. What generally can cause a person to "catch" the diseases of alcoholism or drug dependency?

6. What is meant by the "stigma of alcohol or drug programs"? How might such stigmas be overcome?

7. Why should supervisors not attempt personally to diagnose alcohol or drug problems, nor counsel individuals with them?

8. Assume that you are a personnel manager facing some skeptical supervisors who feel any person with drinking or drug problems should be fired on the spot. Prepare a logical argument designed to convince the supervisors that dismissal should be a last—not first—resort.

Other Readings

Cohen, Sidney. *The Drug Dilemma*. New York: McGraw-Hill, 1969.

Drug Misuse: A Psychiatric View of a Modern Dilemma. The Committee on Mental Health Services, Group for the Advancement of Psychiatry. New York: Charles Scribner's Sons, 1971.

A Federal Sourcebook: Answers to the Most Frequently Asked Questions About Drugs. Chevy Chase, Maryland: National Clearinghouse for Drug Abuse Information, 1970.

First Special Report to the U.S. Congress on Alcohol and Health. Rockville, Maryland: National Institute on Alcohol Abuse and Alcoholism, 1971.

Jacobsen, George R. *The Alcoholisms*. New York: Human Sciences Press, 1976.

"Management Guide on Alcoholism and Other Behavioral Problems." Long Grove, Ill.: Kemper Insurance, 1972.

Maxwell, Ruth. *The Booze Battle*. New York: Ballantine Books, 1977.

"Q & A—Special Action Office for Drug Abuse Prevention Answers the Most Frequently Asked Questions about Drug Abuse." Executive Office of the President. Washington, D.C.: United States Government Printing Office, 1972.

Wilkinson, Rupert. *The Prevention of Drinking Problems—Alcohol Control and Cultural Influences*. New York: Oxford University Press, 1970.

Application

The Case of Johnny Ballantine

Johnny Ballantine, a sales representative for the Montana Manufacturing and Mining Company for the past fifteen years, is directly accountable to Joseph Jenever, the sales manager in the branch office at Billings. Ballantine's principal responsibility is to sell electrical products to wholesale electric supply houses.

About eight months ago, Ballantine and his wife, Nivaria, were returning to Billings from a weekend visit with friends in Great Falls. During the trip Ballantine fell asleep at the wheel, the automobile careened off the highway, and Nivaria was critically injured. She died two days later, thus leaving Ballantine with the full responsibility of raising their two daughters, Rosa, age 9, and Rioja, age 14.

A Change in Behavior

In recent months Jenever has begun to notice some significant changes in Ballantines's activities and behavior. For example, there has been a marked increase in Ballantine's entertainment expense account. When questioned about the change earlier this month, Ballantine explained, "I've got to drink a lot when I'm out with customers; it's good for business."

Jenever noticed another unusual situation relating to Ballantine's territory. Every two weeks, he is required to submit an itinerary, a list of the customers he intends to contact on particular days. Recently, on two separate occasions, Jenever discovered that Ballantine had not followed his proposed itinerary. The first time, Jenever had reason to call the customer in an effort to locate Ballantine because of an emergency concerning Rioja, his elder daughter. The second time was when an important account urgently wanted to discuss an error in a shipment of electrical products. In neither case was Ballantine where his itinerary indicated he would be. Nor was he even expected by his customers on those days.

In addition, Ballantine's behavior when he is in the office has significantly changed lately. He often avoids Jenever and frequently becomes belligerent with the office staff. During the past month and a half, Ballantine has had two accidents with his company car, both involving his having driven into parked cars. Also, it appears to Jenever that Ballantine's hands have developed mild tremors in recent weeks.

Jenever suspects that Ballantine is drinking to excess, but he is not quite certain how to handle what he believes to be an exceedingly difficult and delicate situation.

Question

1. What, in your judgment, is the primary problem in this case?
2. What should Jenever do about the problem?

four

From Here to Eternity

When you finish this chapter, you should be able to:

1. **Understand** the importance of maintaining or developing personal faith and trust in one's self and in others.
2. **Recognize** the symptoms of the prevalent deterioration of faith and trust.
3. **Cite** at least five ways in which you can exert a positive influence on your own attitudes toward work and living in general.
4. **State** specific ways in which work addicts can develop the ability to derive greater satisfaction from life.
5. **Distinguish** between the B. F. Skinner-behaviorist and the Rollo May-humanist schools of psychological thought.
6. **Explain** the importance of a regular program of bodily exercise to your physical and mental health.
7. **Describe** at least two ways of reducing your own personal tensions and frustrations.
8. **Explain** why the concepts of happiness and success may have different meanings to different people.

The first and best victory is to conquer self;
to be conquered by self is, of all things,
the most shameful and vile.

—Plato

It is not in doing
what you like, but in liking
what you do that is the
secret of happiness.

—James Barrie

Up to this point, you may have expended considerable effort learning about the human side of work organizations. *Your behavior* as a member of a formal work group is significantly influenced by your own personal life—something which we'll refer to as *personal human relations.*

Socrates regularly suggested to his friends and acquaintances that perhaps they should attempt to know their *own selves* a bit better. His advice was a succinct, "Know thyself." To his friends with more time to spare, he would sometimes add, "Know your strengths and your weaknesses; your potentialities; your aims and purposes; take stock of yourself." Socrates, one of the best and the brightest of his time, believed that before individuals could really understand how to deal effectively with the problems of others, they first had to look within and become better acquainted with their selves.

We've already discussed in previous chapters some of the topics that can help you understand your own and the behavior of others. We've also explored the concepts related to needs and examined the ways people tend to react when their needs are frustrated and unsatisfied.

Do you see *you* when looking at a mirror?

Attempting to know one's self is not a simple task. We are so close to ourselves, both physically and mentally, that absolute objectivity is well-nigh impossible. For example, have you ever looked at your reflection in a mirror and attempted to perceive yourself as others might see you? It's difficult to do, isn't it? There are some persons who appear to prefer not to know how others perceive them; they may feel—either consciously or unconsciously—that ignorance provides them with a protective shield.

Reasonably well-adjusted persons, however, generally have a better knowledge and understanding of their own sentiments and behavior. They are usually aware that life is beset with stress, strain, and frustration, but they attempt to gain greater insight into their feelings in order to cope more effectively with them. Many other persons tend to create their own tensions and to lose faith in themselves and in others.

This chapter explores the concept of *faith* and investigates some of the *consequences of its absence.* In this section we shall also discuss some of the significant reasons for retaining a certain degree of *faith in yourself* and *trust in others*, as well as *hope in your destiny*, all of which are essential for your mental health. Finally, we shall consider what you might do to maintain—or, if necessary, restore—*a more positive outlook* in your own future.

Keep the Faith—Utopia Is in the Beholder's Eyes

Although there are favorable signs that the national mood has improved somewhat since it reached its low in the Watergate- and Vietnam-plagued days of the early 1970s, many Americans continue to be discontented, disenchanted, and uncertain about the future. Evidence of such a negative mood might be found in the increasing number of Americans on the move—that is to say, in the state of *flight*—changing colleges and majors, changing occupations and firms, changing houses and spouses, and even changing countries. According to the U.S. Census Bureau, Americans move, on the average, twelve times during a lifetime, a rate higher than most other nationalities.

Is discontent all bad?　Many Americans *do* seem discontented, but is the present search for utopia necessarily all bad? Perhaps not. "Discontent," said Oscar Wilde, "is the first step in the progress of a man or nation." If Wilde was correct, we should look forward to considerable progress in the years to come.

The Meaning of Faith

faith　The word *faith* has many meanings. To some persons faith is a belief and trust in and loyalty to God, or a belief in the traditional doctrines of a formal religion. To others it may be an absolute allegiance to something concrete, such as one's country—or something abstract, such as the symbolic meanings of the flag or the presidency of the United States.

Other types of faith that individuals may have are in *themselves*, in *humanity*, and in their *own futures*. Without the existence of some positive beliefs, a person has little to look forward to. People who lose all or most of their faith often turn to negative, and frequently destructive, styles of behavior.

What types of behavior might "faithless" persons engage in?　For example, individuals who lose faith, or who are aimless and pessimistic about the future, may abuse such things as alcohol or drugs; they may believe that violence and theft are reasonable; they may develop negative attitudes about almost everything. They may develop the tendency to make wisecracks during serious situations, and they may develop an unhealthy "I-don't-give-a-damn" philosophy.

The Erosion of Trust

What has caused the prevalent erosion of trust?

"Nobody trusts anybody anymore," is a comment made regularly of late. A prevalent attitude among many Americans is their lack of faith in their fellow humans, sort of an adversary we-versus-them syndrome, with groups of people doubting other groups of people.

Have you ever considered a castle with a moat?

Examples of deteriorating trust are to be found everywhere. Homeowners in America during the past decade have installed "decorative bars" on their windows and bought guns and expensive electronic detection equipment to fend off unwelcome visitors. More and more American citizens no longer dare to take leisurely strolls at night. Automobiles have become electronically fitted to discourage thieves. Some businesses even employ security personnel disguised as company workers to spy on other employees.

City newspapers report violent crime like they do scores of ball games, comparing this year's murders to date with last year's. In a recent year, for example, the Annual Uniform Crime Reports informed us that a violent crime occurred every 33 seconds somewhere in the U.S. and a murder was recorded every 26 minutes.

The Need for Situational Faith

situational faith

In such unhealthy atmospheres of distrust, individuals tend to become apprehensive of all their associates. Perhaps, instead, we need to develop the ability to apply what might be called *situational faith*. Historically, we have put forward the belief that in our democratic system, a person is innocent until proven guilty. Perhaps we should attempt to develop a similar conviction that a person is worthy of our trust until we have positive evidence to the contrary.

Could distrust possibly create untrustworthiness?

If you are a manager, for example, you must have a certain amount of trust in your employees; you cannot reasonably search every worker as they leave for home each day. Excessive restriction of employees might even create a challenge for them to see what they can get away with, since a person's behavior often becomes as others expect it to be.

Is any person an island?

Also, individuals who have been hurt by someone for whom they cared deeply may develop bitterness, doubt, and disbelief toward others. Even with such feelings of distrust, which are difficult to discard, we must retain a certain degree of *vulnerability*—to be realistic in our feelings, but vulnerable in our behavior. There will be some risk of being hurt again, but too much protection may isolate us from satisfying experiences in the future.

Cockeyed Idealists?

Is there anything
more ideal
than idealism?

Those who retain hope while half submerged in a sea of despair are sometimes accused of being "cockeyed idealists." But isn't idealism likely to be a far more positive approach than destructive pessimism? Optimism and faith in humanity do not necessarily imply naïveté. An idealist should always keep one foot on the ground—or at least a big toe! The realistic person striving for a better world, reaching eagerly for a piece of that proverbial "pie in the sky," might at least discover a "treasure in the attic." To some persons, the "pie" always seems to be tastier in another neighborhood, so they become nomads, not really certain of what they are searching for. Let's now examine the recent American nomadic trend.

The Tendency Toward Flight

The dictionary definitions of the word *nomad* are interesting. Webster's New Collegiate Dictionary defines it this way: "1: a member of a people that has no fixed residence but wanders from place to place, 2: an individual who roams about aimlessly."

A Nation of Nomads?

Is America on the move?

Could a sizable number of the American people now be included in those definitions? Currently over thirty-five million Americans each year—over 17 percent of the total population—pick up and put down in different parts of the same city, different parts of the same county, another county in the same state, or in another state. On the average, nearly one hundred thousand people move each day. Corporate executives are estimated to make about two hundred and fifty thousand of these moves each year.

Just where is utopia?

In chapter 5, we defined the term *flight* as *the running away from a particular situation that causes frustration or anxiety*. Can individuals really run away from their tensions and locate their true utopias? Many Americans appear to have been trying in recent years. A number have flown to other countries, a few have assimilated themselves reasonably well into the different customs of foreign cultures, while others have either become disillusioned and moved on after a few years to different countries or have returned to the United States.

Communards and Commuters

Is utopia a
commune in suburbia?

Some young Americans have searched for their utopias in communes and other novel styles of living, but most have discovered that many of the same problems and pressures of urban life seem to follow them.

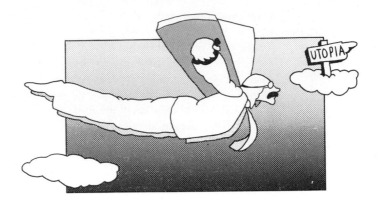

A more common approach for most mobile Americans over the past two decades has been to "flee" to the suburbs in order to attempt to escape from the hustle, bustle, and fears of the decaying cities. But the move to the suburbs has often added even more pressures with which many families have found difficulty coping. For example, some persons have found that the daily commute to their urban employment is often more frustrating and filled with tension than their jobs. The typical commuters spend between one and two hours a day merely traveling to their places of employment. By the time they arrive home after a hard day's work, they are so tired that they can hardly muster up enough energy to communicate with their families.

Why do urban ills follow exurbanites?

Many persons have become disillusioned with suburbs after finding that the problems of crime, drug abuse, alcoholism, juvenile delinquency, and vandalism seemed to follow them. An interesting revelation is that a number of psychologists contend that individuals who make their homes near their work have much better chances of staying happily married than do those who have long commutes in order to get to their places of employment.

The Quest for Freedom

Can you run away from yourself?

Frequently, persons trying to run away or attempting to free themselves from what they believe to be the causes of frustrations and tensions are, in reality, attempting to run from themselves. Unfortunately one's own self always seems to follow. For example, let's take the hypothetical case of a young woman named Ms. Frieda Phlier who felt extremely dissatisfied with certain aspects of her job. Her love life, too, in recent months had not been all that she had hoped for. So Frieda decided to quit her job in Kansas City and head out to the coast. Frieda found what she believed to be a good job in San Francisco, with some conditions much better than they were at her former place of employment, and the men in the city, she discovered, "are absolutely dreamy."

Soon, however, Frieda found that her new job was even worse than the old one, and that *not all* those men were so dreamy after all. After several months in her western "utopia," Frieda left her job again and once more began searching, not realizing that utopia is really in the "eye of the beholder." Instead of attempting to flee from that which cannot be left behind, a person might do better to try to "know thyself," to discover how to adapt more readily to present conditions. Sometimes in our obsessive quest for greater freedom, we actually forego more freedom than we attain.[1]

The Maintenance of Faith

Is your *terra* as firma as it used to be?

With violence, destruction, resource shortages, and political scandals all about us, with the *terra firma,* as viewed on the evening news, seemingly crumbling a bit more each day beneath our shoes, the maintenance of faith and positive attitudes is no mean feat. Negative responses may even seem, at times, to be the easy way out, serving to release pent-up tensions.

But think about your own life. Assuming that you have an eight-hour work day (probably a low estimate, considering travel and preparation time or jobs with differing responsibilities), you will spend roughly 1,912 hours a year at your job. In a lifetime of about forty years of employment, you will have spent at least 76,480 hours (9,560 workdays) in your job. If during your entire career you dread your work, a substantial part of your lifetime will seem beset by dullness and drudgery. Is this what you really want out of life?

The Meaning of Work

Is "work" really a nasty four-letter word?

Some persons when asked what the word *work* means to them tend to develop negative definitions. To many individuals, work is equated with drudgery—a dull, unpleasant, and irksome set of activities—which mainly serves as the means (the paycheck?) to far more satisfying ends (a color TV set or some new skis?).

To many other persons work has no such unfavorable connotation. They not only look forward to paydays but also look with eager anticipation to nearly every day. Open your eyes widely, look intently, and you *will* see persons who truly enjoy their work.

---

[1]For a thorough discussion of the concept of freedom, see Erich Fromm, *Escape from Freedom* (New York: Farrar and Rinehart, 1941) and Ashley Montagu, *The Humanization of Man* (New York: Grove Press, 1962, pp. 66–78)

Why is there so significant a difference in reactions toward work? The *nature* of a particular job has some influence, but an even more important reason could relate to individual *attitudes*, especially since two individuals in similar positions with the same organization may perceive their own activities with completely different viewpoints.

Assuming that you, if given a choice, would prefer to experience a more positive work situation, what might you do—and it is principally up to *you*—to acquire a more positive attitude toward your occupation? If you were to make a sincere effort to attempt to improve your understanding of self, you could probably develop, better than anyone else, a list of factors that would influence in a positive manner your own attitudes toward work and living in general. To aid you, consider the following suggestions and attempt to sort out those that might be useful to you, either now or in the future.

Develop Readily Attainable Goals

Another activity that can assist you in maintaining faith is the development of readily attainable short-run goals. Flexible long-run goals, such as the desire to be a corporate executive, an office manager, a lawyer, or a physician, can be beneficial to your mind, since they tend to give you a sense of direction.

Why are attainable goals beneficial for the mind?

As essential as any long-range goal are relatively easily attained shorter-range goals, which tend to provide you with periodic feelings of self-accomplishment. For example, your plans may include the acquisition of a B.A. or Master of Business Administration degree. Shorter-run goals could include the satisfactory completion of each college course in which you have enrolled along the way, as well as a two-year A.A. degree. Working toward the two-year degree, for example, could enable you to feel the satisfaction of accomplishment and even provide stimulation for your longer-run efforts.

Do you wish to wish your entire life away?

Too frequently, however, we tend to wish away our lives, often in segments. Some young people while in high school may wish those years away so that they can be "free" from what they feel is its drudgery. If they serve in the military, those years are often wished away. If they begin apprenticeship training in a trade, they tend to wish those months or years away. If they are in occupational positions with promotional possibilities, they may go on wishing their time away. Some persons awaken one day, look at their aging faces in the mirror, and suddenly realize that they have wished away substantial portions of their irreversible lives.

Perhaps instead of wishing your life away, you could retain greater faith and mental health by attempting to derive as much personal satisfaction as possible out of each moment in the day. Think about the words of Henry Van Dyke: "There is only one way to get ready for immortality, and that is to love this life and live it as bravely and faithfully and cheer-fully as we can."[2]

Select a Satisfying Occupation

If you gotta do it, why not enjoy it?

An important consideration, especially for a younger person, is the *choice of occupation*. If you have the opportunity to take a wide variety of college courses, you may, as a result, tap previously unknown in-terests. When you discover a particular field that excites you, interview other individuals who work in the occupation. Ask them *open questions* and attempt to uncover their true feelings about their occupations. You might ask them such questions as, "What do you like least (most) about your position?" Wait for answers, listen carefully, and you may discover relevant and useful information. The first step toward maintaining a positive attitude in a work situation is to choose a field that truly interests you.

Seek Opportunities—A Fish Story

Do fish have faith?

Someone once conducted an experiment with fish to determine if such cold-blooded aquatic vertebrates could be made to lose faith as do their Homo sapien cousins.

The experimenter obtained a medium-sized tank, filled it with fresh water, and arranged it so that the container was divided in half by a glass partition. Into one side of the tank was placed a hungry fish about four-teen inches long, and on the opposite side were placed five fish small enough to be readily devoured by their piscatorial superior.

The ravenous larger fish suddenly observed what she believed to be her *petit déjeuner*, and mightily swam toward the little snacks. As you might have expected, each time the large fish streaked toward the smaller ones, she smashed her tender mandible into the clear glass barrier.

Hungry and not eager to give up, she enthusiastically, but abortively, endured the same frustrating experience for fifteen minutes until finally she abandoned her tiresome efforts.

Then the experimenter lifted the glass barrier from the center of the tank, thus making accessible the small fish to the large one. What would you guess happened then?

The large hungry fish hardly budged. The tender little morsels, how-ever, curiously swam near her, occasionally within gill's length. The large fish did nothing, even though she now could begin her meal with no difficulty. She had given up—*resigned*—assuming that the opportunity wouldn't be hers even when the small fish brushed against her pectoral fins.

[2]Margherita Osborne, ed., *The Book of Success* (Joliet, Ill.: P. F. Vollard, 1927), p. 9.

This true fish story has its human equivalent: some individuals, for example, who have had one opportunity after another slip away, or who have felt certain barriers to be insurmountable, may also develop an "I-don't-give-a-damn" attitude, as did the fish, and give up. These attitudes are understandable; however, such persons might close their despondent eyes to real opportunity when it comes along.

The pessimistic person, like our despondent aquatic friend, often passes up opportunities that come very near. There are numerous things that you might do, however, to make your job seem more interesting, challenging, and satisfying.

How might you make your job more satisfying?

For example, periodically you might analyze the methods currently being used to determine how they might be improved, an activity that can be far more satisfying than mere criticism with little positive action. Or perhaps you might volunteer for special projects, or temporary assignments. Company publications usually need interesting material. Perhaps you have the latent interest and ability to apply some of your inactive literary talents to the writing of an article. You might be amazed at how such efforts could help to satisfy your higher-order needs. You might enter company slogan or name-a-product contests. A major point, regardless of the activity that interests you, is that there are infinite ways in which you might make your own job more interesting *if you seek such opportunities.*

Take the "Workaholic" Cure

Have you ever found that you tend to create some of your own tensions and pressures? Many individuals do. They are unable to relax even when they have some spare time. They tend to fill up every available moment of their waking hours with work activities.

In order to cope more effectively with life's innumerable frustrations, organizational members ordinarily should attempt to enjoy a reasonable amount of leisure. Many individuals, however, find the use of their spare time extremely difficult.

work addiction and workaholism

For example, a surprisingly large number of managers and professional people in organizations are suffering from an affliction believed to be worse in some respects than excessive drinking. Its name? *Work addiction*, often called *workaholism*. Some persons apparently overwork for the same reason that alcoholics overdrink: to escape from frustration (they hope).

What are the similarities between the alcoholic and the workaholic?

There are *parallels* between the alcoholic and the workaholic. Both *crave* their activities—excessive drinking on the one hand and excessive work activity on the other. Both develop a *capacity*—some alcoholics "enjoy" at least an eighteen-drink day, while some managers regularly work an eighteen-hour day. Both can develop *withdrawal symptoms*—the alcoholic develops tensions and anxieties without his or her beverage; the person addicted to work often develops tensions and anxieties during weekends or vacations.

Perhaps the persons who bury themselves in work are pursuing an activity similar to that of *flight;* their work may serve as a means of shielding them from other, less satisfying, types of activities.

What is the major difference between the work addict and the hard worker?

Many persons in organizations are *hard workers*, but the major difference between them and the *work addict* is that the addict feels *guilty* when not working; the hard worker does not.

Any compulsive worker should attempt to learn how to enjoy leisure. Some psychologists feel that workaholics need help just as do alcoholics. They both must first recognize that they have problems. Both engage in somewhat destructive behavioral patterns that have to be unlearned and their energies channeled into more positive directions. Bertrand Russell once advised, ''To be able to fill leisure intelligently is the last product of civilization.''

If you are a compulsive worker, and not really deriving the satisfaction from living that you would like, examine the *guidelines* below and consider if they might assist you to maintain or develop the faith and hope that we have been discussing.

How to avoid becoming psychologically dependent on your work.

Try to establish a *balance* between work and leisure activities, which is essential to prevent destructive tensions.

Learn how to slow down or *unwind*. Individuals whose tensions strain their tolerance for them sometimes discover that mama nature assists the slowing down process by heart attacks and increased accidents. A bit morbid, but too often true, is this bit of graffitti philosophy felt-penned onto a washroom wall in San Francisco: ''Death is nature's way of telling you to slow down.'' Think about those words.

Learn how to *relax*. Hobbies and athletics *do not* always help work addicts if they pursue those activities with the same fanatic zeal that they do their work.

Learn to enjoy being with other *people*, especially friends with interests that help you to relax.

Take regular vacations. Some psychologists advise taking frequent short vacations or easing into long vacations by cutting down gradually in your work. Don't take a briefcase filled with work or studies. A book of short stories, easily put aside, can be enjoyable ''escape.''

Plan your *next vacation* soon after finishing one. Such planning gives you something to look forward to, rather than merely feeling that you are back in your usual routine of travail.

Plan some *weekends* exclusively with your family. During such periods, attempt not to have work readily accessible.

Work addiction can lead to trouble: to dreadful careers, to poor health, even to early death. Without work, the work addict starts coming unglued. There might be a little workaholic in each of us. Wouldn't you prefer, however, to try to recognize the warning signs of addiction and cope with them before it's too late?

Establish Ethical Values

We've already touched upon the necessity of faith and trust both in yourself and in others. A significant way to maintain greater trust is to be trustworthy yourself. Any discussion of this nature runs the risk of appearing "goodie-goodie," or possibly even prudish—but think seriously about the following: If you continually engage in unethical practices with others, say, your subordinates or members of the general public, two principal types of problems might confront you. The first relates to *living with your own conscience*, and the second to the tendency of *assuming that others are as unethical* in their dealings as you are.

Imagine, for example, that you work as a sales representative for a steel supply company, and that you have called upon one of your customers who wants to place an unusually large order. However, this morning you learned that in five days your company intends to make substantial price reductions on the materials that your customer wants to buy. You have at least two options: You can take the order for the materials at today's prices, or you can inform your customer that the price is about to drop soon, thus saving her or him a considerable amount of money. If you enable your customer to purchase at next week's lower price, your commission, or earnings, would also be substantially lower.

Is life a "one-shot deal"?

What should you do? For some individuals the choice would be difficult. But need it be? Presumably your responsibility is not merely to push through "one-shot deals." Regular repeat business is far more desirable and profitable to your firm and to you over the long run. If your customers discover that you sold materials at higher prices than necessary, what will probably be their attitudes toward you and your company in the future? Ethical company representatives generally learn that they have far more regular, loyal, and profitable accounts when their customers are treated in a responsible fashion.

Another example that could strain your ethical values might be if your boss were to direct you to do something that you believe is either unethical or illegal. For example, assume that you are an accountant and your boss, Mr. Nomore Straight, asks you to keep a separate set of books —one with padded expense figures—for income tax purposes.

In a figurative sense you have been placed between the Scylla of willful disobedience and the Charybdis of ethical or legal responsibility.[3]

---

[3]Scylla in ancient mythology was a rock on the Sicilian coast (personified as a female monster) opposite a whirlpool called the Charybdis. Mariners were believed to have to sail between two equally hazardous alternatives.

Have you ever found yourself between the devil and the deep blue sea?

If you do as directed, you may be as legally responsible (or criminally negligent) as your boss. If you don't do as directed, you also run risks, since your boss determines your pay raises and promotions. What do you do then? How might your personal financial responsibilities influence or change your decision? What about the longer-run effects on your own conscience? If you are caught, and the chances are fairly good that you will be, how might your future career be affected?

You should continually remind yourself when confronted with certain temptations that *ethical values are not necessarily obsolete*. You will discover that you can live a far more confident existence if, in your mind, your activities do not border on the unethical or illegal.

Influence Others Positively

Will you always find out the effects of your efforts?

Another activity that is beneficial to one's own mind is the exertion of a positive and helpful influence over others. As only one person in a nation of over 220 million, you may at times feel somewhat powerless in your desire to exert any influence over others. However, you may have considerably more influence on others than you might imagine. Sometimes you may not even realize for years afterwards how you may have assisted someone with your comments or attempts to help.

391

For example, a public school speech therapist attempted once a week for two years to assist a young child to overcome a speech impediment. During a summer vacation, the child and his parents moved to another state, but the young boy finally decided to try to apply what the therapist had attempted so diligently to teach. Within a matter of weeks, the speech difficulty disappeared, but the persistent therapist never knew that her persevering efforts had succeeded.

The values that children develop are influenced by their parents far more than the latter might realize. If you have had children, you may have noticed that almost all of what they learn and do within their first few years is a result of direct imitation of you and your spouse. You may not always be a first-hand witness of the results of many of your efforts with others, but your influence may be felt nonetheless.

Don't Bite the Hand That Needs You—Off-the-Job Life Enrichment

Is there any part of your life you would prefer not to live over again?

How would you answer the following question: "Would you be willing to live your life—every bit of it—all over again?" Your response might provide considerable insight into how you perceive your past experiences.

Life seems to become more complex and frustrating as civilization advances. We now possess houses, factories, and offices filled with labor-saving gadgets and devices, yet there seems to be the continual frustrations of mechanical failures and breakdowns. A large proportion of American families possess houses and automobiles, yet during the 1970s they wondered if there would be enough fuel to heat their houses or to operate their automobiles. The events of the day—ranging from political scandals and international conflict to rapid inflation and the erosion of family incomes—have added to the list of human frustrations typically found in the work organization.

How will *you* cope with the continually increasing stresses of life? As we have already observed, the reaction of *flight*—the attempt to run away from problems—is seldom a successful solution to frustration, since utopia seems to exist only in the eye of the beholder. A key question, therefore, is, "What can we do to adapt more readily to our present environments?"

Two Schools of Thought

The B. F. Skinner school of behavioral psychology argues that we mortal beings have little in the way of real influence over our destinies. The

behaviorists

currently controversial *behaviorists*, such as Skinner and James V. McConnell, assert that most of our actions are determined or controlled without our knowledge—not unlike those of caged rats or birds in a laboratory experiment—by the people and institutions around us. The activities of society's members, they feel, are primarily conditioned responses to the stimuli about them.

humanists

An opposing school of psychological thought consists of the *humanists*—such as Rollo May and Carl Rogers—who believe that there will always be strong individuals who will step forth from the "conditioned mass." Humanist psychology, in effect, argues that the individual can become a more active force in shaping his or her own life and that there are human responses that are free from being conditioned or controlled by other forces.

A Mélange of Both Schools?

What is the future of ratkind?

There is little doubt that much of our behavior *is*, as the behaviorists would argue, conditioned by our experiences. We are aware, for example, that many persons respond in an almost "knee-jerk fashion" to other individuals with certain styles of haircuts, shapes of noses, or manners of handshaking, even when unacquainted with the other persons. Many of our normal reactions do appear to be conditioned responses.

How can *you* influence your moods?

However, we also enjoy the capability of independent thought. We are able to influence our moods by altering our environment (music, for example, can change moods), and we can influence our lives by altering such factors as our attitudes. Let's examine some of the ways in which we might be able to prevent ourselves from acting solely as laboratory rats would in a behavioral psychologist's maze, beginning first with a short story about two identical twin sisters.

Recognize the Positive

Once upon a time there was a small community, and residing in this community was a family with identical twin daughters. One daughter was a pessimist and the other an optimist. One year when their birthdays rolled around, a friend of the family—the town psychiatrist—and the girls' parents decided to conduct an experiment. For her birthday, the mother and father gave the pessimistic daughter a shiny new bicycle, a water gun, and a colorful hat. The optimistic child was given a room full of fresh horse manure and a small green shovel.

About fifteen minutes later, the psychiatrist and the anxious parents went into the pessimist's room and enthusiatically asked her how she liked her presents. The sulking young girl snapped, ''The bicycle is no good, the water gun doesn't shoot far enough, and the hat is too small.'' Then they went into the optimist's room and asked her how she liked her gifts. Within the room busily shoveling horse manure about in an excited fashion was the optimistic child, who looked up and cheerfully replied, ''It's a lot of work, but I know there's a pony in here somewhere!''

What effect does your attitude have on how you cope with pressures?

A corny story—agreed—but it does help to illustrate the important fact that our *attitudes* strongly influence how we cope with our environmental pressures. Some individuals, such as the pessimistic daughter, continually focus on the negative—and they can usually find it, for there always seem to be undersirable aspects in any situation.

A characteristic that helps many persons to see the brighter aspects of situations and overcome frustrations more readily is a *sense of humor*. An anonymous humorist once paradoxically exclaimed, ''The only way that I can retain my sanity is to act crazy!'' Persons who can laugh at their own shortcomings, for example, are often more healthy-minded individuals than those who cannot.

Vary Your Activities

Faith in one's self and in others seems to be far easier for persons who regularly have new experiences to look forward to—that is, a wide variety of interests. Bertrand Russell during a television interview once caustically remarked, ''Some individuals' interests consist of no more than sitting in their water closets all day powdering their noses while observing the looking glass and wondering about the reason for their boredom!''

life enrichment

Perhaps our jobs are not the only activities that need occasional enriching. We could all probably benefit from what might be called *life enrichment*. The enrichment of lives is really each person's own individual responsibility. Men and women usually must develop their own cures for loneliness, boredom, and loss of faith.

How might you "enrich" your life?

Simple activities can sometimes enrich at least portions of your life. For example, you may feel that you are in a rut—experiencing the same activities every day—driving to work and then driving the same way back home again. If so, why not vary your route? Does it really matter if another road takes ten minutes or so longer; the opportunities to see different scenery, different neighborhoods, even different traffic signals, all contribute to the variety of your life.

Many persons feel that most life enrichment activities are too costly; as a result, they spend much of their idle time dozing in front of the TV.

What are some leisure activities that are not too expensive?

Many interests, however, are not necessarily expensive. Unfortunately, many persons have not yet discovered, developed, or acquired them. For example, have you ever considered taking an evening course in art or music at a community college? "Not particularly interested in art or music," you say? Are you really certain? With little or no present knowledge of a specific area, an individual has no way of knowing his or her potential interests. An evening course in classical guitar, for example, is not likely to enable you to supplant Segovia, but you might be amazed at how it can expand your appreciation of polished professional artists.

Contributing your talents to such activities as little theatre groups—if not in acting, perhaps as a stage assistant—can be another enjoyable experience. You will have the opportunity to meet and mix with other people, and you would be assigned certain responsibilities that might develop in you feelings of participation and contribution.

Evening courses and little theatre groups are only two illustrations of the wide variety of inexpensive activities that could enrich your life. *You*, however, have to discover for *yourself* what might enhance your own happiness.

Exercise—The Shape of Things to Come

holistic effect

Is inactivity broadening?

We have already mentioned that your mind can affect your bodily functions. The reverse—the body's affecting the mind—is equally important. The relationship between the two is sometimes referred to as the *holistic effect*. As we grow older, or as we assume positions with greater responsibility but less physical activity, we can generally find an infinite variety of excuses for not exercising. "I'm too tired." "I'm too busy." "It's too early." "It's too late." "I really *should* start exercising." "Maybe next week, *if* it's not raining."

Almost without our awareness the condition of our bodies can begin to deteriorate, a process that can take place amazingly rapidly in the inactive person. Of course, you may live to a ripe old age in spite of not taking proper care of your body. But put your feet into the well-worn slippers of the sickly eighty-eight-year-old person who said, "If I had only known I was going to live this long I would have taken better care of myself!"

Life insurance companies have a vested interest in your longevity; they want you to remain durable, since the longer you live, the longer you will pay them money. An insurance company with ample statistical experience to back its assertions—the Metropolitan Life Insurance Company—contends that *exercise* is one of the most significant factors in *prolonging your active years*. The preface of a Metropolitan exercise guide offers its readers this tease:

Would you take a pill that promised to:
Improve your appearance?

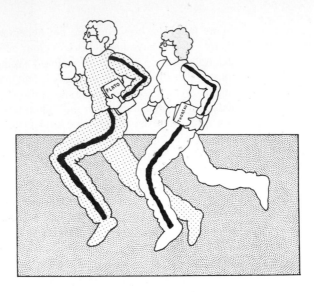

Improve your muscle tone, including the heart muscle?
Improve your blood circulation and breathing?
Help control your weight?
Help relieve fatigue and tensions?
Help improve your coordination and endurance?
No super-wonder drug can do it, but regular exercise can.[4]

If you're a skeptic check with your doctor; then find out what sort of program of *regular* exercise will benefit you. Physical activity can be of value to practically every part of the body and can make a big difference in whether you feel sluggish or energetic. One of its greatest benefits, however, is to the *mind*, for exercise, such as a daily routine of jogging or swimming, can be a form of relief for the man or woman beset with anger, pressures, worries, or frustrations. Try some exercise—gradually at first, especially if you are out of condition—and you may find that you are experiencing one of the most enjoyable "highs" of your lifetime. Because of such positive results, some organizations now encourage their employees to take exercise breaks on company time.

Why not find a friend to run around with!

Some persons hesitate to take up jogging, for instance, because they feel embarrassed when others see them bouncing gingerly along the sidewalk, pathway, or road. Think, however, about a statement made by Francis Parkman that could have considerable relevance to many of your activities, not only jogging:

[4]*Metropolitan Life's Exercise Guide for Men and Women* (1966), p. i.

He who would do some great thing in this short life must apply himself to work with such a concentration of his forces as, to idle spectators, who live only to amuse themselves, looks like insanity.[5]

Warning: The Surgeon General Has Determined That Cigarette Smoking Is . . .

Are you securing your own coffin with white nails?

A habit that will offset much of the benefits of any exercise program is that of cigarette smoking. No moralist can—or should—attempt to shame a person into breaking the habit; an individual must be both willing and able on his or her own. Organized groups have been formed in some cities to aid persons who sincerely feel that they are ready to begin tasting food and breathing fresh air as they really are. One such organization, the Kaiser Permanente Health Center in Oakland, California, regularly conducts Stop Smoking Classes. Included in the advice and assistance offered to class members are the *ten tips* listed below. If you seriously desire or intend to quit smoking, you ought to take a thoughtful look at the following suggestions:

What can a person do to quit smoking?

1. Don't stock up. Never buy by the carton; wait until one pack is finished before buying another.
2. Change brands with each pack for a week or two before quitting.
3. Always ask yourself: "Do I *really* want this cigarette?"
4. Each day try to put off lighting your first cigarette.
5. Only smoke half of each cigarette.
6. Be *aware* of your smoking. Ask yourself: "Why do I need to smoke right now?"; "What is this cigarette doing for me?"; "What would I do if I didn't smoke this cigarette?"
7. Don't smoke while involved in another activity, that is, while you are on the phone, reading, watching TV, or talking. Concentrate on the cigarette.
8. Look forward to the time you will be quitting and able to think of yourself as a nonsmoker.
9. Tell people around you that you're going to quit smoking.
10. If you have physical symptoms that might be related to your smoking, relieve your mind by discussing them with your doctor. It is easier to quit when you know your health status.

The Tensions of Forced Waiting

forced waiting

Another cause of tension and frustration in individuals is the recurring experience of *forced waiting*. Dentists and doctors make you wait; post office personnel make you wait; automobile repair firms make you wait;

[5]Osborne, *op. cit.*, p. 16.

customers make you wait; even gas stations make you wait. Everybody seems to make you wait—it almost seems like a conspiracy! In fact, if on the average you spend 45 minutes of each day idly waiting for something, you have allowed over 270 of your hours in a year to melt away into oblivion.

Why wait when you have to wait?

If waiting really frustrates you, *why wait when you have to wait?* You probably know by now what sorts of situations are likely to require idly biding your time. Why not figuratively don your old girl or boy scout sombrero and "be prepared," as the motto suggests, for forced waiting.

For example, if you have an appointment for your periodic physical examination, take along something that interests you, perhaps that article or book you've been wanting to read but have never had quite enough time. Or maybe you could take some letter writing materials with you.

How about that letter to Uncle Horace?

How about that letter from Uncle Horace that you haven't yet answered, and it's been three years since he wrote!

Or if you are a salesperson who calls on customers; you may experience the frustrations of clients not seeing you promptly. Most sales people, like yourself, have regular and substantial amounts of paperwork to prepare. Instead of complaining about how many forms you have to fill out each evening on your own time, why not accomplish what you can while waiting?

Arthur Brisbane on the subject of the use of idle time once stated, "Time is the one thing we possess. Our success depends upon the use of our time, and its by-product, the odd moment."

Waiting actually can be a delightful part-time experience if you make it so. The above discussion has been aimed more at those with a reasonably strong work ethic. You might prefer, however, merely encouraging your mind to wander and engage in free or creative thinking, a pastime that you may seldom have time for otherwise. If the act of waiting usually bothers you, and if you go to your waiting situations prepared with activities you find interesting, you are likely to find that time will pass more quickly than you desire.

Happiness and Success Are . . .?

Having read this far in the current chapter, you are not quite ready to hang out a shingle advertising that you are a full-fledged professional psychiatrist. You have, however, had the opportunity to examine a few topics that might enable you to follow the advice of Socrates suggested at the beginning of this chapter: "Know thyself."

A Hundred Years From Today . . .

Life in our space module Earth is relatively brief. As the Romans would say, *tempus fugit,* or "time flies." Do you remember when you were in grade school that summers seemed nearly endless? And have you noticed that each summer since has seemed to grow shorter and shorter? Time has a stealthy habit of creeping up on us. One morning you may wake up, look in the mirror, and suddenly realize that the person you see is not the person you saw twenty years before.

Mirror, mirror, on the wall . . .?

Each of us has more influence than we might imagine on whether we will be able to look back on our lives as generally having been happy experiences. But what actually is this thing called "happiness"? Happiness is different things to different people. There are some ingredients, however, that make for more gratifying circumstances. Look at the following list and decide which statements are integral parts of your present situation. Are there any factors that you might add to the list that could contribute to your personal pleasure? If some of the items on the list could make you happier but aren't a part of your present situation, what might you do to utilize them?

What would make your life a happier experience?

I have enjoyable feelings about my job.

I have reasonably good physical and mental health.

I am free from economic want, that is, my needs are reasonably satisfied.

I have some close friends whose company I regularly enjoy.

I have a fairly good sense of humor.

I try to understand the points of view of others and to accept them as they are, not as I want them to be.

I am engaged in an activity that I feel is useful to society.

I feel that I know how to enjoy my leisure.

I feel that my life has a sense of purpose, and includes some specific, but flexible, goals.

The Concept of Success

A basic premise of this chapter has been that the maintenance or restoration of faith *is possible* if society's members—that means *us*—are willing to cease venting their insecurities, frustrations, and emotions on their fellow human beings.

How can you feel more secure with your insecurities?

Although it sounds contradictory, we must learn to feel more secure with our insecurities. As we acquire more education, we tend to realize that we cannot know or do everything and, as a result, may feel more secure with this knowledge. The hope that many persons have lost can be restored if they are willing to educate themselves to face reality—to perceive things as they truly are, not as they've never been, or as they appear to be on the screen of a television set—and to attempt to engage in activities that improve the lot of their fellow human beings.

What is "success"?

An ancient Chinese seer once advised, "A journey of a thousand miles begins with a single step, and it is taking that step today." *Success* is another word that means many things to many people. Numerous persons feel that success is important to them, but they are not quite certain what the concept means.

If you were to observe each day on your way to work an old man dressed in ragged clothes sitting on the grass in a city park merely whiling away the time feeding bread to the pigeons, would you say that he is a success? Who can really say for certain? Perhaps you would have to ask him before you could know.

Is a person in possession of two cars, two houses, a boat, and a responsible executive position necessarily a success? Once again, perhaps you must obtain an honest answer from the person before you can know. Individuals' *attitudes*, far more than their possessions, influence the feelings of success. Material objects, in themselves, can either contribute to or detract from a person's feeling of faith and success. A worthwhile way to conclude this chapter might be with a comment that Henry Ford once made about these concepts. Read his words and see how they might relate to you:

> We begin as pensioners. Some people live two-thirds of their lives on the provision made for them by others. We graduate into cooperators, earn our own living, hold up our own end of the job, produce a little extra for the pensioners that are coming on behind us. A few enter the third stage, where they do something more for the world than the world does for them. They put the world in their debt by making every man's living better, or his hope larger, or his opportunity wider. Just to hold up one's end of the load is a great and satisfactory thing; it makes one a man. However, it only squares the account. But to do for the world more than the world does for you—that is success.[6]

Summary

In this chapter we explored the significant topic of faith and have stressed some of the major consequences of its absence from an individual's personal value system. Examples of eroded faith, hope, and distrust are far too prevalent in our society.

Faith in one's self, in humanity, and in the future are essential, however, if individuals are to derive personal satisfaction from the act of

[6]Osborne, *op. cit.*, p. 52.

living. Individuals with little faith or hope tend to be like nomads in their behavior, changing schools, jobs, addresses, and mates with excessive frequency. The search for utopia is difficult, since many of the problems from which individuals are attempting to escape tend to follow them to each destination.

We also explored some of the ways in which we mortals might cope more effectively with life's many stresses and strains, such as recognizing the positive aspects of particular situations, maintaining good physical condition, using leisure time more effectively, and learning how to enjoy the act of waiting. And finally we analyzed some of the essential ingredients of those nebulous concepts, happiness and success.

We customarily spend much of our lives in work situations. Consequently, the choice of a satisfying occupation, as well as an enjoyable personal life imbued with a variety of interests, can aid the individual in achieving a more satisfying existence and in maintaining a reasonable degree of faith and hope in both the present and the future.

Terms and Concepts to Remember

Faith	Humanist
Situational faith	Life enrichment
Work	Holistic effect
Work addiction	Forced waiting
(workaholism)	Happiness
Behaviorist	Success

Questions

1. Why is the process of "knowing thyself" so difficult?
2. What do you feel Oscar Wilde meant by the statement, "Discontent is the first step in the progress of man or nation"?
3. Could a person have faith and yet not believe in a formalized religion? Explain.
4. How might an overt distrust of employees by managers work to the detriment of the organization?
5. What is one of the major problems associated with the activity of flight?
6. Assuming that you are fed up with your studies, family, and friends, what sort of personal behavior might help to restore some of your faith and hope?
7. Assume that you have successfully stopped smoking. Why might an acquaintance of yours be unappreciative of any crusading efforts on your part to persuade him or her to quit?

8. Explain the apparent conflict between the B. F. Skinner-behaviorist and the Rollo May-humanist philosophies. What arguments might you offer to show the relevancies of both schools of thought?
9. In what ways can a regular program of physical fitness improve your present state of health and prolong your active years?
10. If forced waiting frustrates you, how might you develop a situation in which it is not necessary for you "to wait when you have to wait"?

Other Readings

Berthoff, Rowland. *An Unsettled People: Social Order and Disorder in American History*. New York: Harper & Row, 1971.

Bolles, Richard. *What Color Is Your Parachute? A Practical Manual for Job-Hunters and Career-Changers*. Berkeley, Calif.: Ten Speed Press, 1972.

Boronson, Warren. "The Workaholic in You." *Money*, June 1976, pp. 32–35.

Chenoweth, Lawrence. *The American Dream of Success: The Search for the Self in the Twentieth Century*. North Scituate, Mass.: Duxbury Press, 1974.

Fabun, Don. *Three Roads to Awareness—Motivation, Creativity, Communications*. Beverly Hills: Glencoe Press, 1970.

Fromm, Erich. *Escape From Freedom*. New York: Farrar and Rinehart, 1941.

"Getting Your Head Together." *Newsweek*, 6 September 1976, pp. 56–62.

May, Rollo. *Psychology and the Human Dilemma*. Princeton, N.J.: D. Van Nostrand, 1967.

McConnell, James V. "Feedback, Fat, and Freedom." *Britannica Book of the Year*. Chicago: Encyclopedia Britannica, 1973, pp. 33-40.

Applications

A Search for Utopia

Twenty-five idealistic young Canadians from Victoria, British Columbia, have decided to leave what they feel to be the depressing weather of western Canada to establish new lives on a South Sea island in order to prove that their dreams of a utopia can come true.

"We will live on the island for the rest of our lives," said twenty-year-old waitress, Barbara Broadway, one of six women who will make the trip.

The originator of the trip, Joseph Centerfielder, a lithographer, said that he and the group hope to find sun, security, romance, and escape from the frustrations and tensions of modern industrial life. Centerfielder explained that the twenty-five persons will establish a share-and-share-alike island family community.

None of the women is single, and there are six married couples. The remaining members are men. The average age of the group members is thirty-three. Among the group is an accountant, a stockbroker, a law enforcement officer, a firefighter, a plumber, and a social worker.

Their intentions are to depart after the first of next year to settle on an eight-square-mile island off the west coast of Queensland, Australia. Currently, they are negotiating with the government of Queensland to acquire a renewable ten-year lease for $100,000.

Questions

1. What, in your opinion, are the twenty-five persons "looking for" on the island?
2. Do you feel that they will achieve their goals? Explain your answer.
3. What sort of problems might evolve in the following areas: (a) lack of leadership, (b) morale, (c) status, and (d) personal property?

The Rat Race

Dear Uncle Brian:

I know I haven't written to my favorite uncle for a long, long time. Frankly, I haven't felt like doing much of anything lately. I've really been fed up with most things these days.

Well, it's Friday evening again. Another week shot to hell. The weekends just can't roll around too fast for me. Don't you dread Monday mornings? I sure as heck do. But I've got quite a bit of sick leave accumulated so I've started taking off every other Monday, and I spend nearly the whole darned day in bed. Man, what a waste, but it's one heckofa lot better than going to that dull office in town. Besides, I really haven't been feeling too well lately, terrible headaches most of the time. Probably from that rotten music my sons play on their blasted hi-fi. What ever happened to Guy Lombardo and his Royal Canadians?

Cripes, driving is getting to be a drag. You know, I spend about two miserable hours a day on that big hunk of concrete they call a highway, and I can only creep along at ten miles an hour. At times, I feel like I'm living with those goons in the cars on both sides of me.

You remember that Gladys and I moved out to the suburbs, good old Surreptitious Valley, to get away from all that crap in the city. But things out here just aren't like they used to be. Kids getting busted for speeding all the time, teachers getting beat up, burglaries, the whole shmear.

We've taken Jimmy and Billy out of that public school jungle. Do you know they're now busing those troublemakers from the other side of town to *our* public school? Why can't those people stay with their own kind where they belong? Some things just aren't supposed to mix, you know, like water and grease.

So we're now sending our boys to that private school in the next town. Boy, does that cost us a bundle. Even had to buy Gladys a car to drive them. And you know what's happened to the price of gas since those you-know-whats started that Young Cooper War, or whatever they call it.

Speaking of the boys, I don't know what's with the young kids these days. I work my tail off so's I can afford things like decent clothes for them, but they want to look like a bunch of bums! I'm ashamed to go anywhere with them—they look like a couple of fairies the way they get their hair styled.

Man, am I ever glad it's Friday. Life has really become a rat race. Same old crap day in and day out. Wash the gas guzzler, and it gets dirty all over again. Mow the lawn, and it grows right back in five days, paint the house, and it needs painting again in two years. Back and forth, back and forth, every day on the same highway. Every darned day I'm chained to that desk down at the office, except for my morning coffee breaks, forty-five minutes for lunch, and a couple trips to the restroom. You know, during the week the big event of my day is hopping on the couch after dinner, watching TV, and then falling asleep.

I have to hurry on this letter. I'm going bowling with the boys again tonight. Do it every Friday night. That's about the only real pleasure I get these days—that and drinking beer watching the games on TV on Saturdays and Sundays. Does Gladys ever get peeved with those sports programs! But it's my fun. At least I keep telling myself it's fun.

By the way, I guess I didn't tell you what Gladys and I might do. I'm so sick of this damned rat race, we might buy a little motel up in Twain Harte. We'll get a lot of fresh air up there and get away from the hustle-bustle routine down here. I think it will be kind of fun being one of those entrepreneurs. (How do you like that word, unc?)

Well, Uncle Brian, I gotta get going now. The guys will be coming by soon to pick me up for Friday night bowling. Such a life, eh? By the way, be sure to give Aunt Fanny my regards.

Your nephew,
Quentin

Questions

1. What do you feel is troubling Quentin?
2. What adjustive reactions, discussed in chapter 5, does Quentin appear to be experiencing?
3. How might Quentin improve his attitude toward living?

PIZZA PANTRY
ITALIAN FOOD

Jim Reilly
FOR CITY ATTORNEY

DELIVER
441-2122

Jim Reilly   Jim Reilly
Jim Reilly   Jim Reilly
Jim Reilly   Jim Reilly
Jim Reilly   Jim Reilly
Jim Reilly   Jim Reilly

Pizza Pantry
RESTAURANT

anton-Polk
GROCERY
WINES - BEER
UALITY FOODS

BARBER SHOP

Sea Food
LUNCH - DINNER

When you finish this chapter, you should be able to:

1. **List** the major reasons that some people have little faith in business corporations.
2. **Contrast** two prevalent philosophies of the proper role of business.
3. **List** at least seven areas of managerial social responsibility.
4. **Summarize** some of the guidelines designed to enhance the success of organizational social programs.

Business not only *can* help solve
our urban ills, business *must* do this.

—Robert B. Shetterly

The management of a company is no
longer anointed with absolute
power. Rather it can exercise this
power only so long as it does so in a
socially accepted way.

—Carl A. Gerstacker

"Capitalism is murder. Murder of millions of people in wars. Capitalist wars. World War I. World War II. The Korean War. And the bloody, shameful and disgraceful Vietnam War—and more! Murder of men, women, and children in an attempt to establish a trans-Atlantic slave system. America (capitalism) believes in slavery! Wars to rob people of the land on which they live, and all of their natural wealth. Murder and death is the face of capitalism."

These acrimonious and exceedingly bitter remarks were made in an essay voluntarily submitted by a college student to a professor of economics during the mid-1970s. The writer's attitude may be unusually extreme, but unfortunately there seems to have developed in the United States—especially since the mid-1960s—a growing antipathy toward business. Survey after survey has revealed negative, and often uninformed, attitudes toward business behavior in relation to profits, the environment, and social concern in general. In a climate of perpetual hostility, American business enterprise cannot function as effectively as it might.

External Human Relations

Should managers be concerned with *external* human relations?

Managers have no time to lose in attempting to increase their understanding of the underlying motives for the present antagonism if they are to deal effectively with it. Not all firms can be accused of inaction toward society. There are numerous examples of business firms whose leaders have consistently been concerned with their social behavior and responsibilities. Too frequently, however, many of the social efforts of business managers have been gestures of rhetorical public relations campaigns rather than sincere and consistent programs of specific action designed to improve the quality of life in America.

The Social Role of Business

What has been the traditional role of business?

As with most issues, not everyone agrees on the "proper" social role of business. *Traditionally* the role of business has been solely to "turn a profit." However, the business community today faces considerably more pressures than it has before from various segments of society. Managers who ignore these forces may soon find themselves in positions far more difficult. Merely witness the government takeovers of large private corporations in some South American and Arab countries in recent years.

The major purpose of this chapter is to provide you with an overview of the growing social pressures and responsibilities confronting business managers of today and tomorrow. In addition, we shall examine some specific guidelines that managers should consider if they are sincerely interested in fulfilling their human relations responsibilities, not only to business, but also to society and its environment.

A Loss of Faith—Why?

Why have some people turned against business?

In 1972, the Opinion Research Corporation, a subsidiary of McGraw-Hill, reported the results of its survey on current public attitudes toward business organizations. ORC found that the share of the American public expressing disapproval for business had *climbed* from *47 percent* in 1965 to *60 percent* in 1972. In 1974, ORC reported that people believing profits of large corporations are beneficial to everyone *declined* from a high of *66 percent* in 1965 to a low of *43 percent*. According to almost any public opinion poll of the mid-1970s, public hostility toward business seemed greater than at any time since the Great Depression of the 1930s.

Is Business the Sole Culprit?

Even eggs aren't what they were cracked up to be!

If we analyze the national mood, however, we notice that business is not being singled out as the sole cause of our nation's ills. In fact, public sentiment is even lower toward government, labor, the judiciary, the medical profession, the press, and even educational institutions. What appears to be the case is that virtually all institutions have been the targets of growing criticism and hostility. There seems to be a general breaking down of the respect for institutions in general.

Should business managers feel smug knowing that they are in good company with other institutions in this crisis-of-confidence period? Not really. Managers should be concerned—as many are today—with public attitudes since a disenchanted public can exert pressures through its elected representatives, who may create regulations that tend to be a coercive, rather than a voluntary, means for forcing business to display greater social responsibility.

Why should managers be concerned with public attitudes?

Judged by Actions

Stop and think for a moment about the current mood toward business. At what have the attacks been aimed primarily? Basically, much of the criticism has been directed more toward specific business firms and practices than against the business system itself. Let's take a look now at some of the probable reasons why business has taken an extraordinary amount of verbal abuse during the past decade.

Conglomerate Waves of the 1960s and 1970s

Some employees developed an antipathy toward the business corporation during the 1960s and mid-1970s, periods during which large organizations purchased smaller companies with increased frequency. During these *conglomerate waves,* many employees observed what they believed to be giant companies gobbling up their own sources of employment. Employees often felt that the big firms showed little humane concern for the employees of the acquired organizations.

conglomerate wave

In some instances, the managers of the larger firms lacked the expertise to run the newly acquired firm, which sometimes resulted in its failure or being sold soon after acquisition. This trend tended to make some employees feel that they were not unlike pawns in a chess game or real estate in a game of Monopoly.

Economic Conditions

Before 1970, college-educated persons seldom experienced the same difficulties as others in maintaining or finding new jobs during periods of economic recession. And during most of the 1960s, until the acceleration of the Vietnam War in 1968, inflation rates seldom exceeded 2 percent per year. The simultaneous recession and inflation of the 1970s with, at times, double-digit price leaps, and unemployment pushing—or even exceeding—10 percent in urban areas, brought about new types of dissatisfaction. High rates of unemployment were prevalent among people

How do economic conditions influence attitudes toward business?

unaccustomed to joblessness—staff executives, engineers, Ph.D.'s, school teachers, advertising people, brokers, and security analysts. Skyrocketing prices for food, housing, and energy-related products significantly eroded the purchasing power of the typical household.

Although the business community alone cannot be blamed for the inflationary-recession, which, in general, was the result of ineffective and untimely government policies coupled with energy crises, the parade of bad economic news through the 1960s and 1970s put American-styled business in an unfavorable light. Whether realistic or not, a close correlation seems to exist between economic conditions and public attitudes toward the business community.

The Consumer Movement

Consumer groups have existed unobtrusively for some time in the United States, but their activities, prodded by the aggressive attacks of Ralph Nader, a consumer advocate, seemed to gain impetus between the latter 1960s and the 1970s. Evidence of shoddy products or false product claims seemed to multiply like rabbits. General Motors Corporation sued Ralph Nader for his allegedly libelous claims about the automobile industry in his book, *Unsafe at Any Speed*—and lost. Ralph Nader subsequently countersued General Motors Corporation—and won. Defective automobiles have since been recalled in record numbers, as has been the case with the consumer goods of almost every major manufacturer.

In the late 1970s, public issues have been promoted by approximately fifty organizations with more than 190 professional advocates on their payrolls in Washington D.C. alone. Their activities have brought to the forefront examples of consumer discontent.

caveat emptor

As is usually the case, the highly publicized examples of *caveat emptor* attitudes (let the buyer beware) on the part of some businesses have damaged the reputations of other reputable organizations.

Reluctance to Be Concerned About the Environment

Part of the deteriorating public confidence in the business community has been a result of the latter's apparent reluctance to worry about the environment until pressured by governmental agencies.

For example, in 1968, Roger M. Blough, chairman of the United States Steel Corporation, urged private business to take a bigger part in achieving social change. Yet five years later—1973—*The Wall Street Journal* reported that the same company, United States Steel Corporation, was ordered by a government agency—the Environmental Protection Agency—to reduce pollution at its Gary (Indiana) Works by 85 percent by the end of 1975. The Gary Works had been emitting seventy-one thousand tons of dust and soot into the air each year.

Shouldn't managers *do* as they *say*?

The public tends to become cynical when it *hears* business executives talk about their social responsibility but *observes* their corporations behaving in what appears to be a contrary fashion. Public cynicism had grown so strong by 1974 that many Americans refused to believe that the energy crisis was anything other than a contrived conspiracy of oil company "robber barons." Apparently aware of such attitudes, Gerald Ford, in his first speech to Congress as President, said, "The nation needs action, not words."

The list of events that in recent years have been creating the crisis of public confidence in business could go on *ad infinitum*: oil spills tarring beaches and destroying wild birdlife, illegal contributions to political parties—allegedly designed to influence legislation toward business, questionable payments and bribes by major corporations to foreign officials, and even such apparently unrelated happenings as the Watergate burglaries during the 1972 presidential election campaign.

Far too frequently, the initial business response to criticism has been overdefensive, with strident denials of guilt, or threats of shortages, higher prices, and unemployment. Industry has also consistently lobbied against consumer protection and environmental legislation. As a result, the damage to the image of business has been so extensive that considerable remedial action is necessary if business is ever again to operate within an aura of public faith and confidence.

Attitudes among business leaders differ, however, as we shall see in an upcoming section dealing with two contrary views on the proper role of business.

Are Things Getting Any Better?

There do appear to be some refreshing signs of change on the horizon. There seems to have evolved during the 1970s a fresh mood of social concern, believed by some observers to be *genuine* altruism, and by others to be *unavoidable* altrusim—possibly the result of past protests and attacks by consumer advocates, governmental action, minority groups, and zealous college students. Higher proportions of college students have chosen to study business during the 1970s than during the previous decade. Women and minorities, too, are studying business in record numbers. Better understanding of the activities and workings of business coupled with an improving domestic economy could help to improve public attitudes toward business organizations in the future.

Even with these changes, however, the crisis of confidence remains and will necessitate consistent efforts and a reasonable amount of time to remedy.

Two Philosophies: Profit Quest versus Social Accountability

Milton Friedman, professor of economics at the University of Chicago and previously economic advisor to former President Nixon and Senator Barry Goldwater, has stated:

> If the corporate executive makes expenditures on reducing pollution beyond the amount in the best interests of the corporation or that is required by law; or, at the expense of corporate profits, hires hard-core unemployed instead of better-qualified available workmen, he is spending the stockholder's and employee's money for a general social interest and deprives them of their right to decide what to do with what really is their money.[1]

trustee of profit

In short, Friedman's classical *trustee-of-profit* viewpoint contends that the corporation's *sole responsibility is to produce profits* and that any expenditure on corporate social goals amounts, in essence, to a hidden tax on workers, customers, and shareholders.

enlightened self-interest

A second, and more modern philosophy, argues that *social goals* should not be considered as a force competing for profits but instead as *one of the over-all goals of management*, sometimes referred to as an attitude of *enlightened self-interest*. A spokesperson for this point of view is Thomas M. McMahon, Jr., who, while executive vice-president of the Chase Manhattan Bank, stated: "All the way up and down the line, corporation responsibility must be treated as an integral corporate goal, just like profitability or efficiency."[2]

These two viewpoints typify the opposition that currently prevails among corporate philosophers, and are sometimes referred to as the *profit-quest* and the *social-accountability* approaches. Let's briefly examine each.

The Profit-Quest Approach

Most objective observers of American society would probably agree that the standard of living presently attainable by the majority of its citizens has been largely a result of the private (more aptly called "mixed") enterprise system in the United States. In few other nations is there as wide a choice of different consumer products as there is in the United

---

[1] Milton Friedman, "The Social Responsibility of Business Is to Increase its Profits," *New York Times Magazine,* 13 September 1970, p. 33.

[2] "For Many Corporations, Social Responsibility Is Now a Major Concern," *The Wall Street Journal,* 26 October 1971, p. 1.

States. Trends in other countries—both eastern and western—have generally emulated developments in American technology and marketing. Americans could survive quite well without automatic icemakers, power-driven lawn mowers, and pocket calculators, but generally the existence of such goods has been assured by the consuming public's consistent flow of "dollar votes."

Why have profits been important to the American system? Much of America's wide choice of products and reasonably well-paying jobs have been dependent upon the earning of *profits* by the business community. Reasonable profits themselves—unless you happen to subscribe to Marxian philosophy—are not necessarily evil. Many of America's past and present social ills were caused not so much by the making of profits as by what was done with the nation's resources.

However, many corporations seem to have the notion that they are not obliged to do anything but turn a profit. Some firms *profess* social concern, but, as we have seen, *do not appear* to mean it. At times their efforts have seemed merely to be part of a well-publicized public relations fad with little apparent significance.

profit quest

As we mentioned in the chapter on leadership styles, there is more than one philosophy or way of perceiving others; some managers perceive individuals positively, while others stress the negative. The same thesis could hold true of the way in which business managers perceive the general public *vis-à-vis* their social responsibilities. Some managers feel that their only concern need be with the *quest of profits*. "We are *not* social workers!" some business leaders exclaim.

Social-Accountability Approach

social accountability

We live in a period of rapid change. For many organizations, *social accountability*, or an attitude of responsibility toward society, has become a major concern. Corporate goals still include the production of profits, but many executives today seem to be saying that making a good product, offering it at a good price, and earning a good profit are not enough; it now appears that many corporations are developing a *social conscience*.

Does your *social* conscience bother you?

Enlightened executives have begun to display their social consciences in a variety of ways. In the following section you will read of the areas of public concern that have received increased attention from the business community in recent years.

Areas of Responsibility

We now shall move into a controversial topic, the *specific areas of social responsibility* that the business community should face. Our list of concerns will be neither complete nor absolute. Keep in mind that topics that seem almost radical during one era sometimes become commonplace during another. And conversely, topics that were significant during one period become unnecessary during another if the specific problems no longer exist.

The following discussion is intended to illustrate the various types of social responsibilities with which some managers have become increasingly concerned in recent years. The list should be modified as social conditions change. Among current managerial concerns could include responsibilities:

1. To employees
2. To the environment
3. To provide information
4. To assist the disadvantaged and the handicapped
5. To contribute money and talent
6. To rebuild communities
7. To aid minority businesses

Responsibility to Employees

One of the primary social responsibilities of an organization should be to its *own employees*. Much of what we have already covered in this text relates to the topic of employee human relations.

From the standpoint of improving the "corporate image," employees are exceedingly important since they are an influential *communications link* to the general public. Information regarding either favorable company practices or the distribution of shoddy products and unfair management tactics will generally be transmitted easily to the general public through employees' communication networks.

What are some ways that organizations show social responsibility to employees?

Some firms have well-known reputations for being concerned with employees' attitudes, their personal problems, and other factors that influence both on-the-job performance and public attitudes toward the organization. There are firms, for example, that encourage employees to *further their education* by assisting them with the costs of attending night colleges or universities. Others have assisted women employees by providing *day-care nurseries* for their children. Many firms now provide *counseling services* for such problems as alcoholism and drug abuse among their employees.

A relatively recent innovation is the provision of *executive leaves for public service*. IBM has established a program that enables its employees to take time off, generally with pay, for socially constructive tasks. Xerox and a number of other companies have similar programs.

IBM's first six-month and one-year leaves were started in the 1960s. Until then, the company was granting days or half-days for community work. Recently, IBM had more than 100 employees on public-service leaves.

Responsibility to the Environment

Unfortunately, a tremendous amount of the results of America's over $2,000,000,000,000 ($2 trillion) economy has produced not only an "affluent," but also an "effluent" society, one with polluted rivers, foul air, and an urban atmosphere that generates fear, tension, and sometimes misery. Some critics have referred to the American economy as the "two-trillion-dollar garbage pile."

Should limits be placed on economic growth?

One of the great debates of the seventies has been whether there should be limitations placed upon economic growth in order to conserve our nation's resources and reduce the pollution of the environment. Senator Edmund S. Muskie once put forward, "In a consumer-oriented society, everything we produce leads to waste. Maybe we ought to set some limits on the standard of living." Our purpose is not to be drawn into the firing line of the debate, but instead to point out that limited resources and the environment have received considerable attention in recent years.

416

A question arises, however, about the extent to which business can afford to be involved with protecting the environment. Some executives have contended, for example, that the increased costs resulting from the installation of antipollution devices can price their products out of consumer markets.

Over the long run it is doubtful that environmental controls will have a significant influence on industry's costs. Some of the most profitable firms have been those most concerned with the environment. Those who oppose such controls principally on the grounds of cost should not overlook an essential point: that society reaps substantial benefit from a pollution-free environment. Of course, a free economy does produce a lot of wealth, and wealth is a social good. But so is *health,* which may be attainable only at the sacrifice of some types of freedoms, such as the freedom to pollute.

Many firms have displayed in recent years an increased concern for the environment. For example, some firms have begun to place emphasis on *waste prevention* and the *recycling* of waste materials rather than on *waste disposal*. Others have started utilizing waste products for fuel in order to conserve energy resources.

Who should bear the costs of enrivonmental protection? Do managers really have much choice about being concerned with the environment? Past neglect has already caused the government to enact laws requiring, or institutionalizing, this type of social concern. The government, however, could go farther to encourage voluntary compliance through various tax incentives and by moral suasion.

To Provide Information

What types of information can organizations provide? Another socially beneficial approach taken by some organizations is the *dissemination of information* of practical use to the general public or to other businesses.

For example, Metropolitan Life Insurance Company has consistently made available free brochures providing information on health and hygiene. Naturally, the longer people live, the longer they will pay insurance premiums to insurance companies, such as Metropolitan Life. This factor, however, need not detract from the social usefulness of such efforts.

Another insurance firm, the Kemper Insurance Company, has actively distributed free information to companies concerned with the establishment of drug and alcohol abuse programs.

Banking institutions are generally known as rather conservative organizations. One bank—the Security National Bank of Walnut Creek, California—attempted during the early 1970s to alter its staid image with a novel approach. Every two months the firm mailed to its customers a bulletin that consisted of useful consumer information. It sent them articles that both explained significant social problems and offered various solutions to them. The publication also had a section entitled, ''Our

417

Readers Speak Out,'' in which customers could vent their own pent-up frustrations by submitting letters of any nature to be printed. Furthermore, the executives of the bank stuck their white-collar necks way out during the Vietnam War when they attached a gigantic peace symbol, visible for miles, to the outside of their office building. As evidence of the need for top management support of unique programs, the bulletin was discontinued and the peace symbol removed after the bank's president, Fortney H. Stark, left the organization to pursue a career in politics.

To Assist the Disadvantaged and Handicapped

Considerable space in this text has already been devoted to the topic of hiring individuals who have been discriminated against for various reasons. Many organizations have begun to recognize their responsibilities in this area.

The managers of General Electric are required to report regularly on the percentage of nonwhite and white employees in their departments. The managers have also to submit five-year plans for increasing minority hiring.

Handicapped workers, too, have received more attention from General Electric. For example, the firm installed computer programming equipment into the automobile of an employee with a spinal-cord injury. Another company, McGill Manufacturing in Indiana, pays workers disabled on the job the difference between what they receive from workers' compensation benefits and their regular wages.

Miscellaneous Responsibilities

One need merely to read the newspapers for other examples of social concern regularly displayed by some members of the business community. We have by no means exhausted the many examples. Banking officials *provide counsel to minority-owned businesses. Corporate money and talent* have been contributed to socially useful causes, such as providing inexpensive loans for the *rebuilding of communities* or *depositing corporate funds* in minority-owned banks.

Money, however, is *not* the sole answer. Walter A. Haas, Jr., chairman of Levi Strauss and Company, has stated: ''I'm convinced that to be successful in social programs is not dependent on the amount of money you spend, but the *attitude and concern of management''* (emphasis added).[3]

In the following section we shall explore some recommendations for making social programs more successful.

---

[3]''How Social Responsibility Became Institutionalized,'' *Business Week,* 30 June 1973, p. 76.

418

Guide to Social Action

One of the primary functions of management is that of *planning*. Yet managers concerned with social programs often neglect this important function. Instead, they too frequently have been involved with the "putting out of fires" ignited by disgruntled members of the public.

Social programs developed within a *calm and thoughtful atmosphere* tend to convey greater evidence of sincere concern and have more likelihood of success than those hastily conceived in an atmosphere of crisis. Too frequently, pressured and harried executives have developed and employed programs before analyzing their implications, thus resulting in attitudes of distrust—rather than appreciation and respect—in the general public.

Naturally, there are no magic formulas for guaranteeing the success of any program, but some specific approaches have been tried by various organizations and been effective. The purpose of the following section, therefore, is to offer a *set of guidelines* that can result in more successes than a helter-skelter approach of haste, indecision, and uncertainty.

Management Must Be Committed

Why is *top* management support especially important?

One of the most important guidelines for social action is that *managers*—from the chief executive to the supervisors—*must have firm, sincere commitments* to a corporation's responsibility efforts. These commitments should be a part of the ongoing goals and operations of the organization. A few token dollars spent here or there on temporary programs do not make a company socially responsible in the eyes of the public.

Why the need for long-term consistency?

The commitment first must be *well thought out* and above all—*consistent and long term*. For example, people will generally be turned off by programs that receive adequate funding one year and are put on a barebones budget the next. Consistency should pervade the entire company so that employees in one branch will not be saying or doing one thing while others are saying or doing something else.

The Program Should Be Integrated into Regular Operations

Why shouldn't programs be separated from normal operations?

Any program, in order to prevent the appearance of windowdressing, should not be considered something separate and apart from an organization's regular operations. A firm sincerely concerned with social responsibility should not grandstand its efforts, but instead should attempt to incorporate its obligations to society into the basic structure of the organization.

The Program Must Be Communicated

What are ways to communicate a program to employees?

All levels of an organization must understand the program if it is to be as effective as possible. As we have learned, employees provide a significant communications link with the public, and as a result, employees' misinterpretations can cause untold damage to a program.

Some firms use *movie films* or *slides* to help explain the objectives of a program as well as details of the employees' responsibilities. *Vestibule*, or *company schools*, are sometimes established so that interested employees may learn more about environmental subjects. *Public service awards* can be an incentive or means of motivating employees to participate actively in such programs.

The Program Must Be Credible

Why is credibility essential?

Those directing the programs should be concerned with *credibility*. Few activities will ever be 100 percent successful. Although the negative need not be accentuated when company activities are discussed, efforts to gloss over shortcomings may result in the entire program's being mistrusted. In other words, companies should be honest about their programs.

Participants Should Be Concerned with Action

Which speak louder and clearer— *actions* or *words*?

Little is to be gained by managers who speak eloquently before civic or other groups about the need for social action yet are not actively and sincerely involved, themselves, with specific programs. The public can generally see through pure rhetoric.

Some firms, as we have learned, permit their employees to be genuinely involved by encouraging them to volunteer for work in the community—often on company time. Some firms offer their employees paid sabbaticals; others may allow a half-day each week for such activities as counseling minority businesses.

Failures Should Not Be Discouraging

Should you be discouraged by an occasional Edsel?

As you may know, the Ford Motor Company's Edsel automobile was something of a failure. Undaunted, Ford managers went on to develop two best sellers—the Mustang and the Maverick.

A similar spirit should prevail among those involved with social programs. All may not succeed. Managers, however, should examine the entire picture before evaluating the general success or failure of their efforts. Rather than abandoning some failures, or entire programs, a modification of certain aspects might improve a program's over-all effectiveness.

Summary

In an earlier chapter, we examined the nature and causes of prejudice. We learned that prejudice is a form of judgment made with insufficient facts. Although some business managers have neglected social responsibilities in the past, much prejudice toward the business community has resulted from the lack of understanding of business and its place in society by the general public.

A Communications Problem

social enrichment

Business managers are generally concerned with effective communications *within* their organizations. More and more managers have developed an awareness of modern human relations techniques, such as job enrichment, designed to motivate employees. Perhaps there is an additional need—one for managers to develop programs of "social enrichment" *outside* their organizations.

Organizational leaders have done little in the past to modify the many erroneous conceptions and prejudices of business held by the general public. Too often managers have either been *overdefensive* or have placed excessive stress on how *right* everything is. In far too many instances has management been reluctant to talk about its problems with candor, and, as a result, the public frequently feels that business has something to hide. Annual reports, for example, customarily have been filled with puffery, windowdressing, and glad tidings, instead of honest appraisals of things as they really are.

Management must learn, however, that talk alone will not convince a skeptical general public of the desirability of private organizations. True, zealots have often thrown uninformed and biased rhetorical rocks at the business community. In the long run, however, management will fail to get its message across by fighting rhetoric with rhetoric. To quote an old cliché, "You can try to fight fire with fire, but firefighters usually use water!"

Employees and the general public also have certain responsibilities. Rather than being blindly and emotionally prejudiced toward business *in toto*, they should strive to become better informed about the actual activities of the business community and realize that many organizational contributions toward society cannot take place within the framework of our present economic system unless firms are able to earn reasonable profits.

Long-Term Commitments

The solutions need not involve a battle between business and the general public. Instead, business leaders must establish *long-term commitments* to social action. Too often programs have been hastily adopted, ill-conceived, and then hastily dropped. Managers must be willing not only to anticipate the need for change, but also to employ programs with foresight *before* they are pushed "up against the corporate wall." Some citizens believe that aggressive and hostile attacks upon business are the only effective means to get its attention. The public must be convinced otherwise—not through the use of clever managerial rhetoric, but by an honest display of sincere concern for the well-being of American society by organizations.

The Necessity for Ethical Action

Finally, management should profoundly examine the ethical aspects of any of its actions. The temptation is sometimes great to pursue ethically questionable practices solely on the grounds that they benefit the cash flow or profit position of a company. The long-run effects of such actions, however, could be not only disastrous but could ultimately sound the death knell of American private enterprise. As one Bank of America official has asserted: "In the long pull, nobody can expect to make profits—or have any meaningful use for profits—if our society is wracked by tension."

Terms and Concepts to Remember

Social role of business	Enlightened self-interest
Conglomerate wave	Profit quest
Caveat emptor	Social accountability
Trustee of profit	Social enrichment

Questions

1. What have been some of the principal external forces that have pressured business organizations into developing a greater social conscience? Do you feel that these forces have always been reasonable? Explain.
2. Polls taken in the 1970s revealed relatively low public faith in institutions in general. List and evaluate some of the major causes of such attitudes.
3. Contrast the opposing views of the profit-quest and the social-accountability philosophies related to the public responsibilities of business organizations.

4. Explain the following statement: "The actual dollars-and-cents value of social responsibility programs is difficult to determine."
5. What are the probable long-run consequences of business organizations' ignoring their responsibilities toward the general public?
6. Why is top management commitment toward any organizational program essential for its success?
7. Evaluate the following statement: "All this talk about pollution control and safer products is understandable, but if the public wants all those things, it better be prepared to pay extra for them in higher-priced products."

Other Readings

Farmer, Richard, and Hogue, W. Dickerson. *Corporate Social Responsibility*. Chicago: Science Research Associates, 1973.

Greenwood, William T. *Issues in Business and Society*. 3d ed. Boston: Houghton Mifflin, 1977.

Heilbroner, Robert L. *Business Civilization in Decline*. New York: W. W. Norton & Co., 1976.

Nader, Ralph. *Taming the Giant Corporation*. New York: W. W. Norton & Co., 1976.

Scitovsky, Tibor. *The Joyless Economy: An Inquiry into Human Satisfaction and Consumer Dissatisfaction*. New York: Oxford University Press, 1976.

Silk, Leonard, and Vogel, David. *Ethics & Profits: The Crisis of Confidence in American Business*. New York: Simon and Schuster, 1976.

Stead, Richard. *Business and Society in Transition: Issues and Concepts*. San Francisco: Canfield Press, 1975.

Stone, Christopher D. *Where the Law Ends*. New York: Harper & Row, 1975.

Weaver, Paul H. "Corporations Are Defending Themselves with the Wrong Weapon." *Fortune,* June 1977, pp. 186–196.

Application

Caught on Two Horns of a Dilemma

Wanda Wohri, a representative of a pharmaceutical company, has the responsibility of calling on druggists and medical doctors for the purpose

423

of promoting the products of the S. S. Crowlow Company, Incorporated. Wanda is a voracious reader, and recently she learned from a foreign publication that a German governmental agency in Bonn has banned the sale of a drug that her company currently manufactures and distributes under a different brand name in the United States and Canada. The Bonn governmental agency has uncovered what it believes to be positive evidence that the drug can cause physical deformities in newborn babies.

Not long after reading the German report, Wanda was requested by her boss, Mr. Fred Finchpenny, to come to his office. During the session, Mr. Finchpenny informed Wanda that the sale of a particular drug, which the Crowlow Company as been marketing under the brand name of Encrouchonol, has not been particularly good in her territory. He also suggested that she begin to promote Encrouchonol to her accounts with greater vigor.

Encrouchonol is the Crowlow Company's name for the drug that was removed from the German market. Wanda explained this to Finchpenny, who glossed over the German experience and mumbled something about those "dumb foreigners." He informed her of the tremendous capital investment that Crowlow has sunk into the research, development, and advertising of Encrouchonol. "If we don't recover our investment," warned Finchpenny, "all of us are going to suffer financially here at Crowlow."

Wanda was disturbed by Finchpenny's attitude, so she told him that the company should not be "pushing" a drug that might cause harm to newborn babies. Finchpenny stressed that the firm has hardly begun to recover the tremendous investment already made. He also made allusion to her being a widow with a $40,000 house mortgage and two children whom she currently supports financially at an out-of-state university. Finchpenny closed the discussion with the comment, "I expect to see some positive results on your next monthly production statement!"

Questions

1. What sort of a problem does Wanda face?
2. Assume that Wanda came to you for advice. How would you help her?

18

Which Direction Is the Future?

A Prognosis

When you finish this chapter, you should be able to:

1. **Explain** why knowledge may be sometimes satisfying and at other times frustrating.
2. **Describe** what human relations is not.
3. **Review** the major objectives of the study of human relations.
4. **Summarize** some of the significant forces likely to influence organizations and personal lives in future years.

> The future lies ahead;
> the past is behind us.
> —Mort Sahl

> Maybe if we listened to it,
> history would stop repeating itself.
> —Lily Tomlin

Now that you've almost come to the end of this book, you must feel like an expert in the field of human relations, right? No more problems for you with humans in organizations, eh? If you really feel this way, you are urged to reread the chapter on perception. If this is the end of your first course in human relations or if you have just finished reading this book, you are now, in essence, only at the *beginning* of your quest for greater human understanding.

Students of human behavior should never cease to be aware that there is considerably more to learn about our fellow humans—and even ourselves. At this juncture, we've really barely scratched the surface of human knowledge. As former Beatle, George Harrison, once philosophized, "I'm beginning to know that all I know is that I know nothing." The world's body of knowledge is, indeed, expansive.

Why is knowledge sometimes frustrating? The acquisition of knowledge is often a satisfying experience, but it can also be a frustrating experience. For example, occasionally you may find yourself interacting with others during a specific situation in a manner that you, yourself, don't like. With a reasonable amount of knowledge of human behavior, you may understand *why* you are responding as you are, but may feel that you don't have complete control over your actions.

We all, however, sometimes do and say things that later we regret. When you find yourself in such a situation, don't be afraid to attempt to communicate your feelings to others. Frequently you may find that merely an apology from you will resolve a conflict. Sometimes only a few words can have significantly positive effects on others. Take a look at the following "Short Course in Human Relations." It may seem corny at first, but there is much that is useful packed into the seven short statements.

A Short Course in Human Relations

The Six Most Important Words:
  "I admit I made a mistake"

428

The Five Most Important Words:
　"You did a good job"

The Four Most Important Words:
　"What is your opinion?"

The Three Most Important Words:
　"If you please"

The Two Most Important Words:
　"Thank you"

The One Most Important Word:
　"We"

The Least Important Word:
　"I"

Have you ever felt that you'd seen a side that others hadn't?

Knowledge generally improves perception. But knowledge can also be frustrating if you feel that your educational frame of reference enables you to perceive some things that others seem not to see. We have learned that not everybody perceives the same situation in precisely the same fashion. In order to enhance your human relationships, you should attempt to have patience with others who, due to different environmental experiences, perceive things differently. And even if some individuals have less education than you, they may still see some aspects of a situation that you do not. Remember that in any situation, some of us see the truth, some of us see part of the truth, and some of us fail to see the truth.

What Human Relations Is Not

The concepts discussed in the chapter on perception can also hold true for those who have studied a particular book on the topic of organizational behavior; not everyone will have derived precisely the same ideas from such a study. There generally exists the danger that some persons will interpret an author's words in a manner that he or she had not intended. At this point, therefore, it may be worthwhile to stress once again what objectives *were not* a part of this text in order to lessen the chance of your completing it with unintended impressions. Read the following section for a short summary of what your study of human relations was *not* intended to accomplish.

To Eliminate All Conflict

Previously we learned that in any situation where there are two or more persons there is the potential for conflict. However, individuals who are in positions of influence over others in group situations *should not*, as a part of their goals, *attempt to eliminate all differences*. In fact, some conflict can be quite beneficial, either as a means for releasing tension or as a source of new ideas.

For example, as a manager you could discover that new and useful ideas frequently emerge from situations in which individuals feel free to assert different viewpoints. Responsible group members, therefore, should attempt to *encourage*—not stifle—conflicting ways of thinking. The free flow of communication is not likely to take place in a tense or unhealthy human relations atmosphere.

To Create a "Country Club" Atmosphere

Is human relations actually a "one-big-happy-family" approach?

Some former critics of the human relations movement have referred to it as a "happiness-school" approach, one advocating that managers should never discipline employees but, instead, should continually pat workers on their backs and strive to develop a permissive "one-big-happy-family" atmosphere.

The purpose of understanding human behavior in organizations, however, is *not* to enable you to win people over with superficial kindness and ingenuine glad tidings. Neither was personality development a basic objective of this book, although an improved understanding of human relations certainly can aid you in such efforts.

Should employees ever be fired?

Nor do "people-oriented" managers always smile and never fire anyone. Firing an employee should seldom be a part of a manager's initial efforts at resolving a problem, but when other reasonable efforts have failed, and an employee refuses to correct unacceptable deficiencies, dismissal may be necessary.

To Manipulate People

Why shouldn't "manipulation" be a goal of human relations?

There are others who feel that the main purpose of learning human relations is to enable them to manipulate people in a fashion not unlike that of a carnival puppeteer. The concept of manipulation, however, has extremely *negative* connotations; human relations, on the other hand, endeavors to instill more *positive* attitudes toward one's fellow beings. Subordinates can usually see through most attempts at manipulation. A sincere and positive concern for others in relation to the over-all goals of an organization is a far more effective approach in the long run than is manipulation.

To Provide Instant Solutions

You may have noticed that you have learned very few *rules* as a result of reading this book. Although human behavior is sometimes predictable, it

Does human relations provide you with "instant" solutions?

seldom is absolute. Humans are not like chemical compounds to be controlled as scientists control their laboratory experiments. Therefore, although you were exposed to a number of *guidelines* for action, you were not provided with such things as a list of "eighteen sure-fire rules" or principles applicable with ease to every problem and therefore serving as "instant problem solvers." Each situation, as we have learned, is unique and should be treated as such. Remember the concept of *situational thinking*.

Far more important than what the objectives of this book are not is the flip side of the coin: What *are* the goals of our study of human relations? You should already have discerned the major reasons for improving your understanding of human behavior, but a summary at this point might prove useful. Read the following section for a quick review of our main objectives.

Objectives of Human Relations

Organizations, as well as the world in which they are situated, are in a continual state of transition. Managers and workers will continue to be confronted with new types of problems requiring imaginative solutions. As we have learned, the nature of work is rapidly changing, new laws affect organizations in new ways, and subgroups both within and without organizations are energetically asserting their influence and making heretofore unheard of demands. Therefore, today's organizational members need a far greater awareness of the human side of organizations than ever before.

We need not delve into a detailed summary of the purpose of understanding human behavior, since the entire book explored the topic in some depth. Instead, carefully examine the following *list of objectives* and ask yourself how your awareness of each of them has been enhanced. An understanding of human behavior can:

Have you helped yourself to these six objectives?

1. Assist you to develop a *keener sensitivity* toward other people.
2. Help you to develop a greater realization of how your own *attitudes* and *behavior* play a part in everyday affairs.
3. Help you to develop an improved understanding of the problems of *reconciling your own interests and capabilities* with the *needs and goals of organizations* of which you are, or will become, a part.
4. Enable you to *anticipate and prevent problems*, or at least to *resolve* more effectively those that you did not avoid.
5. Assist you to *see things as they are*, not as they *should* or as you *would like* them to be.
6. And assist you to cast aside some of the *excess mental luggage* that increases your mental load but not your effectiveness.

On the subject of mental luggage, Morris Raphael Cohen put it this way:

> Never having discovered for myself any royal road up the rocky and dangerous steep of philosophy, I did not conceive it to be part of my function as a teacher to show my students such a road. The only help I could offer them was to convince them that they must climb for themselves or sink in the mire of conventional error. All I could do to make the climbing easier was to relieve them of needless customary baggage. This exposed me to the charge of being merely critical, negative or destructive. I have always been ready to plead guilty to that charge. It seemed to me that one must clear the ground of useless rubbish before one can begin to build.[1]

A Humanistic Approach

The study of human relations does not—indeed, cannot—provide all of the answers to each specific behavioral problem. Instead, it stresses a more humanistic point of view—one that focuses on the *dignity and worth of people* and on the individual's capacity for *self-realization* through reason.

Nonetheless, the *human being* must somehow be coordinated with the *technical aspects and needs of organizations* if the over-all goals and objectives of either are to be attained. As we have learned from the previous chapter, in a mixed free enterprise system, the coordination of goals and responsibilities is not a simple task; organizations must face a variety of complex responsibilities.

What sort of knowledge and abilities will tomorrow's leaders need?

Perhaps the leaders of tomorrow, surrounded by computers and other highly technical hardware, will require greater *interdisciplinary knowledge* which will provide them with the skill to use technology, as well as rational thought, to solve complex human and environmental problems.

Problem Solving Requires More Than Definitions

What is as important as the *definition* of a problem?

Some persons feel that at present students and professors spend too much time and energy learning how to define problems, and too little time on how to solve them. For example, H. Ross Perot, American industrialist, has been critical of education that teaches "that the definition of the problem is everything."[2]

---

[1]*A Dreamer's Journey, The Autobiography of Morris Raphael Cohen* (Boston: The Beacon Press, 1949), pp. 145–147.

[2]"Wharton Copes with Its Identity Crisis," *Business Week,* 23 June 1973, p. 51.

Although perhaps a bit overcritical of educators, in a sense Perot is correct, since *no one part of any process is everything*; each part is essential for the accomplishment of an over-all objective. For instance, a person could develop an excellent solution that may be utterly useless if it doesn't relate to the problem at hand. So an accurate *definition* of a problem is essential, but by itself does nothing unless it assists one *to apply useful solutions*. Human relations, as you should recall, is an "action-oriented" discipline. Organizational members cannot be content merely to intellectualize problems.

Never swim close to Sam!!

Far too often, individuals who study human behavior in organizations are a lot like the person—let's call him Sam—who urinates while standing in a crowded swimming pool. Sam gets a warm feeling, but nobody around him knows the difference! How about you? Are you a little like Sam? When studying human relations concepts, do you get a "warm feeling" from the concepts discussed, but after you return to your workplace, nobody around you knows the difference? Useful concepts should do more than create an "uh huh, that's right" feeling; they should be *applied* to the organizational setting.

So you've about approached the end of what may be your first—but it is to be hoped not your last—exposure to concepts of human relations. Now might be a worthwhile time for us to take a soft cloth, dust off our trusty crystal ball, and attempt to peer into the future. (You may use tea leaves, if you prefer!) In the rest of this book, therefore, we shall attempt to predict some of the forces that are likely to affect future organizational behavior.

A Crystal-Ball Approach

Which direction *is* the future? Can the future be predicted with *complete* accuracy? Not likely. All we really know for certain is that social and economic conditions will not remain the same.

There are factors, however, whose *direction of change* is, to a degree, predictable. These changes, which are likely to have profound effects on organizational and personal lives in the years to come, include:

1. The changing nature of *work*.
2. The changing nature of *workers*.
3. The changing attitude toward *leisure*.
4. The continual changing of *values*.
5. The development of a *corporate social conscience*.
6. Increased *government* involvement.
7. The greater influence of *multinational corporations*.
8. The increased *scarcity of resources*.

Let's now briefly examine each factor.

433

The Changing Nature of Work

A production manager recently declared, "My job is to get rid of people." These words, crass and cold as they may sound, partially typify what such a job is all about. One of the key tasks of a manager is to eliminate not only people but also any other cost items that can be eliminated without sacrificing production.

The Elimination and Creation of Jobs

Why isn't work like it used to be?

A natural evolution in work situations has been the automating of various types of jobs that require increasingly more expensive labor. As a result, the nature of work has changed. Many types of industrial and clerical jobs have been eliminated. However, many new types of jobs have been created, some of which require additional training and the development of new skills.

Automation—A "New" Word

Is _automation_ really new?

Neither automation nor resistance to changing technology are particularly new. In a sense, _automation_ is merely a newer word for an older process, that of _substituting machinery for labor_. Today, however, much of the machinery consists of computers rather than old-fashioned looms and jennies.

Two Schools of Thought

What are the two general schools of thought on automation?

In general, there are two principal schools of thought regarding the effects of automation on organizational members. There are those, such as Henry Ford II, who have characterized as "the most dangerous kind of nonsense statements that U.S. industry is not providing enough jobs because we have too much technological progress, too much automation, too rapid displacement of men by machines."[3]

Proponents of automation frequently argue that it will continue to improve our standard of living in the same manner that greater application of mechanization has since the Industrial Revolution. They contend that automation can result in lower production costs, higher profits and wages, and increased demand for products, thus enhancing the level of total output and employment.

Then there are the bleak prophets of doom who insist that the effects of automation have already begun to accelerate too rapidly. They point to

[3]"Ford Scoffs at Automation Peril," _San Francisco Chronicle Business World_, 16 January 1964, p. 46.

new official definitions of ''normal'' employment, which indicate that no longer is 4 percent of the labor force a realistically attainable target for unemployment. They point to the between 7 and 9 percent rates of unemployment prevalent during recent years, despite generally high rates of economic activity. They quote statistics showing that *manufacturing employment* has *decreased* while *output* has actually *grown* substantially.

Those who fear the effects of automation offer early American history as evidence of what can occur. They point out that the United States during its early history was an agrarian society and that an industrial movement resulted in agriculture's becoming relatively insignificant as as an employer of human resources. Today, only between 4 and 5 percent of the nation's population produce the food for more than 100 percent of the United States population. They wonder if we are not becoming a *post-industrial society* where manufacturing will become a victim of its own successes and will follow the pattern of agriculture by employing fewer and fewer human beings all the time.

post-industrial society

Which position is correct? This is a difficult question to answer, since both sides can present credible arguments. One of the most certain factors, however, is that *work*, as we know it today, *will continue to change*. There will be the need for *attitudes* that are *flexible and adaptive*. *Education* is likely to become even more important and require significant changes in emphasis, with greater stress on *interdisciplinary studies*. *Funds* will have to be made available for the *upgrading of skills* and the *retraining and relocation* of individuals who are displaced by automation. Additional solutions to the problems of a growing *aging population* must likewise be developed.

A key factor in whether automation evolves into a blessing or a curse will be what our ''social-industrial complex'' does with it. Automation may eliminate certain jobs, but in the process the enormous brainpower of computer technology could become society's partner, taking on the more mundane tasks while freeing the individual to pursue other, more satisfying endeavors. What we term ''leisure'' today may even become a form of work tomorrow. Perhaps it is not the *use*—but rather the *misuse*—of technology that creates hardships for society.

The Changing Nature of Workers

Rapidly changing technology has changed the nature of *work*, but that isn't all it has affected. It has also changed the nature of *workers* themselves. Slightly over a century ago, a large majority of people worked for themselves as farmers or as small shopkeepers. All this has changed radically over the years. Today most people in technologically advanced nations work for someone else.

Numerous changes in technology have resulted in a diminishing need for production, or manual, workers and a greatly increasing need for the

435

type of person referred to by Peter F. Drucker as the "knowledge worker." In the future, unlike the past, most work will *not* be done by manual workers producing products, but by knowledge workers producing concepts, systems, and ideas.[4]

What's Happening to the Old Breed?

Since the beginnings of the Industrial Revolution, the person who worked with his or her hands lacked job security. As a result of collective bargaining, employee benefit programs, and social legislation, workers today feel generally more secure in many ways than did their predecessors. Yet, will the future bring them greater or lesser feelings of security? If Drucker's assessment is correct, production workers of tomorrow may feel even less secure than in the past since management appears to be doing everything possible to automate them out of their jobs.

American workers—possibly due to social and family pressures—have attained fairly high levels of education, especially when compared with their counterparts in other nations. Most manual workers in the United States, for example, have completed secondary school and over one-quarter of them have attended college. How is this rising educational attainment, accompanied by increasingly simplified types of production jobs, likely to affect their future attitudes toward work?

Does more education necessarily result in greater satisfaction for the manual worker?

For one thing, tomorrow's production workers could feel even more alienated from their jobs. Because they may be overeducated for their work responsibilities, greater dissatisfaction and militancy toward work organizations could result. Tomorrow's manual workers may see work solely as a means to a personal end—a higher standard of material living—and look forward principally to paydays, holidays, vacations, sick leave, and retirement.

Tomorrow's production workers may also look with spiteful envy at knowledge workers who seem to enjoy more in the way of status, pay, and privilege. To cope with a changing old breed of worker will require an enlightened and concerned management willing to try to understand human needs and motivation. Greater use of job enrichment techniques is likely to be made in the future, with efforts to humanize production through the use of worker teams. The aim of some managers will be to introduce creativity, responsibility, and variety to manual work in the hope that industrial monotony and boredom will be reduced.

[4]Peter F. Drucker, *People and Performance: The Best of Peter Drucker on Management* (New York: Harper & Row, 1977), pp. 271–275.

A New Breed of Cat—The Knowledge Worker

knowledge
workers

Engineers, researchers, economists, accountants, nurses, teachers, chemists, financial experts, and managers are among those included in the fastest growing work group—*knowledge workers*. The strength of knowledge workers is not in their backs or their manual dexterity, as with manual workers. Instead, their principal strength lies in their ability to put knowledge to work.

Knowledge workers, in general, are well paid and usually perform more varied and interesting tasks than do production workers. At first glance, then, it might appear that, because of their unique positions, managing knowledge workers would be a relatively simple task. Yes, it might appear that way, but let's take a deeper look into this topic before we pass judgment.

Managing the Knowledge Worker

The traditional Theory X style of manager discussed in chapter 7 got results with manual workers; that is, until workers gathered together collectively and demanded more equitable treatment and working conditions. Fear did—as it often still does—motivate the manual worker, though the risks associated with fear as a motivating technique are great.

How do the
knowledge
workers
differ
from
manual
workers?

The knowledge worker, however, tends to operate within a different, far more independent, framework than the production worker. Of course, knowledge workers are individuals and therefore differ from each other in many respects. But Drucker's studies indicate some common characteristics among them. For example, because of their relatively independent nature, knowledge workers are less motivated by fear or traditional styles of leadership. Their specialized knowledge is usually in high demand, so their tolerance of an unfavorable work atmosphere is slight. When dissatisfied with their jobs, knowledge workers seldom hesitate to look elsewhere for a new position.

A little
Herzberg
goes a
long way
with
knowledge
workers.

Do you remember Herzberg's two-factor theory of motivation discussed in chapter 5? Achievement, we discovered, tends to be a motivating factor. Since knowledge workers tend to be quite *achievement-oriented*, this factor should be considered by those managing them. Knowledge workers also tend to need and expect *recognition* for their achievements, and usually prefer *challenging tasks* with opportunities for growth and *personal satisfaction*.

Although managers should always recognize the individual nature of all people, there are certain guidelines that can be useful to those directing the activities of knowledge workers. These are:

Guidelines
for managing
the
knowledge
worker.

1. Assess the contributions of knowledge workers regularly—at least once every six months to a year.

2. Develop goals and objectives jointly with knowledge workers (management by objectives), being certain to follow up for control and recognition purposes.

3. Eliminate activities that tend to block the progress of knowledge workers, such as unnecessary meetings, reports, and paperwork. Occasionally ask knowledge workers what might be impeding their progress.

4. Try not to underemploy knowledge workers (that is, place them on jobs below their capabilities) or they are likely to become bored and disenchanted with their jobs.

5. As with any employee, watch for warning signs of poor morale. Organizations typically have a lot invested in knowledge workers, and irreversible damage can often be caused if problems are not resolved as early as possible.

6. Select and place knowledge workers carefully. Try to place qualified people where they can best accomplish and meld their personal goals with those of the organization.

Other New Breeds—Young People, Women, and Minorities

Current management literature discusses the rapid entry of other so-called new-breeds of workers, besides knowledge workers, into the labor force. These are young people (there has been a 98 percent increase in the number of teenagers in the work force in the past twenty years), women, and minority group members. We've already discussed many of the organizational problems associated with the members of these groups in other sections of the text.

Greater
diversity
ahead.

From the standpoint of our look into the future, it seems safe to predict that managers of tomorrow will be increasingly faced with a work force that is less homogeneous than that in the past. Instead of a plant or office occupied by first- and second-generation middle European whites, managers are likely to see the work place occupied by women, Hispanics, blacks, and the "old breed" in more equal proportions. Managerial ranks are likely to see similar diversity.

Once again, however, we should stress the necessity for managerial personnel to treat their subordinates as individual human beings, each having separate and distinct needs and aspirations, regardless of his or her so-called breed.

The Greater Acceptance of Leisure

Was the so-called hippie movement of the late 1960s a foreshadow of attitudes that will be prevalent twenty-five years from now? Some observers of society agree with such a premise and feel that over the long run, traditional values, such as the Protestant work ethic, may be eroded as a result of higher levels of affluence, education, and productivity.

Leisure has become somewhat institutionalized. Long hours of toil used to be required of workers, whereas today a five-day—and in some instances four-day—workweek is well established. Expanding vacations and reduced workweeks may diminish the strength of the work ethic.

Is Leisure an Innate Right?

The question has been raised of whether leisure is an innate *right*, or something that must be *earned* by the individual. A philosophy rapidly gaining currency is that *both* leisure and work are valid activities. But the definition of work is no longer clear-cut. What is believed by one person *drudgery work* to be *drudgery work* may be perceived as a form of *leisure work* to *leisure work* another. "Work" is a four-letter word with either nasty or pleasant connotations depending on a person's outlook.

Purchasing Power of the Unemployed?

Rapid technological developments could free many individuals for more leisure activities. A snag could develop, however, in this near-utopian concept. Imagine a highly developed society in which organizations are capable of producing *all* the goods and services its citizens want with *only about 75 percent* of the work force. Just think—one quarter of the people of working age could do whatever they wanted with their leisure time—or could they? Such a society would have to discover answers to **How will the un-** such questions as: What really happens to the unemployed 20 to 25 **employed receive** percent? How will they obtain their *title to consumption*; that is, *dollars*? **title to consumption?** If large segments of the population want, but are unable to find, employment and if they are excluded from the mainstream of economic opportunity, are they likely to identify with the prevailing system?

These are perplexing questions to answer since, with our present value system, it is difficult to fathom a society in which people are paid merely to be consumers.

The Need for Alternative Solutions

Between 1947 and 1974 the percentage of production workers declined from 77 percent to 68 percent of the labor force, much of this drop due to increased mechanization. Will this reduced need for production workers be offset by the trend toward larger firms with increasing needs for clerical workers and managers? The future is beset with many uncertainties. Should organizational leaders adopt "wait-and-see" attitudes? Or might it not be more beneficial to apply the scientific method of establishing alternative solutions to problems before they reach the crisis stage? Solutions that *prevent,* rather than *correct,* will be far more useful to humankind in the long run.

The Continual Changing of Values

How *good* were those "good old days"?

Changing values are nothing new. Every generation has tended to believe that the values of the younger segments of society have deteriorated from the way they were in the "good old days." However, were the "good old days" really that good? Today's youth not only seem to have developed markedly different values from those of past generations, but they are felt by many to have had significant influence on the present value system of Americans in general.

Are the values of today's youth really all that different from those of previous generations, or are young people just more "out front" with their feelings and activities? History seems to be like a swinging pendulum—it repeats itself with remarkable regularity. Perhaps some of the space on the pendulum is reserved for value systems as well.

The Self-Centered Generation?

Are today's young more inner-directed?

self-centered generation

Young people in the 1960s seemed to develop a far greater concern with the inequities in the American system than had previous generations. The 1970s, however, apparently ushered in a reversal of values and attitudes. The ending of the war in Vietnam, along with the surplus of college graduates during the inflationary-recessions of the 1970s, seemed to cause young people to turn inward. Because of this, they have been called the "self-centered generation." The name may also be partly a natural outgrowth of young people's having to compete for scarce jobs—jobs made even scarcer by an expanded labor force composed of increasing numbers of women and minorities vying for positions in industry and government.

Social and environmental issues, too, seemed to demand less attention from young people in the 1970s. As one young person exclaimed, "It's hard for me to get all worked up about the plight of the Alaskan caribou when I'm not even sure if I can get a job!''

Effects of Tube Watching on Society's Values

By the time a child graduates from high school, she or he will have spent some 12,000 hours in classroom and 15,000 hours in front of the television set. For many children, television watching accounts for more of their time than any other activity except sleeping. In the average American household, the television is turned on for more than six hours a day, climbing to over seven hours a day during the winter months.

Has television influenced the values of its watchers? Television is undeniably a significant part of many individuals' environment, and we've already discussed the significance of environment on the way people perceive others. Critics of television charge it with making Americans more violent, more passive, more cynical, more materialistic, and more homogeneous. Television has also been characterized as a serious rival of parents as an influence on children's development.

Will watching the tube create more boobs?

According to George Gerbner, dean of the Annenberg School of Communication at the University of Pennsylvania, ''Television is a 'new industrial, corporate religion' whose most ardent supplicants, the real TV addicts, are very likely to have low IQs and school grades and be in the low social and economic strata.'' Gerbner's studies suggest that TV can incite unstable people to violence when they have no other way of achieving their goals. He points out that television violence is especially unsettling to the elderly because it fosters an unreasoning fear of being victimized. He feels that senseless crimes against the elderly are portrayed too often and can foster paranoia.[5]

Leadership Influence on Society's Values

Shouldn't public leaders set examples for others?

Unfortunately, young and older Americans alike have become increasingly cynical about what they have perceived as hypocrisy among their leaders, both in industry and in government. A Department of Justice report released in January 1974, did little to improve attitudes. The report stated, without comment, ''The former Vice-President, two former Cabinet officers, three Congressmen, a former Senator, and a federal judge were indicted, convicted or sentenced. More than fifty-one indictments of state and local officers were also returned.'' The public scandals surrounding the Presidency of the United States resulted in the resignation of Richard Nixon in August 1974.

[5]Norm Hannon, ''How TV Can Foster Paranoia,'' *Oakland Tribune,* 21 June 1977, p. 5.

And in June 1977, John N. Mitchell, previously the number one enforcer of law and order in the United States, became the first former attorney general to go to jail. Sentenced to a federal prison, he began serving a 2½-to-8 year sentence for his role in the Watergate coverup. Mitchell thus became the twenty-fifth person to be jailed in connection with Watergate. As he entered the prison area for the first time, Mitchell was met by jeering inmates. Are these the examples of leadership that youth are to emulate? Do you remember the concept that organizational members *tend to follow as they are led?*

The Development of a Corporate Conscience

corporate conscience

In spite of the highly-publicized cases of questionable business practices, corporation leaders, as we mentioned in the previous chapter, seem to be developing—and must continue to develop—what could be termed as a *corporate conscience.* Organizations, as we know, function in an environment that is continually undergoing rapid change. The role and responsibilities of organizational members will have to change at a dynamic pace merely to keep up with society. Active external and internal forces make it necessary for responsible organizational individuals to be sensitive toward the need for developing the means for adapting to such pressures. Social, economic, cultural, religious, political, and technological forces are all clamoring for organizational attention.

The Danger of Defensive Reaction

Why is overdefensive reaction dangerous?

organizational inbreeding

There always exists the potential danger that organizational members will *react overdefensively* to social criticism and thereby insulate themselves from the real world. An additional significant danger is that of *organizational inbreeding,* or the development of a "yes-boss" atmosphere where differences are stifled and subordinates fear to make any attempts to challenge the established hierarchy. Another danger looms in the tendency to *blame others* for our own problems—the "we-are-right-and-they-are-wrong" philosophy.

Eroded Faith Must be Restored

The Watergate scandals of the 1970s relating to the re-election of former President Nixon, and the massive doses of unfavorable publicity surrounding questionable foreign payments and bribes by large American corporations, eroded part of society's faith in America's institutions and organizations. The so-called "Bert Lance affair" during the presidency of

Jimmy Carter added to public cynicism. A not atypical example of deteriorating attitudes was extracted from a letter to the editor of *Time* magazine: "Most Americans lie, cheat, steal and indulge in arrogance, yet are outraged when they find their elected officials doing the same thing."[6]

Faith must be restored, however, before a healthy society is likely to exist. Organizational members can help by engaging in honest and ethical practices. But faith will continue to be eroded if organizational leaders are dishonest and unethical, because dishonesty is more visible to the public than is often realized. On this topic, William Simon, former chairperson of the Antitrust Section of the American Bar Association, has warned:

> Nothing is more efficient than honesty: those who break the law or abuse the basic moral code in the name of profit are doing more to make "profit" a dirty word than all of the critics of the free-enterprise system put together.[7]

Increased Government Involvement

Adam Smith, one of the first business philosophers, contended that maximum economic and social progress would result from the least government involvement. Writing in 1776, long before the advent of giant international conglomerate corporations, Smith believed that business entrepreneurs and resource suppliers each pursuing their own self-interests would create a free and ideal economic situation resulting in virtually the automatic full employment of labor and other resources. The marketplace, he argued, if not directed or influenced by government, *invisible hand* would adjust automatically as though an "invisible hand" were guiding it.

The "Visible" Hand of Government

Do business leaders always prefer a "hands off" policy?

The invisible hands of Adam Smith are likely to become even less visible in the future. Instead, expanded government involvement in the private sector seems even more probable.

Business leaders are no longer urging the government to keep its "hands off" as they did in previous eras. In fact, the reverse has occurred. For example, when the aerospace industry tumbled into trouble in 1971, its leaders beseeched members of Congress for financial assistance

---

[6]"Letters," *Time,* 2 July 1973, p. 4.

[7]Marvin G. Gregory, ed., *Bits & Pieces* (Fairfield, N.J.: The Economics Press, May 1977).

(none dared call it ''welfare''!) in order to bail out Lockheed and save the SST (Supersonic Transport) airplane. Likewise, homebuilders, during occasional slumps, have pressed the government to increase housing subsidies. The nation's floundering passenger railway system was given an economic transfusion through the creation of Amtrak, the government-sponsored railway corporation. And the oil industry has consistently demanded preferential tax treatment.

Government Involvement Not New

Government involvement in private affairs isn't particularly novel or recent. Either because of previous organizational abuse, or upon the demands of an aroused public, much legislation was passed in order to require the government to be a ''watchdog'' over such activities as unfair competition, or to protect workers' and consumers' interests—and even their bank accounts if the banks should become insolvent.

In what area is government likely to expand its activities?

The government is likely to expand its activities in social welfare, including additional legislation affecting employee rights. Continued governmental concern is likely to be shown in product safety and environmental protection. There is even the probability of greater involvement in the areas of resource allocation and wage-, price-, and profit-determination, as has been witnessed during the seventies.

An Opinion

Richard D. Steade, Professor of Management at Colorado State University, contends about the future:

> [The result may be] a cooperative system of business-government enterprise beyond anything we have realized to this point. Business will be expected to join with government in solving a bundle of social ills that challenge the quality of life in our society. Large corporations, in their collaboration with the major agencies of the federal government will not necessarily lose their power, but probably will be more involved in shaping the basic dimensions of American life.[8]

What is likely to influence governmental roles?

As Professor Steade predicts, government and business are likely to have a closer relationship. The inclination for a government takeover, or ownership, of the private means of production does not appear to be likely if one takes into account foreseeable American attitudes. It is

[8]Richard D. Steade, *Business and Society in Transition: Issues and Concepts* (San Francisco: Canfield Press, 1975), p. 31.

probable, however, that the behavior of business leadership at present will significantly influence the course and extent of government involvement in the future.

The Greater Influence of Multinational Companies

Volkswagens— made in Pennsylvania?

A person can now buy a MacDonald's hamburger in Paris (served with wine, rather than a milkshake—*naturellement*) and purchase the Colonel's "it's finger-lickin-good" Kentucky fried chicken in Frankfurt (with a stein of cold beer, *natürlich*). American automobile, petroleum, farm machinery, and other miscellaneous producers have plants throughout the world. You can even drive a car rented from Hertz to the Chase-Manhattan Bank in downtown Moscow, USSR. One of the most important developments affecting corporations since World War II has been the substantial expansion of *multinational business*; that is, business organizations with branches or subsidiaries in a variety of other nations.

multinationals

Concentration of Power

What are some criticisms of multinational corporations?

Critics of giant multinational corporations contend that the enormous economic power of some firms has become so concentrated they are able to shape national policies, stifle new businesses, and reduce—rather than foster—free enterprise. There are some organizations, for example, whose total productive output far exceeds the total industrial output of many nations.

Some international organizations have been accused of increasing the severity of international monetary crises by shifting huge sums out of one currency into another, thereby contributing to monetary speculation and instability.

Multinationalism—A Natural Evolution?

There are others who feel that the trend toward internationalism is a natural evolution akin to the interstate operations of corporations within the United States. As a result, there are likely to be ever-growing numbers of multinationals, with additional firms from many nations entering the field. Supporters of this trend contend that such expansion will not necessarily bring about conflict between nation states and the corporations, but instead will require that nations develop supranational organizations to oversee and regulate multinational corporations for the purpose of harmonizing national interests with those of the giant companies.

Responsibilities of Multinational Corporations

What are the social responsibilities of multi-national corporations?

The trend toward multinational corporations is likely to continue. A question arises, therefore, of whether the social responsibilities of such firms differ from or are similar to those of domestic entities.

It could probably be safely argued that managers of multinational businesses should recognize that they have responsibilities similar to their domestic counterparts. The previous chapter discussed these major responsibilities. The list could be expanded for multinational corporations and include:

1. An awareness of customs and cultural differences in host countries.
2. An awareness of variations in laws.
3. A concern for financial and economic stability in international markets.
4. A concern not to exploit their host nations by extracting resources and profits, and leaving nothing in their stead.

The same words of warning could be proffered to managers of multinational corporations as were presented in the previous chapter to managers of domestic concerns. The lack of a social-accountability approach might predictably result in more extensive restrictive legislation, which could bind the productive hands of the managers.

The Yanks Are Coming—Over There

American companies operating in other countries have had an impact on foreign organizational practices, as have foreign nationals on Americans both abroad and in the United States. A major contribution made by American companies is in the area of management development. U.S. companies operating abroad have introduced modern programs patterned after their domestic approaches. Another ''contribution'' relates to a cultural characteristic of Americans. As a group, they tend to be less formal and more open in their patterns of communication, a custom that has generally been favorably received by foreign business people.

Too frequently, however, American transplants have failed in their efforts on foreign soil because they neglected to do their homework. They attempted to use exactly the same business strategy that worked for them in the ''good old U.S.A.'' One rude awakening experienced by many Americans dealing in Europe, for example, was discovering the more generous employee benefits and job protection enjoyed by most workers. Another significant cultural difference they found was that foreign business people tend to submerge themselves less in their work. Family life and recreation are seldom subordinated to a work ethic. Also prevalent in Europe is the custom of employee representation on work councils and managerial committees, as a result of which upward communication is felt to be more effective in many foreign-based organizations.

Although many American managers are able to function reasonably well abroad without a knowledge of the local language, they would be well advised to try learning as much as possible about the similarities and differences between their own culture and the host country's culture before reporting to an overseas assignment. Not only does such preliminary research enhance the American's chances for accomplishing goals, but it also makes the overseas assignment a far more enjoyable and enriching experience.

"Care for some corn on the cob, Jean Paul?"

"For my pigs, *monsieur,* **only for my pigs,** *merci!"*

Increased Scarcity of Resources

The fourth Arab-Israeli conflict, the Yom Kippur War of 1973, brought home the shocking awareness of how fleeting a thing the comfort of ever-abundant resources can be. For many years most Americans assumed that the supply of resources was limitless. Turn on the tap, and water will always flow. Turn on the light switch, and there will always be illumination. Squeeze the handle on a gasoline pump, and there will always be petrol. The Arab oil embargoes and reductions of supplies that began in 1973 changed world—and especially American—attitudes almost overnight.

Potential Sources of Conflict

Scarcity of natural resources has long been a potential source of human conflict. Much of the unity of the European Common Market countries fell apart in 1974 after a dispute arose about the distribution of oil resources. Also, in 1974, China and South Vietnam began to clash over the fifty or so tiny, nearly uninhabited reefs, shoals, and atolls that make up the Paracel archipelago in the South China Sea. Each country claimed the islands as its own. The Middle East continues to be filled with tension and uncertainty over territorial rights, as does South Africa over its racial policies.

How might scarce resources affect organizational members?

Natural resources, as they grow scarcer, may create additional domestic and international conflicts. Similar problems develop within business or governmental units. Members of departments or competing branch offices sometimes "fight" over available organizational resources.

The Need to Share and Preserve

Dr. William G. Pollard, a physicist and Episcopalian priest, expects that by this century's end, fresh water, petroleum, lead, tin, chromium, manganese, and iron ore will be in critically short supply. At a conference at Stanford University on ''Peaceful Change in Modern Society,'' in November 1969, Dr. Pollard warned that the moral and ethical imperatives can be reduced to two:

1. To learn to share and preserve those parts of the environment—''the commons''—which belong to all mankind.
2. To understand and practice a morality of scarcity.[9]

As we have noted, the mid-seventies already have shown evidence of shortages, especially as a result of the energy crisis. For example, gasoline service station operators have been in conflict with their suppliers. In the transportation industry, violence erupted in 1974 among truckers, some of whom blocked highway traffic in an effort to force the government to exclude them from reduced speed limit regulations designed to conserve energy resources.

Additional conflict has developed between environmentalists and powerful lobbyists in Washington, the latter having been quoted as stating that the best way to stay warm during energy-short winters would be to burn the environmental protection laws.

international human relations

As we become more crowded on our planet, and as the newly developing nations begin to demand their rightful share of the world's resources, shortages of space and resources could feed the flames of old tribal rivalries unless humankind learns to apply something that could be termed *international human relations*. Our present habits and priorities will significantly determine how we allocate our available resources.

[9]''A Depleted Environment—Man's Dismal Outlook,'' *San Francisco Chronicle,* 21 November 1969, p. 2.

Dr. Pollard went on to say that, "by 1990, the 200th anniversary of the Industrial Revolution, the human species will have had two centuries of marvelous luxury in the magic garden. Thereafter it must adjust itself to the hard realities of the life outside the garden."[10] Pollard's predictions may come true sooner than he thought.

Which Direction Is the Future?

Sociological journals and the popular press today literally abound with utterances by prophets of doom. Whether the prophets are right or wrong depends upon each of us. We are *not* sheep. What *you* do IS important, for the sum of all of our actions will determine what sort of a future we and subsequent generations will have.

What we are to be we are now becoming. What are we becoming?

Summary

This, the final chapter, has stressed once again what are, as well as what are not, the objectives of a study in human relations. An important factor for the student to recognize at this juncture is that he or she cannot become highly adept at understanding or applying concepts from having read merely one book. In fact, a person should never cease striving to learn more about human behavior. The world's body of knowledge is extensive and new concepts are continually replacing the old. Behavioral knowledge, alone, has little practical value unless it is applied to human relations situations.

The world in which organizations and their members find themselves is anything but static. Responsible individuals, therefore, should attempt to anticipate and understand the dynamic forces—both external and internal—that are likely to influence the manner in which the organizations of tomorrow will function.

And finally, the lone individual facing a complex and confusing world beset with numerous problems sometimes feels powerless. However, that individual's actions are important, since the sum of every individual's activities will significantly influence the answer to the question, "Which direction is the future?"

Terms and Concepts to Remember

Automation	Knowledge worker
Post-industrial society	Leisure versus drudgery work

[10]*Ibid.*

Self-centered generation   Visible hand of government
Organizationl inbreeding   Multinational corporations
Invisible hand   International human relations
Corporate conscience

Questions

1. Why shouldn't the study of human relations have as one of its goals the elimination of *all* conflict situations in organizations?
2. Evaluate the following statement: "I can't be bothered with this human relations stuff! It may sound good in theory, but I don't feel that I should be expected to create a 'country club' atmosphere for my employees!"
3. Is a major purpose of learning about the human side of organizations to enable you to manipulate people? Explain.
4. In your own words, summarize the meaning of the quote by Morris Raphael Cohen on page 432.
5. How does the "Sam-in-the-swimming-pool" analogy discussed on page 433 relate to studying human relations concepts?
6. The chapter lists eight changing areas that are likely to have significant effects on our future lives. What might be some additional areas not mentioned that will affect you or future generations during the next twenty years?

Other Readings

Barnet, Richard J., and Müller, Ronald E. *Global Reach: The Power of the Multinational Corporations.* New York: Simon and Schuster, 1974.

Cavanaugh, Gerald F. *American Business Values in Transition.* Englewood Cliffs, N.J.: Prentice-Hall, 1976.

Drucker, Peter F. *Management: Tasks, Responsibility, Practices.* New York: Harper & Row, 1974.

Moffitt, Donald, ed. *America Tomorrow.* New York: Dow Jones & Co., 1977.

Peterfreund, Stanley. *Mind-to-Mind Management: How to Meet the New Breed on Its Own Ground.* New York: AMACOM, 1977.

Toffler, Alvin, *Future Shock.* New York: Bantam Books, by arrangement with Random House, 1970.

Application

The Commencement Speaker

Assume that you have been extended an invitation to be the commencement speaker at this year's graduation exercises at Holland Tunnel University. You have been requested to discuss "The Future Direction of American Private Enterprise." Prepare a ten-minute address expressing a viewpoint that you believe would be of interest to graduating students and their guests.

Index

81   82   83   84   11   10   9   8   7